Sustainable Development Goals Series

The **Sustainable Development Goals Series** is Springer Nature's inaugural cross-imprint book series that addresses and supports the United Nations' seventeen Sustainable Development Goals. The series fosters comprehensive research focused on these global targets and endeavours to address some of society's greatest grand challenges. The SDGs are inherently multidisciplinary, and they bring people working across different fields together and working towards a common goal. In this spirit, the Sustainable Development Goals series is the first at Springer Nature to publish books under both the Springer and Palgrave Macmillan imprints, bringing the strengths of our imprints together.

The Sustainable Development Goals Series is organized into eighteen subseries: one subseries based around each of the seventeen respective Sustainable Development Goals, and an eighteenth subseries, "Connecting the Goals", which serves as a home for volumes addressing multiple goals or studying the SDGs as a whole. Each subseries is guided by an expert Subseries Advisor with years or decades of experience studying and addressing core components of their respective Goal.

The SDG Series has a remit as broad as the SDGs themselves, and contributions are welcome from scientists, academics, policymakers, and researchers working in fields related to any of the seventeen goals. If you are interested in contributing a monograph or curated volume to the series, please contact the Publishers: Zachary Romano [Springer; zachary.romano@springer.com] and Rachael Ballard [Palgrave Macmillan; rachael.ballard@palgrave.com].

Kailash Jeenger

A Humanitarian Critique of International Humanitarian Law

Springer

Kailash Jeenger
National Law University and Judicial
Academy, Assam
Guwahati, Assam, India

ISSN 2523-3084 ISSN 2523-3092 (electronic)
Sustainable Development Goals Series
ISBN 978-981-96-8318-5 ISBN 978-981-96-8319-2 (eBook)
https://doi.org/10.1007/978-981-96-8319-2

This Springer imprint is published by the registered company Springer Nature Singapore Pte Ltd.
The registered company address is: 152 Beach Road, #21-01/04 Gateway East, Singapore 189721, Singapore

My parents, Suaa & Bhagvat Lal
My wife, Seema & my son, Azad

Acknowledgements

Writing a monograph may seem to be an individual project, but it is never completely so. The contribution of many people in the completion of this book has been immense and deserves special mention, recognition and gratitude. The book would not have been completed without the support and constant encouragement of my partner, Seema. I am forever thankful to her. I am grateful to my PhD supervisor, Prof. Prahlad Rai, for inspiring me to write on the subject of the laws of armed conflict. I am highly thankful to my friends Haris, Sujith and Anumeha for the discussions and deliberations on legal theories. I have been greatly benefitted by their continuous motivation, help, suggestions and concern about timely publication of the book. Special thanks are due to Haris for introducing me with Nupoor Singh of Springer Nature, Delhi, who supported my book-project and ensured its timely publication. On a similar note, I am grateful to Sujith for suggesting me an appropriate title of the book. I express my gratitude to my friends Saheb and Anubhav also for discussing with me jurisprudential and philosophical concepts whenever I requested.

For writing a book, access to a variety of reading materials is crucial. Therefore, I express my deep sense of gratitude to the authorities of the Department of Law, University of Rajasthan, Jaipur; Faculty of Law, University of Delhi; National Law University, Delhi; Indian Society of International Law, Delhi; National Law University and Judicial Academy of Assam, Guwahati and Jawaharlal Nehru University, Delhi for providing me the access to the library-resources. I am also thankful to the anonymous reviewers. Their inputs have been very beneficial to the book. Lastly, I am grateful to all the teachers, colleagues, students, authors, publishers, organizations, institutional staff, family-members and friends for their direct or indirect contribution in enriching my knowledge and writing the book. I disown any moral desert in this book-project.

Delhi, 27 September 2024 Kailash Jeenger

Table of Cases

International Court of Justice

International Criminal Court

International Criminal Tribunal for the Former Yugoslavia

Prosecutor v. Blaškić, IT-95-14-T, Appelas Chamber, Judgment, 29 July 2004
Prosecutor v. Boškoski and Tarčulovski, IT-04-82, Trial Chamber, Judgment, 10 July 2008
Prosecutor v. Delalić et al, IT-96-21-A, Appeals Chamber, Judgment, 20 February, 2001
Prosecutor v. Delalić et al, IT-96-21-T, Trial Chamber, Judgment, 16 November, 1998
Prosecutor v. Dragomir Milošević, IT-98-29/1-A, Appeals Chamber, Judgment, 12 November 2009
Prosecutor v. Dusko Tadić, IT-94-1-A, Appeals Chamber, Judgment, 15 July 1999
Prosecutor v. Dusko Tadić, IT-94-1-AR72, Appeals Chamber, Judgment on the Defence Motion for Interlocutory Appeal on Jurisdiction, 2 October 1995,
Prosecutor v. Dusko Tadić, IT-94-1-T, Trial Chamber, Judgment, 7 May 1997
Prosecutor v. Dusko Tadić, IT-94-1-T, Trial Chamber, Separate opinion of judge McDonald, 7 May 1997
Prosecutor v. Galić, IT-98-29, Trial Chamber, Judgment, 5 December, 2003
Prosecutor v. Galić, IT-98-29-A, Appeals Chamber, Judgment, 30 November, 2006
Prosecutor v. Haradinaj et al, IT-04-84-T, Trial Chamber, Judgment, 3 April 2008
Prosecutor v. Kupreškić et al, IT-95-16-T, Judgment, 14 January 2000
Prosecutor v. Rajić and Andrić, IT-95-12, Trial Chamber, Review of the Indictment pursuant to Rule 61 of the Rules of Procedure and Evidence, 13 September 1996
Prosecutor v. Strugar, IT-01-42-A, Appeals Chamber Judgment, 17 July 2008

International Criminal Tribunal for Rwanda

Prosecutor v. Akayesu, ICTR-96-4-T, Trial Chamber, Judgment, 2 September 1998
Prosecutor v. Musema, ICTR-96-13-A, Trial Chamber I Judgment, 27 January 2000

International Military Tribunal for the Far East

United States et al v. Araki Sadao et al, International Military Tribunal for the Far East, (Decision of 12 November 1948), Dissentient Judgment of Justice Radhabinod Pal

Claims Commission

Eritrea-Ethiopia Claims Commission, Partial Award: Prisoners of War, Ethiopia's Claim 4, 1 July 2003

National Courts

Navtej Singh Johar v. Union of India, AIR 2018 SC 4321
Public Committee against Torture in Israel v. Government of Israel, HCJ 769/02, 14 December 2006
Ryuichi Shimoda et al v. The State (7 December 1963)
United States v. Wilhelm List et al, Trial Judgment, Case No. 7, (1948), XI LRTWC

Contents

1 Introduction: Why a Humanitarian Critique?

Abstract

International humanitarian law is widely perceived as a part of international law seeking to contain the effects of war, however, its problematic foundations and unclear language cannot be overlooked. This introductory chapter tries to explain why it is imperative to critique international humanitarian law. Describing the meaning of critique, it specifies the approaches employed and summarises the overall plan of the book. Thereafter, it briefly explains what every subsequent chapter seeks to offer.

Keywords

Critique · Critique of IHL · Principles of IHL · Laws of armed conflict

Laws of armed conflict or "international humanitarian law" are a special and a significant component of international law. They encompass rules and principles relating to regulation of belligerent conduct during international and non-international armed conflicts and seek to limit the effects of war. After World War II, the growth of the laws of armed conflict has been exponential. As the use of force is frequently resorted to by States and organized armed groups, the law has not been found to be irrelevant, however, its relevance is not a convincing answer to its problematic foundations, vague provisions, inadequacy and validation of violence. It has failed to prevent the wholesale loss of civilian lives and destruction of property in armed conflicts because many of its provisions offer justification for the same. Wars such as Israel-Palestine, Russia-Ukraine and the 1990 Gulf are a testimony to this fact. The powerful States invoked the laws of armed conflict to justify the deaths and destruction. Military necessity driven vague principles of proportionality, unnecessary suffering and distinction offer enough leeway to do that. Ironically, however, the law is glorified as International "Humanitarian" Law.

The mainstream accounts on the laws of armed conflict including the enormous literature produced by the International Committee of the Red Cross (ICRC) uncritically view this body of law as a major achievement of human civilization. The laws of armed conflict are seen as an ensemble of rules and principles, which can save the humanity, whereas they do not condemn war. The mainstream perspective finds the laws of armed conflict apolitical, objective, neutral and rational. However, the critical literature argues that the law is problematic in several ways, and its much marketed nomenclature (International Humanitarian Law) is misleading because the law barely serves the humanitarian purpose. Approaches, such as the Third World, Marxist,

K. Jeenger, *A Humanitarian Critique of International Humanitarian Law*,
Sustainable Development Goals Series, https://doi.org/10.1007/978-981-96-8319-2_1

critical and feminist, suggest that international law in general is problematic because, for instance, it is a product of colonization; it serves the interests of the global capitalist class, and it is political, biased and gendered. So are the laws of armed conflict. Therefore, a critique of the laws of armed conflict is necessary in order to inquire into the claim of a "humanitarian" law.

Critique, according to Dianne Otto, "is a mode of engagement that aims to make visible the conceptual and structural underpinnings of legal discourse, in order to understand how, despite its claims to objectivity and universality, certain structures of inequality come to be naturalized and particular subjects are privileged while others are marginalized or excluded."[1] Critique is more than the act of mere condemning. According to Michel Foucault, "A critique is not a matter of saying that things are not right as they are. It is a matter of pointing out on what kinds of assumptions, what kinds of familiar, unchallenged, unconsidered modes of thought the practices that we accept rest."[2] Critique has been found necessary for a theoretical understanding "because it exposes the assumptions we make as being not natural or neutral but, rather, associated with our particular position in the world. Critique can therefore enable us to understand, at least, that our own view is partial."[3] More importantly, critique encounters with power and challenges the obedience it stipulates, according to Foucault.[4]

In this backdrop, the book broadly aims at (1) investigating the assumptions and beliefs underlying the laws of armed conflict, (2) exposing that humanitarianism is not the foundation of the law but a topping, and (3) challenging the Western way of making and looking at it.

Considering the marginalization of humanitarian idea and primacy of military goals, a critical intervention in respect of the laws of armed conflict is crucial. It is necessary to revisit the historical background of the law, discuss the negotiating history of key instruments and critically analyze the rules and principles of the law. Therefore, in this monograph, I first aim at providing a materialist account of the historical development of the laws of armed conflict, which is essential to investigate its problematic foundations and reveal how the imperialist and capitalist tendencies shaped the content of the law. While doing so, I also employ the Third World approaches to international law to explain the exclusion of the Third World from the making and the material field of application of the laws of armed conflict. The Third World approaches need to be employed also to establish how the law helped the colonizers to maintain their hegemony over colonies.

I also try to make a deeper investigation into the negotiating history (*travaux préparatoires*) of the 1949 Geneva Conventions and the 1977 Protocols. It is essential in order to explain the arguments and position of the delegates of various States on the negotiating table. It tells us how the powerful nations abused their dominant status in order to manipulate the terms of the treaties and also how they shaped the treaties to be suitable to the European view of armed conflict. It also exposes the role played by the ICRC in the drafting of these instruments.

Further, I intend to critically examine the rules and the principles of the laws of armed conflict (i.e. principles of military necessity, proportionality, necessary suffering, distinction and humanity). This inquiry is necessary in order to look into their real character and examine to what extent they fulfill the "humanitarian" goals, especially because this body of law is glorified in the name of International Humanitarian Law. It involves not just an analysis of the provisions but their drafting history too. It especially refers to the ongoing Russia-Ukraine and Israel-Palestine armed conflicts and closely looks at the application of the rules and principles. The critical analysis of rules and principles explains the gaps in the protection of victims of war and exposes their vague and unworkable language that often facilitates and legitimates violence. Furthermore, the book also seeks to engage with the gendered foundations of the law and examine how problematic the law is in respect of women and queer bodies.

[1] Otto (2016, p. 493).

[2] Foucault (1988, p. 154).

[3] Davies (2017, p. 207).

[4] Butler (2001).

Overall, the book tries to challenge the humanitarian face of this body of law. It argues that the origin and development of the laws of armed conflict in the nineteenth century were driven by capitalist and imperialist motives. The application of the idea of "humanity" as originally conceived was limited to the "civilized" colonial masters only. The law justified violence and brutalities on the Third World peoples. The book endorses and carries further the position that the idea underlying the principles of proportionality and unnecessary suffering is military necessity, instead of humanity. In the entire architecture of the law, humanity gives way to the demands of military necessity. I argue that the vagueness and inadequacy in various rules and principles were deliberately introduced in order to satisfy the military needs of the powerful nations. I emphasize that the lack of clarity facilitates manipulation and meets the demands of military necessity, instead of humanity. In the book, I further try to suggest that the law not only remains silent on incidental civilian losses, but legitimates the same also. In respect of the humanitarian rhetoric, I attempt to underline that the humanitarian vision of the law is very narrow in that the legal framework of protection against military operations is advantageous, if at all, mainly to the white heterosexual male human beings.

1.1 Structure of the Book

The book is divided into three parts. Part I (Introduction to International Humanitarian Law "as It Is") consists of two Chaps. (2 and 3) and intends to briefly introduce readers with international humanitarian law "as it is." This introductory discussion on the laws of armed conflict is from a positivist perspective. Its overall purpose is to acquaint readers with the main provisions of the laws of armed conflict before presenting a critique thereof. In Chap. 2, therefore, I intend to briefly talk about the development of international humanitarian law, its role and its relation with other associated components of international law, such as *jus ad bellum*, human rights law and international criminal law. Thereafter, I seek to discuss the material, temporal, personal and geographical scope of application of the law in international as well as non-international armed conflicts, mainly with the help of the legal provisions, decisions of international tribunals and the ICRC commentaries.

Chapter 3 introduces the substantive rules pertaining to the conduct of hostilities. Thus, this chapter seeks to describe the rules and principles relating to combatants, non-combatants, prisoners of war, civilians, means and methods of war and environment. It tries to offer a short discussion in respect of the concerned rights and obligations of protected persons and belligerents. In doing so, the chapter intends to deal with the relevant treaty-provisions, customary international law, views of the ICRC and international judicial decisions in respect of international and non-international armed conflicts.

Part II (Historical Critique of International Humanitarian Law) contains five Chaps. (4–8) presenting the history of the laws of armed conflict critically. In Chap. 4, I try to delve into the history of the laws of armed conflict from a materialist approach. Initially, I try to explain the importance of materialist way of doing history and the metaphor of base and superstructure. In this chapter, I draw a picture of a period from the sixteenth century to the first half of the nineteenth century. My focus is on the rules of war suggested by Francisco de Vitoria, Hugo Grotius and other European writers, emerging colonization and growing capitalism. I mainly engage with the political economy of that time to explain how colonization and growing capitalism shaped the warring tendencies of the European nations and their conduct during war. The chapter underlines that the rules of war were not so developed during this period, but this era does reveal how the political and economic realities of the time led to militarism and shaped the attitude of powerful countries towards regulation of conduct during war. The Battle of Plassey, Napoleonic Wars and Crimean War explain this position. In this way, this chapter prepares the necessary background for the next chapter.

Continuing with the same approach, in Chap. 5, I deal with the development of the laws of armed

conflict from the 1864 Geneva Convention to the Additional Protocols of 1977, along with the impact of the political economy on the form and content of the instruments. I try to demonstrate how, since the very inception, selective humanitarianism was at work in terms of its content and scope. I reemphasize how the imperialist motives kept the colonies away from the making and application of the law. While discussing these developments, I intensely talk about the trade rivalry, colonial competition and imperialism, and also the impact of these historical events on the formulation of the laws of war. I argue that the law facilitated colonial expansion.

In Chap. 6, I critically engage with the ancient restraints in war prevalent in the non-European world, with special focus on India. Initially, I explain the ancient Indian historical context and *Varna* system which shaped the sources of ancient traditions in war. I offer a caste critique of various rules relating to war to explain the position of Shudras and tribes in war. Subsequently, I discuss the comprehensive restraints in war prescribed by the ancient Indian scriptures. I also strive to underscore simultaneously the instances when the practices differed from the principles. Thereafter, the chapter also analyses the position of Buddhism, Jainism and Islam in respect of war and rules in war. It specifies some of the rules from the Islamic texts and examples of departure from the same during war.

Chapter 7 deals with the historical expansion of material scope of application of the laws of armed conflict. I argue that the so called civilized States shaped the applicability criteria of the law as it suited to their imperialist agendas. I try to emphasize that the references of humanitarian considerations in the texts and during the negotiations were esthetic in nature. For this purpose, I examine in detail the preparatory works as well as the negotiating history of the 1949 Geneva Conventions and the 1977 Additional Protocols, with special reference to civil wars and anti-colonial wars. I closely analyze the submissions made by the delegates of the Western countries as well as the post-colonial countries. This analysis seeks to critically explain the role of powerful countries, the Third World countries and the ICRC in drawing the boundaries of the laws of armed conflict.

The next chapter is related to the adoption of discriminatory rules in respect of international and non-international armed conflicts. In this chapter, I intend to answer the following questions: Was it originally intended to have different set of rules regarding the two categories of armed conflict? Second, were the States initially in favor of different restraints in both the armed conflict situations? Third, how did France and the United Kingdom ensure that only a limited number of rules would apply to non-international armed conflicts? And fourth, how are the different rules for both these categories of armed conflicts problematic and how do they demonstrate the façade of a "humanitarian" law? Subsequently, the chapter tries to argue that the difference in the rules makes it unavoidable to classify an armed conflict, and this exercise often gets very complex. The complexity involved in the classification delays the operation of the law and enforcement of whatever protection it makes available.

Part III (Critique of International Humanitarian Law) extends to seven Chaps. (9–15) and it offers a critique of the rules and principles of the laws of the armed conflict. The ninth chapter introduces and describes the basic principles of the laws of armed conflict: military necessity, distinction, unnecessary suffering, proportionality and humanity. Subsequently, I offer some jurisprudential insights to the principles through the Hart-Dworkin exchanges on rules and principles. I try to locate critically the principles of the laws of armed conflict in this jurisprudential framework by using the basic ideas of principle and the "dimension of weight." I demonstrate how the "humanitarian" principles are not in harmony with this theoretical premise.

In Chap. 10, I try to analyze the laws of armed conflict from a feminist perspective. I try to explain how capitalist patriarchy makes the law stereotypical, gender-biased and hostile towards women. I reemphasize that the treaty law by and large reflects a male view of armed conflict. It ignores the fact that women experience war in a much more different and atrocious way. Accordingly, I provide a detailed analysis of how the law

is based on patriarchal notions and how it makes the conditions of women even worse in some situations during an armed conflict. The chapter argues that from a humanitarian perspective, the notion of humanity in the laws of armed conflict largely means masculinity. Lastly, I ring an alarm in respect of the attempts of dilution and hegemonic appropriation of the feminist movement.

Chapter 11 offers a critique of the laws of armed conflict from a queer perspective. I initially talk about the patriarchal normalization of gender binary and introduce the queer theory. I unearth the fundamental heterosexual-normalcy and binary assumptions, and explain how they are problematic so far as the protection of bodies with different gender identities or sexual orientations during an armed conflict is concerned. Subsequently, I seek to explain how they experience war in a different way, and in spite of this, the law is blind towards these bodies and their concerns. I also try to highlight the blind, deaf and discriminatory nature of the legal provisions from a queer perspective.

The next chapter relates to the principle of distinction. At the beginning, I discuss critically the meaning of civilians and civilian objects, and the principle of distinction. Subsequently, I discuss three important humanitarian challenges to the distinction principle in the contemporary warfare: (1) how to distinguish in asymmetrical warfare; (2) disputed meaning and scope of the phrase "direct participation by civilians in hostilities," and (3) whether child soldiers may be targeted. The analysis refers to, at suitable places, the current armed conflicts between Israel and Palestine, and Russia and Ukraine, and contextualizes the problematic side of the principle.

Chapter 13 critically approaches the principle of proportionality and tries to unveil its inhuman side. I begin with the Roman theological underpinnings to the principle of proportionality and then discuss its drafting history in order to explain how several delegates found the draft proportionality provision to be problematic. Thereafter, I discuss in detail the critical dimension of the proportionality principle with special reference to the wars on Ukraine and Gaza. I stress upon the vagueness in the provision and explain how the proportionality assessment is challenging for a commander. I reemphasize that certain effects of war, such as mental harm and reverberating effects do not factor in the assessment. I explain how the vague notion of military advantage may be abused by a powerful belligerent, especially on the ground of self-defense. I also argue that at times the principle may even encourage violence and justify death and destruction.

In Chap. 14, I offer a critique of the much marketed principle of humanity. I try to argue that humanity stays at the periphery of the laws of armed conflict, while military necessity enjoys the prominent position because it dictates the contents of the rules of the law. I question the humanitarian side claimed in respect of the principle of proportionality. I argue that proportionally principle justifies and helps overlook the simultaneous harm to civilians, even when it is huge. It does not entail an obligation about minimizing civilian loss. Considering the overall architecture of the law, I argue that it compromises with humanitarian considerations and validates violence and suffering in several ways. Lastly, I argue that the name of the discipline (International Humanitarian Law) is flawed, deceptive and political.

Chapter 15 offers the concluding observations.

References

Butler J (2001) What is critique? an essay on Foucault's virtue. https://transversal.at/transversal/0806/butler/en

Davies M (2017) Asking the law question. Thomson Reuters, Sydney

Foucault M (1988) Practicing criticism. In: Kritzman LD (ed) Politics, philosophy, culture: interviews and other writings, 1977–1984. Routledge, New York, pp 152–158

Otto D (2016) Feminist Approaches to International Law. In: Orford A, Hoffmann F (eds) The Oxford handbook of the theory of international law. OUP, New York, pp 488–504

Part I

Introduction to International Humanitarian Law "as It Is"

Scope of Application 2

Abstract

In this chapter, I intend to briefly talk about the development of international humanitarian law, its role and its relation with other associated components of international law, such as *jus ad bellum*, human rights law and international criminal law. Thereafter, I seek to discuss the material, temporal, personal and geographical scope of application of the law in international as well as non-international armed conflicts mainly with the help of the legal provisions, decisions of international tribunals and the ICRC commentaries. The discussion is from a positivist perspective and tries to explain in detail the scope of the laws of armed conflict.

Keywords

IHL & human rights · Scope of IHL · Application of IHL

2.1 Introduction to the Laws of Armed Conflict

Primarily, the body of laws of armed conflict (international humanitarian law) refers to that segment of international law which come into play mainly during an armed conflict, be it international or non-international. It provides for certain restrictions on the hostile conduct of parties at war. The law seeks to restrict the means and methods of warfare and ensure the protection of and humane treatment with persons who are not, or no longer, taking a direct part in hostilities.[1] The necessity of the law has been sought in mitigating the hardships of war and in limiting the measure of violence by its absolute practical necessity.[2] It is, therefore, *jus in bello* which regulates the way belligerents operate during an armed conflict and determines the lawfulness of their hostile conduct.

The laws of armed conflict mainly comprise and include the four Geneva Conventions adopted in the year 1949,[3] Convention on the protection of cultural property[4] (1954), three Protocols additional to the Geneva Conventions of 1949,[5]

[1] Melzer (2016, p. 17) and Burra (2018, p. 52).

[2] Sastry (1952, p. 254).

[3] The Geneva Convention for the Amelioration of the Condition of the Wounded and Sick in Armed Forces in the Field of 12 August 1949 (Geneva Convention I), the Geneva Convention for the Amelioration of the Condition of Wounded, Sick and Shipwrecked Members of Armed Forces at Sea of 12 August 1949 (Geneva Convention II), the Geneva Convention relative to the Treatment of Prisoners of War of 12 August 1949 (Geneva Convention III) and the Geneva Convention relative to the Protection of Civilian Persons in Time of War of 12 August 1949 (Geneva Convention IV).

[4] Convention for the Protection of Cultural Property in the Event of Armed Conflict (1954).

[5] Protocol Additional to the Geneva Conventions of 12 August 1949, and relating to the Protection of Victims of International Armed Conflicts (Protocol I) of 8 June

K. Jeenger, *A Humanitarian Critique of International Humanitarian Law*,
Sustainable Development Goals Series, https://doi.org/10.1007/978-981-96-8319-2_2

Hague Conventions and Regulations of 1899 and 1907,[6] Convention on conventional weapons (1980),[7] Convention on biological weapons[8] and customary international law. Out of these instruments, Article 3 common to the four Geneva Conventions, 1949 and Protocol II additional to the Geneva Conventions were exclusively adopted in respect of armed conflicts not of an international character. On the other hand, instruments applicable in both the types of armed conflicts include the Conventions on cultural property, conventional weapons and biological weapons. The rest of the instruments apply exclusively to international armed conflicts.

2.2 Linkage with Allied Components of International Law

In contrast to the legality of conduct during armed conflicts which is the subject matter of laws of armed conflict, the legality of waging a war itself is determined by *jus ad bellum*, for instance, Articles 2(4), 42 and 51 of the United Nations Charter. Distinction may also be drawn with another related discipline, International Criminal Law. It defines international crimes (which include war crimes also), and provides for the composition, jurisdiction and powers of an international criminal tribunal and the procedure for initiating criminal proceedings against an accused. Thus, it also helps in the enforcement of the laws of armed conflict. While describing war crimes, the international criminal law refers to the law of armed conflict and uses its expressions or identical language.[9] In this way, some part of international criminal law derives its origin from the laws of armed conflict.[10] Therefore, it has been said that both of them share common roots in that they aim at protecting victims of armed conflict.[11]

Unlike *jus adbellum* and international criminal law, international human rights law can regulate some of the belligerent actions during an armed conflict. It has been said to be an "overarching regime under international law"[12] which interacts with the laws of armed conflict in variety of ways. Such intermingling was little at the beginning of the second half of the twentieth century,[13] though, it augmented later on. This relationship between the two disciplines may be understood in light of the differences and commonalities between them. At the same time, the march from early divergence to gradual convergence and complementarity in them is equally significant for this purpose. Considering the negotiations of the Universal Declaration of Human Rights, 1948 and the four Geneva Conventions of 1949, it has been generally argued, excepting a few[14] scholars, that there was no mutual influence.[15] The human rights law was seen as specific to peace time only. However, in 1953, the General Assembly condemned the atrocities committed

1977, Protocol Additional to the Geneva Conventions of 12 August 1949, and relating to the Protection of Victims of Non-International Armed Conflicts (Protocol II) of 8 June 1977 and Protocol additional to the Geneva Conventions of 12 August 1949, and relating to the Adoption of an Additional Distinctive Emblem (Protocol III) of 8 December 2005.

[6] Hague Convention (II) with Respect to the Laws and Customs of War on Land of 29 July 1899 and annexed Regulations Concerning the Laws and Customs of War on Land and Hague Convention (IV) with Respect to the Laws and Customs of War on Land of 18 October 1907 and annexed Regulations Respecting the Laws and Customs of War on Land.

[7] Convention on Prohibitions or Restrictions on the Use of Certain Conventional Weapons Which May Be Deemed to Be Excessively Injurious or to Have Indiscriminate Effects as amended on 21 December 2001 (1980).

[8] Convention on the Prohibition of the Development, Production and Stockpiling of Bacteriological (Biological) and Toxin Weapons and on their Destruction (1971).

[9] For example, compare Article 3 Common to the Four Geneva Conventions of 1949 with Article 8(2)(c), Statute of International Criminal Court (1998) (Rome Statute) or Articles 50, 51, 130 and 147 of the Four Geneva Conventions of 1949 respectively with Article 2 Statute of the International Criminal Tribunal for the Former Yugoslavia (1993) (ICTY Statute).

[10] Cassese et al (2008, p. 5).

[11] Cryer et al. (2011, p. 15).

[12] Lixinski (2010, p. 590).

[13] Kolb (1998, p. 409) and Sivakumaran (2011, p. 234).

[14] For instance, Dijk (2018, pp. 553–582).

[15] For more, see Droege (2008, pp. 504–505).

by the North Korean and Chinese forces against the United Nations prisoners of war in Korea by calling it a disrespect of human rights as well.[16] Similarly, the General Assembly called upon the Soviet Union and Hungary to respect Hungarian people's fundamental human rights during invasion of Hungary in 1956.[17] However, it was the International Conference on Human Rights, 1968 held in Tehran when the issue prominently came up for discussion for the first time.[18] By adopting a resolution,[19] the Conference invited the United Nations Secretary General to present a report on the issue of human rights in armed conflict.[20] The two reports produced by him acknowledged the fact that the international human rights law may apply to armed conflicts as well.[21] The reports were followed by a General Assembly resolution titled Basic Principles for the Protection of Civilian Populations in Armed Conflict.[22] The resolution re-emphasized that fundamental human rights continue to apply fully in situations of armed conflicts. Since then, the application of human rights provisions in situations of armed conflict has been frequently accepted, for example, by the ICJ in the matters of Legality of the Threat or Use of Nuclear Weapons and Legal Consequences of the Construction of Wall in the Occupied Palestinian Territory[23]; by the Human Rights Committee[24]; by the United Kingdom in the Nuclear Weapons case[25] and by State-parties in some of the foremost human rights and armed conflict law treaties.[26]

The international human rights law does not apply unconditionally to an armed conflict. The provisions common in both the regimes (for instance, prohibition of slavery[27] and recruitment of children below the age of fifteen years into armed forces[28]) may apply simultaneously. However, where a provision contained in the laws of armed conflict is more specific[29] or contradictory[30] to a human rights law norm, the laws of armed conflict apply according to the principle of *lex specialis derogat lege generali.*

[16] A/RES/8/804, Question of Atrocities Committed by the North Korean and Chinese Communist Forces against United Nations Prisoners of War in Korea (1953).

[17] A/RES/8/1312, The Situation in Hungary (1958).

[18] Sivakumaran (2012, p. 86).

[19] Human Rights in Armed conflicts, Resolution XXIII, 12 May 1968.

[20] Milanovic (2016, p. 93).

[21] UN Doc. A/7720, Respect for Human Rights in Armed Conflicts, Report of the UN Secretary General, para 23 (1969) and UN Doc. A/8052, Respect for Human Rights in Armed Conflicts, Report of the UN Secretary General, para 25 (1970). For more discussion, see Milanovic (2016, pp. 93–96).

[22] A/RES/25/2675 (1970).

[23] Advisory Opinion (1996) ICJ Rep 226, para 25 and Advisory Opinion (2004) ICJ Rep 136, para 106, respectively.

[24] UN Doc., CCPR/C/21/Rev.1/Add. 13, General Comment 31, Nature of the General Legal Obligation Imposed on States Parties to the Covenant, para 11 (2004).

[25] Milanovic (2016, pp. 86–87).

[26] Art. 4 International Covenant on Civil and Political Rights (1966), Art. 15 European Convention for the Protection of Human Rights and Fundamental Freedoms (1950), Art. 27 American Convention on Human Rights (1969) and Art. 72 Addition Protocol I, above n 5.

[27] Art. 4(2)(f), Additional Protocol II, above n 5 and Article 8(1), International Covenant on Civil and Political Rights (1966).

[28] Art. 77(2) Additional Protocol I, above n 5 and Article 38(3), Convention on the Rights of the Child (1989).

[29] In Nuclear Weapons advisory opinion, the ICJ followed this principle to determine what is meant by arbitrary deprivation of one's life in Article 6 of the International Covenant on Civil and Political Rights (1966): 'Every human being has the inherent right to life. ... No one shall be arbitrarily deprived of his life.' The court held that to clarify the right not arbitrarily to be deprived of one's life in hostilities recourse must be had to the applicable lex specialis, namely, the law applicable in armed conflict which is designed to regulate the conduct of hostilities. See para 25, above n 23. Accordingly, targeting soldiers during an armed conflict may not be arbitrary but targeting civilians may be.

[30] According to Article 118 of Geneva Convention III, for instance, prisoners of war shall be released only after the termination of active hostilities, while Article 9(3), International Covenant on Civil and Political Rights (1966) gives a detainee a right to be brought before a judge promptly.

2.3 Scope of Application of Laws of Armed Conflict

The laws of armed conflict become applicable as soon as an armed conflict occurs; however, its field of application is broad and multidimensional. A discussion as to its scope of application seeks to explain, (a) the hostile situation the law seeks to regulate (material scope); (b) the beginning and end of application of the law (temporal scope); (c) persons subject to the law (personal scope), and (d) areas to which the law may extend (geographical scope).

2.3.1 Material Scope of Application

The material field in the context of the laws of armed conflict refers to the situations which trigger the application of the law. Broadly, the situations have been categorized as international armed conflict and non-international armed conflict.

2.3.1.1 International Armed Conflict

Under the Geneva Conventions of 1949, there are three situations that amount to international armed conflict: "all cases of declared war or of any other armed conflict which may arise between two or more of the High Contracting Parties … all cases of partial or total occupation of the territory of a High Contracting Party".[31] The first condition refers to a war which is waged after making a declaration to this effect. The expression war remains undefined in the Geneva Conventions; however, several scholars have made efforts in this direction. According to Oppenheim, "War is a contention between two or more States through their armed forces, for the purpose of overpowering each other and imposing such conditions of peace as the victor pleases."[32] Post World War II, Quincy Wright defines war as "the legal condition which equally permits two or more hostile groups to carry on a conflict by armed force."[33] Thus, declaration and hostile involvement of armed forces is necessary to constitute the first condition. The second condition of armed conflict has been explained in Tadić case, by the ICTY as "a resort to armed force between States."[34] On the similar vein, the 1952 Commentary to the First Geneva Convention published by the International Committee of the Red Cross (ICRC) says that an armed conflict is any difference arising between two States and leading to the intervention of armed forces.[35] However, this approach has been refuted by the second edition of the ICRC Commentary. The Commentary calls it a narrow interpretation because it necessitates simultaneous involvement of at least two States and thus, excludes from the scope of armed conflict unilateral use of force by one State against another. Therefore, the new ICRC approach is that "when a State resorts to means and methods of warfare against another State, that situation qualifies for an international armed conflict, irrespective of the organ within that State that has resorted to such means and methods."[36] It clarifies that resort to means and methods of warfare include naval or air blockade, and deployment of armed forces on the territory of another State irrespective of any armed resistance. Further, the use of these means and methods even by paramilitary or border security forces, or coast guards but not by private persons, shall also constitute an international armed conflict. The term armed conflict extends to use of force directed against enemy's territory, civilian population or civilian objects as well.

Besides actual hostilities between States, occupation of a foreign territory is also subject to the laws of international armed conflict. Even before the adoption of the four Geneva Conventions in 1949, the occupying forces were subject

---

[31] Art. 2 common to Geneva Conventions, above n 3.

[32] Oppenheim (1952, p. 202).

[33] Vasquez (2009, p. 31).

[34] Prosecutor v. Dusko Tadić, IT-94-1-AR72, Appeals Chamber, Judgment on the Defence Motion for Interlocutory Appeal on Jurisdiction, 2 October 1995, para 70.

[35] Pictet (1952).

[36] ICRC (2016a, para 223).

to the ordinary rules of warfare.[37] Occupation is invasion plus taking possession of enemy country for the purpose of holding it, at any rate temporarily.[38] According to The Hague Regulations, territory is considered occupied when it is actually placed under the authority of the hostile army.[39] This definition, "despite its vagueness",[40] has been considered to be the exclusive criteria to determine the existence of an occupation by national and international courts, and also under the Geneva Convention IV of 1949.[41] The term "authority" used in the definition implies control over the territory. However, to apply the relevant humanitarian law, the control must be effective, which means presence of foreign troops without consent, ability to exercise authority over the territory under control disregarding the incumbent government and inability of the incumbent government to exert its authority over the territory.[42] Within the meaning of the four Geneva Conventions, a situation amounts to occupation even if it is exercised over the entire territory or any part thereof, and irrespective of armed resistance against the invading army.

One more category added to international armed conflicts finds place in the Additional Protocol I. Accordingly, "armed conflicts in which peoples are fighting against colonial domination and alien occupation and against racist regimes in the exercise of their right of self-determination, as enshrined in the Charter of the United Nations and the Declaration on Principles of International Law concerning Friendly Relations and Co-operation among States in accordance with the Charter of the United Nations"[43] also fall within the scope of international armed conflicts. The ICRC Commentary calls the armed conflicts involving peoples, "wars of national liberation".[44] One of the positive aspects of applying the laws of international armed conflict to wars of national liberation is that fighters of the liberation movement attain the status of combatants and in case of capture, the status of prisoners of war.[45]

The term "armed conflict" in the above provision is qualified by intensity and length, according to the ICRC.[46] In respect of the expression "peoples," it has been suggested that peoples are represented by national liberation movements, as contrast to ethnic groups which are sometimes represented by non-State actors.[47] According to the provision, such an armed conflict takes place in the exercise of the right to self-determination in accordance with the United Nations Charter and the Declaration of 1970. The right to self-determination implies the right of people freely to determine, without external interference, their political status and to pursue their economic, social and cultural development.[48]

2.3.1.2 Non-International Armed Conflicts

Before the adoption of the Additional Protocol II in 1977, armed conflicts not of an international character were governed by Article 3 common to the four Geneva Conventions, 1949. However, it does not contain any description or criterion,

[37] Stone (1954, p. 694) and Sect. III, Hague Regulations 1907, above n 6.

[38] Oppenheim (1952, p. 434).

[39] Art. 42 para 1 Hague Regulations 1907, above n 6. Similar definition was given by Holland: "Occupied territory is the one placed, as a matter of fact, under the authority of the hostile army." See Holland (1898, p. 71).

[40] Spoerri (2014, p. 188).

[41] Rev. Mons. Sebastiao Francisco Xavier dos Remedios Monteiro v. The State of Goa (AIR 1970 SC 329). In the Wall Advisory Opinion the ICJ confirms the customary status of the definition. See para 78, above n 23. A trial chamber of the ICTY endorses this definition: Prosecutor v. Naletilic and Martinovic, IT-98-34-T, Trial Chamber, Judgment, 31 March 2003, paras 215–216. Article 154 of the Geneva Convention on Civilians (above n 3) says that this Convention is supplementary to the relevant Hague Regulations. See also, ICRC (2016a, b, paras 296, 298).

[42] ICRC (2016a, b, paras 302–303) and Ferraro (2012a, b, p. 10).

[43] Art. 1(4).

[44] Sandoz et al. (1987, para 66).

[45] Baxter (2013, p. 283).

[46] Sandoz et al. (1987, para 118).

[47] Mastorodimos (2016, p. 32).

[48] A/RES/25/2625, Declaration on Principles of International Law concerning Friendly Relations and Co-operation among States in accordance with the Charter of the United Nations (1970); International Covenant on Civil and Political Rights (1966).

except the expression "armed conflicts not of an international character." After more than four decades, in the famous case of Tadić, an appeals chamber of the International Tribunal for the Former Yugoslavia (ICTY) held that when there is "protracted armed violence between governmental authorities and organized armed groups or between such groups within a State,"[49] it is an armed conflict not of international character. A trial chamber of the ICTY interpreted the Appeal Chamber's twofold test as, first, intensity of violence instead of protracted armed violence, and second, organization of the armed group.[50]

According to the Tribunal, some of the indications of the first condition (intensity of violence) are as follows: the spread of clashes over territory and over a period of time, use of heavy weapons and military equipments such as tanks, quantity of troops, number of deaths, number of civilians forced to flee, damage to property, steps taken by the Security Council, occupation of territory, deployment of government forces to the crisis area, ceasefire agreements.[51] However, it has been importantly pointed out that violence that is protracted but not intense, or intense but not protracted, does not amount to a non-international armed conflict.[52]

On the other hand, organization of armed group has been interpreted to mean the following: "existence of a command structure and disciplinary rules and mechanisms within the group; existence of headquarters; the fact that the group controls a certain territory; the ability of the group to gain access to weapons, other military equipment, recruits and military training; its ability to plan, coordinate and carry out military operations, including troop movements and logistics; its ability to define a unified military strategy and use military tactics; and its ability to speak with one voice and negotiate and conclude agreements such as ceasefire or peace accords."[53] In any case, the criteria of intensity and organization must be present cumulatively in order for a situation of violence to reach the threshold of a non-international armed conflict.[54] Thus, internal disturbance, mob violence or riots do not trigger application of common Article 3.[55]

In respect of non-international armed conflicts, the criteria provided by Protocol II set a threshold higher than that under common Article 3. Unlike the non-definition approach[56] of the latter, the Protocol specifies conditions constituting non-international armed conflicts. Notably, the Protocol seeks to develop and supplement common Article 3 without altering its applicability criteria.[57] It aims at applying to all armed conflicts,

> which take place in the territory of a High Contracting Party between its armed forces and dissident armed forces or other organized armed groups which, under responsible command, exercise such control over a part of its territory as to enable them to carry out sustained and concerted military operations and to implement this Protocol.[58]

Thus, under a Protocol II type of non-international armed conflict, one of the parties to armed conflict is always a State and the other party may be a dissident army (for instance, Free Syrian Army) or an organized armed group. It implies that

[49] Tadić, above n 34, para 70.

[50] Prosecutor v. Dusko Tadić, IT-94-1-T, Trial Chamber, Judgment, 7 May 1997, para 562 and Darcy (2014, p. 105). With the help of Vattel's definition of civil war, ICRC reports of Conference of Government Experts of 1962 and 1972, and the ICRC Commentary on Additional Protocol II (1987) a distinguished author establishes that the requirements of intensity and organisation are of longstanding origin. See Sivakumaran (2012, pp. 165–166).

[51] Prosecutor v. Boškoski and Tarčulovski, IT-04-82, Trial Chamber, Judgment, 10 July 2008, para 177.

[52] Dinstein (2014, p. 35).

[53] Prosecutor v. Haradinaj et al., IT-04-84-T, Trial Chamber, Judgment, 3 April 2008, para 60.

[54] ICRC (2016b, para 434).

[55] Ibid., para 386, Art. 1(2) Protocol II, above n 5 and Art. 8(2)(d)(f) Rome Statute, above n 9. Sivakumaran maintains that the two ingredients had been recognized decades and centuries earlier. Besides Vattel and Hall, the ICRC suggested the two components to Conference of Government Experts in 1962 and 1972, and also in the Commentary on Additional Protocol II. See Sivakumaran (2012, pp. 165–166).

[56] Sivakumaran (2012, p. 156).

[57] Art. 1(1) Protocol II, above n 5.

[58] Ibid.

an armed conflict between two or more organized armed groups is not a subject matter of the Protocol, but that of common Article 3. The non-State actor side of the conflict must be under a responsible command, which presupposes some degree of organization[59] with either hierarchical or horizontal[60] structure.

The type of control over territory intended in the provision need not be a long-standing one and over a vast amount of land. According to the ICRC, there must be some degree of stability in the control even on modest area of territory which is beyond the control of the government.[61] It has been suggested that in certain circumstances control over a small portion of national territory (for example 1 percent) would also suffice.[62] Further, the territorial control must be of such character which enables the forces or armed groups to carry out sustained and concerted military operations. The word "sustained" signifies "continuous"[63] but not "non-stop,"[64] and therefore, any pauses or intervals of a few days during hostilities do not divest the military operations of being sustained. The operations must also be "concerted" which implies premeditated or pre-planned operations, or operations agreed upon.[65]

Additionally, the territorial control must be effective enough to facilitate implementation of the Protocol. For example, the non-State actor must be able to protect and care the wounded, sick and shipwrecked,[66] and to conduct fair and impartial trial.[67] The ability is measured by resources and infrastructure. Therefore, territorial control indeed has material bearing on the ability to implement the Protocol.[68]

Overall, the protocol is an extension of common Article 3.[69] Common Article 3 is an overarching provision in respect of non-international armed conflicts. A common Article 3 non-international armed conflict is a genus of which an Additional Protocol II non-international armed conflict is a species. Therefore, an armed conflict to which the Additional Protocol II applies, common Article 3 also applies. However, a non-international armed conflict not covered by the Additional Protocol II is governed by common Article 3.

2.3.2 Temporal Field of Application

Temporal field of application simply refers to the points of time which marks the beginning and cessation of application of relevant law to an armed conflict. Broadly, the law becomes applicable as soon as the conditions necessary to what constitute an international armed conflict are present; and ceases to apply when such conditions disappear. In fact, an armed conflict (including occupation) and the applicability of the relevant law are generally coexistent and correlated except for certain provisions which continue to apply even after cessation of hostilities. They include the final release, repatriation and re-establishment, as the case may be, of persons after fighting ceases.[70] There are certain provisions which are applicable during peacetime. They relate to the dissemination of the text of instruments even in peacetime.[71] However, it is always not so obvious to determine the existence and absence of the conditions.

---

59 Sandoz et al. (1987, para 4463).

60 Sivakumaran (2012, p. 176). See also above n 59.

61 Sandoz et al. (1987, para 4467).

62 Mastorodimos (2016, p. 21).

63 Sandoz et al. (1987, para 4469) (the Commentary uses dictionary meaning) and Prosecutor v. Akayesu, ICTR-96-4-T, Trial Chamber, Judgment, 2 September 1998, para 626.

64 Sivakumaran (2012, p. 188).

65 The dictionary meaning referred to in the Commentary is "agreed upon, planned and contrived, done in agreement according to a plan." See Sandoz et al. (1987, para 4469). The Akayesu judgment calls it "planned." See Akayesu, above n 63, para 626.

66 Art. 7 Protocol II, above n 5.

67 Ibid., Art. 6.

68 For a critique on the formulation of the provision, see Jeenger (2017, pp. 43–56).

69 Sandoz et al. (1987, para 4437).

70 Art. 5, 5(1), 6(4) Geneva Conventions I, III and IV, above n 3, respectively, and Art. 75(6) Protocol I, above n 5.

71 Art. 47, 48, 127, 144, 83, 19, 7 Geneva Conventions I-IV, above n 3, and three Protocols additional to them, above n 5, respectively.

2.3.2.1 International Armed Conflicts

As soon as the factual requirements of an international armed conflict, as set out above, are found to exist, the relevant laws of armed conflict become applicable.[72] To the contrary, "the general close of military operations"[73] is the moment when the law ceases to apply, except the situations specified in the above paragraph.[74] In this respect, the ICRC is of the following opinion:

> 'Military operations' means the movements, maneuvers and actions of any sort, carried out by the armed forces with a view to combat. 'The general close of military operations' ... may be deemed in principle to be at the time of a general armistice, capitulation or just when the occupation of the whole territory of a Party is completed, accompanied by the effective cessation of all hostilities ...[75]

However, in the opinion of the ICTY, the application of the law extends beyond the cessation of hostilities until a general conclusion of peace is reached.[76]

Similarly, the law of occupation applies as soon as all the elements constituting effective control are in place. However, as to the applicability of the occupation law to the stage of invasion, there is difference of opinion. The debate arose in view of the looting and violence at the hands of private persons during the invasion of Iraq in 2003. In this regard, the earlier position held by the ICRC is: "there is no intermediate phase between invasion and occupation",[77] which implies that the occupation law becomes applicable from invasion phase. This position has been refuted by majority of experts on the ground that occupation requires some control over the territory, which is absent in case of invasion.[78]

Cessation of the applicability of the occupation law is also dependent on effective control. The absence of any of the essentials constituting effective control stops the applicability of the law, however, it has been argued that where the occupying forces withdraw themselves formally but somehow continue to exercise the authority as before, the law of occupation continues to apply.[79]

2.3.2.2 Non-International Armed Conflicts

During a situation of internal disturbance or armed rebellion against the incumbent government, the time when the legal threshold of organization of armed group and the intensity of violence is reached or the criteria under Protocol II is met, the law of non-international armed conflict begins to regulate the conflict situation. As regards cessation of operation of the law, mere end of hostilities is not sufficient. The relevant law remains in force until a peaceful settlement is arrived at,[80] or for the benefit of persons whose liberty has been restricted.[81]

2.3.3 Personal Field of Application

Personal sphere of application of the laws of armed conflict refers to those to whom the law is binding. The term "person" is used here in jurisprudential sense, and thus includes a legal person also who enjoys certain legal rights and obligations. The subjects of the laws of armed conflict can be classified into two categories in both the types of armed conflicts: parties to an armed conflict and human subjects.

2.3.3.1 International Armed Conflicts

Parties to an international armed conflict are generally those who are party to a relevant

[72] Art. 3(a), Protocol II, above n 5.

[73] Art. 3(b), Protocol I, above n 5.

[74] Ibid. According to the Commentary on Additional Protocols, Article 3(b) has the effect of replacing Articles 5, 5, 6 of Geneva Conventions I, III and IV respectively: Sandoz et al. (1987, para 151).

[75] Sandoz et al. (1987, para 152).

[76] Tadić, above n 34, para 70.

[77] Pictet (1958).

[78] Zwanenburg et al. (2012, pp. 34, 39).

[79] Ferraro (2012a, b, pp. 156–157).

[80] Tadić, above n 34, para 70.

[81] See, Art. 2(2), 5 Protocol II, above n 5.

treaty,[82] or who accept the provisions of a relevant treaty,[83] or are bound to respect the customary law. According to the Vienna Convention on the Law of Treaties, a treaty is binding upon the parties to it.[84] The other subjects of the law in an international armed conflict are combatants (members of the armed forces who have a right to directly engage in hostilities.),[85] non-combatants (medical personnel and chaplains)[86] and civilians.

2.3.3.2 Non-International Armed Conflicts

The declaration of the common Article 3 that "each Party to the conflict shall be bound to apply" a list of provisions indicates that it is binding on State as well as non-State actors. Protocol II also binds the parties in the same way. Additionally, medical and religious personnel,[87] and persons who do not engage themselves in hostilities directly,[88] who have ceased to do so,[89] or whose liberty has been restricted[90] are also subjects of the laws of armed conflict.

2.3.4 Geographical Field of Application

It refers to the determination of the expanse where the laws of armed conflict shall apply during a situation of armed conflict. This aspect as to the territorial reach of the law is very crucial; however, the law is almost silent[91] on its determination. The following discussion tries to explain how the law's territorial application is not just limited to the combat zone or the belligerents' territory, but it may extend to neutral and non-warring States too.

2.3.4.1 International Armed Conflicts

Apparently, the laws of armed conflict operate in the war zone as they regulate the conduct of hostile parties. However, considering, for instance, the prohibitions as to attack on civilians and civilian objects, and ill-treatment with sick, wounded and shipwrecked soldiers, prisoners of war, detainees and internees, the law is applicable throughout the territory of belligerents,[92] extending to land territory, territorial sea, internal waters, archipelagic water and territorial airspace too under the "principle of unity of territory."[93] Similarly, the law may also apply to continental shelf[94] and exclusive economic zone[95] of coastal belligerent States, high seas[96] and airspace above these maritime zones in case of hostile conduct.[97] Additionally, the law may also operate in States not party to an armed conflict.[98] Such a situation arises in case of internment or detention of various protected persons in neutral or non-belligerent States.[99]

2.3.4.2 Non-International Armed Conflicts

It has been suggested by an international tribunal that the laws of armed conflict apply to the entire territory belonging to a party to a non-international armed conflict falling within the common Article 3 or Protocol II, regardless of

[82] Art. 2(2) common to four Geneva Conventions, above n 3.

[83] Ibid. and Art. 96(2)(3) Protocol I, above n 5.

[84] Art. 26, Vienna Convention on the Law of Treaties (1969).

[85] See Art. 44(5) and 43(2) Protocol I, above n 5.

[86] See Art. 33 Geneva Convention III, above n 3.

[87] Art. 9 Protocol II, above n 5.

[88] Art. 3(1) common to four Geneva Conventions, above n 3 and Art. 4 Protocol II, above n 5.

[89] Ibid.

[90] Art. 5 Protocol II, above n 5.

[91] Tadić, above n 34, para 68.

[92] Ibid.

[93] Kolb and Hyde (2008, p. 95).

[94] See Art. 76, United Nations Convention on the Law of the Sea (1982).

[95] See ibid., Art. 57.

[96] See ibid., Art. 86.

[97] Crawford (2020, pp. 65–67).

[98] CICR (2012, p. 108).

[99] See, for instance, Art. 4(B)(2) Geneva Convention III, above n 3 and Art. 19, Protocol I, above n 5.

actual hostilities taking place there.[100] This view, however, presupposes that a State is a necessary party to such an armed conflict. It, thus, leaves unanswered the question of field of application of the law where both the parties are non-State actors.

However, where such an armed conflict is not confined to the territory of one State and has some extra-territorial connection, it has been suggested by the ICRC in its latest Commentary to the Convention that common Article 3 can be lawfully applied to the non-international armed conflicts having extra-territorial effect because; (1) the expression "one of the High Contracting Parties" under the Article has been used to exclude a State not signatory to the Geneva Conventions, and (2) the object of the common Article 3 is to afford minimum protection to those who do not actively participate in the hostilities irrespective of their location.[101] However, it has been argued that this position runs contrary to the view held by the tribunal that the law applies to the territory under the control of a party to the conflict.[102]

References

Baxter R (2013) The Geneva conventions of 1949 and wars of national liberation. In: Vagts DF et al Humanising the laws of war: selected writings of Richard Baxter. OUP, Oxford, pp 277–285

Burra S (2018) Collective engagement and selective endorsement: India's ambivalent attitude towards laws of armed conflict. In: Burra S, Babu RR (eds) Locating India in the contemporary international legal order. Springer, New Delhi, pp 51–65

Cassese A et al (eds) (2008) Cassese's international criminal law. OUP, Oxford

CICR (2012) Scope of application of international humanitarian law, proceedings of the 13th Bruges colloquium, CICR, 18–19 October 2012

Crawford E (2020) The temporal and geographic reach of international humanitarian law. In: Saul B, Akande D (eds) Oxford guide to international humanitarian law. OUP, Oxford, pp 57–76

Cryer R et al (2011) An introduction to international criminal law and procedure. CUP, New Delhi

[100] Tadić, above n 34, para 70 and Akayesu, above n 63, para 635.

[101] ICRC (2016b, paras 466–467).

[102] Crawford (2020, p. 72).

Darcy S (2014) Judges, law and war: the judicial development of international humanitarian law. CUP, Cambridge

Dijk B (2018) Human rights in war: on the entangled foundations of the 1949 Geneva conventions. Am J Int Law 112(4):553–582

Dinstein Y (2014) Non-international armed conflicts in international law. CUP, Cambridge

Droege C (2008) Elective affinities? Human rights and humanitarian law. Int Rev Red Cross 90(871):501–548

Ferraro T (2012a) Determining the beginning and end of an occupation under international humanitarian law. Int Rev Red Cross 94(885):133–163

Ferraro T (ed) (2012b) Expert meeting: occupation and other forms of administration of foreign territory. ICRC, Geneva

Holland TE (1898) Studies in international law. Clarendon Press, London

ICRC (2016a) Commentary on article 2, Geneva convention I. https://ihl-databases.icrc.org/en/ihl-treaties/gci-1949/article-2/commentary/2016

ICRC (2016b) Commentary on article 3, Geneva convention I. https://ihl-databases.icrc.org/en/ihl-treaties/gci-1949/article-3/commentary/2016#146_B

Jeenger K (2016–2017) How "ability" requirement in additional protocol II may disable its applicability to NIACs. ISIL YB of Int'l Humanitarian & Refugee Law XVI–XVII:43–56

Kolb R (1998) The relationship between international humanitarian law and human rights law: a brief history of the 1948 Universal Declaration of Human Rights and the 1949 Geneva convention. Int Rev Red Cross 324:409–419

Kolb R, Hyde R (2008) An introduction to the international law of armed conflicts. Hart Publishing, Oxford

Lixinski L (2010) Treaty interpretation by the Inter-American Court of Human Rights: expansionism at the service of the unity of international law. Eur J Int Law 21(3):585–604

Mastorodimos K (2016) Armed non-State actors in international humanitarian law and human rights law: foundation and framework of obligations, and rules on accountability. Ashgate, Surrey

Melzer N (2016) International humanitarian law: a comprehensive introduction. ICRC, Geneva

Milanovic M (2016) The lost origins of lex specialis: rethinking the relationship between human rights and international humanitarian law. In: Ohlin JD (ed) Theoretical boundaries of armed conflict and human rights. CUP, New York, pp 78–117

Oppenheim L (1952) International law, vol II: disputes, war and neutrality. Longmans, Green & Co, London

Pictet J (ed) (1952) Commentary on article 2, Geneva convention I. https://ihl-databases.icrc.org/en/ihl-treaties/gci-1949/article-2/commentary/1952,).

Pictet J (ed) (1958) Commentary on article 6, Geneva convention IV. https://ihl-databases.icrc.org/en/ihl-treaties/gciv-1949/article-6/commentary/1958?activeTab=undefined

Sandoz Y et al (eds) (1987) Commentary on the additional protocols of 8 June 1977 to the Geneva conventions of 12 August 1949. ICRC/Martinus Nijhoff, Geneva
Sastry KRR (1952) Studies in international law. Eastern Law House, Kolkata
Sivakumaran S (2011) Re-envisaging the international law of internal armed conflict. Eur J Int Law 22(1):219–264
Sivakumaran S (2012) The law of non-international armed conflict. OUP, Oxford
Spoerri P (2014) The law of occupation. In: Clapham A, Gaeta P (eds) The Oxford handbook of international law in armed conflict. OUP, Oxford, pp 182–205
Stone J (1954) Legal control of international conflict: a Treatise on the dynamics of disputes and war-law. Stevens & Sons Ltd., London
Vasquez JA (2009) War puzzle revisited. CUP, New York
Zwanenburg M et al (2012) Is the law of occupation applicable to the invasion phase? Int Rev Red Cross 94(885):29–50

Law Relating to Conduct of Hostilities 3

Abstract

It introduces the substantive rules pertaining to the conduct of hostilities. It seeks to describe the rules and principles relating to combatants, non-combatants, prisoners of war, civilians, means and methods of war and environment. It tries to offer a short discussion in respect of the concerned rights and obligations of protected persons and belligerents. In doing so, the chapter intends to deal with the relevant treaty-provisions, customary international law, views of the ICRC and international judicial decisions in respect of international and non-international armed conflicts.

Keywords

Combatants · Non-combatants · Civilians · Occupation · Means and methods of war

3.1 Introduction

The substantive rules of laws of armed conflict (international humanitarian law) relate to belligerent conduct. They primarily determine the rights and obligations of parties involved in armed conflicts, as well as of those persons who do not participate directly in the military operations but are affected by them. These rules regulating military operations mainly relate to combatants, non-combatants, prisoners of war, civilians, means and methods of war, environment and cultural property. These rules as applicable in international and non-international armed conflict are discussed below.

3.2 Combatants and Non-combatant

Combatants and non-combatants play a vital role in the war-effort of a belligerent. The laws of armed conflict define them separately and provide for their rights, privileges and obligations as explained below.

3.2.1 In International Armed Conflicts

Both combatants and non-combatants are members of armed forces. However, the laws of armed conflict distinguish between those members of armed forces who play combat roles and those who do not, by using the terms "combatants" and "non-combatants" for them respectively. According to Protocol I: "Members of the armed forces of a Party to a conflict (other than medical personnel and chaplains covered by Article 33 of the Third Convention) are combatants, that is to say, they have the right to participate

K. Jeenger, *A Humanitarian Critique of International Humanitarian Law*,
Sustainable Development Goals Series, https://doi.org/10.1007/978-981-96-8319-2_3

directly in hostilities."[1] Thus, medical and religious personnel who are otherwise members of the armed forces are non-combatants. The Hague Regulations of 1899 as well as 1907 expressly provide that the armed forces of the belligerent parties may consist of combatants and non-combatants.[2] The expression "non-combatants" may appear to be akin to the term "civilians," however, it must be noted that the four Geneva Conventions and the Additional Protocols of 1977 recognize the two categories separately and provide for different protection.[3]

Scholars[4] have also referred to the definition of prisoner of war under the Geneva Convention to have a detailed understanding of the notion of combatants. Accordingly, the first category of persons amounting to prisoners of war is "Members of the armed forces of a Party to the conflict as well as members of militias or volunteer corps forming part of such armed forces."[5] This is because armed forces enjoy the legal status of an organ of a party to a conflict.[6] Armed forces of a State, according to the Protocol, comprises of "all organized armed forces, groups and units which are under a command responsible"[7] to that State. The second category covers the following:

> Members of other militias and members of other volunteer corps, including those of organized resistance movements, belonging to a Party to the conflict and operating in or outside their own territory, even if this territory is occupied, provided that such militias or volunteer corps, including such organized resistance movements, fulfill the following conditions:
>
> a) that of being commanded by a person responsible for his subordinates;
> b) that of having a fixed distinctive sign recognizable at a distance;
> c) that of carrying arms openly;
> d) that of conducting their operations in accordance with the laws and customs of war.[8]

Before World War II, such fighters fought in several parts of the world, and many of them were captured by the opponent and summarily executed. Therefore, the Geneva Convention III gives them prisoner of war status when captured by enemy, and the Additional Protocol I treats them as a part of armed forces.[9] However, to be treated as armed forces such groups must belong to a party to the conflict.[10] The test of "belonging to a party to the conflict" is satisfied where a group conducts hostilities on behalf and with the agreement of that party.[11] The third category of fighters recognized by the Geneva Convention is "Members of regular armed forces who profess allegiance to a government or an authority not recognized by the Detaining Power".[12] The

[1] Art. 43(2) Protocol Additional to the Geneva Conventions of 12 August 1949, and relating to the Protection of Victims of International Armed Conflicts (Protocol I) of 8 June 1977. See also Henckaerts and Doswald-Beck (2009), Rule 3.

[2] Art. 3 Regulations concerning the Laws and Customs of War on Land, annexed to The Hague Convention (II) with Respect to the Laws and Customs of War on Land of 29 July1899 and Regulations Respecting the Laws and Customs of War on Land, annexed to The Hague Convention (IV) with Respect to the Laws and Customs of War on Land of18 October 1907.

[3] See for further clarification Art. 7 the Geneva Convention for the Amelioration of the Condition of the Wounded and Sick in Armed Forces in the Field of 12 August 1949 (Geneva Convention I) and the Geneva Convention for the Amelioration of the Condition of Wounded, Sick and Shipwrecked Members of Armed Forces at Sea of 12 August 1949 (Geneva Convention II), Art. 33 the Geneva Convention relative to the Treatment of Prisoners of War of 12 August 1949 (Geneva Convention III), Art. 15(a)(b) the Geneva Convention relative to the Protection of Civilian Persons in Time of War of 12 August 1949 (Geneva Convention IV) and Art. 15, 43, Protocol I, above n 1.

[4] See Crawford (2015), p. 17 and Crawford and Pert (2015), p. 90. Article 44(1) of Protocol I (above n 1) is also helpful to arrive at this conclusion: "Any combatant, as defined in Article 43, who falls into the power of an adverse Party shall be a prisoner of war.".

[5] Art. 4(A)(1) Geneva Convention III, above n 3.

[6] Ipsen (2013, p. 85).

[7] Art. 43(1) Protocol I, above n 1. Protocol I has been found to be the first treaty defining armed forces: Melzer (2014), p. 302. This definition may be referred to because the Protocol supplements the Geneva Conventions.

[8] Art. 4(A)(2) Geneva Convention III, above n 3.

[9] Crawford and Pert (2015, p. 91).

[10] Art. 4(A)(2) Geneva Convention III, above n 3.

[11] Melzer (2009, p. 23).

[12] Art. 4(A)(3) Geneva Convention III, above n 3.

fourth group entitled to prisoner of war status is "Inhabitants of a non-occupied territory who, on the approach of the enemy, spontaneously take up arms to resist the invading forces, without having had time to form themselves into regular armed units, provided they carry arms openly and respect the laws and customs of war."[13] This conduct of inhabitants is called as *levée en masse*, an expression that originated in the French Revolution at the end of the eighteenth century.[14] The general meaning of the term is "people in arms" and it had twofold application: national conscription and popular uprising, however, it was attached to the latter gradually.[15]

Besides the Geneva Convention on prisoners of war, Protocol I also provides for some situations wherein two more categories get the status of combatants. First is members of a paramilitary or armed law enforcement agency which is incorporated into the armed forces of a State.[16] The provision further requires that a notification of this incorporation shall be sent to the other parties to the conflict, however, filing the notification with the Swiss depository at the time of ratification (as done by France and Belgium) of the Protocol has also been recognized as a valid method of notifying.[17] Although notifying the other belligerents is mandatory, non-compliance thereof does not deprive the members of the agency of combatant status once they are incorporated in armed forces.[18] The second situation is where, because of the nature of hostilities, armed combatants cannot so distinguish themselves, and they shall retain the status of combatants, provided that, in such situations, they carry the arms openly.[19] The terms "situations" and "nature of hostilities" are interpreted to mean occupation and war of national liberation.[20] Thus, the provision extends the combatant status to national liberation and guerrilla fighters as well. A resolution of the United Nations General Assembly also recognizes the combatant status of such fighters.[21]

Additionally, the Convention on United Nations Personnel[22] recognizes as combatants the United Nations forces engaged in enforcement actions taken by the Security Council under Article 42 of the Charter. Similar acknowledgment has been made in the United Nations Secretary General's Bulletin.[23]

3.2.1.1 Privileges, Rights and Immunities

As noted above, combatants have a right to participate directly in hostilities, that is to say, they may attack or capture enemy soldiers and destroy enemy military objectives. In respect of these acts, they may not be held liable under the penal law of adversary. Where, however, during the conduct of combat activities, they act contrary to the laws of armed conflicts, such actions may amount to war crimes[24] and invite individual criminal responsibility under the international criminal law. For instance, killing a soldier who has surrendered[25] or pillaging a town[26] amount to war crimes. As the right to attack is available to combatants of enemy also, every combatant is a legitimate target. They are not immune from being attacked because they are considered as "threat of harm".[27] However, the status of "legitimate target" ends the moment a

[13] Ibid., Art. 4(A)(6).

[14] Scheipers (2015, p. 22).

[15] Ibid., pp. 52, 133.

[16] Art. 43(3) Protocol I, above n 1.

[17] Henckaerts and Doswald-Beck (2009), Rule 4.

[18] Ibid.

[19] Art. 44(3) Protocol I, above n 1.

[20] Sandoz et al. (1987, paras 1698, 1703).

[21] A/RES/3103, Basic Principles of the Legal Status of the Combatants Struggling against Colonial and Alien Domination and Racist Regimes (1973, paras 3–4).

[22] Convention on the Safety of United Nations and Associated Personnel (1994).

[23] ST/SGB/1999/13, United Nations Secretary General's Bulletin on Observance by United Nations Forces of International Humanitarian Law (1999).

[24] See for instance, Art. 8 Statute of International Criminal Court (1998) (Rome Statute).

[25] Ibid., Art. 8(2)(b)(vi).

[26] Ibid., Art. 8(2)(b)(xvi).

[27] Lamb (2013, p. 37).

combatant becomes "*hors de combat*"[28] or "prisoner of war"[29] as there is an obligation[30] not to harm them. Wounded or sick combatants are entitled to be respected, protected, cared for and treated humanely.[31] Any form of violence against them, particularly murder, extermination, torture or biological experiments is prohibited.[32] Similar safeguards are available in respect of combatants who are at sea and who are sick, wounded or shipwrecked.[33] This protection regime reflects what Rousseau suggested in his treatise on Social Contract or Principles of Political Right (1762): "The object of war being the destruction of the hostile State, the other side has a right to kill its defenders while they are bearing arms; but as soon as they lay them down and surrender they become once more merely men, whose life no one has any right to take."[34]

On the other hand, non-combatants (for instance, medical personnel and chaplains) are not entitled to prisoner of war status under the Geneva Convention,[35] but The Hague Regulations[36] do confer upon them this status. Nevertheless, there is an obligation on belligerents not to attack them, but to respect and protect them.[37] Similar treatment is to be accorded when they fall into the hands of an adversary,[38] and they should also be allowed to perform their medical and spiritual functions.[39] Their other entitlements include protection by neutral States,[40] protection in case of special agreements,[41] protection by the International Committee of the Red Cross[42] (ICRC) and protection by a substitute organization.[43] More importantly, these rights are not allowed to be renounced by any of them.[44]

3.2.1.2 Mercenaries

Members of armed forces fight for their own nation. However, there is a different category of fighters who despite not being national of any party to the conflict, fight on behalf of a party to conflict for private gains. Protocol I refers to them as mercenaries.[45] They are also called as "military entrepreneurs".[46] It has been maintained that the practice of using private military is "as old as war itself".[47] Under the present law, a mercenary is not entitled to the right to be a combatant or a prisoner of war[48]; however, it does not disentitle mercenaries of fundamental guarantees available in Article 75 of the Protocol.

---

[28] A person is hors de combat if he is in the power of an adverse Party and he clearly expresses an intention to surrender or he has been rendered unconscious or is otherwise incapacitated by wounds or sickness, and therefore is incapable of defending himself; provided that in any of these cases he abstains from any hostile act and does not attempt to escape: Art. 41(2) Protocol I, above n 1.

[29] Art. 4(A) Geneva Convention III, above n 3 and Art. 43–44 Protocol I, above n 1. See next Section on prisoners of war.

[30] Art. 12 Geneva Conventions I, II, above n 3, Art. 41(1) Protocol I, above n 1 and Art. 13 Geneva Convention III, above n 3.

[31] Art. 12 Geneva Convention I, above n 3.

[32] Ibid., Art. 12.

[33] Art. 12 Geneva Convention II, above n 3.

[34] Rousseau (1762).

[35] Art. 33 Geneva Convention III, above n 3.

[36] Art. 3 Hague Regulations 1899 and 1907, above n 2.

[37] See Art. 19, 24 Geneva Convention I, above n 3, Art. 36 Geneva Convention II, above n 3 read with Art. 8(c)-8(e) Protocol I, above n 1 (because the Protocols supplement the Conventions).

[38] Art. 33 Geneva Convention III, above n 3.

[39] Art. 19, 37, 33 Geneva Conventions I, II, III respectively, above n 3.

[40] Art. 4 Geneva Convention I, above n 3.

[41] Art. 6 Geneva Convention I, II, above n 3.

[42] Ibid., Art. 9.

[43] Ibid., Art. 10.

[44] Ibid., Art. 7.

[45] Art. 47(2) Protocol I, above n 1. Similar definition of mercenary is available in Article 1 International Convention against the Recruitment, Use, Financing and Training of Mercenaries (1989) and Article 1, Convention for the Elimination of Mercenarism in Africa (1977).

[46] Scheipers (2015, p. 7).

[47] Crawford (2015, p. 152).

[48] Art. 47(1) Protocol I, above n 1.

3.2.1.3 Private Military Companies

Private military personnel may carry weapons into combat zones and train members of armed forces.[49] This outsourcing also extends to logistic, administration, technology, delivery of humanitarian aid, cooking, cleaning and the like civil functions. The issue of private troops is now a "central contemporary concern,"[50] especially with their increasing use by the United States of America in Iraq and Afghanistan, where they "outnumbered the multinational forces on the ground".[51] These companies and their personnel do not exactly fall within the existing categories of persons recognized by the laws of armed conflicts,[52] and therefore, pose a challenge before the existing framework of the law in respect of their rights and obligations.[53]

Personnel of these companies differ from mercenaries in several respects. As contrast to mercenaries, they are not always hired solely to directly participate in hostilities; they may belong to the nationalities of parties to the conflict also; in some cases they are entitled to prisoners-of-war status, and they are not always legitimate targets.

3.2.2 In Non-International Armed Conflicts

In respect of non-international armed conflicts, there is no specific recognition of a combatant and non-combatant status and corresponding privileges in the Common Article 3 and the Additional Protocol II. However, "a member of armed forces falling in the hands of adverse party and a civilian deprived of liberty for a reason related to the conflict enjoy the same legal protection under Article 4 (fundamental guarantees), Article 5 (persons whose liberty has been restricted), Article 6 (penal prosecutions) and Article 7 (protection and care) of the Protocol."[54] During a non-international armed conflict, domestic law remains in force. Consequently, the State-authorities "retain the right to prosecute and sentence persons who have been found guilty of offences related to the conflict."[55] In particular, the Protocol does not prevent prosecution of a member of a non-State actor for the act of taking up arms. It does not confer upon them either combatant or prisoner of war status. Medical and religious persons are also entitled to respect and protection.[56]

3.3 Prisoners of War

Capturing enemy soldiers during an armed conflict, especially those in higher ranks, is an old tradition. They were detained for variety of reasons, such as to compel enemy to surrender, to weaken the enemy State, to secure ransom, to exchange own soldiers captured by the enemy or to arrive at a settlement at desired terms. Their captivity and torture continued in modern times also, including the "First and Second World Wars,"[57] and the "era following the adoption of the 1949 Geneva Conventions".[58] The first international treaty that outlines the rights of prisoners of war and respective obligations on the State-parties is Hague Regulations of 1899[59] which was repeated in the second Hague Convention of 1907[60] also. However, the first full-fledged Convention adopted solely on the issue of prisoners of war was Geneva Convention relative to the Treatment of Prisoners of War, 1929, which ceased to operate at the coming into force of the

[49] Perrin (2006, p. 614).

[50] Cockayne (2014, p. 624).

[51] Melzer (2016, p. 40).

[52] Cottier (2006, p. 638).

[53] See also Montreux Document on Pertinent International Legal Obligations and Good Practices for States related to Operations of Private Military and Security Companies during Armed Conflict (2008).

[54] Sandoz et al. (1987, para 4441).

[55] Ibid.

[56] Art. 9 Protocol Additional to the Geneva Conventions of 12 August 1949, and relating to the Protection of Victims of Non-International Armed Conflicts (Protocol II) of 8 June 1977.

[57] Darcy (2014, p. 126).

[58] Hill-Cawthorne (2016, p. 48).

[59] Art. 4–20 Hague Regulations 1899, above n 2.

[60] Art. 4–20 Hague Regulations 1907, above n 2.

Geneva Convention Relative to the Treatment of Prisoners of War (Geneva Convention III) 1949. Some of its provisions reflect customary international law and *jus cogens*.[61] The Convention becomes applicable from the time persons entitled to prisoner of war status fall into the power of the enemy and until their final release and repatriation.[62]

Persons entitled to the prisoner of war status are generally those declared to be combatants, as explained in the previous section. Additionally, persons belonging to two more categories are entitled to this status when captured by the adversary. They are:

> Persons who accompany the armed forces without actually being members thereof, such as civilian members of military aircraft crews, war correspondents, supply contractors, members of labor units or of services responsible for the welfare of the armed forces, provided that they are authorized and provided with an identity card by the armed forces which they accompany.[63]

> Members of crews, including masters, pilots and apprentices of the merchant marine and the crews of civil aircraft of the Parties to the conflict.[64]

3.3.1 Determination of Prisoner of War Status in Doubtful Cases

Such cases generally cover deserters and persons who accompany the armed forces and have lost their identity cards.[65] They are entitled to the similar protection[66] (not the status) as accorded to prisoners of war until their status has been determined by a "competent tribunal." However, the Additional Protocol I entitles such persons to the status of prisoner of war pending the determination by a competent tribunal.[67] Such tribunal may be an administrative authority.[68] Thus, Article 5 seeks to prevent arbitrary determination of the status of the prisoners. However, the determination of the status by these tribunals has not been an easy task.[69]

3.3.2 Who Shares the Responsibility

The first and foremost responsibility to comply with the third Geneva Convention belongs to the detaining State. Article 12 of the third Geneva Convention contains an important principle that a person who is captured by enemy soldiers and possesses the status of prisoner of war, is considered to be in the hands of the enemy State, instead of the military personnel. This is the theory of "vicarious control"[70] according to which, it is States who are parties in an international armed conflict[71] and responsible for the compliance with the laws of armed conflict.

In addition to that, it is mandatory for parties to an armed conflict to apply the Convention with the cooperation and under the scrutiny of the protecting States, whose duty is to safeguard the interests of the parties to the conflict.[72] Thus, the provision authorizes a protecting State to take any step which may enable it to verify the application of any provision of the Convention, or improve the application of the Convention.[73] In practice, a belligerent who wants to protect its interests requests a neutral State to represent it in the territory of the enemy State. At the consent of the

[61] Krähenmann (2013, pp. 363, 365).

[62] Art. 5 para 1 Geneva Convention III, above n. 3.

[63] Ibid., Art. 4(A)(4).

[64] Ibid., Art. 4(A)(5).

[65] Pictet (1960a). In the latest Commentary of the ICRC, the word "deserters" does not find mention: ICRC (2020a, b).

[66] Art. 5 Geneva Convention III, above n 3.

[67] Art. 45(1) Protocol I, above n 1.

[68] Sandoz et al. (1987, para 1750). It can also be a government commission: Krähenmann (2013, p. 368).

[69] For difficulties encountered during the 2003 Iraq War in the determination of the status by the UK forces of more than 1500 captives who were not in uniform, see Mercer (2014, pp. 149–168).

[70] Hingorani (1963, p. 97).

[71] Pictet (1960b).

[72] Art. 8 para 1 Geneva Convention III, above n 3.

[73] Pictet (1960c).

neutral State and the other belligerent as well, its role as a protecting State begins. Here, an enemy State may not permit a particular neutral State to act as a protecting State, but this liberty cannot extend to preventing every neutral State.[74] When a neutral State gets the authorization of enemy State, it may assign the responsibility to its diplomatic or consular staff, representatives from among its own nationals or the nationals of other neutral States.[75] Parties to the conflict are bound to facilitate these representatives to the greatest extent possible. The Convention does not preclude the ICRC or any other impartial humanitarian organization to undertake humanitarian activities in favor of prisoners of war, provided that the parties to the conflict consent to it.[76] The Convention also permits transfer of prisoners of war to another State-party to the Convention who is willing and able to carry out the obligations under the Convention.[77]

3.3.3 Obligations on Parties to Conflict Prior to Capture

Besides the obligations in respect of treatment of prisoners of war, the States have assumed under the Geneva Convention III certain obligations which are to be discharged before capture of persons mentioned in Article 4. Before the outbreak of hostilities, parties to the conflict are required to provide every such person with identity cards displaying name, rank, army, regiment and date of birth.[78] When the battle begins, it is obligatory upon the belligerents to communicate to one another the titles and ranks of all such persons in order to ensure equality of treatment between prisoners of equivalent rank.[79] At the same time, they are also required to notify the adverse party of their laws and regulations allowing or prohibiting its own nationals to accept release on parole or promise,[80] because a detaining State may release the prisoners of war according to the law of the State on which they depend.[81]

3.3.4 Basic Principles of Treatment with Prisoners of War

Principle of Humane Treatment

Humane treatment to the prisoners of war is what the Convention actually aims at. It is perceived widely as the basis of all obligations assumed by States under the Convention. The Convention requires that prisoners of war must at all times be humanely treated.[82] Similar provision is contained in the Additional Protocol I also in respect of persons who are in the power of a belligerent.[83] It is also a rule of customary law[84] and international human rights law.[85]

Principle of Equality of Treatment

The principle of equality of treatment contained in Article 16 permits different treatment on some grounds, and prohibits discrimination on other grounds. The Convention, thus, permits special treatment to some prisoners of war on the ground

[74] Ibid.

[75] Art. 8 para 1 Geneva Convention III, above n 3.

[76] Ibid., Art. 9.

[77] Ibid., Art. 12 para 2.

[78] Ibid., Art. 17 para 3.

[79] Ibid., Art. 43 para 1.

[80] Ibid., Art. 21 para 3.

[81] Ibid., Art. 21 para 2.

[82] Ibid., Art. 13 para 1. Also contained in Art. 4 para 2 Hague Regulations 1899 and 1907, above n 2 and Art. 2 para 2 Geneva Convention relative to the Treatment of Prisoners of War (1929).

[83] Art. 75(1) Protocol I, above n 1.

[84] Eritrea-Ethiopia Claims Commission, Partial Award: Prisoners of War, Ethiopia's Claim 4, 1 July 2003, para. 53 and Henckaerts and Doswald-Beck (2009), Rule 87.

[85] Art. 10(1) International Covenant on Civil and Political Rights (1966).

of rank, sex, health, age and professional qualification,[86] while it prohibits adverse distinction based on race, nationality, religious belief or political opinion or any other distinction of similar nature, for example, color or language. On the basis of this principle, the Convention, for instance, requires all prisoners of war, except officers, to salute all officers of the detaining State,[87] and separate conveniences for women prisoners of war.[88]

Principle of Respect for the Person of Prisoner of War

Respecting prisoners of war is an idea underlying the rules relating to treatment with prisoners of war, and it is required to be observed in "all circumstances."[89] Respect to their person has been interpreted to indicate respect for the physical as well as moral person of a prisoner of war.[90] Respect for physical person signifies safety of life and limb of a prisoner of war. This is ensured in several provisions, for example, prohibition of any act of violence or medical experiments[91] and physical or mental torture while questioning.[92] On the other hand, respect for mental person extends to social, political, religious and other convictions and the desire to carry out them.[93] Similarly, prisoners of war are also entitled to honor according to their age and rank.[94] Furthermore, they should not be subjected to insults by way of libel and slander. They should not be deprived of their civil rights except in so far as the captivity requires.

The entitlements of prisoners of war under the Geneva Convention may not be renounced partially or absolutely by the prisoners themselves[95] nor can be restricted by a special agreement between the States.[96]

3.3.5 Obligations on Detaining State at the Initial Stage of Captivity

- Not to inflict any form of physical or mental torture for the purpose of securing any information from prisoners of war (Article 17, paragraph 4)
- To hand over a prisoner of war to the medical service in case of inability to reveal own identity due to physical or mental condition (Article 17, paragraph 5)
- To question prisoners of war in a language they understand (Article 17, paragraph 6).
- To provide identity document to those who do not have (Article 18, paragraph 2)
- Not to take from prisoners of war badges and articles of personal or sentimental value (Article 18, paragraph 3)
- Not to take away money carried by prisoners of war otherwise than on order by an officer, and to maintain record in a special register if money is taken away (Articles 18, paragraph 4, and 59)
- To evacuate them from combat zone to camps and to provide them food, portable water and medical facility (Articles 19 and 20)
- To intern them on land and in hygienic conditions and to evacuate them to a healthy place if interned on unhealthy area (Article 22, paragraph 1 and 2)
- To assemble prisoners of war according to their nationality, language and customs, but not to separate them from other prisoners of their armed forces (Article 22, paragraph 3)

86 On the basis of rank: Art. 39 paras 2, 3; 40, 43, 44, 45, 49 paras 2, 3; 60, 89 para 2; 97 para 3; 98 para 2; sex: Art. 14 para 2; 25 para 4; 29 para 2; 49 para 1; 88 paras 2, 3; 97 para 4; 108 para 2; health: Art. 30, 49 para 1; 55 para 2; 92 para 3; 98 para 4; 108 para 3; 109, 110, 114; age: Art. 49 para 1; 45; or aptitude for work: Art. 49, 53, 55, 62.

87 Art. 39 para 2 Geneva Convention III, above n 3.

88 Ibid., Art. 29 para 2.

89 Ibid., Art. 14 para 1.

90 ICRC (2020b).

91 Art. 13 Geneva Convention III, above n 3.

92 Ibid., Art.17 para 4. However, a deviation from the general rule of physical safety is permitted in case a prisoner of war attempts to escape provided that warning is given before using any weapon (Art. 42).

93 ICRC (2020b).

94 Art. 44 Geneva Convention III, above n 3.

95 Ibid., Art. 7.

96 Ibid., Art. 6 para 1.

- Not to prevent the prisoners from wearing badges of rank and nationality (Article 40).
- To enable them to send to their families capture cards informing their capture, location and state of health (Article 62).

3.3.6 Obligations on Detaining State During Captivity

A detaining State may intern the prisoners of war to limit their mobility,[97] consistent with ensuring hygiene and healthfulness.[98] The premises must be sufficiently heated and lighted, and free from any danger from fire.[99] A detaining State is required to ensure daily food supply and clothing for prisoners of war.[100] The prisoners may be asked to work (other than unhealthy and hazardous activities) taking into account their health, age, sex and rank.[101] The hours of work must not exceed the maximum limit permitted for civilians of the State for similar activities.[102] The detaining State is bound to pay a fair working rate of pay to the prisoners who work.[103]

In addition to the above requirements, detaining States are required to take measures to ensure hygiene in the camp, medical treatment and periodic health inspection of the prisoners (Article 29–31). The Convention also protects the religious faith of the prisoners. For this purpose, it requires detaining States to allow the retained religious personnel (chaplains) to conduct religious worship and rituals among the prisoners of the same religion (Article 35). Additionally, where there is no retained chaplain and the prisoners demand to have one, the detaining State is bound to appoint a suitable person for this purpose (Article 37). For the intellectual and physical development of the prisoners, detaining States shall provide necessary place and facilities so that prisoners can engage themselves in recreational and educational activities, and sports and games according to their choice (Article 38). It may not prevent the prisoners from sending and receiving correspondence (Article 73, paragraph 1).

Most importantly, in order to ensure due compliance of the Convention, every detaining State is required to employ from its regular armed forces a responsible commissioned officer who shall carry a copy of the Convention and ensure that every camp staff knows its provisions (Article 39). The texts of the Convention as well as its Annexes are required to be posted in the prisoners' own language at a suitable place where prisoners may read them (Article 41).

3.3.7 Proceedings and Punishments

A prisoner of war who tries to escape from the detention or aids or abets an escape may be liable to disciplinary punishment, provided that reasonable opportunity of being heard is given.[104] Further, a prisoner of war accused of violating the laws of detaining State or the laws of armed conflict may be tried judicially[105] consistent with essential guarantees of independence and impartiality.[106] Investigative safeguards entail that during the pre-trial confinement or interrogation, an accused prisoner should not be subjected to mental or physical torture to make any confession.[107] Other safeguards in this regard under the Convention include the following:

- To notify the protecting State of the decision of initiating judicial proceedings against a prisoner of war, at least three weeks before the proceedings begin (Article 104, paragraph 1)
- Not to punish a prisoner of war more than once for the same act (Article 86)
- Not to award more punishment to a prisoner of war than what is prescribed for the members

[97] Ibid., Art. 21 para 1.
[98] Ibid., Art. 22 para 1.
[99] Ibid., Art. 25.
[100] Ibid., Art. 26, 27.
[101] Ibid., Art. 49, 50, 52.
[102] Ibid., Art. 53 para 1.
[103] Ibid., Art. 62 para 1.
[104] See ibid., Art. 96.
[105] See ibid., Art. 84–85.
[106] Ibid., Art. 84 para 2.
[107] Ibid., Art. 99 para 1.

of the armed forces of the detaining State for committing the same act (Article 87, paragraph 1)
- No collective punishment for individual acts, corporal punishment, imprisonment in premises without daylight and, in general, any form of torture or cruelty (Article 87, paragraph 3)
- Not to deprive prisoners of war of their rank or prevent from wearing their badges (Article 87, paragraph 4)
- No punishment for female prisoners of war more severe than what is prescribed for male or female members of the armed forces of the detaining State for committing the same offence (Article 88)
- To report the protecting State the judgment pronounced upon the prisoner (Article 107)
- To deduct the period undergone in confinement pending the trial (Article 103, paragraph 2)
- Right of appeal or petition against a decision of the court of appeal (Article 106)
- To provide healthy and humane conditions of confinement, and separate quarters and supervision of women for women prisoners (Article 108).

3.4 Civilians

The fourth Geneva Convention, 1949 is the first international Convention aiming at the protection of civilians not directly participating in hostilities. The Convention defines civilians as those who find themselves in the hands of a Party to the conflict or occupying State of which they are not nationals.[108] It refers to civilians as protected persons.[109] On the other hand, the Additional Protocol I uses the expressions civilians and civilian population. Civilian population consists of civilians.[110] Here, the term civilians refer to persons who are not members of the armed forces under Article 43 of the Protocol, or entitled to prisoner of war status under Article 4A(1), (2), (3) and (6) of the Geneva Convention on Prisoners of War.[111] Likewise, under customary international law, civilians are persons who are not members of the armed forces.[112] In case of any doubt about civilian status of a person, the Protocol requires to treat such a person as a civilian.[113]

3.4.1 Protection of Civilians During International Armed Conflict

During an armed conflict, civilians generally require protection in two ways. First, they should be protected against military attacks. It is taken care of by The Hague Regulations and the Additional Protocol I. Second, they should not be subjected to mistreatment of any sort during an armed conflict. It is largely ensured by the Geneva Convention IV and, to some extent, by the Protocol. Additionally, customary international humanitarian law also contains some rules to safeguard civilians against direct attacks as well as abuse.

3.4.1.1 Prohibition of Attack Against Civilians and Civilian Objects

As stated above, Hague Regulations of 1899 as well as 1907 prohibit bombardment of undefended villages, towns, dwellings and buildings.[114] However, more detailed rules are contained in Protocol I. Part IV of the Protocol starts with the rule of distinction, which is the basis of civilian protection. It requires the parties to a conflict to distinguish between the civilian population and combatants and between civilian objects and military objectives and to direct their operations only against military objectives.[115] The rules protecting civilians against direct hostilities apply

108 Art. 4 para 1.

109 Art. 4 Geneva Convention IV, above n 3.

110 Art. 50(2) Protocol I, above n 1.

111 Art. 50(1).

112 Henckaerts and Doswald-Beck (2009), Rule 5.

113 Art. 50(1) Geneva Convention IV, above n 3.

114 Art. 25 Hague Regulations 1899 and 1907, above n 2.

115 Art. 48.

not just to land warfare, but also to sea and air warfare.[116] The Protocol protects the civilians against attacks in the following manner.

3.4.1.2 Prohibition of Direct Attacks

A belligerent State is prohibited from deliberately targeting civilians under Protocol I as well as the customary international law.[117] It has been suggested that the prohibition is without any exceptions and even military necessity cannot justify killing civilians.[118] This prohibition under Article 51 extends also to "acts or threats of violence, the primary purpose of which is to spread terror among the civilian population".[119] "To spread terror" here means to intimidate, awe and cause panic among the civilians, and it should be the main motive of such acts or threats. Ban on such acts or threats is a part of customary international law.[120] The Protocol also forbids reprisal against civilians,[121] which means to attack civilians in response to an armed attack made by an adversary.

3.4.1.3 Prohibition of Indiscriminate Attacks

As contrast to direct and deliberate attacks, indiscriminate attacks are blind, untargeted, unintentional and blanket. The enemy does not actually try to injure civilians or civilian objects.[122] However, they are bound to be hit. The treaty law as well as customary law prohibits such attacks.[123] Protocol I calls the following attacks indiscriminate[124]: those which are not directed at a specific military objective and, thus, may hit a civilian object[125]; those which employ a method or means of combat which cannot be directed at a specific military objective[126] or which cannot be limited as required by this Protocol[127]; "an attack by bombardment by any methods or means which treats as a single military objective a number of clearly separated military objectives located in an inhabited area;"[128] "an attack which may be expected to cause incidental loss of civilian life, injury to civilians, damage to civilian objects, which would be excessive in relation to the concrete and direct military advantage anticipated."[129] The last-mentioned clause in respect of incidental civilian harm indicates proportionality test. The test requires an advance assessment by a commander of probable civilian loss and military gain as a result of a planned attack.

3.4.1.4 Precautions in Attack

In addition to the express prohibition of targeting civilian population, there is also an obligation to take due care to spare civilians and civilian objects.[130] This may be done by taking "all feasible precautions" in selecting a target to be attacked and in adopting means and methods of attack, so that loss of civilian life and objects can be avoided or minimized.[131] Here, the term "feasible precaution" means a precaution which is practically possible in the given circumstances.[132]

---

116 Art. 49(3).

117 Art. 51(2) Protocol I, above n 1 and Henckaerts and Doswald-Beck (2009), Rule 1.

118 Prosecutor v. Galić, IT-98–29-A, Appeals Chamber, Judgment, 30 November, 2006, para 130.

119 Art. 51(2) Protocol I, above n 1.

120 Galić, above n 118, para 87.

121 Art. 51(6) Protocol I, above n 1.

122 Hanke (1993, p. 26).

123 Art. 51(4) Protocol I, above n 1 and Henckaerts and Doswald-Beck (2009), Rule 11.

124 See Art. 51(4)(a), (b), (c) and 51(5)(a), (b) Protocol I, above n 1. See also Henckaerts and Doswald-Beck (2009), Rule 12.

125 Ibid., Art. 51(4)(a).

126 Ibid., Art. 51(4)(b).

127 Ibid., Art. 51(4)(c).

128 Ibid., Art. 51(5)(a).

129 Ibid., Art. 51(5)(b).

130 Ibid., Art. 57(1) and Henckaerts and Doswald-Beck (2009), Rules 15–17.

131 Ibid., Art. 57(2).

132 Eritrea-Ethiopia Claims Commission, above n 84, para 110.

Besides these prohibitions, any attack or reprisal against civilian objects is forbidden under the laws of armed conflict.[133] Civilian objects mean objects other than those which significantly contribute to military action and whose total or partial destruction, capture or neutralization offers a definite military advantage.[134]

3.4.1.5 Respect for and Humanitarian Treatment with Civilians

Whether it is a situation of an armed conflict or occupation, protected persons enjoy the safeguards including the following: respect for their persons, their honor, their family rights, their religious convictions and practices, and their manners and customs[135]; protection against violence or threat thereof and insults and public curiosity[136]; protection of women against rape, enforced prostitution, or any form of indecent assault[137]; prohibition of physical or moral coercion[138]; prohibition of any action causing murder, torture, corporal punishment, mutilation, medical or scientific experiments not necessitated by the medical treatment, or any other form of physical suffering[139]; prohibition of taking of hostages[140]; prohibition on compelling to take part in hostilities against their own nation[141]; establishment of hospitals and safety zones to protect children from the effects of war[142]; free passage of all consignments of essential foodstuffs, clothing and tonics meant for children[143]; education and exercise of religion to children who are orphaned or separated from their families due to the war[144]; preferential treatment if the children belong to an alien nation[145]; additional food to expectant or nursing mothers[146]; prohibition of recruitment into armed forces,[147] and right to leave to foreign nationals.[148]

However, when civilians directly participate in hostilities, they lose the protection afforded by the laws of armed conflict.[149]

3.4.2 Protection of Civilians in Non-International Armed Conflicts

Common Article 3 and the Additional Protocol II do not define the term civilians. Moreover, in practice it is difficult to distinguish civilians from armed groups because they are seldom organized, and they carry out operations with a variety of civilian support.[150] However, persons who do not constitute any of the parties to the conflict (armed forces of State, its dissident armed forces or other organized armed groups) and do not participate in the hostilities directly are civilians[151] and entitled to civilian protection. According to the International Criminal Tribunal for Rwanda, a person who is not a member of either party to the armed conflict is a civilian.[152]

The variety of protection available to civilians during a non-international armed conflict includes the following: humane treatment in all

133 Art. 52(1) Protocol I, above n 1 and Henckaerts and Doswald-Beck (2009), Rule 7.

134 Art. 52(2) Protocol I, above n 1 and Henckaerts and Doswald-Beck (2009), Rules 8–9.

135 Art. 27(1) Geneva Convention IV, above n 3.

136 Ibid., Art. 27(1).

137 Ibid., Art. 27(2), Art. 76 para1 Protocol I, above n 1 and Henckaerts and Doswald-Beck (2009), Rule 93.

138 Art. 31 Geneva Convention IV, above n 3.

139 Ibid., Art. 32.

140 Ibid., Art. 34.

141 Art. 23(h) Hague Regulations 1907, above n 2.

142 Art. 14 para 1 Geneva Convention IV, above n 3.

143 Ibid., Art. 13 para 1.

144 Ibid., Art. 24 para 1.

145 Ibid., Art. 38(5).

146 Ibid., Art. 89 para 5.

147 Art. 77(2) Protocol I, above n 1.

148 Art. 35 para 1 Geneva Convention IV, above n 3.

149 Art. 51(3) Protocol I, above n 1.

150 Fleck (2013, p. 591).

151 See Art. 3 common to four Geneva Conventions, above n 3, Art. 13(3) Protocol II, above n 56 and Melzer (2014), pp. 319–320.

152 Prosecutor v. Musema, ICTR-96–13-A, Trial Chamber I Judgment, 27 January 2000, paras 277, 280.

circumstances[153]; prohibition of violence to life and person, taking of hostages, outrages upon personal dignity and the passing of sentences without a fair trial[154]; general protection against the dangers arising from military operations[155]; prohibition of attack and acts of violence or threat thereof[156]; prohibition on the order of no quarter[157]; prohibition of starvation of civilians as a method of combat[158]; prohibition of destruction of assets necessary for the survival of civilians[159]; prohibition of "violence to the life, health and physical or mental wellbeing of persons, collective punishments, taking of hostages, acts of terrorism, outrages upon personal dignity, in particular humiliating and degrading treatment, rape, enforced prostitution and any form of indecent assault, slavery and the slave trade in all their forms, pillage and threats to commit any of the foregoing acts;"[160] respect, food, drinking water, hygiene, freedom to practice religion, separate quarters for women, accommodation at a place away from war zones, physical as well as mental health and medical care in respect of persons whose liberty has been restricted[161]; judicial guarantees in respect of prosecution and punishment of offenses related to armed conflict.[162]

On the question of different laws applicable in international and non-international armed conflicts, the International Criminal Tribunal for the Former Yugoslavia (ICTY) has stated: "What is inhumane, and consequently proscribed, in international wars, cannot but be inhumane and inadmissible in civil strife."[163] This observation suggests that the scope of civilian protection in non-international armed conflicts has been broadened by the customary international law and also by the treaty law applicable to international armed conflicts by "analogy"[164] though only in "general essence of those rules."[165] Such expanding rules relate to "protection of civilians and civilian objects, prohibition of certain means and methods of war,"[166] and "judicial guarantees in respect of prosecution and punishment of offences related to the armed conflict."[167]

3.5 Belligerent Occupation

At present, The Hague Regulations of 1899[168] and 1907,[169] Geneva Convention IV,[170] Additional Protocol I[171] and customary international

153 Art. 3(1) common to four Geneva Conventions, above n 3 and Art. 4(1) Protocol II, above n 56.

154 Art. 3(1) common to four Geneva Conventions, above n 3. Also found in customary international law: Humane treatment (Rule 37); murder (Rule 89); torture, cruel and inhuman treatment (Rule 90); mutilation (Rule 92); rape and other forms of sexual violence (Rule 93); taking of hostages (Rule 96); fair trial (Rule 100): Henckaerts and Doswald-Beck (2009).

155 Art. 13(1) Protocol II, above n 56.

156 Ibid., Art. 13(2) and Henckaerts and Doswald-Beck (2009), Rule 1.

157 Art. 4(1) Protocol II, above n 56 and Henckaerts and Doswald-Beck (2009), Rule 46.

158 Art. 14 Protocol II, above n 56 and Henckaerts and Doswald-Beck (2009), Rule 53.

159 Art. 14 Protocol II, above n 56.

160 Ibid., Art. 4(2) and Henckaerts and Doswald-Beck (2009), Rules 89 (murder); 90 (torture, cruel and inhuman treatment); 92 (mutilation); 91 (corporal punishment); 103 (collective punishments), 96 (taking of hostages); 2 (acts of terrorism); 93 (rape and other forms of sexual violence); 94 (slavery and the slave trade); 111 (pillage of personal property).

161 Art. 5 Protocol II, above n 56 and Henckaerts and Doswald-Beck (2009), Rules 118 (adequate food, water, clothing, shelter and medical attention); 119 (separate quarters for women); 121 (accommodation away from war zones); 127 (respect for religious practices).

162 See Art. 6 Protocol II, above n 56 and Henckaerts and Doswald-Beck (2009), Rule 100.

163 Prosecutor v. Dusko Tadić, IT-94–1-AR72, Appeals Chamber, Judgment on the Defence Motion for Interlocutory Appeal on Jurisdiction, 2 October 1995, para 119.

164 Zegveld (2002, pp. 77–84).

165 Tadić, above n 163, para 126.

166 Ibid., para 127.

167 Henckaerts and Doswald-Beck (2009), Rule 100.

168 Art. 42–56 Hague Regulations 1899, above n 2.

169 Art. 42–56 Hague Regulations 1907, above n 2.

170 Art. 47–78.

171 Art. 69.

law[172] regulate the conduct of an occupying State in an occupied territory by conferring a set of rights upon occupied population and the occupying State. They also bind both of the parties with certain obligations. It has been made clear that these treaties do not examine the legality of the occupation, but recognize the de facto authority of the occupant.[173]

3.5.1 Safeguards During Occupation

In addition to the safeguards commonly available to civilians during an armed conflict as well as occupation, there are many rules which are applicable in occupied territories only. Geneva Convention IV especially contains a wide range of such provisions in favor of the protected persons living in an occupied territory. The Convention has sought to fill in the gap left by The Hague Regulations in respect of rights of civilian population residing in an occupied territory. These rights are inviolable irrespective of (1) any changes in the administrative structure of the occupied territory, (2) any agreement between the occupying State and government of occupied territory and (3) partial or total annexation of the occupied territory.[174]

During belligerent occupation, deportations or forcible transfers of the inhabitants to any other country by an occupier is totally prohibited.[175] Notably, during the World War II thousands of Jews were deported from occupied France to concentration camps in Germany and occupied Poland. The prohibition is subject to no exceptions. However, in the interest of security of inhabitants or imperative military reasons an occupier may evacuate all or some of the civilians and displace them within the occupied territory or, in exceptional circumstances, outside the territory also. Such displacement is subject to two conditions: first, ensuring accommodation, health and safety of protected persons and, second, settling them back to their homes at the earliest.[176] The ban of deportation is also applicable to nationals of the occupant living in its territory. An occupant cannot settle its nationals in the occupied territory.[177] Thus, Israeli settlements constructed for its Jewish people in the occupied areas of West Bank after the Six-Day War in 1967 violate this provision.[178]

The occupying State is under an obligation to ensure with the help of local authorities that institutions meant for care and education of children function properly.[179] Workers residing in an occupied area cannot be forced by the occupier to serve in the armed forces or to work in activities related to military operations, except for civilian needs of the occupying army or inhabitants.[180] Destruction of any kind of public or private property is prohibited under the Convention except for military reasons.[181] Hague Regulations, however, completely prohibit such destruction excepting the properties of municipalities only.[182] An occupying State may only administer and preserve the immovable public property including buildings, forests and real estate.[183] The benefits arising out of such property may not be used to improve the economy of the occupant, but the same may be used to meet the requirements of occupying forces or for the betterment of the inhabitants.[184] Further, an occupier may only take possession of movable public property,

---

172 For instance, Henckaerts and Doswald-Beck (2009), Rules 41, 51, 130.

173 Melzer (2016), p. 237.

174 Art. 47 Geneva Convention IV, above n 3.

175 Ibid., Art. 49 para 1.

176 Ibid., Art. 49 paras 2, 3.

177 Ibid., Art. 49 para 6.

178 UNSC/RES/2334 (2015). See also, Legal Consequences arising from the Policies and Practices of Israel in the Occupied Palestinian Territory, including East Jerusalem, Advisory Opinion (19 July 2024) ICJ, paras 268, 270, 285.

179 Art. 50 para 1 Geneva Convention IV, above n 3.

180 Ibid., Art. 51. See also Art. 52 para 1 Hague Regulations 1907, above n 2.

181 Art. 53 Geneva Convention IV, above n 3.

182 Art. 56 para 1 Hague Regulations 1907, above n 2.

183 Ibid., Art. 55 and Henckaerts and Doswald-Beck (2009), Rule 51(a), (b).

184 Antonio Cassese, cited in Gasser and Dörmann (2013, p. 293). See S/RES/1483 (2003) para 20, wherein the Security Council declared that the Iraq"s oil would be used only for the benefit of the inhabitants.

such as cash, means of transportation and things of military importance, like weapons and stores.[185] The right to take possession has been interpreted to mean the right to confiscate.[186] During occupation, an occupying army cannot deprive the civilians of food and medical supplies. Rather, it is the duty of the forces to bring in the necessary foodstuffs and medicines for themselves and, if necessary, arrange the same for the population also.[187]

3.5.2 Administration of Occupied Territory

In the absence of control of the territorial State over the occupied area, an occupant is required to administer the occupied territory in accordance with Article 64 of the Geneva Convention and Article 43 of the Hague Regulations of 1907. It is necessary so that civil administration and administration of justice to the civilian population is not hampered. Administration of a territory is a three-fold task: legislative, judicial and executive. However, not being a lawful authority, the occupying State does not assume the rights of a sovereign State.[188] Therefore, the occupying State cannot lawfully legislate and establish courts for the occupied territory, and it is required to continue with the "penal laws and courts of the occupied State".[189] It has been observed that Article 64, thus, gives primacy to the necessity of securing the rights and wellbeing of the occupied population.[190]

However, an occupant may repeal or suspend the penal law, (1) which may harm the occupant itself, such as a law requiring civilians to render services to resist enemy or (2) which is contrary to the Convention, for example a law discriminatory to religious minorities.[191] Similarly, the occupant is not required to continue with the courts enforcing laws derogatory to the Convention.[192] The Hague Regulation, on the other hand, requires the occupying State to restore and ensure public order and safety while respecting the laws in force in the country.[193] However, an occupying State may make laws necessary for (1) the implementation of the Convention, such as for labor and public health, (2) maintenance of orderly government of the territory and (3) its own protection.[194]

A protected person accused of having violated any of the laws passed by the occupant under Article 64, paragraph 2 may be prosecuted by a "competent court" (a properly constituted, non-political military court of the occupying State sitting in the occupied territory).[195] Such an accused shall have a right to regular trial before being convicted[196] and the right also to produce evidence, call witness and consult a lawyer of their own choice.[197] In the event of conviction, the convicted person has a right to appeal.[198]

3.5.3 Internment

Internment is to confine a person within certain limits for security reasons, and not by way of punishment ordered by a court. Therefore, it is also called as "administrative detention".[199] The ICTY has held that internment is an "exceptional measure"[200] which may be adopted only when "the party has good reasons to think that the person concerned, by his activities, knowledge or qualifications, represents a real threat to its present

[185] Art. 53 para 1 Hague Regulations 1907, above n 2.

[186] Melzer (2016, p. 245).

[187] See Art. 55 Geneva Convention IV, above n 3.

[188] Gasser and Dörmann (2013, p. 284).

[189] Art. 64 para 1 Geneva Convention IV, above n 3.

[190] Arai-Takahashi (1993, p. 68).

[191] Art. 64 para 1 Geneva Convention IV, above n 3.

[192] Ibid.

[193] Art. 43 Hague Regulations 1907, above n 2.

[194] Art. 64 para 2 Geneva Convention IV, above n 3.

[195] Ibid., Art. 66.

[196] Ibid., Art. 71 para 1.

[197] Ibid., Art. 72.

[198] Ibid., Art. 73.

[199] Pejic (2005, p. 375).

[200] Prosecutor v. Delalić et al., IT-96–21-T, Trial Chamber, Judgment, 16 November, 1998, para 578.

or future security."[201] Geneva Convention IV permits internment of protected persons either for imperative security reasons[202] or when a court orders internment in place of imprisonment.[203] However, a detaining State cannot intern civilians arbitrarily. There are some procedural safeguards which include observance of procedure prescribed for decision-making,[204] right to appeal against the decision[205] and informing of the grounds of internment.[206] Failure to comply with the procedural safeguards may render an internment unlawful.[207]

Internment of civilians comes with heavy responsibilities on the shoulders of a detaining State. While allotting accommodation to the internees, a detaining State shall ensure to the extent possible that family members and persons having same nationality, language and customs are grouped together.[208] The internment camps should be reasonably "far from the dangers of war,"[209] "hygienic, adequately heated, lighted and ventilated, and having separate rooms and sanitary conveniences for men and women,"[210] health center[211] and canteen[212] also to buy foodstuffs and things of daily use. To keep internees in good state of health, the detaining State shall provide sufficient and quality food to them, and workers, expectant and nursing mothers shall be given additional food.[213] Internees shall also be given necessary clothing and footwear suitable to the climate.[214] The detaining State shall not create any hurdle in the performance of "religious duties"[215] and "recreational activities, games and sports."[216]

3.6 Means and Methods of Hostile Conduct

Regulating the means and methods of war which uselessly aggravate the human suffering has always been a part of the laws of armed conflict.[217] It has been considered to be a significant step in alleviating the horrors of war.[218] While means of war indicates different types of tools or weapons of conducting military operations, methods of war cover any specific hostile strategy or policy as well as the manner in which the means are employed in the battlefield. Thus, missiles and cyber technology are means of war, whereas pillage and order of "no quarter" exemplify methods of war.

Some of the principal international instruments incorporating these prohibitions are The Hague Conventions of 1899[219] and 1907,[220] the

201 Prosecutor v. Delalić et al., IT-96–21-A, Appeals Chamber, Judgment, 20 February, 2001, para 327.

202 Art. 78 Geneva Convention IV, above n 3.

203 Ibid., Art. 68.

204 Ibid., Art. 78 para 2.

205 Ibid.

206 Art. 75(3) Protocol I, above n 1.

207 Delalić, above n 201, para 322.

208 Art. 82 paras 1, 2 Geneva Convention IV, above n 3.

209 Ibid., Art. 83.

210 Ibid., Art. 85.

211 Ibid., Art. 91 para 1.

212 Ibid., Art. 87.

213 Ibid., Art. 89.

214 Ibid., Art. 90.

215 Ibid., Art. 93.

216 Ibid., Art. 94.

217 For instance, Declaration Renouncing the Use, in Time of War, of Explosive Projectiles under 400 Grammes Weight (1868) (St. Petersburg Declaration) and Convention on Prohibitions or Restrictions on the Use of Certain Conventional Weapons Which May Be Deemed to Be Excessively Injurious or to Have Indiscriminate Effects as amended on 21 December 2001 (1980).

218 Preamble St. Petersburg Declaration, ibid.

219 Hague Convention II and Regulations 1899, above n 2, Declaration concerning the Prohibition of the Discharge of Projectiles and Explosives from Balloons or by Other New Analogous Methods (1899), Declaration concerning the Prohibition of the Use of Projectiles with the Sole Object to Spread Asphyxiating Poisonous Gases (1899) and Declaration concerning the Prohibition of the Use of Bullets which can Easily Expand or Change their Form inside the Human Body such as Bullets with a Hard Covering which does not Completely Cover the Core, or containing Indentations (1899).

220 Hague Convention IV and Regulations 1907, above n 2, Convention relative to the Laying of Automatic Submarine Contact Mines (1907), Convention concerning Bombardment by Naval Forces in Time of War (1907) and Declaration Prohibiting the Discharge of Projectiles and Explosives from Balloons (1907).

Convention on Biological Weapons (1972),[221] the Additional Protocol I (1977), the Convention on Certain Conventional Weapons (1980), and the Chemical Weapons Convention (1993).[222] The ideal fundamental to these bans may be sought in the preamble to the St. Petersburg Declaration, 1868:

> That the only legitimate object which States should endeavor to accomplish during war is to weaken the military forces of the enemy;
>
> That for this purpose it is sufficient to disable the greatest possible number of men;
>
> That this object would be exceeded by the employment of arms which uselessly aggravate the sufferings of disabled men, or render their death inevitable

The corresponding "basic rules"[223] in the Additional Protocol I have been said to be emanating from the preamble above.[224] Accordingly, the Protocol declares that the right of the belligerent States to choose means and methods of warfare is not unlimited.[225] It, thus, seeks to ban those means and methods of warfare which may cause superfluous injury or unnecessary suffering.[226] Unnecessary suffering has been understood by the International Court of Justice (ICJ) as a harm greater than that avoidable to achieve legitimate military objectives.[227] Thus, an injury which does not increase military advantage is superfluous and unnecessary. Additionally, the Protocol also forbids widespread, long-term and severe damage to the natural environment.[228] These provisions have attained the status of customary international law.[229]

To illustrate, the St. Petersburg Declaration sought to prohibit projectiles which are either explosive or charged with fulminating or inflammable substances and of a weight less than 400 g. Similarly, a Hague Declaration of 1899 provided for prohibition of dum-dum bullets or bullets that would expand or flatten after coming in contact with the human body.[230] Ban on the use of blinding laser weapon[231] and fragments not detectable through X-ray,[232] for instance glass or plastic, also follows the basic rule of no unnecessary suffering. Likewise, order of "no quarter" as a method of warfare has been outlawed.[233]

Protocol I also seeks to check those methods and means of war which attack indiscriminately.[234] Indiscriminate attacks, according to the Protocol,[235] are

(a) those which are not directed at a specific military objective;
(b) those which employ a method or means of combat which cannot be directed at a specific military objective; or
(c) those which employ a method or means of combat the effects of which cannot be limited as required by this Protocol; and consequently, in each such case, are of a nature to strike military objectives and civilians or civilian objects without distinction.

Thus, States must refrain from employing those weapons that are incapable of differentiating between civilian and military targets, as endorsed by the ICJ too.[236] This prohibition has taken the shape of customary international law in both

[221] Convention on the Prohibition of the Development, Production and Stockpiling of Bacteriological (Biological) and Toxin Weapons and on their Destruction (1972).

[222] Convention on the Prohibition of the Development, Production, Stockpiling and Use of Chemical Weapons and on their Destruction (1993).

[223] Art. 35 Protocol I, above n 1.

[224] Crawford and Pert (2015), p. 195.

[225] Art. 35(1) Protocol I, above n 1.

[226] Ibid., Art. 35(2).

[227] Legality of the Threat or Use of Nuclear Weapons, Advisory Opinion (1996) ICJ Rep 226, para 78.

[228] Art. 35(3) Protocol I, above n 1.

[229] Henckaerts and Doswald-Beck (2009), Rule 70.

[230] Declaration on the Use of Bullets Which can Easily Expand (1899), above n 219.

[231] Protocol on Blinding Laser Weapons (Protocol IV to the 1980 Convention) (1995).

[232] Protocol on Non-Detectable Fragments (Protocol I) (1980).

[233] Art. 23(d) Hague Regulations 1899 and 1907, above n 2, Art. 41 Protocol I, above n 1 and Art. 4(1) Protocol II, above n 56.

[234] Art. 51(4).

[235] Ibid.

[236] Nuclear Weapons, above n 227, para 78.

international as well as non-international armed conflicts.[237]

Several weapons and methods of warfare fall in this prohibited category because they may harm not only members of the armed forces but also civilians. Majority of them also have the potential of causing superfluous and unnecessary harm. For instance landmines,[238] incendiary weapons (flame-throwers),[239] chemical weapons,[240] biological weapons[241] and pillage.[242] The lawfulness of nuclear weapons as a means of war continues to be contested and uncertain. Despite its unquestionable potential to blatantly violate every canon on means and methods of war and cause "death and destruction in huge proportion,"[243] its unlawfulness could not be determined with finality on international level so far.

Interestingly, the rules and principles relating to unnecessary suffering and indiscriminate killing are prospective in operation in relation to new weapons or ways of combat. Article 36 of the Protocol obligates the State-parties that in the event of development, acquisition or use of a new means or method of war, a State-party is bound to ensure that its use is not prohibited by the Protocol or any other rule of international law. It, thus, prevents a State from raising a defense that the rules of the Protocol do not apply to the new weapon merely because the weapon or method was invented or acquired subsequently.[244]

References

Arai-Takahashi Y (1993) Preoccupied with occupation: critical examinations of the historical development of the law of occupation. Int Rev Red Cross 94(885):51–80

Bernard V (2015) A price too high: rethinking nuclear weapons in light of their human cost. IInt Rev Red Cross 97(899):499–506

Cockayne J (2014) Private military and security contractors. In: Clapham A, Gaeta P (eds) The Oxford handbook of international law in armed conflict. OUP, Oxford, pp 624–655

Cottier M (2006) Elements for contracting and regulating private security and military companies. Int Rev Red Cross 88(863):637–663

Crawford E (2015) Identifying the enemy: civilian participation in armed conflict. OUP, Oxford

Crawford E, Pert A (2015) International humanitarian law. CUP, Cambridge

Darcy S (2014) Judges, law and war: the judicial development of international humanitarian law. CUP, Cambridge

Fleck D (2013) The law of non-international armed conflicts. In: Fleck D (ed) The handbook of international humanitarian law. OUP, Oxford, pp 581–610

Gasser HP, Dörmann K (2013) Protection of the civilian population. In: Fleck D (ed) The handbook of international humanitarian law. OUP, Oxford, pp 231–320

Hanke HM (1993) The 1923 Hague rules of air warfare. Int Rev Red Cross 33(292):12–44

Henckaerts JM, Doswald-Beck L (2009) Customary international humanitarian law, vol I. ICRC/CUP, New York

Hill-Cawthorne L (2016) Detention in non-international armed conflict. OUP, Oxford

Hingorani RC (1963) Prisoners of war. NM Tripathi Pvt Ltd, Bombay

ICRC (2020a) Commentary on article 5, Geneva convention III. https://ihl-databases.icrc.org/en/ihl-treaties/gciii-1949/article-5/commentary/2020?activeTab=undefined.

ICRC (2020b) Commentary on article 14, Geneva convention III. https://ihl-databases.icrc.org/en/ihl-treaties/gciii-1949/article-14/commentary/2020?activeTab=undefined.

Ipsen K (2013) Combatants and non-combatants. In: Fleck D (ed) The handbook of international humanitarian law. OUP, Oxford, pp 301–331

Kolb R, Hyde R (2008) An introduction to the international law of armed conflicts. Hart Publishing, Oxford

[237] Henckaerts and Doswald-Beck (2009), Rule 71.

[238] Convention on the Prohibition of the Use, Stockpiling, Production and Transfer of Anti-Personnel Mines and on their Destruction (1997).

[239] Protocol on Prohibitions or Restrictions on the Use of Incendiary Weapons (Protocol III) (1980).

[240] Hague Declaration Concerning Asphyxiating Gases 1899, above n 219, Protocol for the Prohibition of the Use in War of Asphyxiating, Poisonous or Other Gases, and of Bacteriological Methods of Warfare (Geneva Gas Protocol) (1925); Convention on Chemical Weapons 1993 above n 222.

[241] Convention on Biological Weapons (1972), above n 221.

[242] Art. 28 Hague Regulations 1899 and 1907, above n 2, Art. 33 Geneva Convention IV, above n 3 and Art. 4(2)(g) Protocol II, above n 56.

[243] Bernard (2015, pp. 499–506) and Tomonaga and Yamamoto (2015, pp. 507–525).

[244] Kolb and Hyde (2008, p 152).

Krähenmann S (2013) Protection of prisoners in armed conflict. In: Fleck D (ed) The handbook of international humanitarian law. OUP, Oxford, pp 359–412

Lamb A (2013) Ethics and the laws of war: the moral justification of legal norms. Routledge, Oxfordshire

Melzer N (2014) The principle of distinction between civilians and combatants. In: Clapham A, Gaeta P (eds) The Oxford handbook of international law in armed conflict. OUP, Oxford, pp 296–331

Melzer N (2016) International humanitarian law: a comprehensive introduction. ICRC, Geneva

Melzer N (ed) (2009) Interpretative guidance on the notion of direct participation in hostilities under international humanitarian law. ICRC, Geneva

Mercer N, (2014) The future of article 5 tribunals in the light of experience in the Iraq war, (2003). In: Harvey C et al (eds) Contemporary challenges to the laws of war: essays in honour of professor Peter Rowe. CUP, Cambridge, pp 149–168

Pejic J (2005) Procedural principles and safeguards for internment/administrative detention in armed conflict and other situations of violence. International Review of the Red Cross 87(858):375–391

Perrin B (2006) Promoting compliance of private security and military companies with international humanitarian law. Int Rev Red Cross 88(863):613–636

Pictet J (ed) (1960a) Commentary on article 5, Geneva convention III. https://ihl-databases.icrc.org/en/ihl-treaties/gciii-1949/article-5/commentary/1960?activeTab=undefined

Pictet J (ed) (1960b) Commentary on article 12, Geneva convention III. https://ihl-databases.icrc.org/en/ihl-treaties/gciii-1949/article-12/commentary/1960?activeTab=undefined.

Pictet J (ed) (1960c) Commentary on article 8, Geneva convention III. https://ihl-databases.icrc.org/en/ihl-treaties/gciii-1949/article-8/commentary/1960?activeTab=undefined.

Rousseau JJ (1762) The social contract or principles of political right, book 1. https://jjrousseau.net/english-lecture/the-social-contract-or-principles-of-political-right/.

Sandoz Y et al (eds) (1987) Commentary on the additional protocols of 8 June 1977 to the Geneva conventions of 12 August 1949. ICRC/Martinus Nijhoff, Geneva

Scheipers S (2015) Unlawful combatants: a genealogy of the irregular fighter. OUP, Oxford

Tomonaga M et al (2015) After the atomic bomb: Hibakusha tell their stories. Int Rev Red Cross 97(899):507–525

Zegveld L (2002) Accountability of armed opposition groups in international law. CUP, Cambridge

Part II

Historical Critique of International Humanitarian Law

Materialist History of International Humanitarian Law (Part I)

4

Abstract

In this chapter, I try to delve into the history of the laws of armed conflict from a materialist approach. Initially, I try to explain the importance of materialist way of doing history and the metaphor of base and superstructure. In this chapter, I draw a picture of a period from the sixteenth century to the first half of the nineteenth century. My focus is on the rules of war suggested by Francisco de Vitoria, Hugo Grotius and other European writers, emerging colonization and growing capitalism. I mainly engage with the political economy of that time to explain how colonization and growing capitalism shaped the warring tendencies of the European nations and their conduct during war. The chapter underlines that the rules of war were not so developed during this period, but this era does reveal how the political and economic realities of the time led to militarism and shaped the attitude of powerful countries towards regulation of conduct during war. The Battle of Plassey, Napoleonic Wars and Crimean War explain this position. In this way, this chapter prepares the necessary background for the next chapter.

Keywords

History of IHL · Colonization · Vitoria · Barbarians · Militarization

4.1 Why a Materialist Account?

The history of laws of armed conflict (politically called as international humanitarian law) as a conscious creation of *men* has been told.[1] Such an account generally projects the series of past events as if *men* were free to shape the legal developments historically. Usually, narrating history as a record of important happenings in a given time and place tells "exactly what happened, exactly where and exactly when."[2] It generally presupposes that external factors such as technology, occupation, economic activities have no bearing on the past. It reflects Hegel's "historical idealism"[3] which maintains that history of the world is a manifestation of world spirit.[4] In other words, historical development is an outcome of conscious rational creation accomplished freely.[5] However, there is an alternate way

[1] This way of narrating history is usually known as conventional or orthodox history: Alexander (2015, pp. 109, 111). See for the general history of the law, O'Connell (2013, pp. 1–42), Solis (2010 pp. 38–72), Baets (2022, pp. 1586–1620), Islam (2018, pp. 294–307), and Crawford and Pert (2015, pp. 4–19).

[2] Wright (1942, p. 25).

[3] See, Marx and Angels (2010a, pp. 55–57).

[4] Hegel (1899, pp. 78–79).

[5] Cohen (2001, pp. 17–19). For an easy understanding of Hegel's idealism and Marx's materialism, see Gaarder (2015, pp. 326–327).

K. Jeenger, *A Humanitarian Critique of International Humanitarian Law*,
Sustainable Development Goals Series, https://doi.org/10.1007/978-981-96-8319-2_4

of exploring the history. The alternative model broadly disagrees with the idea of past events as a product of deliberate conscious creation. Instead, it believes that the origin and development of any historical occurrence is shaped by external factors, such as economic forces.[6] It tries to link human actions mainly with the existing economic conditions.[7] Law may also be viewed from this perspective. This economic interpretation and explanation of history is a Marxist idea of "historical materialism." Engels notes that Marx placed history on its real foundation: the material base, the economic production of life.[8] Cohen calls it not only a philosophy of history but also a theory of history, which is a contribution to understanding the inner dynamic of what happens.[9] Productive power and economic structure are two key concepts of this theory.[10] The concepts and methodology offered by this theory are crucial in conducting Marxist analysis of every dimension of social systems, including law.[11]

Thus, the materialist perspective to the development of the laws of armed conflict engages with the then existing economic and political conditions and tries to explore how they shaped the law. It explains the role of colonialism, industrial revolution, capitalism and imperialism in the growth of the international law regulating violent conduct in war.[12] It examines how the laws of armed conflict were employed as a tool to achieve imperial motives. Further, this account will be helpful also to understand how the development of international legal relations is interlinked with colonialism and capitalism.

[6] Collins (1982, pp. 17–18).

[7] Marx and Angels (2010a, p. 43).

[8] Bober (1950, p. 4).

[9] Cohen (2001, p. 27).

[10] Ibid., p. 27).

[11] Collins (1982, p. 17).

[12] For a materialist history of international law in general, see Chimni (2017, pp. 477–498).

4.2 The Idea of Economic Explanation of History

According to the Marxist idea, the substance of history lies in the practical economic activities.[13] It takes into account the material conditions and economic production of life. According to Marx and Angles, material conditions are those which exist already (i.e. natural resources) and which are produced by human activities (such as, food, clothing, machines).[14] In fact, the production of these material conditions is the first historical act.[15] But it is done not just once or randomly, but continuously.[16] Thus, the materialist conception of history presents the idea that the social orders are by and large a product of the material and economic realities. Therefore, according to Marxism, law and legal institutions which, though, appear to be deliberate purposive creations, are also conditioned by the material circumstances. Marx believes that legal relations are rooted in the material conditions of life, and thus, could not be explained by the so called general progress of the human mind.[17]

4.2.1 Base and Superstructure

In order to explain how material conditions shape law, Marx employs a metaphor of "base and superstructure" in the preface of his book, A Contribution to the Critique of Political Economy. In the metaphor, base represents relations of production and superstructure includes legal and political institutions. Marx argues that the production relations form the "economic structure of society—the real foundation, on which rise legal and political superstructures."[18] But how is the economic structure constructed, and how does it affect the superstructure?

[13] Forgacs (2017, p. 37).

[14] Marx and Angels (2010a, p. 31).

[15] Marx and Angels (2010a, p. 42).

[16] Marx and Angels (2010a, pp. 50–53).

[17] Marx (1904, p. 11).

[18] Ibid.

The formation of economic base relates to the production of material life. The production of material life depends upon "productive forces," such as natural resources and knowledge of technology to exploit them.[19] The utility, quality and efficiency of these forces affect the production of material life. Thus, the better the available technology, the more advanced the production of material life, for instance clothing and various machines. In this process, an individual inevitably enters into relations with others.[20] These contacts are "relations of production" which correspond to productive forces. In other words, these production relations are appropriate to the forces of production.[21] For instance, invention of wheel led to the relations between a farmer and a cart owner to transport the agricultural produce; similarly, invention of spinning machine resulted into the relations between a factory owner and workers ready to work. These arrangements or relations of production constitute the economic structure of society[22] or "material base." On this material foundation, legal and political superstructure is built. In both the examples given above, corresponding rules are framed to regulate the emerging relations of productions. The influence of economic base on the superstructure manifests itself most explicitly in the epoch of capitalist mode of production. Thus, in the example of spinning machine, laws regulating contract of employment, wages, working hours, working conditions are formulated. As the relations of production and the legal and political superstructure correspond to the productive forces, what does happen when the forces themselves change over a period of time?

According to Marx, when the material powers of production develop further, tension arises between the forces and the existing production relations, which leads to social revolution.[23] This may be explained well with the help of the technological developments which brought in capitalist mode of production replacing feudalism.[24] During feudalism land was held by lords. Serfs rendered services to lords because they ensured their physical safety. Later on, however, with the invention of basic tools and instruments, merchant-capitalists wanted to produce more by assembling workers under single roof and also by supplying raw material and advance money to households[25] for domestic production. As a result, emerging merchants needed land already held by lords, and serfs wanted to join factories to work. The feudal relations of production (serfdom) were contradictory to the advancement in the forces of production. Thus, through revolutionary English civil war in the seventeenth century, feudal system was targeted. Subsequently, relations of production between workers and merchants were established. This necessitated changes in the superstructure as well. The enactment of Tenures (Abolition) Act, 1660 ensured smooth transition by nullifying the feudal laws of land tenure.[26] Similarly, the change in the forces and relations of production brought by industrial revolution was followed by a huge architecture of labor and commercial laws.

However, leading Marxist scholars do not support the economic determinism or the view that law is always determined by the economic base.[27] By the end of the nineteenth century, the inadequacies of the determinism became more obvious when the ruling classes of Europe deliberately created laws and legal institutions to advance their interests and suppress the working classes or *proletariat*. Law began to be perceived as a conscious creation of the dominant social classes. This became possible precisely because of the age-old interest of the state in the economic development and the interconnections and commonalities between political class and industrialists. In many cases, both of them are not just hand-in-glove, but common. However, the deliberate

[19] Collins (1982, p. 18). According to Cohen, Marx considered within the ambit of productive forces means of production (instruments of production, raw materials, spaces) and labour power: Cohen (2001, p. 55).

[20] Marx (1904, p. 11).

[21] Cohen (2001, p. 136).

[22] Marx (1904, p. 11).

[23] Ibid., p. 12.

[24] See, Collins (1982, p. 21).

[25] Also known as putting-out system: Banaji (2020, p. 72).

[26] Collins (1982, p. 21).

[27] See, ibid., pp. 23–24.

making of the oppressive laws by ruling classes does not operate in vacuum or independent of economic base. Such a law-making is connected to the position of ruling classes in the relations of production. A social class is dominant in the relations of production because it has access and control over the means of production, whereas the subordinate class does not.[28] Thus, it is their dominant status in production relations which is decisive and also constitutes the base. In this way, the economic base indirectly shapes the content of law, "through a process of class rule".[29]

However, it must be noted that by economic analysis of legal and other social institutions, Marx and Engels never intended to convey that only material factors determine the superstructure.[30] Engels categorically stated that economic structure is the base, but several components of the superstructure also interact with and influence each other.[31]

This economic explanation of the superstructure (for instance legal system) was originally conceived in a closed national set up. However, to apply the same model for understanding the origin of international law, we need to look into the theoretical developments in the works of subsequent Marxist scholars, such as Rosa Luxemburg and Lenin. The appropriate place to discuss their viewpoints is the next chapter, which deals with the epoch of mature capitalism and world economy. However, here it suffices to mention that factors, such as the emerging international economic intercourse, colonial division of the world among the powerful nations, development of advanced productive forces and class division on international plane had significant impact on the development of international law. The early history of these economic and political developments coupled with their impact on the shaping of international law of war is discussed below. It began as early as from the sixteenth century with the gradual collapse of feudalism and growing mercantilism and taking over of the non-European territories.

4.3 Materialist Beginning of Laws of Armed Conflict

The historical moment from which materialist history of modern law of war should begin is not the birth of the ICRC. That does not mean there is some other specific event from where we may begin. However, the material conditions of industrial production, technological development, colonization and capitalism prevailing at the time of ICRC's establishment did not emerge overnight. Therefore, the appropriate point to begin with is the transformation from feudalism to capitalist mode of production.

Before the emergence of capitalism in Europe, feudalism and craftsmanship had reached their zenith. Much of the European society was chiefly divided into two classes, namely feudal lords and serfs—the former dominating the latter in nearly all walks of life. The feudal lords protected the territories in lieu of revenue, harvest and labor which serfs were compelled to offer. Just war theories, seeking moral justification of war in expanding the Roman Empire and in defense of religion,[32] and corresponding rules of hostilities, were already in place. During this time, some ethical rules regulating the conduct in war among Christians were formulated by medieval churchmen, canonists, theologians and princes. For instance, on behalf of the Church, the Second Lateran Council prohibited use of the crossbow in 1139, and the Third Lateran Council of 1179 denied enslavement of Christian prisoners and prescribed immunity from attack for Church members, merchants and peasants.[33] Italian

[28] Bober (1950, pp. 98–99).

[29] Collins (1982, pp. 29–30).

[30] Cain and Hunt (1979, p. 56).

[31] Ibid. Gramsci mentions that in significant works, like The Eighteenth Brumaire, Revolution and Counter Revolution in Germany, The Civil War in France, Marx and Engels have clearly maintained this position: Forgacs (2017, p. 190).

[32] Mani (2004, p. 17).

[33] Solis (2010, p. 5) and Bryant (2016, p. 58).

jurists Bartolus[34] and Giovanni da Legnano[35] contributed in the formulation of these principles. On the other hand, Christian princes adopted and followed the rules of chivalry in war or "*jus militare*".[36] Chivalry implied the obligation to act honorably, even in war.[37] Notably, this era witnessed clashes between emperors and local princes on the issue of control over land on one hand, and between emperor and Christian religious leaders on the question of authority of appointing church officials, on the other. These restraints on the conduct in war were neither universal nor unconditional in nature. They revolved around the Augustinian theory of just war, such as self-defense and recovery of property, and sought to legitimize the Christian overreach in feuds. Additionally, the rules could be ignored while fighting with non-Christians.[38]

Marx calls this phase before capitalism "primitive accumulation."[39] Primitive accumulation is a historical process which resulted into an unfair situation in society. On one hand there are few people owning almost all the wealth and means of production, while on the other there are masses who have been deprived of the means of production and who have nothing to sell except their own labor.[40]

4.3.1 Justifying Barbarism During War

According to Marx, the phase of capitalism generally begins with the sixteenth century.[41] While the sixteenth-century India was encountering wars by external invaders, rival dynasties and politically ambitious rulers, growing manufacture and trade was knocking at the doors of Europe where the conditions for overthrow of feudal mode of production were already mature:

> The discovery of gold and silver in America, the extirpation, enslavement and entombment in mines of the aboriginal population, the beginning of the conquest and looting of the East Indies, the turning of Africa into a warren for the commercial hunting of blackskins, signalised the rosy dawn of the era of capitalist production.[42]

Marx opines that the manufacturing period roughly begins with the middle of the sixteenth century and extends to the third quarter of the eighteenth century.[43] Factors that necessitated manufacturing include exchange of manufacturing tools between towns, rising demand and growing population.[44] Kings also began to support merchants and manufacturers in variety of ways. They encouraged adventurous travelers and sponsored voyages to unexplored territories in search of markets. Thus, Christopher Columbus from Spain and Pedro Alvarez from Portugal discovered and took possession of America in 1492 and Brazil in 1500 respectively.[45] On the other hand, Vasco da Gama of Portugal reached Calicut in 1498 to further trade interests. Besides this, many European nations formed companies (English East India Company (1601), Dutch East India Company (1602) and French East India Company (1604)) and appointed viceroy to establish trade and monopoly in Asia and America. These company-sovereigns enjoyed State-like prerogatives.[46] They could establish trade relations, negotiate treaties, wage war and make peace.[47] Thus, kings protected the interests of merchants and manufacturers. Petty traders of craftsmanship era were replaced by bigger ones.[48]

---

[34] He is considered as first theorist of international law. See Neff (2018, p. 7).

[35] According to Holland, the first substantive treatise upon the subject of war and reprisals was written by him. See Holland (1898, p. 44).

[36] Bryant (2016, p. 61).

[37] Solis (2010, p. 5).

[38] Bryant (2016, pp. 59–61).

[39] Marx and Angels (2010b, p. 704).

[40] Ibid., pp. 704–706.

[41] Ibid., p. 706.

[42] Ibid., p. 739.

[43] Ibid., p. 341.

[44] Marx and Angels (2010a, pp. 67–68).

[45] Anand (2006, pp. 10–11).

[46] Welsh (2017, p. 151).

[47] Anand (2006, p. 4).

[48] Marx and Angels (2010a, p. 70).

With these developments in the field of trade and commerce, a significant but prejudiced scholarship in the discipline of laws of war was emerging in the sixteenth-century Europe. These scholars included Francisco de Vitoria, Balthasar Ayala and Francisco Suárez from Spain, and Pierino Belli and Alberico Gentili from Italy. Their works were largely influenced by the Christian theory of just war and biased towards the imperialist policies of their kings. They began to seek justification for embryonic colonization. As Spain was first to discover and colonize the Indies, its jurist Francisco de Vitoria took the lead. He accomplished the task faithfully while writing in the sixteenth century after the beginning of Spanish colonization. His work On the Indians Lately Discovered sought to answer questions, like "by what right were the barbarians subjected to Spanish rule" (Vitoria called the American Indians, barbarians).[49,50] For this purpose, he used law and cultural differences to justify the Spanish domination. According to Vitoria, the Indians possessed reason[51] though inferior[52] than European. Because of having reason, the barbarians were also bound by the law of nations (*just gentium*)—a product of universal natural law.[53] Then he carefully wrote some of the rights and obligations under the natural law, which facilitated control over the Indies. For instance, Spaniards had right to travel anywhere and trade with the inhabitants, and ships of any nation may lawfully enter anywhere.[54] Similarly, the right to loot the indigenous territory was handcrafted in the following fashion:

> a thing which does not belong to anyone (*res nullius*) becomes the property of the first taker ... therefore, if gold in the ground or pearls in the sea or anything else in the rivers has not been appropriated, they will belong by the law of nations to the first taker, just like the little fishes of the sea.[55]

Vitoria further maintained that if in the exercise of these rights, the barbarians retort violently or deny the Spanish what belongs to them as per the law, it amounts to an offense which entitles the Spaniards to wage a just war against them.[56] On the other side, he clarified that the barbarians could not wage just war against the Spaniards because they lacked sovereignty as they were unbelievers and uncivilized.[57] Thus, relying on the universal nature of the European natural law principles, Vitoria sought to justify the war on the Indies in furtherance of the Spanish economic and political interests. On the other hand, he employed the "dynamic of difference"[58] of culture to declare the Barbarian recourse to violence unjust and to determine rules of war with them. This invocation of universality and difference in the same situation by Vitoria is certainly an enterprise of convenience and deceit.

In war with the barbarians, the Vitorian scheme of rules ruthlessly legitimized the infliction of brutalities on the aboriginal population and also paved the way for similar inhuman rules and treatment in hostilities with colonies, especially from 1860s onwards. He justified indiscriminate killing, seizure of property, taking hostage and enslavement of women and children in wars with the non-believer, irredeemable Americans.[59] How brave was the so called "brave champion of the rights of the Indians in his time"![60]

Thus, he laid the foundation for justification of colonization, development of inhuman rules in case of war with colonies, and a culture of Christian superiority and Non-European lowliness. In this way, the discovery of America marks as an important event in the history of international law. Importantly, it has been observed that the discovery of America paved the way for the modern industry and world's market.[61] His

[49] Pagden and Lawrance (2010, p. xxv).

[50] Ibid., p. 233.

[51] Ibid., pp. xxv–vi, 290–291.

[52] Anghie (2014, p. 132).

[53] Anghie (2004, p. 20).

[54] Pagden and Lawrance (2010, pp. 278–279).

[55] Ibid., p. 280.

[56] Ibid., p. 282.

[57] Anghie (2004, pp. 26–27).

[58] Ibid., p. 37.

[59] Ibid., p. 27.

[60] Georg Cavallar, cited in ibid., p. 28.

[61] Marx and Angels (2018, p. 34).

contemporary European writers Balthasar Ayala, Francisco Suárez and Alberico Gentili by and large followed his footprints. Their formulations were used to swallow the rest of the non-Christian world in furtherance of the emerging economic greed. For instance, the barbaric religious wars of the sixteenth century between Christian and Muslim nations were actually waged to establish spice trade with India and East Indies.[62] This theory of war and related rules was not limited to only one century; rather, it was just a beginning of the more barbaric ensuing times.

4.3.2 Anything for Trade

In the seventeenth century, Hugo Grotius, a paid counsel[63] for the Dutch East Indian Company, demonstrated the Vitorian loyalty in his celebrated work *De jure Belli as Pacis* (The Law of War and Peace) published in the year 1625. Basing on secular natural law, he advanced humanitarian considerations during war. He promoted the idea that restraints on the conduct in war were applicable irrespective of the just or unjust nature of the initial resort of war.[64] However, the overall plan of his work promoted the Dutch expansion.[65]

Soon, the bloodshed in the Thirty Years War (1618–1648) exposed the selectivity of the existing rules. Improved weapons of iron, use of gunpowder and cannonball, organized military and better equipped warships caused unprecedented violence. The war concluded with the Treaty of Westphalia, 1648. The treaty marked the beginning of the modern sovereign states and consequent vanishing of feudal mode of rule. The modern state featuring sovereignty appeared as an embodiment of unbridled political power useful "to confront the challenges that war and domestic upheaval brought."[66] The economic and expansive policies of the powerful European States became more explicit. Soon England, France and Portugal discovered and colonized more American and African territories. Their engagement in war got increased with this expansion. Trade interest was the root-cause of great number of these wars. According to a study, 36 percent of the wars waged during 1648–1713 occurred due to commerce and navigation, while 9 percent, on account of colonial competition.[67] The colonial powers maintained effective control over the subjugated territories so as to preserve the commercial interests of their nationals. Militarism played a decisive role in achieving these goals.[68] This century witnessed, more explicitly, the combine of traders and the State at work. It has been rightly observed:

> It (colonial politics) was no longer a question of conflicts between private trading companies and a few settlers. Colonial governors, national navies, forts, and garrisons representing the monarchies were all involved. As the economic stakes in the colonies increased, so did the commitment of the sovereigns to promote and protect those interests. Colonial policy now became national policy, and the linkage between colonial wars and continental wars became firmly established.[69]

This trend grew in the next century. It was bound to happen given the growing accumulation of wealth, development of technology and economic and political circumstances. It has been observed that by the end of the seventeenth century an international division of labor began wherein the colonized territories were forcibly made the raw material and labor supplier to the European manufacturing units.[70]

4.3.3 Competition, Wars and no Law

The eighteenth century was a "century of trade",[71] "an age of Commercial Revolution."[72] With the expansion of colonies in Asia, Africa

[62] Anand (2006, p. 9).

[63] Ibid., p. 20.

[64] Solis (2010, p. 18) (internal citations omitted).

[65] Ittersum (2010).

[66] Bederman (2002, p. 4).

[67] Holsti (1991, p. 50).

[68] Luxemburg (1951, p. 434).

[69] Holsti (1991, p. 95).

[70] Chimni (2017, p. 485).

[71] Marx and Angels (2010a, p. 71).

[72] Anand (2006, p. 63).

and America during the previous two centuries, France, England and few other European nations made phenomenal economic growth. With the navigation legislation of 1651 and 1661, England had already declared its monopoly in trade with the colonies.[73] Further, the outcome of the war of the Spanish Succession (1701–1704) established England as the biggest slave-trading country.[74] The discovery of Australia and New Zealand by the British explorer James Cook[75] was also advantageous to England. On the other side, with the unprecedented increase in the international trade of France and circulation of gold in the Kingdom, France rose as an economic giant.[76] In this century, the volume of trade of England increased by 500 to 600%, and that of France, even more.[77] Therefore, the British "wished to eliminate their chief competitor on the way to achieving total predominance of their trade in the European markets, the total control of the colonial and overseas markets, which in turn implied the control of the high seas."[78] While, England was on the victorious side in the Seven Years' War (1756–1763), the French won the Bourbon War (1778–1783) against England. These two nations, thus, were not just dominant players in the political economy of the eighteenth-century Europe, but gave a fillip to the colonial trade, enhanced the colonial competition and shaped the existing power relations.

In the burgeoning European economy, the slave plantation zones of Americas and Asia constituted a major share.[79] These regions were export zones of some of the valuable crops, such as sugar, tobacco and coffee, and post-industrial revolution, cotton.[80] The overwhelming profits and wealth accumulated in the Europe could not stay idle by its very nature. It needed markets and industries to enter into the vicious circle of "capital accumulation".[81] It increased competition for colonies and trade supremacy among the advanced European nations. The race for colonies and empire resulted in several wars.[82]

In the eighteenth century, Rousseau rationalized ban on unnecessary violence in war by arguing for the first time that the purpose of using force is to overcome an enemy State, and that to do this it is sufficient to disable enemy combatants. This idea of Rousseau was adopted in the American-Prussian Treaty, 1785 and also during nineteenth century, by public opinion, statecraft and legal theory (for instance, Declaration of St. Petersburg 1868).[83] Nevertheless, during the French Revolution (1789–1799) and Napoleonic battles (1803–1815), things distorted rapidly and significantly because professional army was replaced by citizen soldiery fueled with nationalism and spirit of vengeance. The National Convention of France did not hesitate in passing decree prohibiting ransom and permitting execution of prisoners of war. The modest restraint that the Convention could lay down was a decree of May 25, 1793 providing for the same hospital treatment for wounded and injured enemy soldiers as that accorded to French soldiers, on the basis of reciprocity.[84]

The economic and political account of the eighteenth century was significantly shaped by the events that occurred in India. During the seventeenth century, India was one of the prominent industrial nations. Its textile and ship-building industries attracted not only Asians but also Europeans.[85] The eighteenth century witnessed constant fights by the Mughals in the northern

[73] Chimni (2017, p. 484).

[74] Ibid.

[75] James Cook is well-known for mapping much of the surface of the oceans. See, Hobsbawm (1962, p. 7).

[76] Fournier and Bisson.

[77] Anand (2006, p. 63).

[78] Hobsbawm (1962, p. 83).

[79] Ibid., p. 13.

[80] Ibid., p. 14.

[81] First money is invested as capital to produce goods. The goods are sold at a value which include profit as well as original capital. The money so realised is again put in invested as capital. Thus, after each sale, capital accumulates. For more, see Marx and Angels (2010b, p. 564).

[82] Nehru (2004, p. 390).

[83] Nussbaum (1950, p. 134).

[84] Nussbaum (1950, p. 133).

[85] Anand (2006, pp. 38–39).

region and by the English East India Company in the coastal areas of India in order to capture territories. By the end of the eighteenth century, the Mughal emperors though lost their hold in India, but the British succeeded in their imperialist goals. The victory of the English East India Company in the battle of Plassey in Bengal in 1757 was a turning point in the history of the British Empire in India. It has been argued that after the conquest of Plassey, the influx of Indian treasure in England gave a fillip to the economic activities and prompted inventions (spinning jenny in 1764, improved steam engine in 1768 and power loom in 1785).[86] The plunder of Bengal proved to be a great driving force of the industrial revolution in England, in 1770s.[87] The impact of the colonial loot and exploitation on the aggrandizement of the Western wealth has been succinctly put by Marx:

> The colonial system ripened, like a hothouse, trade and navigation ... The colonies secured a market for the budding manufactures, and, through the monopoly of the market, an increased accumulation. The treasures captured outside Europe by undisguised looting, enslavement, and murder, floated back to the mother-country and were there turned into capital.[88]

These developments signaled towards a more explicit international division of labor and a developing world market and economy.

4.3.4 Advanced Weaponry and Making of a Superpower

The industrial revolution swiftly changed the production process and means of transportation. Hand-machines were replaced by automatic ones, which could produce goods in larger quantity in less time and at a cheaper cost. It necessitated more allocation of different jobs to different workers (i.e. division of labor), expansion of work place and employment of more workers. The economic gains of the commercial class increased manifold. Hence, a clearest division of the society on domestic level into capitalist and working class occurred, like never before.

The sudden rise in industrial production increased the hunt for colonies. Every economic power started swallowing more and more territories.[89] While England paid much attention to grab India—"a river of gold,"[90] Africa was turned into a "continent of European domination and the hunting ground for slaves to be transported like animals to the New World."[91]

After the defeat of Napoleon, the conquering nations held the Congress of Vienna in 1814–1815 to redraw the European frontiers and reallocate the overseas possessions of the Continental Powers on a new basis.[92] In the Congress, four principal powers Britain, Prussia, Austria and Russia, and later on France, emerged as Great Powers[93] and formed the Concert of Europe. They distributed the colonies, especially of North America and the Caribbean, and rearranged the European map. However, they were neither prepared for disarmament[94] nor any humanitarian restraints on their conduct in war. This attitude of the Great Powers has been explained in detail below:

> For schemes of disarmament there was in Europe then no articulate demand. The French had still an inordinate pride in their army; Prussia had just passed a universal service law which evoked a willing response from the people; Great Britain was not prepared, in the slightest degree, to apply the principle of disarmament to sea-power, in which she had attained complete and overwhelming supremacy; the Tsar, though he initiated proposals on the subject in 1816, appears to have had no real intention of allowing them to affect his own vast armies; and in no country was there any attempt to coerce the Governments on this subject. Accusation on this score must, in fact, be leveled against the age as a whole and not against the statesmen.[95]

Nevertheless, they promoted the idea of continental stability with the motto of "never again."[96]

---

86 Ibid., p. 58 (internal citations omitted).

87 Ibid.

88 Marx and Angels (2010b, p. 741).

89 Nehru (2004, p. 464).

90 Ibid.

91 Sen (2006, p. 86).

92 Webster (1920, p. 1).

93 Ibid., p. 61.

94 Ibid., p. 148.

95 Ibid.

96 Stråth (2014, p. 163).

The decades to come were relatively peaceful for Europe till the end of first half of the century. Post Congress of Vienna, England was the only industrialized economy, the only naval power and virtually the only colonial power in the world.[97] Collectively, however, the Western international trade between 1780 and 1840 shot up by more than threefold, and during 1780–1850, it proliferated by more than four times.[98]

From 1850s onwards, revolution in weapon technology provided new military strength in the form of iron and steel ships, heavier naval guns and more accurate and powerful rifles.[99] Technological innovations also facilitated production of destructive weapons and speedier movement of troops and arms to the theaters of war. Consequently, in addition to competition for colonies and trade, arms race also began among the advanced European nations. Out of envy, fear and hate for each other, they enhanced their military power.[100] Thus, the growing militarism became "a weapon in the competitive struggle between capitalist countries for areas of non-capitalist civilization."[101]

The use of advanced armaments became common to unleash plunder, loot and barbarism not just over enemy forces but also common masses. The Crimean War (1853–1856) is considered to be the first to implement the scientific advances in ballistic technology.[102] In this war, Turkey, supported by Britain, France and Austria fought against Russia and won. The warships of Great Britain and France successfully obstructed Russia's imports and exports, whether carried by enemy or neutral vessel.[103] The war ended with the conclusion of two significant international instruments, namely Treaty of Paris, 1856, and Declaration respecting Maritime Law, 1856. The economic interests dictated the terms of both the instruments. While the Treaty of Paris was meant to restore peace and ensure unimpeded commerce, the Declaration partially regulated the conduct during maritime war by prohibiting privateering (permitting armed private ships to attack enemy ships) and seizure of enemy and neutral goods except contraband, for the first time on international level. The Declaration was acceded to by few more maritime nations. However, detailed humanitarian restraints on war were yet to become part of general international law. In the meantime, the Concert of Europe had begun to decay.

By then, Europe had realized the danger attached to advanced weapons. Soon, armament control became a central issue of diplomatic deliberations between France and Britain; however, Britain was not willing to limit her military power. Till then, Britain had become not only an "undisputed commercial and manufacturing hegemon"[104] but also the biggest empire. Any restriction on the use of weaponry might affect its dominance. Moreover, the Revolt of 1857 against the British rule in India was a sufficient indication that only its military power could help keep the colonial and economic hegemony intact.

Meanwhile, the Great Powers assumed for themselves a new mission of "civilizing" the so called primitive, savage, barbaric people of colonies. They used these phrases for the colored, black, technologically ignorant and poor peoples in the colonial world, in short the Global South. Moreover, they projected it as their duty and responsibility to civilize the "backward" masses.[105] In the name of civilizing them, "the superior races" took over those territories and committed criminal acts of torture, enslavement and loot. The "civilizing" mission was actually a program of exploitation, torture and dehumanization of the colonized peoples, carried out by the so called "civilized" nations to further their commercial interests. In the words of European historian Charles Salomon, the language of civilization was pure hypocrisy.[106] In his view, to be

[97] Hobsbawm (1962, p. 1962). Hobsbawn points out that England in 1840 had ships nearly equal to the ships of all other navies put together.

[98] Ibid., p. 172.

[99] Anand (2006, p. 64).

[100] Nehru (2004, p. 464).

[101] Luxemburg (1951, p. 434).

[102] Bryant (2016, p. 116).

[103] Kalshoven (2016, p. 33).

[104] Hopkins (2014, p. 40).

[105] Anand (2006, p. 51).

[106] Cited in Koskenniemi (2004, p. 106).

civilized actually implies duties, instead of extensive rights.[107] On the other hand, the nineteenth-century European writers sought to justify the distinction between civilized and uncivilized by saying that international law applied between civilized i.e. European nations only because the "uncivilized" nations were not part of the "family of nations" and they lacked sovereignty.[108] Actually, what united the states in the family of nations was their common economic interests, primarily.[109]

References

Alexander A (2015) A short history of international humanitarian law. Eur J Int Law 26(1):109–138

Anand RP (2006) Development of modern international law and India. Indian Society of International Law, New Delhi, Nomos Verlagsgesellschaft, Baden-Baden

Anand RP (2008) New states and international law. Hope India Publications, Gurgaon

Anghie A (2004) Imperialism, sovereignty and the making of international law. CUP, New York

Anghie A (2014) Towards a postcolonial international law. In: Singh P, Mayer B, Critical international law. OUP, New Delhi

Baets AD (2022) The view of the past in international humanitarian law (1860–2020). Int Rev Red Cross 104(920–921): 1586–1620

Banaji J (2020) A brief history of commercial capitalism. Haymarket Books, Chicago

Bederman DJ (2002) The spirit of international law. The University of Georgia Press, Athens

Bober MM (1950) Karl Marx's interpretation of history. Harvard University Press, Cambridge

Bryant M (2016) A world history of war crimes: from antiquity to the present. Bloomsbury Academic, London

Cain M, Hunt A (1979) Marx and Engels on law. Academic Press, London

Chimni BS (2017) International law and world order: a critique of contemporary approaches. CUP, Cambridge

Cohen GA (2001) Karl Marx's theory of history: a defence. Princeton University Press, Princeton

Collins H (1982) Marxism and law. OUP, New York

Crawford E, Pert A (2015) International humanitarian law. CUP, Cambridge

Forgacs D (ed) (2017) The Antonio Gramsci reader: selected writings 1916–1935. Aakar Books, New Delhi

[107] Ibid.

[108] Wheaton, Hall, Westlake, Holland, Stuart Mill, Cited in Anand (2008, pp. 19–22) and Anand (2006, pp. 71–72).

[109] Rovira (2014, pp. 765, 779).

Fournier G, Bisson TN, Continuity and change. https://www.britannica.com/place/France/Continuity-and-change.

Gaarder J (2015) Sophie's world. Weidenfeld & Nicolson, London

Hegel WGF (1899) The philosophy of history. The Colonial Press, New York

Hobsbawm EJ (1962) The age of revolution 1789–1848. Vintage Books, New York

Holland TE (1898) Studies in international law. Clarendon Press, London

Holsti KJ (1991) Peace and war: armed conflicts and international order 1648–1989. CUP, Cambridge

Hopkins T (2014) Ordering the world in the nineteenth century. In: Koskenniemi M, Stråth B (eds) Europe 1815–1914: creating community and ordering the world. University of Helsinki, Helsinki, pp 163–185

Islam MS (2018) The historical evolution of international humanitarian law (IHL) from earliest societies to modern age. Beijing Law Rev 9:294–307

Ittersum MJ (2010) The long goodbye: Hugo Grotius' justification of dutch expansion overseas 1615–1645. Hist Eur Ideas 36(4):386–411. https://doi.org/10.1016/j.historeuroideas.2010.05.003?scroll=top&needAccess=true

Kalshoven F (2016) The history of international humanitarian law treaty-making. In: Liivoja R, McCormac T (eds) Routledge handbook of the law of armed conflict. Routledge, Oxon, pp 33–49. https://doi.org/10.4324/9780203798362.ch2

Koskenniemi M (2004) The gentle civilizer of nations: the rise and fall of international law 1870–1960. CUP, Cambridge

Luxemburg R (1951) The accumulation of capital. Routledge, London

Mani VS (2007) Christian traditions of international humanitarian law. In: Mani VS (ed) Handbook of international humanitarian law in South Asia. OUP, New Delhi, pp 14–24

Marx K (1904) A contribution to the critique of political economy. Charles H. Kerr Company, Chicago

Marx K, Engel F (2010a) German ideology, collected works 1845–1847, vol V. Lawrence & Wishart, London

Marx K, Engel F (2010b) Capital vol I, collected works 1845–1847, vol XXXV. Lawrence & Wishart, London

Marx K, Engel F (2018) The communist manifesto. Fingerprint, New Delhi

Neff SC (2018) A short history of international law. In: Evans MD (ed) International law. OUP Oxford, pp 3–27

Nehru J (2004) Glimpses of world History. Penguin Books, New Delhi

Nussbaum A (1950) A concise history of the law of nations. The Macmillan Co., New York

O'Connell ME (2013) Historical development and legal basis. In: Fleck D (ed) The handbook of international humanitarian law. OUP, Oxford, pp 1–42

Pagden A, Lawrance J (eds) (2010) Francisco de Vitoria: political writings. CUP, New York

Rovira MG (2014) The politics of interest in international law. Eur J Int Law 25(3):765–793

Sen A (2006) Identity and violence: the illusion of destiny. Penguin Books, London

Solis GD (2010) The law of armed conflict: international humanitarian law in war. CUP, Cambridge

Stråth B (2014) Vienna 1815 in perspective: three utopias of peace and the European search for a political economy. In: Koskenniemi M, Stråth B (eds) Europe 1815–1914: creating community and ordering the world. University of Helsinki, Helsinki, pp 163–185

Webster CK (1920) Congress of Vienna 1814–1815. OUP, London

Welsh JM (2017) Empire and fragmentation. In: Dunne T, Reus-Smit C (eds) The globalization of international society. OUP, Oxford, pp 145–166

Wright Q (1942) A study of war, vol I. The University of Chicago Press, Chicago

5 Materialist History of International Humanitarian Law (Part II)

Abstract

In this chapter, I deal with the development of the laws of armed conflict from the 1864 Geneva Convention to the Additional Protocols of 1977 along with the impact of the political economy on the form and content of the instruments. I try to demonstrate how since the very inception, selective humanitarianism was at work in terms of its content and scope. I reemphasize how the imperialist motives kept the colonies away from the making and application of the law. While discussing these developments, I intensely talk about the trade rivalry, colonial competition and imperialism, and also the impact of these historical events on the formulation of the laws of war. I also argue that the law facilitated colonial expansion.

Keywords

Henry Dunant · History of IHL · Capitalism · Imperialism · Hague conventions

5.1 Introduction

The previous chapter tries to explain the beginning of shaping the rules of war by the origin and development of colonization and capitalist mode of production. It covers the period from the sixteenth century to the first half of the nineteenth century. It suggests that these developments built the foundation of laws of war and international law in general on cultural differences and political and economic motives. Part II seeks to discuss the political economy of the later period and emphasize upon its impact on the development of the laws of armed conflict (international humanitarian law).

5.2 Geneva Convention (1864): Beginning of "Humanitarianism" by Convenience

Coming back to 1850s, the exclusive club of Great Powers which had already been weakened by the Crimean War, further received a blow by the Franco-Austrian war, 1859. However, this war is also of historical significance so far as the origin of the modern laws of armed conflict is concerned. During the war, Jean Henry Dunant, a merchant from Switzerland happened to see thousands of dead, wounded and sick but unattended soldiers in the battlefield of Solferino, 1859.[1] He

[1] Bhai Kanhaiya (1648–1718) is seen as an Indian counterpart of Henry Dunant. He served water to all the wounded and sick soldiers on the battlefield irrespective to the side they belong to in the battle of Anandpur Sahib (1705): Burra (2018, p. 53).

K. Jeenger, *A Humanitarian Critique of International Humanitarian Law*, Sustainable Development Goals Series, https://doi.org/10.1007/978-981-96-8319-2_5

wrote an account of the protracted suffering and pain in his book *Un Souvenir de Solférino*, 1862 (A Memory of Solferino). In the book, he not just penned the scenes of pain and distress of nearly 40,000 dead or wounded soldiers, but called upon the whole world, (1) to form relief societies to help the wounded and sick in wartime,[2] and (2) to "formulate some international principles, sanctioned by a Convention, inviolate in character."[3] He stressed on taking these steps by underlining the hard material realities of contemporary Europe. He warned in the letter that instruments of destruction were being invented regularly, European nations were engaged in an armament race, wars had become unavoidable,[4] and future wars would only become more and more murderous.[5] With this word of caution and appeal to take action, he published the book at his own expenditure and sent its copies to many heads of States, army commanders, doctors, friends etc. across Europe in 1862. Many of the recipients responded with messages of support.

Henry Dunant, however, was also a product of his times. It is important to note that he was seen as a colonialist and a colonizer who was operating several projects of natural resource exploitation and business-friendly infrastructure building in colonies.[6] When he witnessed the painful pictures on the battlefield, he was proceeding towards materializing a colonial business endeavor. He was going to contact King Napoleon III, to seek concessions in Algeria.[7]

In February 1863, he, with four other Swiss nationals, formed a Committee of Five which they soon named as International Committee for the Relief of Wounded Soldiers. The Committee convened an international conference in October 1863 wherein delegates from fourteen governments and few non-governmental organizations, among others, participated. None of the Committee members were great influential political figures of Europe, yet all major European states participated in the conference because Dunant's book had warned them of the ferocious consequences of future wars in Europe. Moreover, Dunant's idea was not about disarmament or prohibition of war, therefore, the European Powers found it convenient to be a part of a mission which would project their humanitarian image before the world without compromising their economic and military strength. They treated it as an opportunity to participate in a humanitarian mission which they could easily overpower and make their own, as they did within a couple of years by sidelining Dunant and giving it a European color. They were already in a habit of capturing and dominating anything that would benefit them.

In the conference of 1863, ten resolutions[8] were adopted wherein the delegates agreed upon the formation and mode of functioning of national relief societies. Additionally, the conference provided that volunteer medical personnel shall wear a white armlet with a red cross as a distinctive and uniform emblem. However, it cannot be denied that the emblem was inspired by the Swiss flag with colors reversed which actually symbolizes Christian cross.

In August 1864, with the support of Swiss Federal Council, Henry Dunant convened a diplomatic conference to agree on a binding instrument. After a fifteen-day conference, the first Geneva Convention, namely Geneva Convention for the Amelioration of the Conditions of the Wounded in Armies in the Field was adopted. However, the humane effort could not stay away from the complex of contemporary political, economic and cultural relations. These intertwined factors significantly shaped the content of the Convention and determined States' participation. First, the Convention was carefully drafted in that the humanitarian obligations not affecting the military capabilities of belligerents

[2] Dunant (1939, p. 115).

[3] Ibid., p. 126.

[4] Ibid., p. 116.

[5] Ibid., p. 128.

[6] Mégret (2006, pp. 272–273).

[7] Ibid., p. 273.

[8] Bugnion (2012, pp. 1299, 1319).

were made mandatory to comply with (using "shall"), whereas the obligations adding to the enemy combat power and disadvantageous to one's own were merely directory in nature (using "may").[9] Selective humanitarianism was at work at the very inception.

Second, the Convention mandated that military hospitals and ambulances shall adopt uniform flag bearing a red cross on a white ground,[10] actually, a mark symbolizing Christianity. After the first Geneva Convention, Dunant was kept aside as "more practical men began to take over"[11] and by the end of 1866, he had been completely sidelined. With no surprise, the organization itself was renamed as International Committee of the Red Cross in 1876. And why not? After all, only "civilized" countries could conceive a philanthropic humanitarian idea! Going by that belief system, "savages" could indulge only in inhuman acts. As a measure of protest against this religious supremacy, Turkey opposed the use of Red Cross and used Red Crescent during the Russo-Turkish War (1876–1878). Later on, the International Committee of the Red Cross (ICRC) tried to justify the use of the red cross by saying that it was a tribute to Swiss government for its support in executing the idea of Dunant.[12] However, there was no evidence to support this argument. In fact, the ICRC's contention is an afterthought, when Turkey opposed the use of the red cross by calling it a Christian symbol.

Third, States had already realized with their domestic experiences that law was an important instrument of control in the hands of those in power who can shape it as per their suitability. Fourth, the colonizers had understood a major advantage of codified law that it provides legitimacy to a given conduct; and legitimacy is the "currency of power".[13] Fifth, a major part of the world had been colonized by then, and handful of advanced European nations could easily dominate the international law making and mold its terms to suit them. Sixth, the Swiss Federal Council did not invite African, Asian and many Latin American nations in the conference,[14] despite the fact that they were victims of the European colonial wars. European nations believed that non-Europeans were uncivilized barbaric peoples, unworthy of being part of family of nations governed by international law. The standard of being civilized was none other than power.[15] Even Dunant believed in this cultural difference when he stated in the first meeting of the Committee that "... civilized Powers would subscribe to an inviolable, international principle ...".[16]

Seventh, the big powers of Europe were advancing their agenda of colonization in the name of "civilizing" the colonized masses by proclaiming that they were the gentle advanced civilized societies. Supporting humanitarianism in war could be just another way to propagate this (mis)belief. Eighth, on 24 April 1863 (few months before the European States were to assemble in the first Geneva conference to consider Dunant's proposal) the American President Abraham Lincoln notified General Orders No. 100. It was popularly called the Lieber Code as it had been prepared by Francis Lieber, a New York based German professor. Lieber Code was the first comprehensive compilation of

[9] For instance, Article 6 of the Convention provides: Wounded or sick combatants, to whatever nation they may belong, shall be collected and cared for. Those who, after their recovery, are recognized as being unfit for further service, shall be repatriated. The others may likewise be sent back, on condition that they shall not again, for the duration of hostilities, take up arms.

[10] Art. 7 para 3.

[11] Dunant (1939, p. 10).

[12] https://www.icrc.org/en/doc/resources/documents/misc/emblem-history.htm (the URL is not active anymore).

[13] Kennedy (2006, p. 45).

[14] Invitations were sent to all the governments of Europe (including the Ottoman Empire), as well as to the United States of America, Brazil, and Mexico. See, Bugnion (2012, pp. 1299, 1323).

[15] Anand (2008, p. 21).

[16] Transcript of the Minutes of the first meeting of the International Committee for the Relief of Wounded Soldiers (today, International Committee of the Red Cross), 17 February 1863, cited in Bugnion (2012, pp. 1299, 1337).

customary law of war, and America was first to prescribe a formal code of war for its troops. The Code soon gained popularity among the powerful nations. Superpowers, as usual, were envious of each other's achievements and progress. It was difficult for Britain, the most powerful nation at that time, to see America, one of its colonies in the past, to have developed its own laws of war. Moreover, diplomatic tensions between both the countries had already escalated because Britain, despite being a neutral country, allowed construction and repairing of warships to be used by the Confederate Army in the American Civil War (1861–1865). The breach of neutrality later on led to the Alabama Claims Arbitration (1872) as well. Thus, this phase of mutual rivalry and competitiveness prompted Britain and other European States to participate in the Geneva conference and carry the "humanitarian" idea forward. Lieber's forecast that the code "would invite imitation by the English, French and Germans" proved out to be correct.[17]

It has been observed that there is a wider consensus that the law of war developed later in the century carried the imprints of the Lieber Code.[18] The peculiar feature of the Lieber Code was not its humanitarian character but the fact that it was a compilation of the laws and customs of war as already existing in the works of publicists from Grotius onwards, and not Lieber's own creation.[19] Actually, however, the Code heavily compromised with humanitarian standards and preferred military necessity to justify violence. It permitted, for instance, complete destruction of enemy property, starvation of enemy soldiers, and bombardment of civilians without warning to secure the ends of war.[20] Given the primacy to military necessity, the "humanitarian" character of the forthcoming instruments was not difficult to imagine.

[17] Bryant (2016, p. 131).

[18] Jochnick and Normand (1994, p. 65; ibid).

[19] Koskenniemi (2004, p. 87).

[20] Art. 15, 17, 21, respectively.

5.3 St. Petersburg Declaration: In the Name of Humanitarianism

As it is evident, restrictions on the use of weapons were not in the agenda of the 1864 Geneva Conference. However, in 1868, Czar Alexander II of Russia took the initiative to ban a particular projectile. The ammunition under consideration could explode on contact with hard as well as soft surface, like human body, and consequently, cause more harm than needed. In 1860s, Russia was in favor of "rule-based conduct in war"[21] for many reasons. First, Russia had been defeated in the Crimean War by the European nations. Second, the uncompromising arms race among the European nations was threat to Russia, who had formally abolished serfdom and opened the door for capitalism in 1861. Third, the Geneva Convention, 1864 had set the stage painted in the colors of humanity, for regulating conduct in war. Thus, it was convenient for Russia to present its plan sugar-coated with "humanitarian" considerations.

Initially Russia tried to ascertain general attitude of States towards its proposal by sending a circular.[22] On the receipt of responses from many European countries, Russia sent a draft protocol for their consideration and approval. However, Prussia sought to expand the idea by suggesting a general prohibition on any weapon causing superfluous injury. To consider this ambitious proposal, a diplomatic conference was inevitable. Therefore, the representatives of sixteen nations assembled in St. Petersburg. The initial negotiations proved that delegates were not ready to accept wider restrictions on the use of destructive new weapons. Severe opposition came from the British delegate Andrew Buchanan:

> [W]hile the numerical force of the British army was less than that of any Great Power, the mechanical resources, the inventive talent and the wealth of England were probably not exceeded, if indeed they were equalled [*sic*], by those of any other country; and it followed therefore that any

[21] Brisku (2014, p. 52).

[22] For details see, Keefer (2014, pp. 451–52).

> understanding which tended to limit the application of mechanical or chemical arts to war would operate, so far as it was effective, to reduce rather than to augment the military force of this country as compared with that of other nations.[23]

Thus, Britain opposed the sweeping regulations to preserve its military superiority and colonial empire. In the end, the British view prevailed, and the delegates adopted a document, very narrow in scope, the Declaration Renouncing the Use, in Time of War, of Explosive Projectiles Under 400 Grammes Weight, 1868 (popularly called as the Declaration of St. Petersburg). The Prussian proposal of broader regulation consistent with new military technology formed part of the Declaration, not as a binding obligation, but as an idea reserved for discussion in future if parties so decide. The Declaration was a humanitarian failure for three important reasons.

First, the logic behind banning projectiles below 400 grammes was that they could be used against human beings. However, few commentators believed that it was "an unreliable and already obsolete weapon"[24] and never became "integral to military tactics".[25] States commonly used ordinary rifle bullets to incapacitate an enemy soldier. On the other hand, the projectiles above that limit which were used to target military equipments or installations, manned or unmanned, were not forbidden. A Japanese District Court in Ryuichi Shimoda et al. v. The State (1963) explains the relevance of what was prohibited and what was not:

> Such projectiles are small and just powerful enough to kill or wound only one man, and as an ordinary bullet will do for this purpose, there is no overriding need for using these inhuman weapons. On the other hand, the use of a certain weapon, great as its inhuman result may be, need not be prohibited by international law if it has a great military effect.[26]

Second, the Preamble to the Declaration intended to extend the prohibition to wars between "civilized nations" only. It not only excluded a large number of non-European "uncivilized" nations from making the international law but also suggested that war with them knows no limits and their resistance may be crushed brutally.

Third, the "humanitarian" Declaration contained a "general-participation" (*si omnes*) clause, whereby the prohibition would apply only if all the belligerents in a war were State-parties to the instrument:

> This engagement is compulsory only upon the Contracting or Acceding Parties thereto in case of war between two or more of themselves; it is not applicable to non-Contracting Parties, or Parties who shall not have acceded to it.
> It will also cease to be compulsory from the moment when, in a war between Contracting or Acceding Parties, a non-Contracting Party or a non-Acceding Party shall join one of the belligerents.[27]

Thus, the signatories could use any deadly weapon while fighting with colonies, or as soon as a non-State-party joined a war between State-parties. Broadly, a large number of non-European nations remained uncovered by the document, whereas it's Preamble proclaimed that "necessities of war ought to yield to the requirements of humanity." It was a new language of humanity, which was shockingly not universal but racial.

Thus, there were multiple determinants of the emerging European conception of international law, including the distinction between civilized and uncivilized nations (or logic of culture, in the words of Chimni). He acknowledges the influence of logic of culture on the making of international law[28] and explains that: "The 'logic of culture' encompasses the world of ideas and ideology that shape perspectives on capital, territory, market, democracy, nature, language,

[23] Buchanan to Lord Stanely, House of Lords, cited in ibid., p. 453.

[24] Jochnick and Normand (1994, p. 66).

[25] Keefer (2014, p. 458).

[26] Para 11, https://ihl-databases.icrc.org/applic/ihl/ihl-nat.nsf/xsp/.ibmmodres/domino/OpenAttachment/applic/ihl/ihl-nat.nsf/AA559087DBCF1AF5C1256A1C0029F14D/CASE_TEXT/ATTMUB6T.pdf.

[27] Declaration Renouncing the use, in Time of War, of Explosive Projectiles Under 400 Grammes Weight (1868) (St. Petersburg Declaration).

[28] Chimni (2017, p. 35).

law, ethics, democracy, arts and aesthetics and above all the state."[29] Apparently, the capitalist nations excluded the "uncivilized" from the family of nations and treated them as unworthy of being governed by international law. It has been rightly observed that the colonies were not the subjects of international law, but its objects.[30] The colonizers began to craft the law of war in such a way that it would not obstruct their colonial expansion, rather facilitate the same without curtailing their military strength.

5.4 Brussels Conference: Humanitarianism Rejected

Soon after the Declaration of St. Petersburg, the Franco-Prussian war (1870) occurred which was "essentially a test of strength and reputation"[31] between the two countries. Both the countries not only failed to honor the Geneva Convention, but misused the Red Cross insignia too.[32] Finally, Germany defeated France and achieved the "victory of annihilation."[33] During 1864–1871, Germany had defeated Denmark, Austria and France in the same fashion. Lenin, therefore, observed that "in 1871 a new predator appeared, a new capitalist power arose, which developed at an incomparably faster pace than Britain."[34] Actually, between 1850 and 1870, Germany's industrial power had augmented more than that of France.[35] And, it has been indicated that it is the industrial capacity and technological developments which mainly determine a country's political and military power.[36]

Economically struggling Russia could sense the inevitability of wider humanitarian restraints on war. Russia, who was already on a "humanitarian" mission since the St. Petersburg conference, organized a conference at Brussels in 1874. Russia took the lead also because the ruthless conduct in the Franco-Prussian War had received sharp reactions from all quarters of Europe and in 1872 Fedor Martens, the holder of the Chair of International Law at St. Petersburg University had requested the Russian war authorities in a letter to convene a conference.[37] He suggested the adoption of a set of rules based on the pattern of the Lieber Code. However, Martens who is often glorified for the well-known Martens clause in The Hague Conventions, has been found to be under profound influence of colonial and racist beliefs.[38] In one of his articles, he writes:

> [T]he future of Asia and the future destiny of their possessions compel Russia and Britain never to lose sight of the sublime role which Divine Providence has imposed on them, for the good of the semi-savage and barbaric nations of this part of the world.[39]

In the conference, the Russian draft was discussed, debated and modified. Delegates agreed on a set of rules, more comprehensive in scope and less subject to military necessity as compared to earlier international instruments. Finally, a Project of an International Declaration Concerning the Laws and Customs of War was adopted by the delegates of sixteen nations. However, wider the regulations, more reluctant the States. No government ratified the document. European nations were not prepared to accept substantial limitations on their combat capabilities, as it would adversely affect their commercial and imperial interests. After all, colonial trade was the single greatest source of European wealth.[40]

[29] Ibid., p. 479.

[30] Anand (2008, p. 25) (internal citation omitted).

[31] Holsti (1991, p. 156).

[32] Koskenniemi (2004, p. 39).

[33] Bryant (2016, p. 120).

[34] Lenin (1964, p. 404).

[35] Hobsbawm (1995, p. 56).

[36] Ibid.

[37] See Holquist (2018, p. 69).

[38] Mégret (2006, p. 273).

[39] Ibid., 274.

[40] Koskenniemi (2014, p. 28).

5.5 Imperialism: Own It All

The next major steps in the development of the laws of armed conflict were taken at The Hague in 1899 and 1907. The changes in the political economy that took place in the last quarter of the nineteenth century made it imperative to hold the conferences and shaped their outcome.

During the first three quarters of the century, Britain was having maximum number of overseas possessions and enjoying highest economic growth. It advocated the policy of free competition wherein the capitalist countries could sell their goods anywhere. It buttressed the rapid internationalization of British economy.[41] Accordingly, several colonial powers entered into free trade treaties to reduce or eliminate tariffs, except the United States which continued to remain a "bastion of protectionism."[42] Interestingly, on the other hand, colonization was opposed to free trade as it would facilitate monopoly.[43] After the mutiny of 1857, the Crown took over India's administration replacing the British East India Company.[44] Free competition among the Western settlers attained its highest stage during 1870s. However, free competition and colonialism could not coexist longer. Moreover, the invention of electric power revolutionized the industrial production and the factories began to produce multiple times more than the previous decade. Change in the forces of production was bound to influence relations on higher level. The industrialist countries greatly increased import duties so that the imported goods, especially the British, would cost more than goods produced by them and, consequently, the huge amounts of their own goods could be easily sold in the domestic markets.[45] The policy of free trade was discontinued in Russia and Austria (1874–1875), in Spain (1877), in Germany (1879), and elsewhere also except England.[46] British superiority was, thus, under a serious threat during the last quarter. Meanwhile, the United States appeared as a global economic power.

High tariffs abroad reduced export, but the countries still needed markets to sell the surplus goods. Moreover, the "electric" rise in the industrial production needed more raw materials also. The only option available was to own more and more colonies. France started first and launched military attacks on Senegal and Western Sudan.[47] It has been observed that "from 1879–1882 onwards European powers suddenly took active steps for the creation of formal empires."[48]

On the other hand, in 1870s Germany transformed its "idea of destruction" of enemy to that of military necessity or *Kriegsraison*.[49] German commanders equated military necessity with self-preservation, and thus justified violation of the laws of war to defend the territory. Respect for international law received less attention in German military training and military manuals also.[50] In the words of German Chancellor Bismarck, "What leader would allow his country to be destroyed because of international law?"[51] In the fourth quarter of the century, Germany emerged as a new imperial giant.

In such a situation, the greedy capitalist countries started making rival claims over the huge, resourceful African continent to gratify their commercial and imperial hunger. However, any violent solution would have become counterproductive to their interests. Thus, during 1884–1885, they convened the Berlin West African Conference to peacefully settle the issues of freedom of navigation and trade in the Congo and Niger rivers, and the acquisition of

[41] Banaji (2020, p. 72).

[42] Hobsbawm (1995, pp. 51–52).

[43] Koskenniemi (2004, p. 111).

[44] Ibid., pp. 111–112.

[45] सांकृत्यायन (1942, p. 244).

[46] Hobsbawm (1995, pp. 356–357).

[47] Koskenniemi (2004, p. 117).

[48] Ibid.

[49] Bryant (2016, p. 120).

[50] Ibid., 123.

[51] Jochnick and Normand (1994, p. 64).

new territories.[52] With the much needed cooperation, they settled the claims amicably and divided almost the entire continent among themselves to deprive other colonial powers, like Russia, the United States and Japan of any advantage.

Post the scramble of Africa, the European capitalist class became prosperous in the last decade of the nineteenth century, like never before. Those at the top formed combinations and cartels, and commenced combined production, that is to say, processing of raw material, manufacturing, packaging, marketing etc. under one roof. Thus, less than one percent of total number of enterprises begain to control major share of means of production and industrial output. It has been rightly pointed out that the development of the capitalist class was accompanied by their corresponding political advance.[53] Soon, big banks and government ministers became inexorably part of these cartels as they cannot function in isolation.[54] Marx and Angels brilliantly remark that "The executive of the modern state is but a committee for managing the common affairs of the whole bourgeoisie."[55]

The concentration of production in few hands created monopoly by the end of the century. Meanwhile, the hunt for colonies for the purpose of markets and raw materials grew with faster rate. Poorly developed law of war facilitated, let alone prevented, the use of any amount of force to subjugate and own the weak nations. Advanced weapons helped the powerful Western countries to establish and maintain their hegemony on international sphere and expand the colonial empire. According to Hobson, colonial annexations intensified during 1884–1900.[56] It was the epoch of apex of capitalism-imperialism. Imperialism has been understood "as a specifically capitalist phenomenon of unequal and combined development that tends to generate both homogenization and unevenness on a global scale."[57]

In this era, the rate of territorial annexations increased by three times (i.e. from 210,000 square kilometers to 620,000 square kilometers per year).[58] In the opinion of Banaji, the last quarter of the nineteenth century marks the transition from commercial to industrial capitalism which was featured by dynamic growth in the industrial production; emergence of oil, steel and chemical industries; huge concentration of capital in cartels and trusts; revolutionized means of communication and transportation, and use of electric power.[59] According to him, imperialism was a novel term invented to portray a novel phenomenon of the subordination of commercial to industrial capital.[60]

Before deliberating more on imperialism, it is necessary to realize that Marx and Angels did not deal[61] with the encounter between capitalism and colonialism. They treated capitalist economy as a closed system.[62] The attempts to contemplate the bond between capitalism and imperialism under Marxist analysis were made

[52] Koskenniemi (2004, p. 123).

[53] Marx and Angels (2018, p. 34).

[54] Some ministers or their relatives owned banks and industries; while some of them were offered managerial positions there. Banks would grant them big loans on simple terms and ministers would frame policies to suit industries and banks. For a detailed discussion as to how combinations and cartels worked, see Lenin (1988), pp. 21–57 and सांकृत्यायन (1942, pp. 212–232).

[55] Marx and Angels (2018, p. 35).

[56] For instance, Great Britain acquired 3,700,000 square miles of territory with a population of 57,000,000; France, 3,600,000 square miles with a population of 36,500,000; Germany, 1,000,000 square miles with 16,700,000 inhabitants; Belgium, 900,000 square miles with 30,000,000 inhabitants; Portugal 800,000 square miles with 9,000,000 inhabitants: Lenin (1988, pp. 95–96).

[57] Tzouvala (2020, p. 45).

[58] Magdoff, cited in Chimni (2017, p. 490).

[59] Banaji (2020, pp. 121–123).

[60] Ibid., 121.

[61] Though Marx had foreseen such expansion: "The tendency to create the world market is directly given in the concept of capital itself. Every limit appears as a barrier to be overcome." Marx in Grundrisse, cited in Tzouvala (2020, p. 3).

[62] Chimni (2017, p. 491).

by two contemporary Marxist scholars, Rosa Luxemburg and Lenin, in the early twentieth century. Rosa defined imperialism as the political expression of the accumulation of capital in its competitive struggle for what remains still open of the non-capitalist environment.[63] Lenin thought of imperialism as:

> capitalism in that stage of development in which the dominance of monopolies and finance capital has established itself; in which the export of capital has acquired pronounced importance; in which the division of the world among the international trusts has begun; in which the division of all territories of the globe among the great capitalist powers has been completed.[64]

In essence, both of them built the imperialism theory on the premise of capitalism. According to Chimni, they believed that imperialism is a political expression of capitalism.[65]

5.6 Hague Conferences: a "Civilized" Negotiating Space

In the late-nineteenth century, Russia's poor[66] economy was not able to compete with the advanced European countries. Moreover, the introduction of expensive quick-firing artillery in Germany and Austria-Hungary presented a challenge before Russia's military budget.[67] Therefore, it tried to maintain its standing as a "great power" by promoting "a rule-based European order under the standard of civilization."[68] In August 1898 Russia summoned a conference for "the maintenance of the general peace and a possible reduction of the excessive armaments which were burdening all nations."[69] Russia wanted to maintain the status quo of the army and military budget for five years.[70] Susceptible of weaker response from invitees, Tsar Nicholas II of Russia added in his second circular the agenda of arbitration for peaceful settlement of international disputes. European nations knew that Russia wanted to limit armaments because of its trembling economy.[71] However, they accepted the proposal just to cater to the public perception of peace and humanity.[72] At the offer of the Dutch Queen Wilhelmina, the conference was convened at her summer residence in The Hague.[73] While majority of the participants opposed the proposal of arms control, major disagreements flowed from the British delegate, John Ardagh.

As in 1868 St. Petersburg conference, the British delegate at The Hague was in favor of retaining the use of expanding bullets so that the munitions might be employed in battles against "active and brave barbarian foes."[74] In 1868, this issue was resolved by the insertion of "general-participation" clause whereby the prohibition was not applicable in wars with non-signatory countries and colonies. The same could have been done in The Hague negotiations also, yet Britain was in favor of retaining the use of the bullet. This is perhaps because Britain wanted

[63] Luxemburg (1951, p. 426).

[64] Lenin (1988, p. 109).

[65] Chimni (2017, p. 62). However, Pashukanis condemned Rosa's idea by calling it an economic theory of imperialism, and preferred Lenin's "description" which, according to him, revealed the essence of the growth of pre-monopoly capitalism into monopoly capitalism. See, Beirne and Sharlet (1980, p. 250).

[66] Hobsbawm (1989, pp. 18–19). However, Hobsbawm mentions that Russia of the nineteenth century was culturally a great power considering the contribution of Dostoievsky, Tolstoi, Chekhov and several others. See, p. 19.

[67] See Keefer (2014, p. 457).

[68] Holquist, cited in Brisku (2014, p. 54).

[69] Higgins (1909, p. 39).

[70] Ibid., 75.

[71] Russia's project received varied reactions, such as: "diplomatic manoeuvre" in Keefer (2014), p. 457 and "a political trick," "masterpiece of diplomatic finesse" in Jochnick and Normand (1994, p. 70, n. 86, 87).

[72] Jochnick and Normand (1994, p. 70).

[73] Bryant (2016, p. 123).

[74] Coupland and Loye (2003, p. 136). The British proposal was defeated by a majority of 19 to 1 vote: Mégret (2006, p. 276).

to employ the weapon in European wars also.[75] Due to loss of commercial supremacy in the late-nineteenth century and mounting colonial competition, Britain wanted to preserve its strategic interests at any cost.

Similar rejection of legal obligation could be seen while attempting to ban the launching of projectiles and explosives from balloons. It was ensured that the prohibition would not apply to the use of new technology in war, such as ammunition dropping by aircrafts, which could be more fatal than outmoded balloons.[76] Moreover, the obligation was circumscribed by the use of the general-participation clause and a life-time of five years only. Military necessity clearly overrode humanitarian considerations. In similar fashion, use of projectiles causing the diffusion of asphyxiating gas was prohibited whereas States were generally hesitant to use it as it might harm their own army too, besides enemy.[77]

The instrument that received maximum appreciation for its "humanitarian" character is the Convention with Respect to the Laws and Customs of War on Land and its Regulations. However the drafters weakened the document by incorporating the general-participation clause, by frequently referring to "military necessity"[78] and by using vague[79] phrases. The very famous Martens Clause,[80] a compromise of heated debate,[81] magnified the humanitarian rhetoric of the conference, however, could not serve the purpose as it was a preambular paragraph. Imperialist motives once again (de)humanized the law of war. The States made sure that The Hague law did not impede their territorial expansions overseas and military progress. It was pertinently observed that "historically, the articulation of humanity and human, which supposedly served as the foundation for the laws of war, was fully compatible with and, indeed, dependent on an imperialistic racial logic."[82] The Conference ended with a promise to meet soon to negotiate on questions that could not be dealt with.

During the times of the First Hague conference the effects of trade monopoly became apparent. Surplus capital had accumulated in the hands of only a few nations, but the same could be employed in their own territories to a limited extent only. Therefore, the capitalist nations decided to employ (export) the super-abundant capital in the poor and colonized countries where land, labor and raw material were available at relatively low prices.[83] The employment of surplus capital was the dominant force for the early-twentieth century colonial expansion.[84] Thus, for instance, the number of British cotton and jute mills in India increased by two to

[75] A general apprehension of use of such means in European wars was present among the colonialists: Coupland and Loye (2003, p. 136).

[76] Jochnick and Normand (1994, p. 73).

[77] Ibid.

[78] Preamble to the Convention and Art. 23(g), 49, 52 Regulations Concerning the Laws and Customs of War on Land annexed to The Hague Convention (II) with Respect to the Laws and Customs of War on Land of 29 July 1899.

[79] While Article 22 says that "the right of belligerents to adopt means of injuring the enemy is not unlimited"; Article 23 declares that it is prohibited "to employ arms, projectiles, or material of a nature to cause superfluous injury." As it is difficult to clearly define what is "not unlimited" and "superfluous," State-parties could employ the interpretation that would suit them the most. See Jochnick and Normand (1994), p. 74.

[80] "On the other hand, it could not be intended by the High Contracting Parties that the cases not provided for should, for want of a written provision, be left to the arbitrary judgment of the military commanders.

Until a more complete code of the laws of war is issued, the High Contracting Parties think it right to declare that in cases not included in the Regulations adopted by them, populations and belligerents remain under the protection and empire of the principles of international law, as they result from the usages established between civilized nations, from the laws of humanity, and the requirements of the public conscience".

[81] Eyffinger (2007, p. 201), n. 5.

[82] Kinsella, cited in Davey (2020, p. 391).

[83] Lenin (1988, p. 77).

[84] Anand (2008, p. 27) (internal citation omitted).

three times during 1890s–1914.[85] Similarly, the British capital invested abroad grew from 42 billion francs in 1893 to 75–100 billion francs in 1914.[86] France, Germany and America were also celebrating similar growth rates. In the words of Marx and Angels, the capitalist class compelled all nations to introduce the capitalist mode of production, what they call civilization, and created a world after its own image.[87]

In the meantime, Germany issued an army manual shaped by military necessity.[88] Russia, on the other hand, was busy rebuilding its own army after the defeat in Russo-Japanese War in 1904–1905. The new British government, though, banned the use of expanding bullets by its troops, its military authorities stressed on having a robust army.[89]

Before the Second Hague Conference could occur in 1907, the Swiss Federal Council summoned a conference to revise the 1864 Convention as agreed upon by the delegates at The Hague in 1899.[90] The new draft conferred the status of prisoner-of-war[91] on the sick or wounded soldiers falling in the enemy hands, and provided for arrangements to be made for their care and treatment. However, the general-participation clause[92] and considerations of military necessity[93] robbed the Convention of its humanitarian character. Moreover, well aware of Turkish opposition regarding the use of red cross in 1876, the ICRC tried to refute any religious association by incorporating a justificatory provision in Article 18: "Out of respect to Switzerland the heraldic emblem of the red cross on a white ground, formed by the reversal of the federal colors, is continued ..." In the very next year, one commentator noted that the use of the expression "heraldic" is also to exclude any cultural connection.[94] However, the argument is very week considering the impact of the logic of culture and race on the international economic and political relations at that time.

In the next year, the Second Hague Conference was called as ensured during its predecessor. This time the United States' President Roosevelt took the lead, while the "August Initiator"[95] but war-stricken Russia joined as an organizer later.[96] Though the meeting secured greater participation (forty four States) and produced more number of agreements (thirteen Conventions and one Declaration) than in 1899, its achievements on humanitarian front as compared to the 1899 instrument declined on several fronts. First blow on the compassionate hopes was non-inclusion of disarmament[97] and reduction of military estimates in the agenda of meeting.[98] Though, the scope of the Convention on the Laws and Customs of War was enlarged, the advanced European nations drafted the document calculatedly. Restrictions not significantly affecting their military might were accepted unconditionally,[99] while those having material bearing on their combat capabilities were inserted subject to the overriding principle of

[85] सांकृत्यायन (1942, pp. 236–237).

[86] Lenin (1988, p. 78).

[87] Marx and Angels (2018, p. 39).

[88] Jochnick and Normand (1994, p. 64).

[89] Keefer (2014, p. 463).

[90] It took more than five years to Switzerland to convene the conference because of Russo-Japanese war (1904–1905) and other political disturbances. See, Higgins (1909, p. 36).

[91] Art. 2 Convention for the Amelioration of the Condition of the Wounded and Sick in Armies in the Field (1906).

[92] Ibid., Art. 24.

[93] Ibid., Art. 12, 15, 17.

[94] Davis (1907, p. 416).

[95] Roosevelt used the expression for Russia. Scott (2008, p. 13).

[96] For a detailed account of the steps taken by both of them, see Higgins (1909), pp. 51–57.

[97] Eyffinger (2007, p. 203).

[98] Higgins (1909, p. 76).

[99] E.g. Art. 4, 23(a)-(d), 25, 28 Regulations Respecting the Laws and Customs of War on Land annexed to The Hague Convention (IV) with Respect to the Laws and Customs of War on Land of 18 October 1907.

military necessity.[100] In sum, the general-participation clause, principle of military necessity and usual vague expressions provided enough scope to accomplish the colonial ambitions and successfully settle inter-imperialist rivalry.

Another striking feature of the conference was the concern shown by the States towards law relating to maritime warfare, as seven Conventions were adopted on this subject. Though some negotiation on this topic was started in the First Hague Conference also, but could not be translated into an agreement.[101] In 1907, however, the major capitalist nations showed unprecedented enthusiasm to deliberate on sea warfare. According to Higgins, following factors were responsible for their worry: international law relating to naval warfare was in rudimentary state at that time; warships had been changed "from wooden sailing vessels to great floating metal fortresses propelled by steam power"; belligerents used underwater floating mines also that might imperil the neutral commercial ships; and the two great battles[102] occurred since 1899 raised many questions of the law of maritime warfare.[103] Additionally, majority of the European powers were littoral states for whom sea-routes were indispensable for trade as well as war. Moreover, by the end of the nineteenth century, Germany, France and the United States had also become naval powers, besides Britain. In such circumstances, legislation on varied dimensions of naval war was essential. However, all the seven naval-war instruments adopted at The Hague had general-participation clauses, and therefore, were of limited application. Their application was further restricted by military necessity[104] and phrases with enough amount of flexibility.[105] Thus, the greater number of documents did not suggest more limited and maritime war. Rather, the agenda was to ensure maximum naval freedom and protection of sea-trade.[106] The "crusaders of humanity" neither abolished war nor formed consensus on disarmament. Colonies were systematically kept away from international law making and its operation. It has been, therefore, rightly pointed out that "the European law of nations metamorphosed into a law of "civilized" nations."[107] It has been observed that this standard of civilization was formulated to justify and regulate "a world shaped and reshaped by these dynamics of unequal, yet global, capitalist development."[108] In the nineteenth century, the natural law theory was taken over by positivism and positivists prepared the necessary ideological foundations for justifying the colonial project and exclusion of the "uncivilized" world from the application of international law.[109] During the World War I, millions of people including soldiers had to pay the price of the general-participation clauses, as not all the belligerents were signatories to The Hague instruments.

Thus, by the end of the "long nineteenth century,"[110] some of the reasons for not restraining the hostile conduct adequately under the

[100] E.g. Preamble to Hague Convention (IV) with Respect to the Laws and Customs of War on Land of 18 October 1907 and Art. 22; 23(e), (g); 27, ibid.

[101] Higgins (1909, pp. 87–89).

[102] Though Higgins does not mention them, however, most probably he was referring to any two of the following wars: Second Boer War (1899–1902), Boxer Revolt (1899–1901) and the Russo-Japanese War (1904–1905).

[103] Higgins (1909, p. 87).

[104] Art. 2 para 3 Convention (IX) concerning Bombardment by Naval Forces in Time of War (1907) and Art. 7 para 3 Convention (X) for the Adaptation to Maritime War of the Principles of the Geneva Convention (1907).

[105] Art. 2 para 3, 5 para 1 Conventioin IX and 7 para 1 Convention X, ibid.

[106] Eyffinger (2007, pp. 201, 209).

[107] Chimni (2017, p. 492).

[108] Tzouvala (2020, p. 4).

[109] Chimni(2017, pp. 492–493).

[110] The span of the "long nineteenth century" is not uniform for every commentator: It is 1750–1914, in Koskenniemi and Stråth (2014, p. 11; 1789–1914), in Kennedy (1996), p. 390 and 1776–1914, in Hulle and Lesaffer (2019). However, the ending point, 1914, is uniform.

international law of war may be summarized below: First and foremost factor was to own more and more colonies by using unbridled means and methods of war.[111] Initially the annexation was done purely for materialist gains—raw material and markets. However, from 1850s onwards, the same was done in the name of civilizing the native population consistent with the material reasons in disguise. Missionaries were in fact sent to Africa and Asia to civilize (Christianize) the dark and colored peoples, but the missionary organizations actually promoted imperialism.[112] Between 1876 and 1900, the percentage of African territories colonized increased from 10.8 to 90.4, and that of Polynesia, from 56.8 to 98.9.[113] The total colonial domination on the earth increased from 67 to 85% between 1878 and 1919.[114] By its very nature, the capitalist class "must nestle everywhere, settle everywhere, establish connections everywhere",[115] comment Marx and Angles.

Second, the capture of colonies by merciless use of force facilitated the exploitation of forces of production profusely. Because of the huge surplus capital, slaves, vast colonial dominations having precious raw materials and cheap labor, the Gross National Product of the developed nations increased by more than twelve times during the long nineteenth century (from 35 billion dollars in 1750, to 430 in 1913), whereas that of the remaining parts of the world could not double (from 112 to 217 billion dollars only).[116] Capitalist mode of production knows neither geographical nor moral limits.[117] Indeed.

Third, during the long nineteenth century, national liberation wars had increased by three times as compared to the previous century.[118] The colonial powers did not want to run the risk of losing the colonial possessions by accepting humanitarian restraints on war. Fourth, the balance of power sought to be maintained by the Concert of Europe collapsed by the end of the nineteenth century. Consequently, rivalry and competition among the developed countries increased. Fifth, the Great Powers were engaged in arms race at the turn of the twentieth century. For instance, between 1880 and 1914 their military budget mounted as following: Germany's quintuple, England and Russia's triple and France's double.[119] Whereas, the cumulative military burdens of Europe, the United States and Japan between 1898 and 1906 had increased from £251,000,000 to £320,000,000.[120] Agreeing to restrictions on the use of arms in war would frustrate the heavy investment incurred. Sixth, Germany and the United States surpassed the other European nations in terms of economic and military strength, and territorial expansion. This is evident from the fact that during the last two decades of the nineteenth century, Germany had acquired one million square miles of colonial territory,[121] while the United States had increased its imports by four times.[122] In respect of some of the above factors, it has been maintained that they "left their mark on the body of international law"[123] in general from a material point of view.

Given the prevalent political economy of the world, the situation could not continue longer. The First World War occurred for the territorial re-division of the world among the advanced capitalist countries. The new weapon technology (including U-boat, fighter jet and chemicals)

[111] See, Jeenger (2024).

[112] Anand (2008, pp. 27–28) (internal citation omitted).

[113] Lenin (1988, p. 93).

[114] Koskenniemi (2014, p. 31).

[115] Marx and Angels (2018, p. 38).

[116] Buzan and Lawson (2013, p. 13) (submitted version).

[117] Tzouvala (2020, p. 3).

[118] Holsti (1991, pp. 144–145).

[119] Ibid., p. 172. See also सांकृत्यायन (1942, p. 254).

[120] British delegate Sir Edward Fry in the Fourth Plenary Meeting of the Conference on the 18th August, 1907. Higgins (1909, p. 77).

[121] Lenin (1988, p. 95).

[122] सांकृत्यायन (1942, p. 243).

[123] Chimni (2017, p. 492).

which were deliberately kept out of the purview of The Hague law brought unheard catastrophe, misery and suffering.[124]

5.7 Twentieth Century

Post-World War I, the conquering nations dictated the terms of the Treaty of Versailles to share the spoils of war and advance the imperialist agenda. Colonization was given a formal shape under the cover of mandate system in the Covenant of League of Nations.[125] On the crucial point of disarmament, the powerful European nations rejected Woodrow Wilson's idea of "peace without victory" and accepted no limits on military strength. Ultimately, disarmament "was left as a statement of hope for the future rather than as an obligation of the present."[126]

The developments in the law of armed conflict during the inter-war period marked some improvement over the previous instruments as in the year 1929 two separate treaties were negotiated and adopted for ensuring humane treatment with prisoners of war[127] and wounded and sick in armies.[128] These group-specific treaties did not use the general-participation clause, and thereby, sought to ensure safety and dignity of combatants. The occupied colonial territories, however, had no access to the negotiating table. Freedom fighters were, thus, neither recognized as prisoners of war nor considered worthy of care and medical aid in case of injury or illness. These deliberately-incorporated gaps and the abundant number of flexible obligations uncovered the uncompromising political motives of the "civilized" States.

On the other hand, the horrific consequences of armed conflicts on civilians were completely ignored by the so called "civilized" imperialist nations. Though, the ICRC's International Conference approved a draft Convention[129] on the civilian protection in 1934 and kept inviting international attention to consider the draft, however, the unwillingness of the governments and, later on, outbreak of the Second World War (1939–1945) deferred the negotiations.

The unprecedented destruction in World War II certainly influenced the adoption of the four Geneva Conventions of 1949. Under the banner of the ICRC, the four significant treaties were adopted for the dead, wounded and sick soldiers, for prisoners of war and for civilians too. Their contents, however, were largely determined by the contemporary political economy and power relations. For instance, the prominent players did not include armed colonial encounters and wars of national liberation within the definition of international[130] or non-international[131] armed conflicts so that they could retain the colonial possessions and crush any form of resistance arbitrarily. Similarly, in order to smoothly exercise imperialism and militarism, they did not employ any restrictions on the use of means and methods of warfare despite the destruction of

[124] Eyffinger (2007, pp. 201, 206).

[125] See Art. 22.

[126] Holsti (1991, p. 203). See Art. 8 Covenant of League of Nations (1919).

[127] Geneva Convention relative to the Treatment of Prisoners of War (1929).

[128] Geneva Convention for the Amelioration of the Condition of the Wounded and Sick in Armies in the Field (1929).

[129] Draft International Convention on the Condition and Protection of Civilians of Enemy Nationality who are on Territory belonging to or Occupied by a Belligerent (1934).

[130] Art. 2 common to the Geneva Convention for the Amelioration of the Condition of the Wounded and Sick in Armed Forces in the Field of 12 August 1949 (Geneva Convention I), the Geneva Convention for the Amelioration of the Condition of Wounded, Sick and Shipwrecked Members of Armed Forces at Sea of 12 August 1949 (Geneva Convention II), the Geneva Convention relative to the Treatment of Prisoners of War of 12 August 1949 (Geneva Convention III) and the Geneva Convention relative to the Protection of Civilian Persons in Time of War of 12 August 1949 (Geneva Convention IV).

[131] Ibid., Art. 3.

Hiroshima and Nagasaki by atomic attacks,[132] and use of other illegal means and methods of combat in World War II. They conveniently accepted only those restraints on war which suited their imperialist ambitions. It "helped colonizers to control large territories in terms of resources and governance without much obligation under international law."[133] On the other hand, the rules of hostile conduct in non-international armed conflicts were confined to one article only.[134] (For an elaborate discussion, see Chapters 6 and 7).

In the next two–three decades, several colonies were formally decolonized; however, soon they fell into the trap of the international institutions, primarily set up by the Western nations, in the name of development and stability.[135] Meanwhile, the Algerian (1954–62) and Vietnam (1965–72) Wars exposed the gaps in the Geneva Conventions. Their applicability remained uncertain[136] to both the wars and, thus, France and the United States fearlessly committed the egregious breaches in the poor territories.

These concerns of the newly independent countries were arguably accommodated in the two 1977 Protocols, additional to the four Geneva Conventions.[137] Wars of national liberation were included in the definition of international armed conflicts under Protocol I[138] when decolonization was almost over and the provision was almost irrelevant. (See Chapter 7, for a detailed history of these developments). Protocol I also contains several provisions of care and protection, restrictions on the means and methods of war, limits on attack, repatriation, etc. However, a good number of these provisions is subject to the principle of military necessity (for a detailed critique, see Chapters 10–14). The wider range of the rules has also deprived the Protocol from universal ratification (unlike the Geneva Conventions, 1949) and invited more reservations.[139] Protocol II, on the other hand, sought to supplement the Common Article 3 in a detailed fashion, but the high threshold[140] of its applicability limited its operation.

[132] It is both interesting and shocking to note what the United President President, Harry Truman, said on 26 June, 1945 while addressing the Closing Plenary Session of the San Francisco Conference, 1945 on the occasion of the adoption of the United Nations Charter: "If we had had this Charter a few years ago and above all a will to use it, millions now dead would be alive. If we shall falter in future in our will to use it, million now alive will surely die." Watch, Shaping the future—U.N. Charter becomes reality aka San Francisco conference (1945), at 1:45–2:05. https://www.youtube.com/watch?v=U3cGnbCEb-w. Within two months of the captivating speech, Truman authorized atomic bombardment on two Japanese towns, Hiroshima and Nagasaki on 6 and 9 August, 1945, respectively. The attack obliterated the towns, killed thousands of people, left even more number of people suffering and demonstrated the shameless hypocrisy and barbarism.

[133] Burra (2020, p. 197).

[134] See, above n 131.

[135] Rajagopal (2003, pp. 95–134).

[136] Alexander(2016, pp. 42–44, 47).

[138] See Art. 1(4) Protocol I, ibid.

[137] Protocol Additional to the Geneva Conventions of 12 August 1949, and relating to the Protection of Victims of International Armed Conflicts (Protocol I) of 8 June 1977 and Protocol Additional to the Geneva Conventions of 12 August 1949, and relating to the Protection of Victims of Non-International Armed Conflicts (Protocol II) of 8 June 1977.

[139] See Gaudreau (2003, pp. 143–184).

[140] See Art. 1(1) Protocol II, above n 137.

References

Alexander A (2016) International humanitarian law, postcolonialism and the 1977 Geneva protocol I. Melb J Int Law17:15–50

Anand RP (2008) New states and international law. Hope India Publications, Gurgaon

Banaji J (2020) A brief history of commercial capitalism. Haymarket Books, Chicago

Beirne P, Sharlet R (eds) (1980) Pashukanis: selected writings on marxism and law. Academic Press, London

Brisku A (2014) 'Politics of change and stability' in the Ottoman and Russian empires, 1815–1914. In: Koskenniemi M, Stråth B (eds) Europe 1815–1914: creating community and ordering the world. University of Helsinki, Helsinki, pp 44–58

Bryant M (2016) A world history of war crimes: from antiquity to the present. Bloomsbury Academic, London
Bugnion F (2012) Birth of an idea: The founding of the International Committee of the Red Cross and of the International Red Cross and Red Crescent Movement: From Solferino to the original Geneva convention (1859–1864), IRRC, 94:888, 2012, 1299, 1319.
Burra S (2018) Collective engagement and selective endorsement: India's ambivalent attitude towards laws of armed conflict. In: Burra S, Babu RR (eds) Locating India in the contemporary international legal order. Springer, New Delhi, pp 51–65
Burra S (2020) Four Geneva conventions of 1949: a third world view. In: Bhuiyan MJH, Khan BU (eds) Revisiting the Geneva conventions: 1949–2019. Brill/Nijhoff, Leiden, pp 190–214
Buzan B, Lawson G (2013) The global transformation: the nineteenth century and the making of modern international relations. International Studies Quarterly 59(1):620–634 (submitted version). http://eprints.lse.ac.uk/44894/
Chimni BS (2017) International law and world order: a critique of contemporary approaches. CUP, Cambridge
Coupland R, Loye D (2003) The 1899 Hague declaration concerning expanding bullets: a treaty effective for more than 100 years faces complex contemporary issue. Int Rev Red Cross 85(849):135–142
Davey E (2020) Decolonizing the Geneva conventions: national liberation and the development of humanitarian law. In: Moses AD et al (eds) Decolonization, self-determination, and the rise of global human rights politics. CUP, Cambridge, pp 375–396
Davis GB (1907) The Geneva convention of 1906. Am J Int Law 1:409–417
Dunant H (1939) A memory of Solferino. ICRC, Geneva
Eyffinger A (2007) A highly critical moment: role and record of the 1907 Hague peace conference. Neth Int Law Rev 54:197–228
Gaudreau J (2003) The reservations to the protocols additional to the Geneva conventions for the protection of war victims. Int Rev Red Cross 849:143–184
Higgins AP (1909) The Hague peace conferences and other international conferences concerning the laws and usages of war: texts of conventions with commentaries. CUP, London
Hobsbawm EJ (1989) The age of empire 1875–1914. Vintage Books, New York
Hobsbawm EJ (1995) The age of capital 1848–1875. Abacus, London
Holquist p (2018) The laws of war: from the Lieber code to the Brussels conference. Berl J 32 Fall:68–70
Holsti KJ (1991) Peace and war: armed conflicts and international order 1648–1989. CUP, Cambridge
Hulle IV, Lesaffer R (eds) (2019) International law in the long nineteenth century (1776–1914). Brill and Nijhoff, Leiden
Jeenger K (2024) Third world view of the laws of armed conflict: an introduction. RGNLU Stud Res Rev 10(2) (forthcoming)
Jochnick C, Normand R (1994) The legitimation of violence: a critical history of the laws of war. Harv Int Law J 35(1):49–96
Keefer S (2014) 'Explosive missals': international law, technology, and security in nineteenth-century disarmament conferences. War Hist 21(4):445–464
Kennedy D (2006) Of war and law. Princeton University Press, Princeton
Kennedy DW (1996) International law and the nineteenth century: history of an illusion. Nord J Int Law 65:385–420
Koskenniemi M (2004) The gentle civilizer of nations: the rise and fall of international law 1870–1960. CUP, Cambridge
Koskenniemi M, (2014) Ruling the world by law(s): the view from around, (1850). In: Koskenniemi M, Stråth B (eds) Europe 1815–1914: creating community and ordering the world. University of Helsinki, Helsinki, pp 16–32
Koskenniemi M, Stråth B (2014) Creating community, ordering the world and struggling for securing welfare, an introduction. In: Koskenniemi M, Stråth B (eds) Europe 1815–1914: creating community and ordering the world. University of Helsinki, Helsinki, pp 1–15
Lenin VI (1964) War and Revolution, Collected Works April–June 1917, vol 24. Progress Publishers, Moscow
Lenin VI (1988) Imperialism: the highest stage of capitalism. Lawrence & Wishart, London
Luxemburg R (1951) The accumulation of capital. Routledge, London
Marx K, Engel F (2018) The communist manifesto. Fingerprint, New Delhi
Mégret F (2006) From 'savages' to 'unlawful combatants': a postcolonial look at international humanitarian law's 'other.' In: Orford A (ed) International law and its others. CUP, New York, pp 265–317
Rajagopal B (2003) International Law from below: development, social movements and third world resistance. CUP, New Delhi
Scott JB (1908) Work of the second Hague peace conference. Am J Int Law 2:1–28
Tzouvala N (2020) Capitalism as civilisation: a history of international law. CUP, Cambridge
सांकृत्यायन रा (1942) दर्शन दिग्दर्शन. किताब महल, इलाहाबाद

6 Non-European Humanitarian Traditions from a Critical Perspective

Abstract

I critically engage in this chapter with the ancient restraints in war prevalent in the non-European world, with special focus on India. Initially, I explain the ancient Indian historical context and *Varna* system, which shaped the sources of ancient traditions in war. I offer a caste critique of various rules relating to war to explain the position of Shudras and tribes in war. Subsequently, I discuss the comprehensive restraints in war prescribed by the ancient Indian scriptures. I also strive to underscore simultaneously the instances when the practices differed from the principles. Thereafter, the chapter also analyses the position of Buddhism, Jainism and Islam in respect of war and rules in war. It specifies some of the rules from the Islamic texts and examples of departure from the same during war.

Keywords

IHL in Asia · India and IHL · Varna system · Shudra · Islam and IHL

6.1 Introduction: Non-European Origins of Humanitarianism

The previous chapter explains that the adoption of treaties and the emergence of "humanitarian" practices relating to conduct of hostilities began in 1860s in a different historical and geographical context. There is a dominant narrative of European civilizational lead which believes that the international events that occurred in Europe were instrumental to the origin and development of the laws of war. This narrative emerges out of the Western belief that non-Europeans were savages and backward, and, therefore, incapable of formulating the humanitarian principles and unworthy of any humanitarian treatment too.

This belief reveals the non-recognition of humanitarian traditions in war prevalent in other parts of the world. This Eurocentric outlook of the origin of international law in general and laws of armed (international humanitarian law) conflict in particular has been contested by the scholars of the Third World. It has been argued that the ancient non-Western world had also developed and observed certain humanitarian practices relevant to war. These practices originated in religious and ethical context long back in those territories, especially in South Asia. This plurality of practices has been scarcely noticed and told in the mainstream accounts of history of the laws of armed conflict. On the other side, the Third World accounts of non-Western traditions of warfare mostly attempt to appreciate and glorify the ancient humanitarian practices while challenging the Western way of looking at the history of the laws of armed conflict. However, it cannot be suggested that the ancient history of the law is bereft of any

K. Jeenger, *A Humanitarian Critique of International Humanitarian Law*,
Sustainable Development Goals Series, https://doi.org/10.1007/978-981-96-8319-2_6

critique and questioning. Not to admit this is not to admit the real character of the ancient Indian social structure, war and politics around it. Therefore, this chapter revisits mainly the South Asian restraints in war applicable in ancient warfare from a critical perspective. For this purpose, I attempt to consider the making of the ancient texts, the timeline, applicability, exclusionary nature, contradictory rules, counter-practices and the questions of caste and universality.

The idea of humanitarianism in respect of war is believed to be at least three thousand years old and multicultural.[1] It finds expression in several ancient traditions, including Aryan, Buddhist, Islamic and Chinese. As traditions like Buddhism and Jainism teach non-violence and compassion, they do not have elaborate rules of war. On the other hand, the ancient Indian and Islamic texts did not outlaw war and, therefore, provided a range of rules of war. Comparatively, however, the ancient Indian texts prescribing rules of war are greater in number and degree of detail. Therefore, the first three parts of the chapter have been dedicated to this literature.

6.2 Historical Context and Sources of Ancient Indian Traditions

In respect of the beginning of the ancient Indian traditions of humanitarianism in war, many scholars[2] agree that perhaps it dates back to three thousand years. The literature came into existence in a unique historical context. The socio-political milieu of that time had a significant impact not just on the form and content of the ancient Indian literature but its authorship as well. It was not natural that *men* only from a particular class enjoyed the monopoly and privilege to author those scriptures, and that the rules of war were prejudiced in some ways. Therefore, it is imperative to first understand the ancient Indian historical context in which the "sacred texts" originated.

The broad social composition of the Indian society before about three thousand years was Dravidians and Indo-Aryan speaking[3] people. Historians state that the affiliation of Dravidians in India dates back to the Indus Valley civilization,[4] and Aryans migrated[5] from the western central Asia according to the early[6] and recent[7] theories. Aryans were not only priests with poetic skills, but also advanced in military technology and people of warlike stockbreeders.[8] Aryans composed the first Veda, namely the Rig Veda[9] during this period (1500–500 BC)[10] and passed it on to the next generations by words of mouth.[11] The hymns of Rig Veda were in Sanskrit, which is believed to be "a

[1] Legality of the Threat or Use of Nuclear Weapons, Advisory Opinion (1996) ICJ Rep 226, Weeramantry (dissenting opinion), p. 478.

[2] Bandyopadhyay (1920, p. 4), Armour (1922, p. 71), Ibid., p. 478, and Mani (2004, pp. 32–33, n. 4).

[3] Leading scholars do not recognize Aryan as a race but accept it as a speech, language: Thapar (2003, p. 15).

[4] Thapar (2003, pp. 13–14) and Habib (2002, p. 51).

[5] Many scholars endorse the migration theory of *Aryans*: Roy (2012, p. 16), Ambedkar (1946, pp. 68, 70, 73), and Witzel (2019, pp. 25–26). While some scholars believe that Aryans invaded and colonized the dark indigenous inhabitants (*Anaryas*): Sankrityayana (1953, pp. 50–51) and Basham (2004, p. 41).

[6] Witzel (2019, p. 26), Thapar (2019a, pp. 30–93), Roy (2012, p. 16), Tilak (1903, p. 408) and, for similar views of Jyotiba Phule, E. V. Ramasamy Periyar and Mohandas Gandhi, see Ambedkar (2013, p. 237, n. 45). However, Ambedkar, writing in 1940s, has expressed some doubts about these theories. See, Ambedkar (1946, pp. 56–82).

[7] Recent theories are based on excavation at the Indus Valley civilisation sites, like Rakhigarhi, and genetic profile evidence: see Friese (2019, pp. 119–123).

[8] Basham (2004, pp. 31, 34).

[9] According to Rahul Sankrityayan, Brahmin saints like Vashishtha, Vishvamitra and Bhardwaj wrote majority of its verses as they would please the then Aryan King: Sankrityayana (1953, p. 80).

[10] Thapar (2019b, p. x).

[11] Basham (2004, p. 31).

remote cousin of all the languages of Europe."[12] The Rig Veda provided in its *Purusha Sukta*[13] (a verse) for the hierarchical division of the society into the following four classes or *Varnas* based on birth: Brahmin i.e. priests as creator's or Brahma's mouth; Rajanya or Kshatriya i.e. warriors as creator's arms; Vaishya i.e. merchants and farmers as creator's thighs, and Shudra i.e. servants and slaves emerged from the creator's feet. This division of society was called as *Chaturvarnya* (four *Varna*) system. This categorization was claimed to be natural, ideal, sacred and divine[14] in order to render it unchallengeable. In respect of the people constituting each of the *Varnas*, Ambedkar, however, argues that at some earlier point of time, Shudras were a clan of Kshatriyas in the Indo-Aryan society.[15] However, because of clashes between some of the Shudra kings and Brahmins, the Brahmins denied to perform *Upanayana*[16] sacrament for Shudra kings, separated them from Kshatriyas and put them on the last pedestal in hierarchical *Varnas* subsequently.[17] Ambedkar notes that the relentless revengeful attitude of Brahmins towards Shudras was like graveyard for them.[18] This *Varna* system of "graded inequality"[19] is not[20] found in any other ancient text in the world. On one hand, the whole *Chaturvarnya* system was humiliating for Shudras, while on the other, it also established supremacy of Brahmins. According to Ambedkar, "even in the times of the Rig Veda, Brahmins were a class by themselves, had developed class consciousness and were keen on maintaining class interests."[21] In the coming centuries, the term "Shudra" was to extend beyond the Indo-Aryan peoples and the scale of oppression was to become intense.

The growing Vedic period-Brahminism soon received sharp reactions from three traditions growing at that time: Charvaka, Jainism and Buddhism in the sixth-century BC. While Charvakas emphasized upon materialist rather than super-natural explanation of earthly affairs,[22] Jainism offered complete non-violent ideology as contrast to the Aryan sacrificial rituals, and did not believe in the existence of god.[23] The unorthodox and reformist Buddhist traditions, on the other hand, challenged the Aryan notions of priest-craft, ritualism, exploitative class-distinction and metaphysical notions of rebirth.[24] Additionally, the Buddhist movement suggested the noble eight-fold path of righteousness.[25] Ambedkar maintains that the social system prescribed by the *Purusha Sukta* has not been challenged by anyone except Buddha.[26] It certainly disturbed the status of Brahmins.[27]

Meanwhile, an important development took place regarding the ambit of the Shudra class. As already mentioned, the original (Aryan) Shudras were reduced to the lowest class of people under the *Varna* system of social ordering because they were contemptuous to Brahmins. Gradually, however, everyone occupying a low social status or hateful to Brahmins came to be identified as Shudra. The word "Shudra" became a generic term for all "low class people without civilization, without culture, without

[12] Ibid., p. 388. Similar opinion held by Habib (2002, p. 98). Notably, it has been maintained that the Dravidian languages were in practice in north India before Sanskrit: Roy (2012, p. 16).

[13] Rig Veda 10/90/12.

[14] Ambedkar (1946, p. 7).

[15] Ibid., pp. 144, 154. See, p. 154.

[16] A sacrament of wearing a pair of thread across the left shoulder and under the right arm, performed by a Brahmin.

[17] Ambedkar (1946, p. 176).

[18] Ibid., pp. 199, 232.

[19] Ibid., p. i.

[20] Ibid., pp. 8, 16.

[21] Ibid., p. 237.

[22] सांकृत्यायन (1944, p. 435) and Thapar (2003, pp. 165–166).

[23] Shepherd (2019, p. 60).

[24] Thapar (2003, pp. 167–173).

[25] Shepherd (2019, pp. 62–65). Eight-fold path includes the following eight principles: right views, resolves, speech, conduct, livelihood, effort, recollection, and meditation: Thapar (2003, p. 168).

[26] Ambedkar (1946, p. 4).

[27] Nehru (2012, p. 123).

respect and without position."[28] Accordingly, the non-Aryan servants, farmers,[29] craftsmen, artisans, tribal, the followers of Buddhism and Mauryans[30] began to be treated as Shudras, and faced the catastrophic penalties prescribed by the subsequent Brahmin law-givers. This prompted Ambedkar to observe that in the Indo-Aryan society, "Shudra was a proper name of one single people," however, in the Hindu society, Shudra is "an epithet for a low-cultured class of people."[31]

Coming back to the challenges to the Aryan class-system and superstitious beliefs, the Buddhist tradition flourished during the times of Mauryan emperors (322–185 B.C.), who were treated as Shudras.[32] The Mauryan Empire marked a period of freedom, greatness and glory.[33] The Mauryan emperor Ashoka embraced Buddhism and spread it all over his empire and sent organized missions in many parts of Asia to propagate the faith. His edicts on Buddhism are engraved on rocks and pillars in Prakrit.[34] They are said to be "the oldest surviving Indian written documents of any historical significance."[35] Brahmins felt depressed during this revolutionary phase. The Buddhist challenge to the developing Aryan ideology became a concern for its survival during the Mauryan rule. Eventually, Pushyamitra Shunga, the Brahmin army-commander of the last Mauryan emperor, Brihadratha, assassinated the king and grabbed the throne.[36] In order to revive the Vedic civilization, he started patronizing Brahminism and abolishing[37] Buddhism. A major step in this direction was drafting of religious texts which also prescribed certain (discriminatory) forms of conduct in every facet of human life, including armed conflicts. They contained exaggerated and heroic stories of Aryan kings, and bolstered Brahmin-superiority and privilege even in war, as explained below.

In the series of such writings which relate to rules of war also, Kautilya's Arthashastra happens to be an important document. Though it represents the ideas of Kautilya, a prominent minister of Mauryan emperor Chandragupta, scholars doubt the originality of the available version of the work and believe it to be a latter but pre-Guptan (fourth-century AD) compilation done by others.[38]

Historians maintain that the next prominent sources (regulating conduct in war) include the two epic poems, Mahabharata and Ramayana, and Bhagvat Geeta, recorded probably around the beginning of the Christian era.[39] They are unique and secular[40] compilations on statecraft and human life. According to a historian,[41] they affiliate to the episodes of the first half of the first millennium BC. However, the battle of Mahabharata has been viewed as "magnified by titanic proportions" in its elaboration, and the historical basis of certain parts of Ramayana have been questioned by Basham.[42] Works written subsequently were Smritis (works based on memory) or Dharmashastras, numbering twenty

[28] Ambedkar (1946, p. iii).

[29] Thapar (1961, p. 62).

[30] Ibid., 198.

[31] For more explanation on the distinction, see Ambedkar (1946, p. 235).

[32] Roy (2012, p. 61).

[33] Ambedkar (2013, p. 276, n. 107).

[34] According to Basham, Prakrit is simpler than Sanskrit. Basham (2004, p. 393).

[35] Ibid., 53.

[36] SankrityayanA (1984, pp. 167–168), Nehru (2004, p. 91), and Roy (2012, p. 57). For various reasons leading to Pushya Mitra's violent action, see Thapar (1961, pp. 198–202).

[37] According to an estimate, for instance, destruction of 84,000 *Stupas* built by Ashoka: Thapar (1961, p. 200).

[38] Basham (2004, p. 80).

[39] SankrityayanA (1984, p. 168). It has been claimed that Bhagvat Geeta was added to the epic Mahabharata somewhere between 150 and 350 AD: Ambedkar (2013, p. 310, n. 161).

[40] Chaturvedi (1993), pp. 19, 22 and Basham (2004, pp. 409, 411).

[41] Basham (2004, pp. 40, 48).

[42] Ibid., pp. 40, 415. Basham writes: "The story of Rama's adventures in exile has thus no historical basis whatever, even if we rationalise his monkey allies into aboriginal tribesman with a monkey totem.".

according to Yagyavalkya.[43] Manu Smriti, Yagyavalkya Smriti, Narada Smriti and Parashar Smriti are some of the prominent Smritis. Among the above sources, all works excepting those of the Buddhist tradition were written in Sanskrit by Brahmins. Several scholars are of the view that the word "Hindu" had not been discovered by that time and, thus, maintain that it did not occur in any of the ancient literature.[44] They underscore that it is misleading to call these texts as Hindu literature[45] and the then civilization as Hindu civilization.[46]

While assessing the status of these writings, it must be understood that in this vast literature, Vedas are classified as Shruti, which means what was heard and handed down from generation to generation verbally, whereas the texts based on writer's memory is called as Smriti. While the Vedas are regarded as the basis of the ancient legal system, Smritis are considered as the "law proper which was in force."[47] An erudite historian has clarified that the authors of the vast ancient literature "described things not as they were in fact, but as they believed they ought to be."[48] This is not to summarily reject the ancient writings, ideas and practices, but to grasp their essence subject to these limitations. Uncritical reception and glorification of the "sacred texts" may give a distorted view of the history and conceal the larger scheme of the *Varna*-based social system. This historical background is important to understand the rules of war developed in these scriptures.

6.3 A Caste Critique of Ancient Indian Rules of War

The *Chaturvarnya* system sanctioned by the scpritures laid down for the first three classes their respective privileges, and treated them as *Dvijas* or twice-born (first being natural birth and the second on *Upanayana* sacrament).[49] Shudras, on the other side, were considered neither *Dvijas* nor worthy of any dignity and respect. They were rather put in the lowest stratum subject to many unimaginable inhuman restrictions.[50] The peculiar character of the hierarchical division was its so called "divine origin"[51] and unchanging[52] nature. Gradually, this division in terms of *Varnas* got solidified and transformed into castes

[43] Jois (2010, p. 22).

[44] Chaturvedi (1993, p. 20), Nehru (2012, p. 69), and Ambedkar (2013, p. 242, n. 51).

[45] Nehru (2012, pp. 70–71).

[46] Chaturvedi (1993, p. 19).

[47] Jois (2010, p. 19).

[48] Basham (2004, p. 81).

[49] Ambedkar (1946, p. 21).

[50] E.g. Shudras must not read, must not collect wealth, must not live in a house etc. See Manusmriti, 10/129, 2/36, 11/131, 8/270–272, Parashar Smriti, 1/73 and Gautam Dharmasutra, 2/3/2, 4–5.

[51] As reiterated in Bhagvadgeeta (4/13) also.

[52] There is a widely prevalent misconception that the *Varna* system was based on profession and people were free to affiliate themselves to a *Varna* by choosing a corresponding occupation. In other words, the *Varna* system is not based on birth, according to this approach. In this regard, for instance V. S. Mani relies on two verses of the *Geeta* and its interpretation by S. Radhakrishnan. Accordingly, he says that the *Varna* system was based on one's avocation and not determined by birth. Thus, he tries to maintain, though erroneously, that one may become a Brahmin or Shudra by choice of avocation. See, Mani (2004, pp. 32–33, n. 4). However, it is submitted that for a holistic explanation of the *Varna* system a variety of Aryan literature and the contemporary practices and politics of relations of domination must be considered. The "sacred texts" prescribed inhuman treatment for Shudras and established superiority and domination of Brahmins. The Dharmsutra and Smriti rules prohibiting Shudra from reading and hearing Vedas and providing for severe punishment if they strive to do so (e.g. Manusmriti, 4/80 and Gautama Dharmsutra, 2/3/4–5) make it very clear that a Shudra could not become a Brahmin by choice. Similarly, there is a story in Ramayana, where Rama kills Shambuk, a Shudra, because he was practicing austerities, which under the Aryan tradition could be done by Brahmins only (Ramayana, Uttarakhanda, vii, 4, 76). Thus, under the hostile *Varna* system, a person's *Varna* was not determined by avocation but by birth, and it was not open to change. For the birth theory in *Apastambha Dharmasutra, Vashishtha Dharmasutra* and in general, see Ambedkar (1946, pp. 4–5, 220). *Varna* by birth is strongly supported by *Manu and other Smritis:* Ambedkar (2013, p. 310, n. 161).

(*Jati*).[53] It significantly shaped the relations of power gradually in the ancient India.

In the texts, Brahmins raised their own status equal to God[54] and pushed Kshatriyas to a lower level. According to the texts, Brahmins could ensure safety of a king during war merely by their prayers.[55] King's offerings were held to be not acceptable to God unless made through a Brahmin.[56] Because of the exclusive sacramental and literary skills, they occupied a significant place in a king's court. Thus, they commanded extraordinary authority and privileges for themselves. Under the rules of war, there was a special provision for Brahmins in respect of private enemy property. In Mahabharata, it was mandated that they may be given the cows captured forcefully from the enemy.[57] On the other hand, the epic poem prescribes that a Kshatriya who transgresses righteousness and the barriers ceases to be a Kshatriya.[58] This applies to a king who disregards the rules of war. It further advises Kshatriyas to fight fairly and die by virtue of the duties (Kshatriya-Dharma) set for them. It thus reveals the centrality of the class-system in dictating the terms of the rules of war.

The literature also suggested a casteist composition of the army. It confined the membership of the armies mainly to Kshatriya men and offered them the incentive of entry into heaven in the event of death.[59] Members of the two lower classes, though, could join the army but in the lowest ranks only and without any metaphysical motivation of entry into heaven.[60] For instance, the fighters of a native tribe (non-Aryan Shudras) were admitted to fight in war but were not regarded as regulars.[61] The subsequent texts further intensified the class-division.[62]

The restraints in war were highly prejudiced by the class-system, and they affirmed Aryan superiority and immunity. Kautilya's Arthashastra prohibited enslavement of Aryans, but the similar ban did not apply in respect of the non-Aryans.[63] Similarly, the Arthashastra sanctioned wholesale plunder in the war of deception (*Koota Yuddha*) with the wild tribes.[64] This was true not just in principle but practice also. It has been observed that the advancing Aryans exterminated numerous native people when met with resistance.[65] In fact, historians argue that in some of the Aryan mythological texts, the characters of demons (*Asuras* or *Danavas*) were actually a reference to the natives,[66] probably Dravidians.[67] Who would imagine that after almost two millenniums, this cultural logic shall be repeated by the European colonizers during anti-colonial armed conflicts with the so called uncivilized people of India and the other Third World nations? It shows that power speaks a uniform language of oppression irrespective of temporal or geographical boundaries. The Aryan rules of war were undoubtedly discriminatory and demonstrated selective humanitarianism. The class-system determined the terms of the rules of war, and they were not

[53] Thus, some authors hold the view that the terms *Varna* and *Jati* can be used interchangeably. E.g. see, Ghurye (2008, p. 75). Some say that unlike *Varna*, old castes may disappear and new ones may be constituted. So both the terms cannot be used interchangeably. See, Basham (2004, p. 149). However, the fact remains that it is the Varna system out of which the caste-system has emerged with the same hierarchical order and permanent nature: Burra (2016, pp. 114–115).

[54] Ghurye (2008, pp. 57, 89) and Basham (2004), p. 88.

[55] Ibid., p. 46.

[56] Ibid.

[57] Mahabharata, Shantiparva, 96/6.

[58] Bandyopadhyay (1920), p. 110.

[59] "Those kings who seeking to slay each other in battle, fight with the utmost exertion and do not turn back, go to heaven." Manu Smriti, VII/9, 89.

[60] Bandyopadhyay (1920, p. 100).

[61] Ibid., p. 138.

[62] See Ghurye (2008, pp. 60–110).

[63] Arthashastra, 3/13.

[64] Arthashastra, 9/2.

[65] Basham (2004, p. 199).

[66] Ibid., 200 and Sankrityayana (1953, pp. 50–51).

[67] Roy (2013, p. 18).

universal as claimed by some scholars.[68] The texts reflect a caste-view of the society, where caste was the strongest bond.[69]

Subject to these limitations, the ancient Indian scriptures contain probably the most comprehensive architecture of rules of war. Akin to the modern international laws of war, the ancient framework is wide enough and covers rules in respect of wounded soldiers, prisoners of war, civilians and means and methods of war, subject to military necessity in some cases, as explained below.

6.4 Ancient Indian Rules of War

The restraints on war provided for in the ancient Indian scriptures are described below:

6.4.1 War with Equals

In the ancient times, land warfare was the main mode of war. The armies used to have a hierarchical structure, consisting of king, commander (*Senapati*), horse-riders and foot-soldiers. To ensure fight between two warriors having equal rank and capabilities, some texts advise that a king should fight with a king, a commander with a commander, a horse rider with a horse rider and so on.[70] However, Koutilya, "the arch-apostle of expediency,"[71] adopts a practical view in this respect. He not only declares an attack on a king by a soldier appropriate but also advises to reward such a warrior by gold coins.[72]

In addition to the suggestion of battle between equals, the texts also declare that collective attacks against a single soldier and the slaying of a warrior who is temporarily at a disadvantaged position during battle are strictly prohibited.[73] However, the epic poems contain few counter-practices in this respect. For instance, in Mahabharata, Abhimanyu was attacked collectively and ultimately killed by several Kaurava warriors.[74] Dronacharya, a commander of Kauravs, was slain when he gave up his weapons. Similarly, Karna, a warrior from Kaurava's army was attacked by Arjuna when he was in distress because a wheel of his chariot had sunk into the ground.[75] Krishna justifies this attack on the ground of reciprocity.[76] He says that Karna himself violated the law for several times, including when he attacked Abhimanyu with other fighters, and thus he did not deserve fair treatment.

6.4.2 Means and Methods of War

Means of war are weapons, while methods of war refer to various ways of combat, such as pillage and denial of quarter. The ancient texts contain several restraints in this respect that seek to prevent excessive suffering of opponent army and targeting civilians. Rig Veda contains few basic restraints on the conduct in war, such as prohibition of the use of poisoned arrows and targeting civilians.[77] On the contrary, it also sanctions attacks in the nature of "no quarter" whereby no one is left alive.[78] Mahabharata[79] and Yagyavalkya Smriti[80] forbid the use of concealed weapons and poisoned arrows. Manu Smriti also echoes similar instructions and bans weapons which are concealed, barbed, poisoned,

[68] See Singh (1968, p. 601) and Chaturvedi (1993, p. 19).

[69] Armour (1922, p. 84).

[70] Mahabharata, Bhishma Parva, 1/29, Shantiparva, 95/10, 96/7; Shukraneeti, 4/354 and Agnipurana, 236/57–60.

[71] Bandyopadhyay (1920, p. 116).

[72] Arthashastra, 10/3.

[73] Sinha (2005, p. 292).

[74] Mahabharata, Dronparva, 33–49.

[75] Ibid., 192.

[76] Ibid.

[77] Rig Veda, 6/75/15.

[78] Ibid., 6/75/16.

[79] Mahabharata, Shantiparva, 95/11.

[80] Yagyavalkyasmriti, 1/13/324.

or the points of which are blazing with fire.[81] However, such rules are attached to a particular kind of war—*Dharma Yuddha* or fair war and every king, especially a powerful king was expected to respect the same. For instance, in Mahabharata, Bhishma advises Yudhishthira, a Pandava king, that a victory by unfair means is temporary and devastating, and deprives a king of heaven.[82] Thus, the basis of the restraints in war was sought in justness of the cause of war, morality and spirituality.

However, it does not follow that in the ancient times, there was no suggestion of violation of the rules or recourse to unfair or treacherous war (*Koota Yuddha*). Ramayana, Mahabharata, Manu Smriti, Yagyavalkya Smriti, Shukra Neeti and Neetivakyamritam define and explain *Koota Yuddha* but sternly condemn it. Exceptionally, few precepts and practices evince recourse to *Koota Yuddha* as a method of war. For instance, by a king who is weak[83] or at an unfavorable position during a battle[84]; against wild tribes[85]; by a king who has no other means to protect himself; when enemy is an *Asura* (devil, actually Shudras) or an *Adharmi* (sinner), or when enemy also uses such unfair practices. In this way Ramayana justifies killing of Bali, devils and Ravana.[86]

In the event of *Koota Yuddha,* the Arthashastra recommends attack on the enemy troops when they are in trouble, or tired or running away.[87] According to a distinguished Indian scholar:

> The overwhelming duty of self-preservation on the part of a state compelled it to take recourse to *Koota Yuddha* but a small state before undertaking such wars was advised by Kautilya to enter into a subordinate alliance with a powerful state in the relationship of a sovereign and a client state. It is only when outside help was not available that such a method, of warfare was to be adopted.[88]

These practices and principles have been acknowledged by foreign travelers and writers such as Megasthenes, Diodoros Sekulos and Yuan Chwang as well.[89]

6.4.3 Immunity from Attack

The ancient literature declares combatants (in certain situations), non-combatants and civilians immune from attack during war. Generally, combatants or enemy army constitute a legitimate target during an armed conflict. However, a combatant who flees,[90] who folds the palms of his hands,[91] who is fatigued,[92] who is an eunuch,[93] who is seated with hair disheveled,[94] who says "I am yours,"[95] who is asleep,[96] who is naked,[97] who is disarmed,[98] who seeks refuge,[99] who does not have coat of mail,[100] who is busy

[81] Muller, 7/90.

[82] Mahabharata, Shantiparva, 95/15, 16, 22, 96/1–2.

[83] Arthashastra, 10/3 and 12.

[84] See ibid.

[85] Arthashastra, 10/3.

[86] Bali was guilty of committing sexual exploitation of his brother's wife; devils used to not only commit violence when saints performed religious rituals and sacraments but also kill them, and Ravana had kidnapped Rama's wife and used devils, and magical and mysterious tricks in war with Rama.

[87] Arthashastra, 10/3.

[88] Bandyopadhyay (1920, pp. 113–114).

[89] Shastri (1952, pp. 105–106).

[90] Shukraneeti, 4/355–357; Mahabharata, Bhishmaparva, 1/31, Shantiparva, 98/48, 99/14; Ramayana, Yuddhakanda, 80/39; Muller, 7/91 and Agnipurana, 236/57–60.

[91] Mahabharata, Shantiparva, 96/3, Shukraneeti, 4/355–357 and Muller, 7/91.

[92] Agnipurana, 236/57–60 and Shukraneeti, 4/355–357.

[93] Muller, 7/91 and Yagyavalkyasmriti, 1/13/326.

[94] Shukraneeti, 4/355–357.

[95] Mahabharata, Shantiparva, 96/3, Yagyavalkyasmriti, 1/13/326, Muller, 7/91 and Shukraneeti, 4/355–357.

[96] Agnipurana, 236/57–60, Shukraneeti, 4/355–357 and Muller, 7/92.

[97] Muller, 7/92; Shukraneeti, 4/355–357.

[98] Shukraneeti, 4/355–357; Mahabharata, Bhishmaparva, 1/31, Shantiparva 95/13; Muller, 7/92; Agnipurana, 236/57–60 and Yagyavalkyasmriti, 1/13/326.

[99] Mahabharata, Bhishmaparva, 1/31 and Ramayana, Yuddhakanda, 80/39.

[100] Muller, 7/92.

in battle with other,[101] who surrenders,[102] who conceals himself,[103] who is wounded,[104] who has gone mad,[105] who is surrounded by women,[106] or who is feeble[107] is declared to be immune from attack. No doubt, these prohibitions were made in the context of *Dharma Yuddha* (fair war). *Koota Yuddha* and self-preservation discouraged adherence to these norms. As already mentioned, targeting enemy soldiers who are in trouble, or tired or running away is not prohibited in *Koota Yuddha* by Arthashastra.[108]

The next category of persons who cannot be targeted comprises non-combatants (those who accompany the army but do not directly participate in hostilities). They include workers who leave the camp for the purpose of shopping; guards of camps[109]; servants who maintain horses, carry goods and transport weaponries; musicians[110]; car-drivers; camp-followers, or those who perform menial service.[111]

Thirdly, civilians who "do not participate in war but come in the battlefield as spectators"[112] and "old people, women or children"[113] are declared as not legitimate targets.

6.4.4 Treatment with Prisoners of War

The ancient texts contain some rules regarding fair treatment with prisoners of war also. Mahabharata at one place suggests to forgive[114] the enemy after victory while at the other, it forbids fighting with a defeated enemy and guides to imprison him for one year, to teach him adaptability, and then to liberate him.[115] It also recommends treating him like his own son.[116] Koutilya also directs not to enslave any Aryan in any circumstances.[117] This rule is apparently discriminatory and does not apply to Shudra prisoners of war.

It must be understood that the various texts referred to above are the works of individual authors and poets, and not in the form of agreements between kings. They do not outlaw war, like Buddhism and Jainism do. Majority of them set a very high standard of ethics of war, while the others approve of any conduct essential to win the war. Thus, the texts demonstrate two different approaches: deontological and consequentialist. The former believes that an act is an end in itself irrespective of its results. Therefore, it concentrates more upon the character and righteousness of the actions whatever may be the outcome. For instance, prohibiting the use of hyper-destructive weapons. While the latter is absolutely result oriented regardless of goodness or badness of the act. The choice of actions depends upon the desired outcome. Perfidy and denial of quarter reflect consequentialist approach.

6.5 Humanitarian Rules in Other Traditions

Besides the Aryan traditions, Buddhism and Jainism also prospered in ancient India. Buddhism professes peace and compassion, and believes in non-violence. It professes peaceful settlement of disputes because it believes that violence cannot be defeated by violence. Therefore, neither any rules of war nor the idea

[101] Yagyavalkyasmriti, 1/13/326, Mahabharata, Bhishmaparva, 1/31 and Muller, 7/92.

[102] Mahabharata, Shantiparva, 96/3.

[103] Ramayana, Yuddhakanda, 80/39.

[104] Muller, 7/93.

[105] Ramayana, Yuddhakanda, 80/39.

[106] Ramayana, Uttarakanda, 32/28–29.

[107] Mahabharata, Shantiparva, 95/12 and Muller, 7/93.

[108] Arthashastra, 10/3.

[109] Mahabharata, Shantiparva, 100/28, 29.

[110] Mahabharata, Bhishma Parva, 1/32.

[111] Armour (1922, p. 75).

[112] Muller, 7/92 and Agnipuran, 236/57–60.

[113] Shukraneeti, 4/358 and Mahabharata, Shantiparva, 98/48.

[114] Mahabharata, Shantiparva, 102/30. See also verse 32.

[115] Ibid., 96/4.

[116] Ibid., 96/4 and 102/32.

[117] Arthashastra, 3/13.

of "just war" is part of the Buddhist tradition.[118] Its emphasis on the principle of humanity can certainly be pivotal in the further development of humanitarian rules. However, it does not suggest that the kings who followed Buddhism engaged in no wars.

Similar to Buddhism, the values of non-violence are attached to Jainism also because its teachings include the principles of humanity and non-violence. It does not permit violence even by spoken words or thoughts.

Among the rules of war developed in the non-European world, Islamic rules also occupy an important place. Like the Aryan tradition, Islam also does not ban war completely. The prominent sources of the Islamik tradition include the Quran, a compilation of divine revelations, and Sunna or Hadith a collection of the teachings of Prophet Muhammad. Islamic literature offers adequate rules regulating the conduct in war. For instance, the Quran declares that God loves those who fight in His cause in ranks as though they were a compact building,[119] however, God asks them not to transgress verily because God does not love those who transgress.[120]

The Islamic humanitarian rules prohibit torture and mutilation of enemy combatants.[121] They outlaw the use of weapons which are poisoned or cause disproportionate suffering.[122] In respect of prisoners of war, the Quran mandates generous treatment or release on ransom.[123] It forbids the execution of prisoners of war but allows their killing after the forbidden months are over.[124] It has also been suggested that Islam permits discretion to kill or to enslave a captive, except a Muslim, and that he may be released provided the residents of his place are ready to pay ransom.[125] Observing the principles, Muhammad ordered for fair treatment with prisoners of war in the battle of Badr and called them brethren in another battle.[126] Thus, it seems that the Islamic position on the treatment of prisoners of war is not free from contradictions.

On the question of targeting civilians and civilian property, the Quran expressly suggests to "fight those who fight you."[127] Abu Bakr, the first caliph advised that the blood of women, children and old people should not stain their victory.[128] His interdictions extend to prohibition on setting on fire houses and cornfields, and cutting trees.[129] The Islamic tradition also forbids acts of destruction in enemy territory.[130]

On the point of captured enemy property, it is recommended in Islam that even thread and needle should be returned to the rightful owner.[131] However, the gap in principles and practice of war is present in Islamic traditions also. This divergence is evident from the history of bloodshed, pillage and loot during some of the invasions and raids in India.[132] During these raids, not only civilians were killed, but cultural property was also attacked.

Besides the above discussion, in Judaism, Deuteronomy (a second-century BC composition) contained a collection of sermons of Moses relevant to war also.[133] In the ancient China, Sun Tzu wrote a famous treatise on war in the fifth-century BC, The Art of War, which contains detailed rules in respect of prohibition of war and wholesale plunder of enemy, and kind treatment with prisoners of war.[134] Thus, a claim of

[124] Quran, 47/4, 9/5 and Bryant (2016, p. 49).

[123] Quran, 47/4, cited in ibid., p. 44.

[122] Ibid., p. 43.

[121] Alam (2007, p. 41).

[120] Muller (1990c, p. 27).

[119] Muller (1990b, p. 281).

[118] Weeramantry (dissenting opinion), above n 1, p. 481.

[125] Poonawala (2004, pp. 465–466).

[126] Alam (2007, p. 44).

[127] Ibid., p. 43.

[128] Ibid.

[129] O'Connell (2013, p. 17).

[130] Alam (2007, p. 43).

[131] Poonawala (2004, p. 471).

[132] See Nehru (2004, pp. 240–242, 363–365).

[133] See Bryant (2016, p. 28) and Cohn-Sherbok (2004, p. 86).

[134] Tzu, II/17, III/1, 4 and Paul (2004, pp. 60–61).

historical primacy of Europe stands negated by the prevalence of rules of war in other traditions and civilizations. These rules, however, were neither utopian nor unquestionable.

References

Agnipurana

Alam A (2007) The Islamic concept of humanitarian law. In: Mani VS (ed) Handbook of international humanitarian law in South Asia. OUP, New Delhi, pp 39–48

Ambedkar BR (1946) Who were the shudras? Thacker & Co., Bombay

Ambedkar BR (2013) Annihilation of caste: the annotated critical edition. Navayana, New Delhi

Armour WS (1922) Customs of warfare in ancient India. Transactions of the Grotius society, vol 8. Problems of peace and war. CUP, Cambridge, pp 71–88

Arthashastra

Bandyopadhyay P (1920) International law and custom in ancient India. Calcutta University Press, Calcutta

Basham AL (2004) The wonder that was India. Picador, London

Bhagvadgeeta

Burra S (2016) Twail's others: A caste critique Of Twailers and their field of analysis. Wind Yearb Access Justice33:111–128

Bryant M (2016) A world history of war crimes: from antiquity to the present. Bloomsbury Academic, London

Chaturvedi B (1993) Dharma, India and the world order: twenty-one essays. Saint Andrew Press, Edinburgh

Cohn-Sherbok D (2004) War and peace in Judaism. In: Schmidt-Leukel P (ed) War and peace in world religions: the Gerald Weisfeld lectures 2003. SCM Press, London, pp 81–98

Friese K (2019) The complications of genetics. In: Thapar R et al Which of us are Aryans: rethinking the concept of our origins. Aleph Book Company, New Delhi, pp 119–134

Gautam Dharmasutra

Ghurye GS (2008) Caste and race in India. Popular Prakashan, Bombay

Habib I (2002) The people's history of India 2: the Indus civilization. Tulika Books, New Delhi

Jois MR (2010) Legal and constitutional history of India: ancient legal, judicial and constitutional system. Universal Law Publishing Co., New Delhi

Mahabharata

Mani VS (2004) An Indian perspective on the evolution of international law on the threshold of the third millennium. Asian Yearbook of International Law 9:31–77

Manu Smriti

Muller FM (ed) (1990a) The laws of Manu from, Sacred books of the East, vol XXV. Atlantic Publishers, New Delhi

Muller FM (ed) (1990b) The Quran, Sacred books of the East, vol IX. Atlantic Publishers, New Delhi

Muller FM (ed) (1990c) The Quran, Sacred books of the East, vol VI. Atlantic Publishers, New Delhi

Nehru J (2004) Glimpses of world History. Penguin Books, New Delhi

Nehru J (2012) The discovery of India. Penguin Books, New Delhi

O'Connell ME (2013) Historical development and legal basis. In: Fleck D (ed) The handbook of international humanitarian law. OUP, Oxford, pp 1–42

Parashar Smriti

Paul G (2004) War and peace in classical Chinese thought. In: Schmidt-Leukel P (ed) War and peace in world religions: the Gerald Weisfeld lectures 2003. SCM Press, London, pp 57–80

Poonawala IKH (2004) The pillars of Islam, vol I. OUP, New Delhi

Quran.

Ramayana.

Rig Veda.

Roy K (2012) Hinduism and the ethics of warfare in South Asia: from antiquity to the present. CUP, New York

Sankrityayana R (1953) From Volga to Ganga. Rahula Publication, Mussoorie

Sankrityayana R (1984) Selected essays. People's Publising House (P) Ltd., New Delhi

Shastri KAN (1952) International law and relations in ancient India. The Indian Year Book of International Affairs 1:97–109

Shepherd KI (2019) God as political philosopher. Sage Publication, New Delhi

Shukra Neeti

Singh N (1968) India and international law. Revista Española De Derecho Internacional 21(3):600–615

Sinha MK (2005) Hinduism and international humanitarian law. International Review of the Red Cross 87(858):285–294

Thapar R (1961) Asoka and the decline of the Mauryas. OUP, London

Thapar R (2003) The Penguin history of early India: from the origins to AD 1300. Penguin Books, New Delhi

Thapar R (2019a) Multiple theories about the 'Aryan'. In: Thapar R et al Which of us are Aryans: Rethinking the concept of our origins. Aleph Book Company, New Delhi, pp 30–93

Thapar R (2019b) Foreword: the search for the Aryan. In: Thapar R et al Which of us are Aryans: Rethinking the concept of our origins. Aleph Book Company, New Delhi, pp vii-xvi

Tilak BG (1903) The Arctic home in the Veda. Kesari, Poona

Tzu S, The Art of War

Witzel M (2019) Beyond the flight of the falcon: early 'Aryans' within and outside India. In: Thapar R et al Which of us are Aryans: Rethinking the concept of our origins. Aleph Book Company, New Delhi, pp 1–29

Yagyavalkyasmriti

सांकृत्यायन रा (1942) दर्शन दिग्दर्शन. किताब महल, इलाहाबाद

7 Critique of Expansion of Material Field of Application

Abstract

In this chapter, I deal with the historical expansion of material scope of application of the laws of armed conflict. I argue that the so called civilized States shaped the applicability criteria of the law as it suited to their imperialist agendas. I try to emphasize that the references of humanitarian considerations in the texts and during the negotiations were aesthetic in nature. For this purpose, I examine in detail the preparatory works as well as the negotiating history of the 1949 Geneva Conventions and the 1977 Additional Protocols, with special reference to civil wars and anti-colonial wars. I closely analyze the submissions made by the delegates of the Western countries as well as the post-colonial countries. This analysis seeks to critically explain the role of powerful countries, the Third World countries and the ICRC in drawing the boundaries of the laws of armed conflict.

Keywords

History of Geneva Conventions · Wars of national liberation · Common Article 3 · Non-international armed conflict

7.1 Introduction

Application of laws of armed conflict[1] (international humanitarian law) primarily depends on its material field or the conditions of applicability, which in turn facilitate the classification of the armed conflict also. The conditions of applicability indicate the factual situation of hostilities, the existence of which helps categorize the conflict into international or non-international. Under the HLA Hart's classification of rules into primary and secondary, the conditions or requirements of applicability form part of the secondary rules. They are rules about primary rules.[2] They specify, for example, when primary rules (rules regulating conduct) become applicable, or how primary rules may be amended or enforced.[3]

At present, the conditions relating to international armed conflicts are contained in Article 2

[1] Interestingly, the law of armed conflicts applies to the actions which stand prohibited under Article 2, paragraph 4 of the United Nations Charter, except in case of self-defense and collective enforcement actions sanctioned by the Security Council: Burra (2018, p. 52).

[2] Hart (2007, p. 94).

[3] Ibid.

K. Jeenger, *A Humanitarian Critique of International Humanitarian Law*,
Sustainable Development Goals Series, https://doi.org/10.1007/978-981-96-8319-2_7

common to the four Geneva Conventions of 1949[4] and Article 1 paragraph 4 of Protocol I additional to the Geneva Conventions.[5] On the other hand, the criteria in respect of non-international armed conflicts are mentioned in Article 3 common to the four Geneva Conventions 1949 and Article 1 paragraph 1 of Protocol II additional to the Geneva Conventions.[6]

However, before World War II, the laws of armed conflicts applied to inter-State wars only. Thus, the conduct of adversaries during civil wars and wars of national liberation was outside the material field of application of the law. Even while negotiating (perhaps dictating) the terms of 1949 Geneva Conventions, the "civilized" colonizers made sure that the instruments do not apply to wars for independence expressly and extensively. In this chapter, therefore, I seek to critically examine the negotiating history of the Geneva Conventions (1949) and the Additional Protocols (1977) to explain how the Western world influenced the negotiating process and succeeded in limiting the scope the law consistent with the aesthetic invocation of "humanitarian" considerations in war. Simultaneously, I also explore how the post-colonial anxieties of the Third World got exposed on the negotiating table. The history of adopting the restraints on the conduct during an armed conflict is not the subject-matter of this chapter.

[4] The Geneva Convention for the Amelioration of the Condition of the Wounded and Sick in Armed Forces in the Field of 12 August 1949 (Geneva Convention I), the Geneva Convention for the Amelioration of the Condition of Wounded, Sick and Shipwrecked Members of Armed Forces at Sea of 12 August 1949 (Geneva Convention II), the Geneva Convention relative to the Treatment of Prisoners of War of 12 August 1949 (Geneva Convention III) and the Geneva Convention relative to the Protection of Civilian Persons in Time of War of 12 August 1949 (Geneva Convention IV).

[5] Protocol Additional to the Geneva Conventions of 12 August 1949, and relating to the Protection of Victims of International Armed Conflicts (Protocol I) of 8 June 1977.

[6] Protocol Additional to the Geneva Conventions of 12 August 1949, and Relating to the Protection of Victims of Non-International Armed Conflicts (Protocol II), 8 June 1977.

7.2 Before World War II: No Compromise with Imperialism

The armed conflict of international character is the prominent category of armed conflicts sought to be regulated by international law. The phrase "international armed conflict" was used for the first time in the Additional Protocol I of 1977. Earlier, The Hague and Geneva treaties preferred to use the term "war." In respect of war, the criterion prescribed by The Hague Conventions of 1899 and 1907 is "war between two or more Contracting Parties".[7] The criterion reflected the prevalent (European) notion and experience of war, that is, an armed struggle between two or more States. Based on the exclusionary dyad of civilized and uncivilized, the colonial masters kept the colonies away from entering into treaties. They excluded from legal regulation the armed encounters with colonies and wars of independence, as explained in Chap. 5.

The humanitarian idea was missing in The Hague law also because the applicability of The Hague Conventions was dependent on a general-participation (*si omnes*) clause incorporated in the Conventions. Consequently, The Hague Conventions apply only if all the belligerents are parties to them. For instance, Article 2 of the Convention Respecting the Laws and Customs of War on Land, adopted at The Hague in 1907, says:

> The provisions contained in the Regulations referred to in Article 1, as well as in the present Convention, do not apply except between Contracting powers, and then only if all the belligerents are parties to the Convention.

The stipulation obviously shrank The Hague law's operation and limited it to inter-State wars only. This is not to say, however, that the legal regulation would definitely restraint the belligerent conduct. Rather, it is to reemphasize that the imperialist States applied the restraints in war without compromising with their economic and political interests.

[7] Art. 2 Hague Convention (II) with Respect to the Laws and Customs of War on Land of 29 July 1899 and Hague Convention (IV) with Respect to the Laws and Customs of War on Land of 18 October 1907.

7.3 Negotiating the Expansion in Geneva

The experience of the Second World War soon occasioned the adoption of some of the very significant instruments on international plane. The 1949 Geneva Conventions are one of them. The initial exercises conducted by the International Committee of the Red Cross (ICRC) showed a willingness towards widening the scope of application of the laws of armed conflict.

7.3.1 Preparatory Exercise

While preparing for revision of some of the existing Conventions and adoption of new "humanitarian" treaties, the ICRC was interested in eliminating the reciprocity clause and extending the law to "civil" wars as well. This is because application of international law to belligerency[8] was otherwise dependent upon its recognition by a third State, which involved sovereignty-related and political issues. In the absence of the recognition, its status would remain that of a civil war, unregulated by international law.

The process began with the initial recommendations made by the Preliminary Conference of National Red Cross Societies in 1946 and the Conference of Government Experts in 1947. The Preliminary Conference proposed two new phrases in respect of other armed conflict situations: "armed conflict within the borders of a State" and "civil war." The former phrase was proposed to expand the applicability of the 1929 Geneva Convention on the wounded and sick in armies in the field, and the latter to enlarge the scope of the 1929 Geneva Convention on prisoners of war.[9] Originally, these two Conventions applied to inter-State wars only. In the Preliminary Conference proposal, colonial conflicts and wars of liberation were not covered.

On the other hand, the 1947 Conference of Government Experts suggested a broader expression regarding "civil wars," that is, "civil war in any part of the home or colonial territories," and thus sought to extend the principles of both the 1929 Conventions and the draft Convention on civilians to civil and colonial armed struggles.[10]

7.3.2 "Civilized" Influence at Stockholm

Based on the above recommendations and its experience in the field, the ICRC presented four draft Conventions for consideration in the XVIIth Red Cross Conference in Stockholm in August 1948. Article 2 common to the draft conventions contained the conditions of applicability. It sought to expand the existing conditions by proposing the following four paragraphs:

> Beyond the stipulations to be implemented in peace time, the present Convention shall apply to all cases of declared war or of any other armed conflict which may arise between two or more of the High Contracting Parties, even should the state of war not be recognized by one of them.
>
> The Convention shall also apply to all cases of partial or total occupation of the territory of a High Contracting Party, even should the said occupation meets with no armed resistance.

---

[8] Following conditions must be satisfied in order to recognize belligerency: general hostilities (Brierly, 2008, p. 141), possessing a portion of territory and compliance with law of war (Art. 8 Rights and Duties of Foreign Powers as Regards the Established and Recognized Governments in Case of Insurrection, cited in Scott [1916, p. 159]). Actually, territorial states conferred recognition to belligerencies in the American Civil War and the Boer War only: Zamir (2017, pp. 19–20).

[9] Report on the Work of the Preliminary Conference of National Red Cross Societies for the Study of the Conventions and of Various Problems Relative to the Red Cross, Geneva, July 26–August 3, 1946, pp. 15, 70. Another interesting proposal related to the protection of children. In the conference, the Bolivian Red Cross tabled a Draft Convention for the Protection of Children in the event of International Conflict or Civil War. However, majority of experts suggested that instead of having a separate Convention for children, the provisions relating to their protection may be incorporated in a separate Convention on civilians. See, pp. 101–102.

[10] Report on the Work of the Conference of Government Experts for the Study of the Conventions for the Protection of War Victims, Geneva, April 14–26, 1947, pp. 8, 103, 272.

> Should one of the Powers in conflict not be party to the present Convention, the Powers who are party thereto shall, nevertheless, be bound by it in their mutual relations.
> In all cases of armed conflict which are not of an international character, especially cases of civil war, colonial conflicts, or wars of religion, which may occur in the territory of one or more of the High Contracting Parties, the implementing of the principles of the present Convention shall be obligatory on each of the adversaries. The application of the Convention in these circumstances shall in nowise depend on the legal status of the parties to the conflict and shall have no effect on that status.[11]

The first two paragraphs relating to inter-State war and belligerent occupation did not invite much debate. The third and fourth paragraphs of the ICRC draft proposing to remove reciprocity and bring colonial and civil wars within the purview of the laws of armed conflict appeared to be a significant step towards humanitarianism in war. However, these two paragraphs met with intense opposition from the Western bloc in the Stockholm Conference because the drafts intended to expand the applicability of the draft Conventions. They feared that the ICRC's proposals regulating anti-colonial wars would weaken their position in the colonies and colonial conflicts.

The fourth draft paragraph was even more objectionable to the colonial rulers. They preferred to treat the colonial and civil wars as riots, mutiny or emergencies and deal with them under the municipal law.[12] For them, the freedom fighters were bandits or criminals. Therefore, they approved the draft clause after omitting the phrase "especially cases of civil war, colonial conflicts, or wars of religion," which would otherwise be helpful in the interpretation of the new category "armed conflict not of an international character." In the absence of the illustrations, the new category remained vague. Using imprecise terminology is another style of manipulation by the powerful States. The modified paragraph stood as follows:

> In all cases of armed conflict not of an international character which may occur in the territory of one or more of the High Contracting Parties, each of the Parties to the conflict shall be bound to implement the provisions of the present Convention, subject to the adverse Party likewise acting in adherence thereto. The Convention shall be applicable in those circumstances, whatever the legal status of the Parties to the conflict and without prejudice thereto.[13]

The ICRC has tried to offer explanation in respect of the deletion of the words, "especially cases of civil war, colonial conflicts, or wars of religion" in the above draft paragraph. In its 1952 Commentary to common Article 3, it briefly says: "The omission of these words, far from weakening the text, enlarged its scope." This rationalization is further elaborated by the ICRC in its 2016 Commentary in the following words:

> the deletion ... was ultimately guided by the view that too much detail risked weakening the provision because it was impossible to foresee all future circumstances and because the armed conflict character of a situation was independent of its motives.[14]

However, in its Commentary to the Additional Protocols, it admits that the deleted words were "intended to be illustrative, not exhaustive,"[15] a fact which is apparent from the wordings of the draft clause too. Given the illustrative character of the deleted words, they would guide and facilitate interpretation of the phrase "armed conflicts not of an international character," instead of "weakening the provision" as apprehended by the ICRC. In fact, it is in the absence of these words, that recourse has to be made to the preparatory work[16] of the Geneva Conventions as an aid to interpretation. It raises a question whether the ICRC's divergent opinions were an attempt to mask the Western manipulation or its own failure in inspiring confidence in its drafts, or both of them.

11 XVIIth International Red Cross Conference, Stockholm (1948), Draft Revised or New Conventions for the Protection of war Victims (1948, pp. 5, 52, 153).

12 Dijk (2021, p. 249).

13 Final Records of the Diplomatic Conference of Geneva of 1949, vol I, pp. 47, 61, 73, 113.

14 ICRC (2016).

15 Sandoz et al (1987, para 86).

16 See Art. 32 Vienna Convention on the Law of Treaties (1969).

However, it appears from the preparatory work that the ICRC wanted to broaden the scope of the laws of armed conflict; however, its functioning was not immune from the impact of Western domination. The European representation in the ICRC was influential enough to chalk out the drafts in a way favorable to them, an experience that features the ICRC's work since its inception.[17] Besides the documented drafting history, there are undocumented histories as well which rarely surface but affect the outcome. The Stockholm Conference once again demonstrated ICRC's vulnerability to European influence and its inability, if not unwillingness, to challenge the same. Therefore, the clarification put forward by the ICRC regarding the deletion of the words raises doubts and creates confusion.

The draft Conventions to be negotiated and adopted in the Diplomatic Conference had, thus, already been conditioned in Stockholm to suit the powerful States.

7.3.3 Power Structures and Diplomatic Conference, 1949

In the Diplomatic Conference of 1949 in Geneva, the negotiating space continued to be dominated by the colonial countries as it had been done in the past. Additionally, preoccupied by a Eurocentric standpoint,[18] the Swiss Federal Council did not invite any national liberation movement to the conference.[19]

The first two paragraphs of the Stockholm draft, that is on war between States (or international armed conflicts) and belligerent occupation, were adopted by the States without any amendment.[20] To further strengthen the non-reciprocity clause in the draft paragraph 3, the ICRC suggested an addition to the paragraph of a "provision with regard to the case of two States at war, one of which was not a Party to the Convention."[21] Consequent upon some negotiations and amendments, the proposal was finally agreed to by the Special Committee to the Joint Committee[22] and adopted by the States in the Plenary Assembly also.[23] It has been though appreciated as breaking "new ground by imposing unilateral obligations,"[24] however, from a purely humanitarian perspective the text still leaves gap in the protection of victims of war. The adopted text is as follows:

> Although one of the Powers in conflict may not be a party to the present Convention, the Powers who are parties thereto shall remain bound by it in their mutual relations. They shall furthermore be bound by the Convention in relation to the said Power, if the latter accepts and applies the provisions thereof.

In respect of the fourth draft paragraph on non-international armed conflicts, the Diplomatic Conference happened to be a sight of interesting arguments and developments. The initial negotiations on the paragraph began before the Joint Committee of the Conference. The impact of the deletion of the words "especially cases of civil war, colonial conflicts, or wars of religion" from the fourth paragraph of the Stockholm draft surfaced soon on the negotiating table. The deliberations on regulating non-international armed conflicts began to take place as if they meant civil wars only, and colonial wars were not intended to be a part of them. Even the newly independent States did not demonstrate sincerity towards covering colonial wars within the scope of the laws of armed conflicts. The arguments and amendments presented by the delegates were based on the intricacies of civil wars only.[25] In fact, not more than five delegations in the Joint Committee (including Greece, Union of Soviet Socialist Republics (USSR), United Kingdom, and Australia) referred to colonial wars in their submissions, out of which only the USSR repeatedly underlined the brutal suppression of colonial

[17] See Chap. 5.

[18] Dijk (2021, p. 277).

[19] Final Records (1949), above n 13, vol I, pp. 158–172.

[20] Ibid., pp. 108, 325.

[21] Ibid., pp. 10, 108.

[22] Ibid., pp. 108–109.

[23] Ibid., p. 325.

[24] Detter (2000, p. 410).

[25] E.g. see Final Records (1949), above n 13, vol II Section B, pp. 10–15, 40–46, 120–129.

and civil wars, and stressed upon extending the law to them.[26] On the other hand, the reference of colonial conflicts by the other States did not prove to be conducive in advancing the debate on this subject.

On the question of expanding the application of the law to civil wars, the delegations before the Joint Committee did not oppose the same; however, they were divided on the point of magnitude and intensity of civil wars to be recognized for this purpose. Several States including France, the United Nations, Spain, China and Canada were in favor of covering only high-scale civil wars, and not uprisings or rebellions, whereas delegations from the USSR, Mexico, Denmark, Hungary, Romania and Norway realized the cruel nature of civil wars and supported the application of the law to civil wars without pointing out any scale of hostilities or organization of armed groups.

During the deliberations on civil wars, two prominent colonial States were seen struggling while trying to hide their colonial intentions. The French representative Lamarle stated that protection to individuals during civil wars cannot be afforded sacrificing the "rights of the States."[27] In the next meeting, he apologetically said in the conference that his reference to "rights of State" did not imply the interpretation of the term by fascist regimes.[28] Similarly, Robert Craigie representing the United Kingdom totally opposed the adoption of the fourth paragraph in the first meeting.[29] However, on the following day, he tried to correct his words, but, insisted on protecting the State against "irresponsible outbursts."[30]

[26] Ibid., pp. 10, 14, 41, 121, 325, 326.

[27] Ibid., p. 10.

[28] Ibid., p. 13. On this statement of the French delegate, it has been remarkably commented that, "This slip of the tongue reveals the continuing awkward struggle by colonial powers to distinguish their own actions in the colonies from those of their former Nazi occupier. For them, it was vital to apply the notion of rights to European occupation but not to spaces of decolonization beyond the metropole." See, Dijk (2021, p. 279).

[29] Final Records (1949), above n 13, vol II Section B, p. 10.

[30] Ibid., p. 15.

Due to lack of agreement among the delegates in respect of the Draft fourth paragraph, it was decided to further discuss it before the Special Committee of the Joint Committee. In the Special Committee, the representatives expressed similar sentiments in respect of the fourth paragraph of the Stockholm draft. Thus, it was decided by ten votes to one, with one abstention, to replace the paragraph.[31] The decision replacing the draft paragraph exposed the half-heartedness of their "humanitarian" commitments, if any, because any new draft was bound to be narrow and less effective from humanitarian perspective.

To draft the new paragraph, a Working Party was formed. The draft prepared by the Working Party though affirmed the category of armed conflicts not of an international character also, but subject to difficult pre-conditions, like recognition of belligerency, State-like features of the non-State group and ability to enforce the Convention.[32] Commenting upon the draft, the USSR representative Morosov stated that it would render still more difficult the application of the Conventions, and that he preferred the Stockholm version of the fourth paragraph.[33] To the contrary, France and the United Kingdom raised concerns over the application of the Conventions as a whole to civil wars.[34] Considering the objections and suggestions of the members, the Chairman of the Committee requested the Working Party to draft a new proposal "of a more limited character."[35]

The Working Party realized that it might accommodate the concerns of the delegates either by restricting (1) the provisions to be applied to non-international armed conflicts or (2) the situations of non-international armed conflicts to which the Conventions should apply.[36] It followed both of the methods for different Conventions. In respect of the Convention on the protection of civilians, the latter method was followed. The

[31] Ibid., p. 45.

[32] Ibid., pp. 46–47.

[33] Ibid., p. 48.

[34] Ibid., p. 47.

[35] Ibid., pp. 48, 76.

[36] Ibid., p. 76.

draft Article 2A provided that the provisions of the Civilian Convention could apply wholly or partly to a non-international armed conflict by special agreements between the Parties to the conflict.[37] The underlying humanitarian principles of the Convention were nevertheless proposed to be applicable. On the other hand, the draft proposed to apply the other three Conventions to non-international armed conflicts, subject to the recognition of belligerency or State-like features of the non-State group.[38] Thus, attempting to extend the Conventions to civil wars also appeared to be difficult, let alone the wars of national liberation.

In respect of this draft of the Working Party, France proposed an amendment, which found support from other delegates also. Consequently, a Second Working Party under the chairmanship of France was formed to draw up a new proposal.[39] The new French proposal recognized the category of "armed conflict not of an international character occurring in the territory of one of the High Contracting Parties" and did not subject it to any pre-requisites, such as recognition of belligerency.[40] Prima facie, this expression appears to be broad enough to apply the restraints in the conduct of such armed conflicts, but what if the restraints applicable to such armed conflicts are also limited. The French proposal actually contained only a handful of rules applicable to non-international armed conflicts, irrespective of the intensity.[41] The application of the remaining rules of conduct was made dependent on special agreement between hostile parties.[42]

The draft was amended to some extent consequent upon some suggestions.[43] However, countering the French proposal, the USSR proposed a draft suggesting the application of more humanitarian rules in non-international armed conflicts not subject to any condition precedent.[44] Thus, the various proposals submitted before the Special Committee either sought to limit the scope of non-international armed conflicts by raising the threshold, or suggested the application of different (limited) set of rules to such conflicts. None of the drafts could match the humanitarian ideal reflected in the Stockholm proposal. Each draft demonstrated nothing but compromise of diverse proportion.

Since none of the drafts could attain majority of votes, the Special Committee submitted all of them for the consideration of the Joint Committee, where they were put to vote. The draft of the Second Working Party (the French proposal) secured majority of the votes and, therefore, was tabled before the Plenary Assembly for further deliberation and adoption.

The delegations in Plenary Assembly were completely divided over the draft they would prefer. At the same time, there were some States who still wanted to specifically recognize the category of wars of national liberation and colonial wars as mentioned in the Stockholm draft, paragraph 4. First was the Mexican delegate who wanted colonial as well as civil wars to be regulated by the Conventions as a whole. Therefore, he admired the paragraph 4 of the Stockholm draft which was originally introduced before the Joint Committee.[45] Clarifying the Mexican position, he said that his aim was "to ensure that in all non-international wars of whatever character, whether civil wars, wars of resistance or wars of liberation, the right of the stronger and the *lex talionis* (law of retaliation) shall not prevail."[46] Skeptical about the scope of France-led Working Party's proposal, he asked the ICRC representative whether the draft extended to all the cases as foreseen at Stockholm.[47]

The second group was led by the USSR, who reiterated the barbaric nature of colonial and civil wars and the need to regulate them by international

[37] Ibid., p. 77.

[38] Ibid.

[39] Ibid., p. 79.

[40] Ibid., p. 83.

[41] Ibid.

[42] Ibid.

[43] Ibid., Annex E, p. 126.

[44] Ibid., p. 97.

[45] Ibid., p. 333.

[46] Ibid.

[47] Ibid.

law.[48] The Soviet draft secured support from the delegations of Romania and Czechoslovakia too.[49]

On the other side of the extreme was a group of some Asiatic States, represented by a post-colonial State, Burma. The Burmese delegation contested the extension of the "humanitarian" law to colonial and civil wars, and insisted upon the complete deletion of draft Article 2A. In respect of wars of national liberation, the Burmese delegate denied the relevance of the "humanitarian" law stating that "in this highly enlightened age the remaining conquered countries of the world will also receive their independence without the loss of a single drop of blood."[50] Considering the brutal realities of wars of national liberation, as also underlined by the Soviet and Mexican delegates, this optimism was extremely naïve and utopian.

The reasons put forward by the Burmese delegate for his objections to the regulation of non-international armed conflict by international law include: danger to sovereignty of the territorial State, no definition of armed conflict not of an international character, adoption by the Joint Committee without discussion, impossibility to find a satisfactory solution, an incentive to armed conflicts with all their terrible effects, binding irrespective of observance by the insurgents, internal nature of the matter, especially harmful and beyond the scope of the conference.[51]

He further expressed his fears by saying that the recognition of non-international armed conflicts would be helpful "to those who desire loot, pillage, political power by undemocratic means, or those foreign ideologies seeking their own advancement by inciting the population of another country."[52] In this statement, the description of the motives of civil war situation is certainly narrow, and some delegates were found saying that sometimes those who are labeled as rebels in a civil war are actually patriots struggling for the independence and dignity of their country.[53] It may also extend to the exercise of the human right to self-determination of people. Responding to the Burmese stand, the USSR representative commented that this attitude took us back to the dark period of Saint Bartholomew's eve (a sixteenth-century religious massacre in France).[54]

In fact, the Burmese resistance towards extension of the scope of the Conventions does not consider the plight of the victims who need protection. It also hints towards the colonial attitude of stifling resistance. It denotes that in the post-colonial era the change in the ruling people did not result into change in the power structures. The essential attributes of colonialism continue in the consciousness of the formerly colonized privileged classes, who occupy the thrones vacated by the colonial rulers post-independence. Thus, colonialism is not an episode in the history, but a lasting attitude, a habit engrained in the hierarchical power structures. Nevertheless, being a Third World country's representative, the anxieties expressed by the Burmese delegate over potential foreign interventions in civil wars proved out to be true. In the latter half of the century, foreign interventions in some of the countries of global south inflicted violence and socio-political unrest. These lived experiences of the Third World once again exposed the lies of the flag-bearers of humanitarianism.

Between the two extremes of the Soviet idealism and Burmese realism at the Diplomatic Conference, there were the Western bloc and their supporters. During the early drafting exercise that took place before this conference, the maneuvers of the Western bloc had already demonstrated their disagreement with the idea of recognizing the categories of civil and anti-colonial armed conflicts. However, an outright rejection of the proposal in the Diplomatic Conference was difficult for several reasons.

---

[48] Ibid., pp. 325–326.

[49] Ibid., p. 334.

[50] Ibid., p. 329.

[51] Ibid., pp. 327–330.

[52] Ibid., p. 329.

[53] Pictet (1960).

[54] Final Records (1949), above n 13, vol II Section B, p. 338.

In the end, the draft article 2A as tabled before the Plenary Assembly was adopted by 34 votes to 12 with 1 abstention[55] and took the shape of Article 3 common to all the four Geneva Conventions which recognizes the category of "armed conflicts not of an international character" without specifying or illustrating what the phrase actually signifies. The "humanitarian" rhetoric disguised the continuation of economic and political agenda of the powerful Western States. In respect of these negotiations and the outcome, it has been aptly remarked:

> Therefore, purely from the humanitarian point of view, positions taken by the dominant Western States against the extension of conventions to colonial conflicts and the Third World States against civil wars in general, go against the humanitarian spirit of the conventions.[56]

From the drafting point of view, the insertion of Article 3 in all the four Geneva Conventions leading to the status of a common Article is bizarre because it neither refers to the Convention it is part of nor seeks to apply the respective Convention. Rather, it exists independent of the respective Convention. Had it been made part of anyone of the Conventions, its application would have not been affected. Repeating the provision in all the four Conventions can in no way broaden its scope, which had already been curtailed. Actually, the idea of a common provision in respect of non-international armed conflict was conceived and inserted in the Stockholm proposal because it would trigger the respective Convention which it was part of. However, it appears that while discarding the Stockholm draft, the drafters erroneously retained its "common" character.

With this analysis, it also becomes clear that in the entire drafting exercise of 1949 Geneva Conventions, no proposal or debate was initiated by any State on bringing wars of independence within the ambit of international armed conflicts. In its early proposal, the ICRC put armed colonial encounters and civil wars under the category of non-international armed conflicts, and, the entire debate revolved around their inclusion and the extent to which the law may apply to these conflicts only. Thus, the idea of war that prevailed and dominated the negotiating process was certainly Eurocentric in nature, that is, an international armed conflict means a war between "sovereign" States.

Another grave concern of the colonies was continuous occupation of their territories by the colonial powers. It is worth inquiring whether the 1949 Geneva Conventions apply to colonial occupation or not. The wording of the situation covered by common Article 2 of the Geneva Conventions is "partial or total occupation of a foreign territory, regardless of armed resistance." The Hague Conventions also regulate occupation but do not specify it as a distinct condition for the operation of the Conventions. In this regard, it must be understood that occupation cannot be an independent situation and is always preceded by war, in this case, an international armed conflict. It has been argued by Burra that unless the legal criterion of war (international armed conflict) is fulfilled, the territorial control followed by the conflict cannot amount to belligerent occupation.[57] Accordingly, the Conventions apply to an occupation occurring after a war. Thus, colonial occupation could qualify for belligerent occupation only if it is preceded by a war within the meaning of Geneva Conventions. Since the armed colonial encounters had been kept outside the ambit of international armed conflicts, the colonial occupation did not amount to occupation within the meaning of the common Article 2.

Thus, the situations of violent encounters with colonies and occupation of colonies were systematically kept out of the purview of the Geneva Conventions, so that the imperial goals of the "crusaders of humanity" do not get compromised. The whole negotiation process and its outcome have been beautifully put in a nutshell:

> Power relations provide the possibilities for maneuverability. In the process of long drawn-out discussions and amidst several alternative proposals, it is ultimately the power relations that determine the outcome. The Western States succeeded in removing explicit reference to colonial conflicts

[55] Ibid., p. 339.

[56] Burra (2020, p. 206).

[57] Ibid., p. 201.

> while maintaining their humanitarian posture of extending conventions to civil wars. The Third World States could not succeed in their resistance to the extension of the conventions to civil wars.[58]

In the end, Article 2 common to the four Geneva Conventions as adopted in August, 1949 included three situations within the ambit of international armed conflicts: declared war, other armed conflict and belligerent occupation. On the other hand, common Article 3 with less precision and protection covered armed conflicts not of an international character. Importantly, the common Article 3 ensured that international law may regulate such wars without waiting for its maturing into belligerency, which depends on recognition by other States. In fact, it eliminated the chances of a non-international armed conflict culminating into belligerency.[59]

However, the practical reasons why the Western bloc was reluctant to have comprehensive provisions on anti-colonial and civil wars surfaced from their actions and omissions in such situations during 1950s and 1960s.

7.4 Gaining the Ground Post-Geneva Conventions

Extending the Geneva Conventions to non-international armed conflicts was certainly a shift from the pre-World War II position. It marked the beginning of direct international legal regulation of an internal event. However, the vagueness of the expression "armed conflicts not of an international character" got exposed subsequently. After the adoption of the Conventions the number of non-international armed conflicts increased[60] and soon it became the norm.[61] The Geneva Conventions fell short of addressing the changing character of armed conflicts.[62] They were largely based on the assumptions of war between States and corresponding means and methods of war.[63] The common Article was found to be "inadequate with its imperfections and shortcomings."[64] The imprecise meaning and scope of common Article 3, however, provided sufficient leeway to belligerents to implement the "miniature Convention"[65] as per their convenience in the Korean, Indochinese, Algerian and a series of such wars. Governments predominantly resorted to emergency or martial law and tried to curb such a situation at its early stage.[66] However, where a conflict protracted to several weeks or months, States did observe some obligations. Some States including France, the United States and Lebanon recognized the applicability of common Article 3 at different stages[67] of the conflict, though, assuming an obligation is different from its execution.

During these times, while the law of armed conflict was struggling in its coverage, the international human rights movement gained momentum with the adoption of the Genocide Convention[68] (1948), Refugee Convention[69] (1951) and two Covenants[70] on human rights (1966). The rise of international human rights law has been seen as one of the greatest conceptual influences behind the transformation subsequent to the 1949 Geneva Conventions.[71] Additionally, the platform of the United Nations was used by the newly independent states to voice the concerns of colonized peoples and the Third World as a whole from a human right perspective. It has

[58] Ibid., p. 206.

[59] Burra (2013, p. 431).

[60] Zamir (2017), p. 43 and ICRC (2017).

[61] Crawford (2014, p. 100).

[62] Burra (2013, p. 423).

[63] Bassiouni, cited in Crawford (2014, p. 102).

[64] Burra (2013, p. 432).

[65] Soviet delegate in, Final Records (1949), above n 13, vol II Section B, p. 326.

[66] Bond, cited in Forsythe (1978, p. 276).

[67] For instance, in Algerian war, France accepted obligations under common Article 3 after six years of commencement of the war: Alexander (2016, p. 44).

[68] Convention on the Prevention and Punishment of the Crime of Genocide (1948).

[69] Convention relating to the Status of Refugees (1951).

[70] International Covenant on Civil and Political Rights (1966) and International Covenant on Economic, Social and Cultural Rights (1966).

[71] Mégret (2006, p. 296). For the influence of human rights law in the development of the four Geneva Conventions 1949, see Dijk (2018, pp. 553–582).

been rightly observed that "One aspect of this new sensibility was a growing distaste for colonialism."[72] Eventually, several path breaking resolutions were adopted by the General Assembly on several urgent matters, including the right to self-determination,[73] respect for law of armed conflicts in all types of armed conflicts[74] and treating wars of national liberation[75] as international armed conflicts.[76]

This theoretical support was sans much favor in practice. Many colonial rulers, such as Portugal and South Africa, neither discontinued with the colonial domination nor respected the laws of armed conflict during violent freedom struggles. They continued to treat freedom fighters as bandits and criminals, and violent confrontations with them as mutiny and emergency, fit for punishing under the domestic penal law. The anti-colonial and other wars of 1950s and 1960s, such as in Algeria, Congo, Vietnam, Guinea-Bissau, Angola and Mozambique, exposed the insufficiency of the Geneva Conventions as their applicability was contested. These conflict situations also ran contrary to the emerging human rights movement, including the much-fought-for right to self-determination. Thus, it was felt that the gap between the theory and practice of human rights in war must be bridged by further development of the laws of armed conflict.

7.5 Towards Protocol I: Feeding Someone, No More Starving

During this state of affairs, two urgent necessities were felt on international level in respect of armed conflicts. First, human rights must be protected in all armed conflicts, whether international or non-international. Second, the laws of armed conflict must also apply in armed conflicts involving freedom struggles and internal disturbances. Since the General Assembly had expressed the urgent need to apply the "humanitarian" law in all armed conflicts and sought association of the ICRC also for this purpose, the ICRC extended its support. In its XXI conference in 1969, the ICRC submitted a report titled Reaffirmation and Development of Law and Customs Applicable in Armed Conflict,[77] which *inter alia* endorsed the above two propositions. Resolution XIII adopted in the ICRC Conference underlined the need to update the law consistent with the General Assembly resolutions and challenges posed by contemporary warfare.[78] Therefore, first, the ICRC organized the Conference of Government Experts on the Reaffirmation and Development of International Humanitarian Law Applicable in Armed Conflicts in Geneva during 1971–1972. Excepting some of them, majority of experts did not endorse the international character of wars of liberation.[79] On the other hand, the ICRC was aware of the General Assembly resolutions supporting prisoner of war status to freedom fighters and international character of violent freedom struggles. But, in order to propose an acceptable solution in this regard, the ICRC submitted the following drafts to the experts in the second session of the Conference of Government Experts convened in 1972: one, Protocol I in respect of international armed conflicts without recognizing wars of liberation as international but granting prisoner of war

[72] Alexander (2016, p. 37).

[73] Declaration on the Granting of Independence to Colonial Countries and Peoples, A/RES/1514 (1960).

[74] Resolution XXIII, Human Rights in Armed Conflicts, Final Act of the International Conference on Human Rights, Teheran (1968). United Nations, New York, p. 18.

[75] "A war of national liberation is defined by its goal: the implementation of a recognized right to self-determination": Gorelick (1978, p. 364, n. 1).

[76] Basic Principles of the Legal Status of the Combatants Struggling Against Colonial and Alien Domination and Racist Regimes, A/RES/3103 (1973).

[77] XXIst International Conference of the Red Cross (1969), Report on Reaffirmation and Development of Law and Customs Applicable in Armed Conflict (1969). ICRC, Geneva, pp. 96, 102.

[78] Resolution XIII, adopted by the XXI International Conference of the Red Cross (1969).

[79] Sandoz et al. (1987, para 4379).

treatment (not status) to freedom fighters, and two, a Declaration on the Application of International Humanitarian Law in Armed Struggle for Self-Determination requiring the adherence to the humanitarian law as a whole, or at least the law relating to non-international armed conflicts.[80] The declaration did not find much favor from the experts.[81] Consistent with the outcome of the conference of Government Experts, the ICRC equipped itself for the Diplomatic Conference (1974–1977).

Nearly 700 delegates from different blocs assembled in Geneva to participate in the Diplomatic Conference in a highly politicized and contentious environment.[82] The participation of liberation movements in the discussions was seen as one of the flashpoints of the Conference because the imperialist States were largely against the same, while the Third World backed their involvement.[83] In the Diplomatic Conference, the Third World states saw the ICRC's ignorance of the prevalent political and legal developments in relation to the right of self-determination and wars of national liberation. This is because, in its draft, the ICRC set out the scope of the Protocol I in the following words:

> The present Protocol, which supplements the Geneva Conventions of 12 August 1949, for the Protection of War Victims, shall apply in the situations referred to in Article 2 common to the conventions.[84]

Thus, the ICRC had clearly "ignored and bypassed the U.N. decisions and debates referred to above."[85] While many Western States were in favor of the ICRC proposal,[86] the post-colonial States opposed the ICRC draft and stressed on the inclusion of wars of national liberation in the applicability criteria of the Protocol on international armed conflicts.[87] The final text adopted by the conference was indeed a result of a series of proposals, amendments, withdrawals and revisions[88]:

> the situations referred to in the preceding paragraph include armed conflicts in which peoples are fighting against colonial domination and alien occupation and against racist regimes in the exercise of their right of self-determination, as enshrined in the Charter of the United Nations and the Declaration on Principles of International Law concerning Friendly Relations and Co-operation among States in accordance with the Charter of the United Nations.[89]

The proposed paragraph was adopted by voting and not by consensus because several States, especially the colonizers disliked the proposal.[90] The Third World countries succeeded in getting sufficient number of votes in favor of their proposal. The essence of this shift has been captured well in the following words:

> The UN approach, backed by the Third World and Marxist states, predominated over the ICRC approach, backed by the most of the West. What is surprising about the 1974 Conference is that the ICRC and Western states did not foresee the depth of support for the clearly and repeatedly expressed point of view central to the UN approach.[91]

In the end, wars of national liberation were recognized as international armed conflicts under Article 1(4) of the Protocol and regulated by international law of armed conflicts. It occasioned "an encounter between revolutionary, nationalist anti-colonialism and a humanitarian discourse and practice that combined universalist language

[80] Conference of Government Experts on the Reaffirmation and Development of International Humanitarian Law Applicable in Armed Conflicts, Second Session, 3 May–3 June 1972, Report on the Work of the Conference, vol I, pp. 95, 174, 200.

[81] Ibid., p. 201.

[82] Alexander (2016, p. 18).

[83] Davey (2020, p. 377).

[84] Official Records of the Diplomatic Conference on the Reaffirmation and Development of International Humanitarian Law Applicable in Armed Conflicts Geneva (1974–1977), vol I, Part 3, p. 3.

[85] Nirmal (1988, p. 205).

[86] Forsythe (1975, p. 84).

[87] Official Records (1974–1977), above n 84, vol III, pp. 5–9.

[88] Ibid., vol VIII, pp. 99–100.

[89] Art. 1(4) Protocol I, above n 5.

[90] Official Records (1974–1977), above n 84, vol VIII, p. 102.

[91] Forsythe (1975, p. 78).

and Western privilege."[92] Indeed, the recognition of the human right to self-determination by the United Nations was instrumental to the inclusion. It, however, happened at a time when decolonization was almost over[93] and such wars had almost ceased to occur. Moreover, the provision was subject to a condition provided by Article 96(3) of the Protocol, which says that a national liberation movement is required to make a declaration assuming the obligations under the Protocol. Thus, in order to apply the law of international armed conflict to a situation falling under Article 1(4) of the Protocol, it is essential that the State who is a party to such a war has ratified the Protocol and the authority of the national liberation movement has submitted the declaration under Article 96(3) with the Swiss Federal Council. Shockingly, none of the declarations were officially shown in the ratification status of the Protocol by the Council.[94]

7.6 Protocol II: "What the Right Hand Giveth, the Left Hand Taketh Away"

On the other side, major developments for revising the law relating to non-international armed conflicts began with ICRC's XX International Conference at Vienna in 1965, wherein two Resolutions[95] recognizing the insufficiency of humanitarian standards in such conflicts were passed. These steps gained momentum also with subsequent developments in the domain of international human rights law, especially the adoption of the International Covenant on Civil and Political Rights in 1966 and a resolution on human rights in armed conflict[96] in the International Conference on Human Rights in 1968 at Tehran. This resolution was referred to in the XXI international conference of the ICRC in 1969, and the ICRC considered "necessary" and "pressing" the resolution's call to study the need to strengthen the existing rules.[97]

In the first session (1971) of the Conference of Government Experts organized by the ICRC the experts were divided between removing the distinction between international and non-international armed conflicts and suggesting an objective criterion of non-international armed conflict.[98] However, in the second session (1972), the ICRC itself presented for consideration a separate draft protocol additional to common Article 3.[99] The draft would serve as a starting point in the Diplomatic Conference too.

In the Diplomatic Conference (1974–1977), States such as Norway and Syria advocated a single international instrument in respect of international and non-international armed conflicts purely on humanitarian grounds.[100] However, selective humanitarianism never approves of such a maximalist idea. In sync with the dominant view, the ICRC's draft for non-international armed conflicts defended the classification of armed conflicts on the grounds of the distinction between international and non-international armed conflicts recognized in public international law and the views expressed by the experts.[101] The draft submitted by the ICRC and revised by the committees in the Diplomatic Conference stood substantially amended by a draft which was submitted by a country from the Third World, Pakistan. It addressed the fears of violation of sovereignty and external intervention.

[92] Davey (2020, p. 395).

[93] In 1970s, the total number of States increased by three times due to decolonization. Furthermore, delegates from 124 States adopted the Additional Protocols on 8 June, 1977: ICRC (2017).

[94] Burra (2013, p. 427).

[95] Resolution XXVIII, Protection of Civilian Populations against the Dangers of Indiscriminate Warfare, Resolution XXXI, Protection of Victims of Non-International Conflicts. International Review of the Red Cross (1965) 56:588–590, 591–592 respectively.

[96] Resolution XXIII, Human Rights in Armed Conflicts (1968), above n 74.

[97] Report of XXIst International Conference of the Red Cross (1969), above n 77, pp. 12–13.

[98] Sandoz (1987, para 4376).

[99] Report on Conference of Government Experts (1972), above n 80, p. 3.

[100] Official Records (1974–1977), above n 84, vol V, p. 91 (Norway), p. 193 (Syria).

[101] Ibid., vol VIII, p. 202.

However, on the other side of the currents of opinion were few post-colonial States, like India and Iraq, who regarded protocol II completely irrelevant. The Indian delegate viewed common Article 3 in the context of anti-colonial wars only, which would be treated as international armed conflicts under Protocol I, and, therefore, opined that Protocol II was pointless.[102] Furthermore, he considered internal armed conflicts as law and order problems which fall within the exclusive territorial jurisdiction of each State.[103] However, despite opposing the regulation of internal armed conflicts by an international instrument, India offered its comments and suggestions to make the draft protocol more acceptable.[104] For instance, India suggested a new paragraph on non-intervention, which took the shape of Article 3 of the Protocol.[105]

One of the major contentious issues with the Additional Protocol II is its high threshold of applicability. Originally, the ICRC recommended a low threshold to widen the scope of the Protocol, as given below.

> Article 1.—Material field of application:
>
> 1. The present Protocol shall apply to all armed conflicts not covered by Article 2 common to the Geneva Conventions of August 12, 1949, taking place between armed forces or other organized armed groups under responsible command.
> 2. The present Protocol shall not apply to situations of internal disturbances and tensions, inter alia riots, isolated and sporadic acts of violence and other acts of a similar nature…[106]

However, during the negotiations the scope of the Protocol was severely curtailed by incorporating higher standards:

> all armed conflicts … which take place in the territory of a High Contracting Party between its armed forces and dissident armed forces or other organized armed groups which, under responsible command, exercise such control over a part of its territory as to enable them to carry out sustained and concerted military operations and to implement this Protocol.[107]

The flaws that emerge from the above verbiage are: the instrument does not apply to an armed conflict between two armed groups; high threshold renders the instrument rarely applicable[108]; subjective standards of applicability; it is not the ability to carry out but actually carrying out sustained and concerted military operations that is a necessary condition, and how to determine existence of the conditions.[109] Thus, Protocol II is "narrower"[110] than Common Article 3 in scope.

Thus, a Diplomatic Conference on "reaffirmation and development of international humanitarian law" ended up adopting a text on non-international armed conflicts which is less workable. It took away, immediately, what it had sought to give. Notably, the adoption of the two Additional Protocols took four years as contrast to the four Geneva Conventions of 1949 which were agreed in four months only.[111] However, they produced problematic results and could not fetch universal ratification too. Prolonged negotiations reflect that the draft provisions were not acceptable to many delegates.

References

Alexander A (2015) A short history of international humanitarian law. Eur J Int Law 26(1):109–138

[102] Ibid., vol VII, pp. 202–204.

[103] Ibid.

[104] Burra (2013, pp. 440–441).

[105] Thus, calling India as one of the 'monkey-wrenchers', (those who throw a monkey-wrench into the efforts of developing something) by Forsythe seems inappropriate and one-sided. See, Forsythe (1978, p. 281).

[106] Official Records (1974–1977), above n 84, vol I, Part 3, p. 33.

[107] Art. 1(1) Protocol II, above n 6.

[108] Prosecutor v. Boškoski and Tarčulovski, IT-04-82, Trial Chamber, Judgment, 10 July 2008, para 197 and Cullen (2010, pp. 109–112).

[109] See, Jeenger (2017, p. 43).

[110] Chinkin and Kaldor (2017, p. 7. 236).

[111] Davey (2020, p. 378). It is said that the ICRC expected the Conference to get over in one year: Alexander (2015, p. 124).

Alexander A (2016) International humanitarian law, post-colonialism and the 1977 Geneva protocol I. Melb J Int Law 17:15–50
Brierly JL (2008) The law of nations. OUP, New Delhi
Burra S (2013) India and the additional protocols of 1977. Indian J Int Law 53:422–450
Burra S (2018) Collective engagement and selective endorsement: India's ambivalent attitude towards laws of armed conflict. In: Burra S, Babu RR (eds) Locating India in the contemporary international legal order. Springer, New Delhi, pp 51–65
Burra S (2020) Four Geneva conventions of 1949: a third world view. In: Bhuiyan MJH, Khan BU (eds) Revisiting the Geneva conventions: 1949–2019. Brill/Nijhoff, Leiden, pp 190–214
Chinkin C, Kaldor M (2017) International law and new wars. CUP, Cambridge
Crawford E (2014) Trapped: from inter-state and symmetric to intrastate and asymmetric: changing methods of warfare and the law of armed conflict in the 100 years since world war one. Yearb Int Humltarian Law 17:95–118
Cullen A (2010) The concept of non-international armed conflict in international humanitarian law. CUP, New York
Davey E (2020) Decolonizing the Geneva conventions: national liberation and the development of humanitarian law. In: Moses AD et al (eds) Decolonization, self-determination, and the rise of global human rights politics. CUP, Cambridge, pp 375–396
Detter I (2000) The law of war. CUP, Cambridge
Dijk B (2018) Human rights in war: on the entangled foundations of the 1949 Geneva conventions. Am J Int Law 112(4):553–582
Dijk B (2021) Internationalizing colonial war: on the unintended consequences of the interventions of the International Committee of the Red Cross in South-East Asia, 1945–1949. Past & Present 250(1):243–283
Forsythe DP (1975) The 1974 diplomatic conference on humanitarian law: some observations. Am J Int Law 69(1):77–91
Forsythe DP (1978) Legal management of internal war: the 1977 protocol on non-international armed conflicts. Am J Int Law 72(2):272–295
Gorelick R (1978) Wars of national liberation: jus ad bellum. Indian J Int Law 18:364–378
Hart HLA (2007), Concept of law. OUP, New Delhi
ICRC (2016) Commentary on article 3, Geneva convention I. https://ihl-databases.icrc.org/en/ihl-treaties/gci-1949/article-3/commentary/2016#146_B
ICRC (2017) 4th anniversary of the 1977 additional protocols to the 1949 Geneva conventions: policy paper. ICRC, Geneva. https://www.icrc.org/en/download/file/47637/icrc_ap40_policy_paper.pdf
Jeenger K (2016–2017) How "ability" requirement in additional protocol II may disable its applicability to NIACs. ISIL YB of Int'l Humanitarian & Refugee Law XVI-XVII:43–56
Mégret F (2006) From 'savages' to 'unlawful combatants': a postcolonial look at international humanitarian law's 'other.' In: Orford A (ed) International law and its others. CUP, New York, pp 265–317
Nirmal BC (1988) Wars of national liberation and international humanitarian law. Indian J Int Law 28(2):201–215
Pictet J (ed) (1960) Commentary on article 3, Geneva convention III. https://ihl-databases.icrc.org/en/ihl-treaties/gciii-1949/article-3/commentary/1960?activeTab
Sandoz Y et al (eds) (1987) Commentary on the additional protocols of 8 June 1977 to the Geneva conventions of 12 August 1949. ICRC/Martinus Nijhoff, Geneva
Scott JB (ed) (1916) Resolutions of the institute of international law dealing with the law of nations. OUP, New York
Zamir N (2017) Classification of conflicts in international humanitarian law. Edward Elgar, Cheltenham

8 Humanitarian Discrimination in the Rules of International and Non-international Armed Conflicts and Its Implications

Abstract

This chapter is related to the adoption of discriminatory rules in respect of international and non-international armed conflicts. In this chapter, I intend to answer the following questions: Was it originally intended to have different set of rules regarding the two categories of armed conflict; second, were the States initially in favor of different restraints in both the armed conflict situations; third, how did France and United Kingdom ensure that only a limited number of rules would apply to non-international armed conflicts, and fourth, how are the different rules for both these categories of armed conflicts problematic and how do they demonstrate the façade of a "humanitarian" law. Subsequently, the chapter tries to argue that the difference in the rules makes it unavoidable to classify an armed conflict, and this exercise often gets very complex. The complexity involved in the classification delays the operation of the law and enforcement of whatever protection it makes available.

Keywords

Rules of IHL · Common Article 3 · History of Geneva Conventions · Internationalized conflicts

8.1 Introduction

In the historical context, common Article 3 is seen as an innovation and a radical[1] step in the regulation of internal conflicts by international law. It paved the way for constituting an international legal framework providing for humanitarian restraints in the conduct of non-international armed conflicts. It is believed that the demonstration of wholesale death and destruction in the Spanish Civil War (1936–1939) was decisive in the origin of the idea of international legal regulation of non-international armed conflicts.[2] Subsequently, common Article 3 was supplemented by the Additional Protocol II in 1977. There has also emerged a considerable body of international customary rules applicable in such conflict situations. Notably, the legal architecture applicable in international and non-international armed conflicts is contained in separate provisions (common Article 3) or instruments (Protocol II). In other words, the rules regulating the hostile conduct are not same but different in both the categories of armed conflicts. This difference in the legal regimes is of course not without consequences.

[1] Mantilla (2017, p. 495).

[2] Ibid., p. 494.

K. Jeenger, *A Humanitarian Critique of International Humanitarian Law*,
Sustainable Development Goals Series, https://doi.org/10.1007/978-981-96-8319-2_8

At present, for the application of relevant rules of laws of armed conflict (international humanitarian law), it is important and inevitable to determine the nature or character of the armed conflict. This is so not just because the international law recognizes two distinct categories of armed conflicts, but also because the law operating in international and non-international armed conflicts is different. Accordingly, as soon as the conditions prescribed for international or non-international armed conflicts are met, the concerned legal regime starts operating automatically.

In order to talk about the adoption of discriminatory rules and its consequences, this chapter is divided into two parts. In the first part, I try to investigate how despite the draft requiring uniform humanitarian rules for international and non-international armed conflicts, a common Article with limited rules in respect of non-international armed conflicts was adopted. In doing so, I try to emphasize that originally, States did not intend to have so few rules in the form of common Article 3.

The second part is premised on the aspect that it is because of different rules that classification of an armed conflict becomes inevitable. The classification is a very complicated exercise given the various variables affecting the categorization. Consequently, it further adversely affects the protection of victims and fixing of responsibility for violations.

8.2 Did States Really Want Different Rules for Different Armed Conflicts?

It is worth investigating why two different sets of humanitarian rules have been prescribed while the event to be regulated by them is fundamentally one and the same, and the intention is to regulate the conduct of military operations. It is true that international law recognizes two separate categories namely, war (between States) and belligerency. However, the idea that both the conflict situations should be regulated by different sets of humanitarian rules is a post-World War II innovation which was accomplished during the drafting of the four Geneva Conventions in 1949.

In the Preliminary Conference (1946), two new expressions were suggested in respect of armed conflict situations other than the international ones: "armed conflict within the borders of a State" and "civil war." The former phrase was proposed to expand the applicability of the 1929 Geneva Convention on the wounded and sick in armies in the field. The Commission nominated by the Preliminary Conference for the study of the revision of the 1929 Geneva Convention recommended the insertion of the following new article to the 1929 Convention:

> The present Convention is applicable between the High Contracting Parties from the moment hostilities have actually broken out, even if no declaration of war has been made and whatever the form that such armed intervention may take.
>
> In the case of armed conflict within the borders of a State, the Convention shall also be applied by each of the adverse parties, unless one of them announces expressly its intention to the contrary.[3]

On the other hand, the expression "civil wars" was proposed in order to enlarge the scope of the 1929 Geneva Convention on prisoners of war,[4] and thereby to extend the protection available under the Convention in case of civil wars also. The Commission observed that the provisions of the Convention must be applied in principle in case of civil war.[5] Originally, these two Conventions of 1929 applied to inter-State wars only. Interestingly, however, the Preliminary Conference of 1946 recommended extension of the Convention to internal conflicts but subject to reciprocity, leaving the humanitarian question in such wars under uncertainty.[6] But, the International Committee of the Red Cross (ICRC) disclosed a different plan in the next year in Stockholm. In its XVIIth conference in the year 1948, it decided to

[3] Report on the Work of the Preliminary Conference of National Red Cross Societies for the Study of the Conventions and of Various Problems Relative to the Red Cross, Geneva, July 26–August 3, 1946, pp. 14–15.

[4] Ibid., p. 70.

[5] Ibid.

[6] Ibid., p. 15.

float four draft Conventions on different subjects for deliberations.

Paragraphs 3 and 4 of Article 2 common to the ICRC draft Conventions read as:

> Should one of the Powers in conflict not be party to the present Convention, the Powers who are party thereto shall, nevertheless, be bound by it in their mutual relations.
>
> In all cases of armed conflict which are not of an international character, especially cases of civil war, colonial conflicts, or wars of religion, which may occur in the territory of one or more of the High Contracting Parties, the implementing of the principles of the present Convention shall be obligatory on each of the adversaries. The application of the Convention in these circumstances shall in nowise depend on the legal status of the parties to the conflict and shall have no effect on that status.[7]

Moreover, a unique but often overlooked feature of this draft clause was that it sought to apply to a non-international armed conflict not just few rules, but the "principles of the Convention", an expression though vague but broader than the text adopted in the form of common Article 3 in respect of non-international armed conflicts. At the insistence of the United States and other Western delegations, the paragraph removing reciprocity had to be compromised with at Stockholm. In non-international armed conflicts, the application of the Conventions relative to the treatment of prisoners of war and protection of civilians was made subject to reciprocity by adding the words "subject to the adverse Party likewise acting in adherence thereto" in the fourth paragraph of Article 2 of the two draft Conventions.[8] The modified draft of the fourth paragraph to be subjected to debate in the Diplomatic Conference in the next year was as follows:

> In all cases of armed conflict not of an international character which may occur in the territory of one or more of the High Contracting Parties, each of the Parties to the conflict shall be bound to implement the provisions of the present Convention, subject to the adverse Party likewise acting in adherence thereto. The Convention shall be applicable in those circumstances, whatever the legal status of the Parties to the conflict and without prejudice thereto.[9]

This proposal has been understood as radical in the present context and the main reason behind heated debates in the Diplomatic Conference, the next year.[10] The discussions in the 1949 Diplomatic Conference started on these lines.[11] During the preliminary consideration of the above draft in the Joint Committee of the Diplomatic Conference, no delegate opposed the full application of the Conventions to non-international armed conflicts.[12] However, many of them (including France, the United States, Spain, China and Canada) wanted it to apply to high-scale civil wars or belligerencies only. On the other side, some States (the erstwhile Soviet Union, Mexico, Denmark, Hungary, Romania and Norway) wanted the full application of the Geneva Conventions to such conflicts notwithstanding the scale of hostilities.[13]

The next round of discussions happened before the Special Committee of the Joint Committee.[14] The Chairman of the Committee classified the developments so far and reduced them into following three questions so that the committee may offer its views on the debatable issues:

> (1) Should the Conventions be extended to cases of armed conflict which were not of an international character?
> (2) Would it be appropriate to define more clearly than was the case in the Stockholm text the cases of armed conflict which were not of an international character?
> (3) Which of the following criteria should be adopted: formal criteria, factual criteria or a combination of formal and factual criteria?[15]

---

[7] XVIIth International Red Cross Conference, Stockholm (1948), Draft Revised or New Conventions for the Protection of war Victims (1948, pp. 5, 52, 153).

[8] Final Records of the Diplomatic Conference of Geneva of 1949, vol I, pp. 73, 113.

[9] Ibid., pp. 47, 61, 73, 113.

[10] Zamir (2017, p. 28).

[11] See Final Records (1949), above n 8, vol II Section B, pp. 10–15.

[12] Ibid., pp. 10–15.

[13] Ibid.

[14] See also, Chapter 7.

[15] Final Records (1949), above n 8, vol II Section B, p. 44.

Subsequently, the Committee voted for two important decisions. First, the Committee members decided to detach the fourth paragraph from the Stockholm draft by a majority of ten votes to one, with one abstention.[16] Importantly, it was done not because the draft fourth paragraph provided for full application of the Conventions to non-international armed conflicts but because the Committee wanted to define more clearly the situation of non-international armed conflict.[17] Remarkably, the Committee also decided by ten votes to one, with one abstention in favor of full application of the Conventions to non-international armed conflicts.[18] Given the number of votes in favor, it is clear that up to this stage States were inclined to regulating the non-international conflicts by the Conventions in entirety. So far there was no proposal of selective or partial application of the humanitarian rules to such conflicts.

After rejecting the Stockholm draft, the first Working Party of the Special Committee submitted a new draft proposal specifying the conditions of a high-scale non-international armed conflicts (such as recognition of status of belligerency, organized military force and civil authority) and requiring full application of the Conventions.[19] It is this moment, when the advanced European States objected. France first of all reaffirmed the need to "humanize" all types of armed conflicts.[20] Subsequently, the French delegate Lamarle opposed that it was not possible to extend automatically all the clauses of the Conventions to the internal conflicts, especially the Convention on civilians.[21] The United Kingdom "strongly supported the remarks"[22] made by the French delegate. These two States had already influenced the drafting of the paragraphs at Stockholm by requiring deletion of some words. Subsequently, they sought to oppose the application of the Conventions as a whole. Obviously, they were looking for a less-threatening alternative in respect of internal conflicts.

Subsequently, the Working Party submitted a new draft at the request of the Chairman of Special Committee.[23] The new draft Article 2A stated that the provisions of the Civilian Convention could apply wholly or partly to a non-international armed conflict provided that the Parties to the conflict enter into a special agreement.[24] The underlying humanitarian principles of the Convention were nevertheless proposed to be applicable. In respect of the other three Conventions, the draft provided that they may apply to non-international armed conflicts, subject to the recognition of belligerency or State-like features of the non-State group.[25]

8.3 A Manipulative Shift

Before the Special Committee, France proposed an amendment to the draft which found favor from other representatives also. Surprisingly, in order to restart the entire process, a Second Working Party under the chairmanship of France was constituted.[26] It submitted a new proposal. It proved to be nothing but an exercise of calculated cooperative manipulation. The France-led Working Party reduced into writing its intentions in the draft. It contained few rules for the protection of the victims of non-international armed conflicts, instead of extending all four Conventions.[27] Thus, while international armed conflicts were proposed to be governed by four Conventions, the powerful European nations offered in respect of non-international armed conflicts only one article containing handful of rules. It happened despite

[16] Ibid., p. 45.

[17] Ibid.

[18] Ibid.

[19] Ibid., pp. 46–47.

[20] Ibid., p. 47.

[21] Ibid.

[22] Ibid.

[23] Ibid., pp. 48, 76.

[24] Ibid., p. 77.

[25] Ibid.

[26] Ibid., p. 79.

[27] See also Chapter 7.

the fact that the major and common objections towards the fourth paragraph of the Stockholm draft were not related to the size of humanitarian obligations, but to the scale of civil war, combatant privileges of the insurgents and provisions related to Protecting Powers. These anxieties could have been conveniently addressed consistent with ensuring maximum application of the four Conventions. For instance, the Soviet Union delegation clarified before the Special Committee that the Stockholm draft did not take away a State's power to control rebellion or insurgency.[28] The worries expressed by the States were very specific and limited to few provisions only. However, the France-led Working Party used these concerns as a pretext to deny the application of a large number of provisions to non-international armed conflicts. Notably, the rest of the provisions of the respective Conventions were proposed to be applicable only if parties enter into a special agreement to this effect.[29]

Quite contrast to the French draft, the Soviet delegate presented a draft having separate applicability clauses for each Convention ensuring their maximum application to non-international armed conflicts.[30] The Special Committee forwarded all the three drafts to the Joint Committee which approved the French draft to be placed before the Plenary Assembly because the draft happened to secure more votes in its favor.[31] The number of votes has special significance here. While 21 delegates voted in favor of the French draft, 6 were against it and 14 abstained. Thus, it appears that while six representatives expressly disliked the draft, fourteen were perhaps skeptical about the same or unwilling to reveal their dissent. Often, abstention becomes an exercise of conscious political choice of not supporting a motion and, at the same time, of deliberately refraining from disclosing the decision for political reasons.

The delegations in the Plenary Assembly were completely divided over the draft they would prefer. The Mexican delegate wanted colonial as well as civil wars to be regulated by the Conventions as a whole. Therefore, he admired the paragraph 4 of the Stockholm draft which was originally introduced before the Joint Committee.[32] The Mexican delegate stated that:

> The aim of the Mexican Delegation is to ensure that in all non-international wars of whatever character, whether civil wars, wars of resistance or wars of liberation, the right of the stronger and the *lex talionis* (law of retaliation) shall not prevail, and that methods disregarding all humanitarian considerations and the fundamental rights of man should be prohibited … I firmly believe that brutal repression always leads to a reaction, generally stronger than the original movement … If we adhere to the original idea of Stockholm, it is only in the interests of justice and humanity.[33]

The erstwhile Soviet Union, on the other hand, made an important observation, which perhaps went unnoticed, that the maximum application of the four Conventions had been supported by "the overwhelming majority of the delegations present in this Conference."[34] It also warned the delegates that the French draft was intended to replace the Conventions in their application to conflicts of non-international character.[35] Re-emphasizing the maximum application of the Conventions, the Soviet delegate said:

> I should be very glad if the supporters of Article 2 would explain why, in the case of conflicts of a non-international character, it would be impossible to apply the provisions of the Wounded and Sick Convention or those of the Civilians Convention, which stipulate, for instance, that civilian hospitals may in no circumstances be attacked, and that women and children shall at all times enjoy particular respect and protection, that, in order to bring relief to the civilian population, the unrestricted transport and distribution of various shipments, such as medicines and medical equipment, shall be guaranteed.[36]

[28] Final Records (1949), above n 8, vol II Section B, p. 43.

[29] Ibid., p. 83.

[30] Ibid., pp. 97–98.

[31] Ibid., p. 37.

[32] Ibid., p. 333.

[33] Ibid.

[34] Ibid., p. 326.

[35] Ibid.

[36] Ibid. In 1912, when the ICRC proposed to allow National Societies of the Red Cross to provide humanitarian assistance to both sides during civil war and insurgencies, the Russian representative opposed the move saying that Russian laws treat them as criminals and the ICRC should have no duties towards them: Zamir (2017, pp. 24–25).

Thus, the erstwhile Soviet Union vehemently supported the humanitarian cause. The Soviet delegation was "most consequential"[37] of all the sympathizers of full application the Conventions to non-international armed conflict. It was observed that the Soviet delegates grilled the skeptical delegation from the Western colonialist States for their conservatism.[38]

Moving further, it became evident that States like Mexico and Venezuela wanted to revert back to the Stockholm Draft, and, on the similar vein, Romania and Czechoslovakia supported the Soviet draft.[39] It is evident that maximum (if not complete) application of the Conventions to non-international armed conflicts was consistent with the humanitarian purpose of the law, and States were also willing to lend their support to this idea. However, the draft suggested by the France-led Working Party ruptured their humanitarian aspirations as it was a proposal politically more convenient and at the same time "humanitarian" on its face.

The Swiss delegation justified the French draft by saying "half a loaf is better than no bread."[40] Surprisingly, he called the draft as the "only possible balance" between the Mexican idealism and Burmese realism. Notably, the Burmese delegation (representing the Asiatic nations) vehemently opposed the full application of the Conventions to civil wars before the Special Committee[41] and also the compromise formula of the French draft in the plenary meetings.[42] In respect of the French draft, the Burmese delegate had declared very clearly that no compromise would meet the situation.[43] He called the draft as a violation of the United Nations Charter principle of non-intervention and an incentive to armed conflicts.[44] Thus, he strongly recommended complete deletion of the proposed draft.[45]

In the fog of the Swiss narrative of compromise, it must not be lost sight of that, in the end, the compromise was with the humanitarian restraints in civil and anti-colonial wars, and not with the imperial motives. The compromise blurred the continuation of economic and political domination by the West and the adoption of fewer restraints in respect of non-international armed conflicts. It is evident from their strategic negotiations. First, they ensured at the very beginning that the scope of the new category (armed conflicts not of an international character) remained vague by deleting some illustrating words (civil war, colonial conflicts, or wars of religion) from the Stockholm draft (see Chapter 7). Afterward, in the Diplomatic Conference they endorsed a draft containing minimum humanitarian rules. These maneuvers were driven by the inherent "logic of territory"[46] (imperialism), "logic of culture" (ideas and ideology that shapes perspectives)[47] and "logic of capital"[48] (universalizing capitalism).

Their core intentions as reflected in the draft were problematic otherwise also. The delegates of the countries who had colonized major part of the world and committed crimes on the poor people depriving them of their dignity, human existence, resources, fair trial and what not, and who would continue to do the same in the subsequent years (for instance, France in Algeria), authored a clause emphasizing upon the "judicial guarantees recognized by civilized peoples", an expression attributed to them. The clause prohibits:

> the passing of sentences and the carrying out of executions without previous judgment pronounced by a regularly constituted court, affording all the

However, post the Russian Revolution, 1917, the ICRC successfully passed the resolution. Zamir argues that probably the experiences of the Revolution helped in the adoption of the resolution.

37 Mantilla (2017, p. 495).

38 Ibid.

39 Final Records (1949), above n 8, vol II Section B, pp. 331–334.

40 Ibid., p. 335.

41 Ibid., p. 102.

42 Ibid., p. 328.

43 Ibid.

44 Ibid., pp. 329, 330.

45 Ibid., p. 330. For more details on Burmese position, see Chapter 7.

46 Chimni (2017, p. 34).

47 Ibid., p. 35.

48 Ibid., p. 32.

> judicial guarantees which are recognized as indispensable by civilized peoples.[49]

It displays the racial logic of civilized-uncivilized and a boastful but dichotomous proposition.

Another annoying aspect of the drafting exercise was the role of the ICRC. The ICRC representative confessed in the Diplomatic Conference that the Committee was aware that its original proposal or the amended Stockholm version had no chance of being accepted by the Governments and that a compromise should be arrived at.[50] Given the fact that the Committee was mindful of an unworkable draft, the portrayal of its own humanitarian face by presenting the draft again raises doubts on its mode of operation and confirms domination of "white humanitarians."[51] Overall, it failed to put forward a strong case for a controlled behavior in internal wars and protection of victims. It has been observed that the ICRC rejected the texts which were far-reaching and radically expanding in nature.[52]

In the end, the draft article 2A as placed before the Plenary Assembly was adopted by 34 votes to 12 with one abstention,[53] and took the shape of Article 3 common to all the four Geneva Conventions.[54] It was understood as "a short bill of right for war victims."[55] In its Commentary to the Geneva Conventions, the ICRC explained that States were reluctant to adopt the same rules for both the types of armed conflicts because it might confer upon the insurgents the status of belligerents, provide them legal recognition, motivate ordinary criminals to engage in similar acts and compel the territorial government to release the captured rebels.[56]

The application and adequacy of common Article 3 soon underwent a severe scrutiny because majority of the armed conflicts that occurred subsequently were non-international in character. According to a study, 42 armed conflicts not of an international character occurred during the period 1945–1970 nearly in each of the continents.[57] In majority of the cases, States preferred to quell the rebellion by their criminal laws,[58] and wherever common article 3 obligations were accepted, its rules were found to be inadequate. The ICRC confessed this in its report on the XXIst International Conference:

> It has become clear to the ICRC, from its experience, that the existing provisions fail to meet all the humanitarian requirements of such conflicts. Article 3 common to the four Geneva Conventions especially, valuable as it has already proved to the ICRC, has in practice revealed inadequacies.[59]

Thus, the inadequacy of common Article 3 in anti-colonial and internal wars soon came to the fore. Its non-observance in such wars was almost a universal phenomenon.[60] The law was disrespected during, for instance, wars in Southern Africa, Vietnam, Nigeria, and the Middle East.[61] Colonial powers tortured the detained freedom fighters and executed many of them. It is noteworthy that the Diplomatic Conference of 1949 had passed a Resolution stating that its earnest hope is that Governments may never have to apply the Geneva Conventions for the Protection of war

[49] At present, Art. 3(1)(d).

[50] Final Records (1949), above n 8, vol II Section B, pp. 336–337.

[51] Expression used by, Dijk (2021, p. 248).

[52] Ibid., p. 277.

[53] Final Records (1949), above n 8, vol II Section B, p. 339.

[54] Subsequent to the adoption, a British delegate opined that the provision "would make it more difficult to deal promptly and effectively with rebellion". On the other hand, the Americans viewed the text as unilateral gesture of States that, in its failure to credibly commit rebels, was likely to break down in the heat of violence. Notably, the UK signed the four Conventions after four months of their adoption, while the US signed the first three Geneva Convention on their adoption (8 August 1949) but delayed the signature on the Convention on Civilians until December. See Mantilla (2017, pp. 496–497).

[55] Nirmal (1988, p. 203).

[56] Pictet (1952).

[57] Crawford (2014, p. 102).

[58] Bond, cited in Forsythe (1978, p. 276).

[59] XXIst International Conference of the Red Cross (1969), Report on Reaffirmation and Development of Law and Customs Applicable in Armed Conflict (1969). ICRC, Geneva, p. 98.

[60] Nirmal (1988, p. 203).

[61] Davey (2020, p. 379).

victims in the future.[62] Contrary to that, there arose several occasions to apply them, and the States largely disregarded them.

Gradually, the lack of enough legal protection in wars of national liberation and internal wars began to be seen as a human right issue as well. With the adoption of the United Nations Charter, the introduction of human rights discourse on the international platform grabbed the attention of former colonies and other nations from the Third World, as they had suffered from gross human rights violations during colonial era. They united themselves and contributed to the promotion of respect for the human rights of the Third World. It was observed that they dominated the United Nations' human rights agenda.[63] De-Westernization of the laws of armed conflict and inclusiveness formed part of their main agenda.[64] More significantly, they strongly pursued before the United Nations for the right to self-determination of the poor peoples under foreign rule.

Consequently, they gained plenty of theoretical support of the international community at the United Nations. The General Assembly resolutions of 1960s and 1970s gave voice to their firm beliefs. These resolutions *inter alia* laid down that all peoples have right to self-determination and complete independence[65]; immediate steps must be taken to decolonize the colonies[66]; struggles by the peoples under colonial rule to exercise their right to self-determination and independence are legitimate[67]; initiatives must be taken to ensure application of humanitarian law in all armed conflicts[68]; the Secretary General of the United Nations, in consultation with the ICRC and other international organizations, was to consider initiatives to secure the application of humanitarian law in all armed conflicts[69]; it is necessary to apply basic humanitarian principles to all armed conflicts[70]; the territory of a colony or other Non-Self-Governing Territory enjoys a status separate from the administering State[71]; and anti-colonial armed conflicts are to be treated as international armed conflicts within the meaning of the Geneva Conventions of 1949.[72]

The underlying idea of many of the resolutions was that wars of national liberation were just wars.[73]

Subsequently, the drafting exercise of Additional Protocols of 1977 emerged as an occasion to remove the discrimination in the rules applicable to international and non-international armed conflicts. The discussion began on this idea in the very first conference of the preparatory work, the Conference of Government Experts, 1971. The experts were divided on the question of uniform rules, and, on the other hand, the suggestion to prescribe some criteria for non-international armed conflicts was also under consideration.[74] In this state of indecisiveness, the ICRC submitted a separate draft protocol (ultimately leading to Protocol II) seeking to supplement common Article 3, yet with less number of

62 Resolution VIII, Final Records (1949), above n 8, vol I, p. 362.

63 Davey (2020, p. 379).

64 Mégret (2006, p. 295).

65 Declaration on the Granting of Independence to Colonial Countries and Peoples, A/RES/1514 (1960).

66 Ibid.

67 Implementation of the Declaration on the Granting of Independence to Colonial Countries and Peoples, A/RES/2105 (1965) and Declaration on Principles of International Law Concerning Friendly Relations and Co-operation among States in accordance with the Charter of the United Nations, A/RES/2625 (1970).

68 Resolution XXIII, Human Rights in Armed Conflicts, Final Act of the International Conference on Human Rights, Teheran (1968). United Nations, New York, p. 18.

69 Respect for Human Rights in Armed Conflict, A/RES/2444 (1968). See also, ibid.

70 Respect for Human Rights in Armed Conflict, A/RES/2444 (1968) and Basic Principles of the Legal Status of the Combatants Struggling Against Colonial and Alien Domination and Racist Regimes, A/RES/3103 (1973).

71 Declaration on Friendly Relations, above n 67.

72 Basic Principles of the Legal Status of the Combatants Struggling Against Colonial and Alien Domination and Racist Regimes, A/RES/3103 (1973).

73 Nirmal (1988, pp. 204–205).

74 Sandoz (1987, para 4376).

rules as compared to those applicable in international armed conflicts.[75] It once again resulted into discriminatory rules in both the types of armed conflicts. Notably, four Conventions of 1949, excepting common Article 3, and Protocol I were adopted in respect of international armed conflicts.

8.4 Why Two Categories and Two Sets of Laws

In 1940s, when the ICRC proposed the extension of the laws of armed conflict to non-international armed conflicts, there was no plan to have separate rules for both the conflicts. However, this very recognition of two kinds of armed conflicts and the drawing of boundaries in terms of international and non-international armed conflicts facilitated the exclusion of many humanitarian rules from their application to non-international armed conflicts. Discrimination and exclusion often result from drawing of boundaries irrespective of their contexts. The inherent character of fencing and division is that they promote debates which further reinforce and intensify the boundaries and categorization. For instance, the debate around the principles of "effective control and overall control"[76] carried out by the ICTY reinforces the classification of armed conflicts.[77] To put it differently, in *Tadić*[78] the ICTY delved into the suitability of the effective control test, propounded by the International Court of Justice (ICJ),[79] with the sole purpose of applying the same in classifying an armed conflict. This adventurism further solidifies the idea of categorizing armed conflicts, instead of discouraging it.

The classification of armed conflicts ultimately decides the invocation of the relevant law. The ICTY has brilliantly questioned the humanitarian discrimination caused by the recognition of two types armed conflicts:

> Gradually the maxim of Roman law *hominum causa omne jus constitutum est* (all law is created for the benefit of human beings) has gained a firm foothold in the international community as well. It follows that in the area of armed conflict the distinction between interstate wars and civil wars is losing its value as far as human beings are concerned. Why protect civilians from belligerent violence, or ban rape, torture or the wanton destruction of hospitals, churches, museums or private property, as well as proscribe weapons causing unnecessary suffering when two sovereign States are engaged in war, and yet refrain from enacting the same bans or providing the same protection when armed violence has erupted "only" within the territory of a sovereign State? If international law, while of course duly safeguarding the legitimate interests of States, must gradually turn to the protection of human beings, it is only natural that the aforementioned dichotomy should gradually lose its weight.[80]

Thus, from a humanitarian point of view, abolishing the classification and prescribing one set of rules in respect of an armed conflict might help in the better protection of the victims of war and mitigation of suffering.

8.5 Different Rules, Classification and Complexity

As and when an armed conflict occurs, the conflict situation has to be identified and classified as international or non-international armed conflict so as to trigger the relevant law. Difference in the laws applicable in both the situations is a major reason why such a classification has to be done

[75] Conference of Government Experts on the Reaffirmation and Development of International Humanitarian Law Applicable in Armed Conflicts, Second Session, 3 May–3 June 1972, Report on the Work of the Conference, vol I (ICRC, Geneva, 1972), p. 3.

[76] As laid down by the International Court of Justice in Case Concerning Military and Paramilitary Activities in and against Nicaragua (Nicaragua v. United States of America) (1986) ICJ Rep 14.

[77] This argument was developed in conversation with my friend Haris Jamil, a Ph.D. candidate at Melbourne University. See also, Jamil (2016–2017, pp. 185–211).

[78] Prosecutor v. Dusko Tadić, IT-94–1-A, Appeals Chamber, Judgment, 15 July 1999, para 120.

[79] International Court of Justice in Nicaragua v. United States of America, above n 76, para 115.

[80] Prosecutor v. Dusko Tadić, IT-94-1-AR72, Appeals Chamber, Judgment on the Defence Motion for Interlocutory Appeal on Jurisdiction, 2 October 1995, para 97.

without delay. It is only after the classification of armed conflict, the rules of conduct of war and the legal protection to the victims become applicable. However, the categorization of the conflict is not so straightforward always.[81] There is a significant divergence between armed conflicts in practice and armed conflicts as it is conceived in law.[82] Sometimes the state of conflict gets so complex that it becomes difficult to categorize the armed conflict into international or non-international. The classification of armed conflict and operation of the law are so interlinked that the difference in rules applicable in both the types of armed conflicts is felt as a huge challenge in case of complex conflict situation. It is the complicated state of hostilities when the difficulty in classification and the issue of different rules is realized the most, because the effects of war continue to trouble the innocent victims meanwhile.

This complexity may be explained with the help of the Nicaragua conflict in 1980s. When the United States intervened in the Nicaragua's internal conflict and supported the revolutionary armed groups against Nicaraguan government, the following questions arose: Did the status of conflict not change? Did the ongoing non-international armed conflict transform into an international armed conflict? Were there two simultaneous conflicts going on: first, an international armed conflict between the United States and Nicaragua; and second, a non-international armed conflict between Nicaragua and *contras* armed rebel group?

The laws of armed conflict are silent on these issues as explained below. Between the binary of international and non-international armed conflicts, there are situations which do not fit in any of the two categories so easily. Thus, while the idea of discriminatory rules in international and non-international armed conflicts is problematic from a humanitarian standpoint, in some situations another challenging side of it gets exposed at the outbreak of hostilities. Such situations and simultaneous application of different rules are exemplified below.

[81] Moir (2014, p. 76).

[82] Hill-Cawthorne (2016, p. 20).

8.5.1 Foreign Intervention

8.5.1.1 Foreign Support to a Territorial State

When a foreign State provides military support to a territorial State on its request in an ongoing non-international armed conflict against a non-State actor, the status of the conflict does not change because, at least one party to conflict is not a State. For instance, Uganda provided military forces in Congo civil war in 1997. Another view says that such foreign intervention internationalizes the whole conflict, and the law governing international armed conflict becomes applicable.[83] Such a suggestion of internationalization was made by the Security Council in respect of hostilities in the former Yugoslavia.[84] Similarly, the ICRC made such a proposal in the Conference of Government Experts in 1971 but it was rejected on the ground that it would encourage the armed group to get foreign assistance.[85] Actually, the humanitarian law applicable in international armed conflict should apply only when two States actually fight.[86] However, when a foreign State attacks the armed group in the territorial State without its request or consent, it is violation of paragraphs (4) and (7) of Article 2 of the United Nations Charter, and Article 3(2) of Additional Protocol II. In such a case, if the territorial State chooses to resist the armed foreign intervention forcefully, it amounts to an international armed conflict, and two simultaneous armed conflicts, international as well as non-international, begin in the territorial State, which are governed by different legal regimes.[87] It is not difficult to comprehend how problematic in such a situation it is to ensure compliance of separate rules and

[83] ICRC (2016, para 403, n. 92–93).

[84] United Nations Security Council, Interim Report of the Commission of Experts Established Pursuant to Security Council Resolution 780 (1992), UN Doc S/25274, 10 February 1993, Annex 1, para 45.

[85] Report of the Conference of Government Experts of 1971, pp. 50–52. See also, Moir (2014, p. 79, n. 32).

[86] Moir (2014, p. 80).

[87] Some authors call the entire conflict situation as internationalized armed conflict: Schindler (1982, p. 255) and Stewart (2003, p. 314).

identify violations to fix the State and individual responsibility.

8.5.1.2 Foreign Support to Non-State Actor

During an ongoing non-international armed conflict, where a foreign State provides military support to the armed group, it amounts to active and direct support. For example, Pakistan sent thousands of regular soldiers and militants to support Taliban in the Afghan civil war (1996–2001). In such cases, besides the civil war, an inter-State conflict between the armed forces of territorial and foreign State also starts simultaneously. Thus, the territorial State goes through two conflicts together: international armed conflict and non-international armed conflict. This is also referred to "double classification"[88] as per the "theory of pairings."[89] In the Nicaragua Civil War, the ICJ found that the United States authorities provided the armed group *contras* logistic support and sophisticated information.[90] They largely financed, trained, equipped, armed and organized the FDN (Nicaraguan Democratic Forces).[91] Therefore, the Court observed that the conflict situation comprises of two different armed conflicts:

> The conflict between the *contras*' forces and those of the Government of Nicaragua is an armed conflict which is "not of an international character". The acts of the *contras* towards the Nicaraguan Government are therefore governed by the law applicable to conflicts of that character; whereas the actions of the United States in and against Nicaragua fall under the legal rules relating to international conflicts.[92]

However, where facts of such a conflict situation demonstrate that the actions of the armed group and the foreign State are closely related and coordinated, the entire conflict becomes international in character.[93] A trial chamber of the International Criminal Tribunal of the Former Yugoslavia (ICTY) further clarifies that the facts, such as significant and continuous military action by the intervening State supporting the armed group, intervening State's political and military control over the armed group, and agency relationship between the intervening State and the armed group, are sufficient to convert a domestic conflict into an international one.[94] This kind of complete transformation of the ongoing conflict is treated as "internationalization"[95] of a non-international armed conflict and the converted form of armed conflict is termed as "internationalized armed conflict."[96] International law does not recognize such a term. Thus, where the actions of the intervening foreign State and that of the armed group can be easily differentiated, the ongoing non-international armed conflict is not said to be internationalized, instead, two parallel conflicts go on.[97] The ICTY has also carefully mentioned the situations when a non-international armed conflict can turn into an international conflict entirely, without diluting the likelihood of two simultaneous conflicts:

> in case of an internal armed conflict breaking out on the territory of a State, it may become international (or, depending upon the circumstances, be international in character alongside an internal armed conflict) if (i) another State intervenes in that conflict through its troops, or alternatively if (ii) some of the participants in the internal armed conflict act on behalf of that other State.[98]

It is a trickier situation for ensuring observance of different laws in different situations.

---

[88] Melzer (2016, p. 74).

[89] Sivakumaran (2012, p. 223).

[90] Nicaragua v. United States of America, above n 76, para 106.

[91] Ibid., para 108.

[92] Ibid., para 219.

[93] Sivakumaran (2012, pp. 223–224).

[94] Prosecutor v. Rajić and Andrić, IT-95-12, Trial Chamber, Review of the Indictment pursuant to Rule 61 of the Rules of Procedure and Evidence, 13 September 1996, paras 13, 22, 23 respectively.

[95] ICRC (2016, n. 92).

[96] The term was used for the first time, perhaps, by Dietrich Schindler in: Schindler (1982, p. 255). An ICTY Trial Chamber also used the term for the first time in: Prosecutor v. Dusko Tadić, IT-94-1-T, Trial Chamber, Separate opinion of judge McDonald, 7 May 1997.

[97] However, many authors call it internationalisation of conflict as soon as a foreign State intervenes to support the armed group without following the differentiation approach. See, Crawford and Pert (2015, p. 73) and Vité (2009, p. 80).

[98] Tadić, above n 78, para 84.

8.5.2 Cross-Border Conflicts

Besides foreign intervention, extra-territorial use of force during a non-international armed conflict may also complicate the correct classification of the conflict and consequently the determination of the law applicable. Here, it is the use of force from across the border which affects the classification. It may happen in the following ways as illustrated below.

8.5.2.1 Armed Group Exclusively Based Within the Territorial State

During a non-international armed conflict against an armed group based within the territory, the forces of the territorial State may have to pursue the armed group beyond the territorial boundaries if its members cross the international frontier. If the hostilities between the forces of the territorial State and the armed group spill over and continue on foreign land as well, the conflict remains a non-international armed conflict, provided the fighting on the foreign land is "closely related"[99] to that in the territorial State. As the ICRC considers, the humanitarian law applicable to a conflict is determined on the basis of the parties to the conflict instead of the territory where the conflict takes place.[100] At times, however, the conventional criteria of classification appear to be inappropriate and inadequate to categorize such situations.[101]

Where the foreign State does not approve of hostilities of any kind on its land and uses force to resist or where the forces of the territorial State target the military or civilians of the foreign State, or the public or private property situated in the foreign State, it constitutes an international armed conflict and triggers the relevant humanitarian law.

8.5.2.2 Armed Group Partially Based in Both Territorial State and Foreign State

An armed conflict within the territorial State against an armed group having its bases in both territorial as well as foreign State is undoubtedly a non-international armed conflict. But, where the territorial State has to chase the armed group across the border, the status of the conflict shall be determined as explained in the preceding example.

8.5.2.3 Armed Group Exclusively Based Within the Foreign State

Where an armed group is solely based in the foreign State, and engages in armed conflict with territorial State, it is a non-international armed conflict irrespective of the fact that hostilities take place within the territorial State or foreign State. On the other hand, if the foreign State uses force against the territorial State to resist, it is again a situation of two separate conflicts: one non-international and the other international. However, where the armed group actually acts as its agent, it is an international armed conflict in its entirety. Some commentators prefer to call such conflicts transnational, extra-State or extra-territorial armed conflicts.[102]

Israel-Hezbollah Conflict in Lebanon, 2006

This conflict is an interesting example on characterization of transnational conflicts. Hezbollah was a Lebanon-based armed group as well as political party representing in Lebanese Parliament. A border attack initiated by Hezbollah resulted into killing of eight Israel Defense Forces (IDF) soldiers and capturing of two. Israel retorted by launching "disproportionate"[103] attacks on Lebanon targeting Hezbollah, civilians and Lebanese infrastructure.

Classification of the Conflict by UNHRC The Commission of Inquiry formed by the UN Human Rights Council categorized the whole situation as

[99] Tadić, above n 80, para 70.

[100] Vité (2009, p. 86).

[101] Moir (2014, p. 79).

[102] Crawford and Pert (2015, p. 73) and Vité (2009, p. 88).

[103] 5489th Meeting of the Security Council, 14 July 2006 (SC/8776).

an international armed conflict taking into account the facts that (1) Israel attacked Lebanese army, civilians and assets also, (2) Hezbollah constitutes a militia within the meaning of Article 4A(2) of the Third Geneva Convention of 1949, (3) temporary occupation of a foreign territory without meeting resistance is subject to the law of international armed conflict according to common Article 2, paragraph 2 of the four Geneva Conventions, (4) instead of Israeli armed forces, Hezbollah acts as resistance movement against Israeli occupation in South Lebanon whom the Israeli President regards as "national resistance fighters", and (5) Lebanese higher authorities including its Minister of Justice, accepted that Lebanon was a party to the conflict.[104] The Commission arrived at this conclusion despite considering that Lebanon did not participate in the hostilities actively, rather it approached the Security Council to take effective measures.[105]

Challenging the Classification However, treating the conflict as an international armed conflict is challenged on the ground, that Hezbollah is not militia because Article 4A(2) further requires the armed group to belong to a party to the conflict, which implies allegiance, dependence and control.[106] Whereas, Lebanon officially declared that it neither knew nor consented to the initial assault by Hezbollah. Such facts establish that Hezbollah did not act as an agent of Lebanon. Thus, the conflict between Israel and Hezbollah attracts common Article 3, while the attack on Lebanon is undoubtedly an international armed conflict.

This example illustrates not just the complexity in the process of characterization of armed conflict but likelihood of inaccuracy also. Again, while difference in rules necessitates this process, its results may be questionable and the applicable law may be arguable.

8.5.3 Political Changes

8.5.3.1 Regime Change Due to Armed Conflict

It is evident that when a foreign State intervenes to support a territorial State during a non-international armed conflict, the character of the conflict remains non-international. However, will the conflict status not change where the incumbent government is overthrown? To illustrate, the United States-led coalition forces invaded Iraq in March 2003 against the Saddam Husain's government, on the grounds that "Iraq possessed weapons of mass destruction, and it harbored Al-Qaeda militants."[107] It was a full-fledged international armed conflict. The Saddam government was toppled down in April 2003, and Coalition Provisional Authority was to act as a transitional government until the formation of democratic government.[108] The defeated forces reorganized and strengthened soon with the support of other such groups, and started intense insurgent-attacks from 2004 onwards against the incumbent government and occupying forces. This was a non-international armed conflict. Thus, change in regime sometimes converts an international armed conflict into non-international one.

The case of Afghanistan is more interesting because the conflict status changed twice due to change in the incumbent government. From September 1996 to October 2001, Taliban was engaged in a non-international armed conflict with the United Front (Northern Alliance). Ultimately, Taliban controlled over 90 percent area of Afghanistan and formed government. Following the 9/11 attacks, the United States invaded Afghanistan in October 2001 to raid the terrorist group Al-Qaeda. The incumbent Taliban government also became target of the United States army because of "providing shelter and support to the Al-Qaeda terrorists".[109] Thus, the ongoing non-international armed conflict converted into an international armed conflict. Eventually, the Taliban government collapsed, and in December

[104] Human Rights Council, Report of Commission of Inquiry on Lebanon pursuant to Human Rights Council Resolution S-2/1, A/HRC/3/2, 23 November 2006, paras 53, 57, 58, 59.

[105] Ibid., paras 53–55.

[106] Vité (2009, pp. 91–92).

[107] Richelson (2004).

[108] S/RES/1511 (2003).

[109] Dinstein (2014, p. 93).

2001, Afghan Interim Administration[110] was formed, followed by a duly elected Afghan government in 2004. From 2003 onwards, the Taliban waged insurgency against the incumbent Afghan government. The NATO-led coalition backed the government in intense counter-insurgency operations, especially during 2006–2009. Thus, once again a non-international armed conflict began in Afghanistan.

8.5.3.2 Recognition of State

An armed conflict causing fragmentation of a State (as in former Yugoslavia and Ethiopia) or an armed group coming into power by overthrowing the incumbent government (as in Afghanistan) may lead to a change in the status of armed conflict. For this purpose, is it necessary that the newly emerged political entity is recognized as State by the international community?

In the early 1990s, the Former Yugoslavia fragmented into several units, including Serbia, Croatia, Slovenia and Bosnia, and many States swiftly recognized the new entities. The European Union recognized Croatia and Slovenia on 15 January 1991, and Bosnia on 6 April 1992; while the United States recognized all the three units on 7 April, 1992, followed by the membership of the United Nations on 22 May 1992.[111] The international recognition probably made wider impact. In *Tadić*, a trial chamber of the ICTY classified as international armed conflict the hostilities between Bosnia and Herzegovina on one side and Federal Republic of Yugoslavia (Serbia and Montenegro) on the other that took place from the beginning of 1992 until 19 May 1992.[112] Similarly, in 1991 Eritreans got independence after rebelling against the incumbent government of Ethiopia, and in subsequent referendum held in April 1993, secured almost full majority in favor of independence. Therefore, in the next month, the United Nations admitted Eritrea to the membership of the organization unhesitatingly.[113] The consequent border disputes between both the States were treated as constituting an international armed conflict.[114]

However, when Taliban assumed power ousting the Afghan government in civil war, the Taliban government was recognized by three States only—Pakistan, Saudi Arabia and United Arab Emirates.[115] However, the United States' attack on Afghanistan in 2001 is classified as international armed conflict, perhaps because of the negligible recognition.[116]

Thus, it is apparent that with the change in the nature of armed conflicts during the last few decades, it has become difficult to determine the nature of an armed conflict. In some cases, opinions on classification also differ in the absence of precise guidelines. The aforesaid variety of events happening during an ongoing armed conflict exposes how problematic is the idea of prescribing two categories of armed conflict and corresponding separate bodies of rules. They hint towards the inherent complexity in classifying the armed conflicts and consequent regulatory gaps.

References

Aksar Y (2004) Implementing international humanitarian law: from the ad hoc tribunals to a permanent international criminal court. Routledge, Abingdon

Bjarnason M (2001) The war and war-games in Bosnia and Herzegovina from 1992 to 1995: the main events, disagreements and arguments, resulting in a "de facto" divided country. NATO, 2001. http://www.nato.int/acad/fellow/99-01/bjarnason.pdf

Chimni BS (2017) International law and world order: a critique of contemporary approaches. CUP, Cambridge

Crawford E (2014) Trapped: from inter-state and symmetric to intrastate and asymmetric: changing methods of warfare and the law of armed conflict in the

110 Agreement on Provisional Arrangements in Afghanistan Pending the Re-establishment of Permanent Government Institutions, at Bonn Conference, Germany (2001) and S/2001/1154 (5 December 2001).

111 A/RES/46/236 (Slovenia), 237 (Bosnia and Hezegovina) and 238 (Croatia), (1992). See Bjarnason (2001, p. 28).

112 Prosecutor v. Dusko Tadić, IT-94-1-T, Trial Chamber, Judgment, 7 May 1997, para 569.

113 A/RES/47/230 (1993).

114 Dinstein (2014, p. 57).

115 Mapping Militant Organisations (2022).

116 ICRC (2016) and Pejic (2011, p. 196).

100 years since world war one. Yearb Int Humltarian Law 17:95–118
Crawford E, Pert A (2015) International humanitarian law. CUP, Cambridge
Davey E (2020) Decolonizing the Geneva conventions: national liberation and the development of humanitarian law. In: Moses AD et al (eds) Decolonization, self-determination, and the rise of global human rights politics. CUP, Cambridge, pp 375–396
Dijk B (2021) Internationalizing colonial war: on the unintended consequences of the interventions of the International Committee of the Red Cross in South-East Asia, 1945–1949. Past & Present 250(1):243–283
Dinstein Y (2014) Non-international armed conflicts in international law. CUP, Cambridge
Forsythe DP (1978) Legal management of internal war: the 1977 protocol on non-international armed conflicts. Am J Int Law 72(2):272–295
Henckaerts JM (2005a) The ICRC study on customary international humanitarian law-an assessment. In: Maybee L, Chakka B (eds) Custom as a source of international humanitarian law. ICRC, Geneva, pp 43–52
Henckaerts JM (2005b) Study on Customary International Humanitarian Law. Proc Am Soc Int Law 99:423–428
Henckaerts JM, Doswald-Beck L (2009) Customary international humanitarian law, vol I, II. ICRC/CUP, New York
Hill-Cawthorne L (2016) Detention in non-international armed conflict. OUP, Oxford
ICRC (2016) Commentary on article 3, Geneva convention I. https://ihl-databases.icrc.org/en/ihl-treaties/gci-1949/article-3/commentary/2016#146_B
Jamil H (2016–2017) Classification of armed conflict: an analysis of 'effective control' and 'overall control' tests. ISIL YB of Int'l Humanitarian & Refugee Law XVI–XVII: 185–211
Mantilla G (2017) Conforming instrumentalists: why the USA and the United Kingdom joined the 1949 Geneva conventions. Eur J Int Law 28(2):483–511
Mapping Militant Organisations (2022) "Taliban". http://web.stanford.edu/group/mappingmilitants/cgi-bin/groups/view/367#cite15
Mégret F (2006) From 'savages' to 'unlawful combatants': a postcolonial look at international humanitarian law's 'other'. In: Orford A (ed) International law and its others. CUP, New York, pp 265-317
Melzer N (2016) International humanitarian law: a comprehensive introduction. ICRC, Geneva
Meron T (2011) The making of international criminal justice: a view from the bench, selected speeches. OUP, Oxford
Moir L (2014) 'It's a bird! it's a plane! it's a non-international armed conflict!': cross-border hostilities between states and non-state actors. In: Harvey C et al (eds) Contemporary challenges to the laws of war: essays in honour of professor Peter Rowe. CUP, Cambridge, pp 71–94
Nirmal BC (1988) Wars of national liberation and international humanitarian law. Indian J Int Law28(2):201–215
Pejic J (2011) The protective scope of common article 3: more than meets the eye. Int Rev Red Cross 93(881):1–37
Pictet J (ed) (1952) Commentary on article 3, Geneva convention I. https://ihl-databases.icrc.org/en/ihl-treaties/gci-1949/article-3/commentary/1952?activeTab=undefined.
Richelson J (ed) (2004) Iraq and weapons of mass destruction, National security archive electronic briefing book no. 80. http://nsarchive.gwu.edu/NSAEBB/NSAEBB80/
Sandoz Y et al (eds) (1987) Commentary on the additional rotocols of 8 June 1977 to the Geneva conventions of 12 August 1949. ICRC/Martinus Nijhoff, Geneva
Schindler D (1982) International humanitarian law and internationalized internal armed conflicts. Int Rev Red Cross 230:255–264
Sivakumaran S (2012) The law of non-international armed conflict. OUP, Oxford
Stewart JG (2003) Towards a single definition of armed conflict in international humanitarian law: a critique of internationalized armed conflict. Int Rev Red Cross 85(850):313–349
Vité S (2009) Typology of armed conflicts in international humanitarian law: legal concepts and actual situations. Int Rev Red Cross 91(873):69–94
Wenqi Z (2005) Implications for non-international armed conflicts. In: Maybee L, Chakka B (eds) Custom as a source of international humanitarian law. ICRC, Geneva, pp 129–138
Zamir N (2017) Classification of conflicts in international humanitarian law. Edward Elgar, Cheltenham

Part III
Critique of International Humanitarian Law

9 Humanitarian Principles and Jurisprudential Foundation

Abstract

In this chapter I introduce and describe the basic principles of the laws of armed conflict: military necessity, distinction, unnecessary suffering, proportionality and humanity. Subsequently, I offer some jurisprudential insights into the principles through the Hart-Dworkin exchanges on rules and principles. I try to locate critically the principles of the laws of armed conflict in this jurisprudential framework by using the basic ideas of principle and the "dimension of weight." I strive to demonstrate how the "humanitarian" principles are not in harmony with this jurisprudential premise.

Keywords

Humanitarian principles · Jurisprudence of rules and principle · Hart-Dworkin debate on rules and principles

9.1 Introduction

The laws of armed conflict (international humanitarian law) constitute an area of international law most intimately characterized by the complex interplay of some general principles over which lies a web of detailed rules containing specific prescriptions of a procedural or substantive nature.[1] Principles of military necessity, distinction, proportionality and humanity are proclaimed as the basic principles of the laws of armed conflict. As it is explained below, these principles cannot be placed in watertight compartments; rather, they are interrelated. All of them have gained wide popularity and attracted deliberations by stakeholders, especially the principle of humanity. It is said that all black-letter treaty law needs to be checked against these universal principles.[2] They have developed gradually and they are hailed as the "basic pillars"[3] of the laws of armed conflict. According to the International Committee of the Red Cross (ICRC):

> These principles, however, are not based on a separate source of international law, but on treaties, custom and general principles of law. On the one hand, they can and must often be derived from the existing rules, expressing the rules' substance and meaning. On the other, they inspire existing rules, support them, make them understandable, and have to be taken into account when interpreting them.[4]

Principles by their very nature act as a justification for the application of a rule.[5] Given this premise, principles of the laws of armed conflict also explain operation of its rules. However, these

[1] Kolb and Mar (2015, p. 51).

[2] Garraway (2014, p. 170).

[3] Ohlin (2016, p. 15).

[4] ICRC.

[5] Hart (2007, p. 260).

K. Jeenger, *A Humanitarian Critique of International Humanitarian Law*,
Sustainable Development Goals Series, https://doi.org/10.1007/978-981-96-8319-2_9

principles are much contested because of their conflicting and competing nature and vagueness also. Therefore, the chapter first introduces the principles, examines their competing character and tries to engage with some of the jurisprudential debates centered on them. At the outset, a short description of the principles is necessary.

9.2 Principle of Military Necessity

Generally, military necessity refers to the justification underlying a military conduct which is unavoidable during the course of war. The principle of military necessity expressly appeared for the first time in Article 14 of the Lieber Code as a principle which "consists in the necessity of those measures which are indispensable for securing the ends of the war, and which are lawful according to the modern law and usages of war."[6] Some other dimensions of the principle were explored by the United States Military Courts in the Hostage trial, and held that the principle of military necessity.

> permits the destruction of life of armed enemies and other persons whose destruction is incidentally unavoidable by the armed conflicts of the war ... but is does not permit the killing of innocent inhabitants for purposes of revenge or the satisfaction of a lust to kill. The destruction of property to be lawful must be imperatively demanded by the necessities of war.[7]

The principle is, thus, both permissive and restrictive in nature. It permits use of that much of force in accordance with the laws of armed conflict which is inevitable to attain the objectives of war, and at the same time, restricts adopting of measures beyond what is necessary to secure the desired goals. It reflects the maxim that necessity is the limit of legality.[8]

Military necessity should not be confused with the concept of military convenience as it tends to justify what is beyond necessity yet within the bounds of the law. Quite contrary to the principle of military necessity is the German doctrine of *Kriegsraison geht vor kriegsrecht* which means military necessity in war overrides the laws of war.[9] The doctrine goes beyond military convenience too and seeks to justify what is contrary to the laws of armed conflict but necessary to save oneself from extreme danger or to avoid defeat.

The principle of military necessity has not been expressly recognized by the Geneva law on armed conflicts, however, it admits the demands of military necessity and inevitability of violence, for instance, by recognizing combatants' right to directly participate in hostilities,[10] by permitting operations against military objectives,[11] by prohibiting attacks against civilians only,[12] by prohibiting means and methods of war causing superfluous injury (admitting that some injuries are inevitable).[13]

To achieve the ends of war, the principle of military necessity considers attacks on enemy soldiers and military objectives indispensable consistent with the laws of armed conflict (see also Chapter 14). Such attacks are subject to other principles which are corollary to the principle of military necessity. They are principles of distinction, unnecessary suffering and proportionality.

9.2.1 Principle of Distinction

The principle of distinction, "perhaps the most critical of these principles,"[14] implies an obligation to distinguish and act accordingly. The principle finds place in Article 48 of the Additional Protocol I in the followings expression: "In order to ensure respect for and protection of

[6] Art. 14 Instructions for the Government of Armies of the United States in the Field (1863) (Lieber Code).

[7] United States v. Wilhelm List, et al., Trial Judgment, Case No. 7, (1948), XI LRTWC, 1253–54. It was a war crime trial held by the United States in the occupation area of Germany after the Second World War. It was not part of Nuremberg Trials.

[8] Sandoz et al. (1987, para 1395).

[9] Solis (2010, p. 265).

[10] Art. 43(2) Protocol Additional to the Geneva Conventions of 12 August 1949, and relating to the Protection of Victims of International Armed Conflicts (Protocol I) of 8 June 1977.

[11] Ibid., Art. 48.

[12] Ibid., Art. 51(2).

[13] Ibid., Art. 35(2).

[14] Garraway (2014, p. 170).

the civilian population and civilian objects, the Parties to the conflict shall at all times distinguish between the civilian population and combatants and between civilian objects and military objectives and accordingly shall direct their operations only against military objectives." In furtherance of this rule, the Protocol prohibits attacks on civilian population,[15] unless and for such time they directly participate in hostilities,[16] and also on civil objects, which means all objects other than military objectives.[17] The customary status of this principle has been recognized by the ICRC,[18] and by the International Court of Justice as "an intransgressible principle of international customary law" in its advisory opinion in Nuclear weapons case.[19] The moral and ethical assumption underlying the principle has been seen in the dual dichotomy of civilian-innocent and combatant-threat.[20]

Thus, the principle of distinction seeks to answer the question as to who may be targeted during war. It requires a distinction between targets which are legitimate and which are not. To facilitate distinction, combatants are required to distinguish themselves from civilians, for instance, by wearing uniform, or by carrying of arms openly if uniform is not worn.[21] It has been felt that the principle actually developed out of a need to strike a balance between the desires of States to conduct military operations successfully and to protect their own citizens at the same time.[22]

Attacks without distinction are termed as indiscriminate attacks, such as "those which are not directed at a specific military objective (e.g. aerial bombing); those which employ a method or means of combat which cannot be directed at a specific military objective (e.g. land mines, laying of mines by aircraft); or those which employ a method or means of combat the effects of which cannot be limited as required by this Protocol (e.g. use of fire or nuclear weapons)"[23] and, therefore, prohibited by Protocol I. This prohibition of indiscriminate attacks reflects the principle of discrimination. The principles of discrimination and distinction operate together because an attack without observing the principle of distinction is declared an indiscriminate attack. The principle of distinction thus seeks to prohibit indiscriminate violence and protect civilian population and property.

9.2.2 Principle of Unnecessary Suffering

War is a theater of violence, and the laws of armed conflict presume that a certain amount of injuries, pain and suffering are inevitable during war. Therefore, they aim at minimizing the same by prohibiting the use of weapons, projectiles and material and methods of warfare which result into superfluous injury or unnecessary suffering.[24] This idea has been well explained in the Preamble to the St. Petersburg Declaration, 1868 in the following words:

> That the only legitimate object which States should endeavor to accomplish during war is to weaken the military forces of the enemy;
>
> That for this purpose it is sufficient to disable the greatest possible number of men;
>
> That this object would be exceeded by the employment of arms which uselessly aggravate the sufferings of disabled men, or render their death inevitable.

The Declaration actually sought to ban explosive projectiles under 400 g weight because they would cause excessive injury and suffering to a human body. As the principle of unnecessary suffering is directly linked to the means and methods of war, it also forms the basis of some of the Conventions regulating the use of weapons. For instance,

[15] Protocol I, above n 10, Art. 51(2).

[16] Ibid., Art. 51(3).

[17] Ibid., Art. 52(1).

[18] Henckaerts and Doswald-Beck (2009), Rules 1, 7.

[19] Legality of the Threat or Use of Nuclear Weapons, Advisory Opinion (1996) ICJ Rep 226, paras 78–79.

[20] Silvestri (2019, p. 15).

[21] Art. 44(3) Additional Protocol I, above n 10.

[22] Crawford (2015, p. 13).

[23] Art. 51(4) Additional Protocol I, above n 10.

[24] Ibid., Art. 35(2).

the 1997 Convention related to mines[25] and 1980 Convention on conventional weapons.[26]

The crucial question related to the principle is how to measure suffering and identify a point beyond which it becomes superfluous or unnecessary. The principle itself suggests that during an armed conflict, injuries and suffering are inevitable to some extent to achieve some military advantage. The inevitability of suffering corresponds to the attainment of military objectives. Accordingly, injuries and suffering are considered excessive when no extra military advantage is gained by causing more injuries.

9.2.3 Principle of Proportionality

While the principle of military necessity sanctions military operations, the principle of distinction seeks to prevent directly targeting of civilian population and property. However, armed conflict situations are not always black and white, and military targets are not every time clearly separate and distinguishable from civilian objects, for instance, during military operations in urban areas, or when soldiers take over for military purpose civilian buildings, or when military base camps and installations are situated in close proximity to the populated localities, or when enemy soldiers use human shields to protect themselves, or when there is a bridge near a border town which is of critical importance for military as well as civilian movement. Such situations present a conflict between two competing interests, military necessity on one hand and protection of civilians and civilian objects on the other. While the former demands military action, the latter prohibits the same. It has been argued that since ideally neither of them can claim priority over the other, striking a balance between the two is the only option.[27]

Protocol I seeks to strike the balance by prohibiting an attack which may be expected to cause incidental loss of civilian life, injury to civilians, damage to civilian objects, or a combination thereof, which would be excessive in relation to the concrete and direct military advantage anticipated.[28] Thus, an attack causing incidental loss to civilians (or collateral damage) which is not excessive or disproportionate to the military advantage anticipated is permitted by the Protocol. This is principle of proportionality. It requires a commander to foresee two probable outcomes of an attack (concrete and direct military advantage and civilian harm) on the basis of available information. The military advantage is said to be concrete and direct when it is substantial and relatively close.[29] The word "concrete" has been interpreted to mean real and quantifiable advantage,[30] and the word "direct" indicates a causal relationship between the attack and the anticipated military advantage.[31] The assessment of military advantage is to be done in respect of the attack as a whole or "in its entirety",[32] instead of any "isolated or particular parts of the attack,"[33] such as considering launching of a particular rocket or targeting a particular object.

Besides anticipating the two probable consequences, an attack planner has to weigh the probable military advantage and civilian loss and anticipate whether the latter is going to be excessive to the former or not. Therefore, one has to act like a "reasonable commander"[34] while carrying out proportionality assessment. It has been admitted that there can be no formula to determine when an attack is excessive or disproportionate to the military advantage; "it has to be decided on case-by-case basis."[35]

---

[25] See Preamble to the Convention on the Prohibition of the Use, Stockpiling, Production and Transfer of Anti-Personal Mines and their Destruction (1997).

[26] See Preamble to the Convention on Prohibition or Restrictions on the Use of Certain Conventional Weapons Which May be Deemed to be Excessively Injurious or to Have Indiscriminate Effects (1980).

[27] Cannizzaro (2015, p. 335).

[28] Art. 51(5)(b), Additional Protocol I, above n 10.

[29] Sandoz et al. (1987, para 2209).

[30] NATO (2017, p. 473).

[31] Gisel (2016, pp. 22–23).

[32] Sandoz et al (1987, para 2218).

[33] State of Israel (2015, para 318).

[34] Sloane (2015, p. 318).

[35] Brehm (2014, p. 254).

There are many facets of the principle under the Protocol. Thus, for example, where the military advantage to be achieved through armed operations does not outweigh the harm to civilian life and property, such attacks are prohibited being indiscriminate[36] ; a belligerent shall refrain from deciding to launch such attacks,[37] and such an attack shall be canceled or suspended (if already decided).[38] It, thus, suggests that under the laws of armed conflict belligerents do not have unfettered right to attack nor civilians have complete immunity from any loss during armed conflicts. The principle appears to be a limitation on the conduct of military operations.[39] It seeks to strike a balance between military necessity and humanity.[40] The principle forms part of customary international humanitarian law.[41]

9.3 Principle of Humanity

The movement of protection of victims of war started by Henry Dunant was inspired by the principle of humanity only. There is a wider perception that this principle echoes from a range of provisions of Hague Conventions, Geneva Conventions, Additional Protocols and weapons Conventions. To illustrate a few of them, provisions requiring respect, dignity, protection and care for soldiers who are sick, wounded or shipwrecked, prisoners of war, civilians, medical and religious personnel and journalists, without any adverse distinction as to race, religion, color, sex or the like considerations; fundamental guarantees under Protocol I, prohibition of indiscriminate attacks and prohibition of means and methods of war causing unnecessary suffering.

In older instruments, the principle of humanity was expressed but in abstract form. It was acknowledged in Article 4 of the Lieber Code, 1863: "… it is incumbent upon those who administer it (Martial Law) to be strictly guided by the principles of justice, honor, and humanity …" Similarly, the preamble to the 1868 Declaration of St. Petersburg *inter alia* says that employment of arms which would aggravate suffering would be contrary to the laws of humanity. Again, the Martens Clause, which was suggested in the Hague Conference, 1899 by a Russian jurist and diplomat Fyodor Martens, contains the principle without any concrete description:

> Until a more complete code of the laws of war is issued, the High Contracting Parties think it right to declare that in cases not included in the Regulations adopted by them, populations and belligerents remain under the protection and empire of the principles of international law, as they result from the usages established between civilized nations, from the laws of humanity and the requirements of the public conscience.

The clause was incorporated in the preambles of the Hague Conventions of 1899 and 1907. Subsequently, the clause was included in each of the four Geneva Conventions of 1949, the two Additional Protocols of 1977, and few of the weapons Conventions as well.[42] The principle has attained the status of customary international law.[43]

In its concrete and abstract form, the humanity principle implies a moral force and it has also been referred to as "humanity-sentiment."[44] It seeks to restrict the excesses of war. Perhaps, this is

[36] Art. 51(5)(b), Additional Protocol I, above n 10.

[37] Ibid., Art. 57(2)(a)(iii).

[38] Ibid., Art. 57(2)(b).

[39] Cohen and Zlotogorski (2021, p. 3).

[40] Ibid., pp. 4–5 and ICRC (2015, p. 51).

[41] Henckaerts and Doswald-Beck (2009), Rule 14 and Prosecutor v. Kupreškić, et al., IT-95–16-T, Judgment, 14 January 2000, para 524.

[42] Art. 63(4), 62(4), 142(4) and 158(4) of the Geneva Convention for the Amelioration of the Condition of the Wounded and Sick in Armed Forces in the Field of 12 August 1949 (Geneva Convention I), the Geneva Convention for the Amelioration of the Condition of Wounded, Sick and Shipwrecked Members of Armed Forces at Sea of 12 August 1949 (Geneva Convention II), the Geneva Convention relative to the Treatment of Prisoners of War of 12 August 1949 (Geneva Convention III) and the Geneva Convention relative to the Protection of Civilian Persons in Time of War of 12 August 1949 (Geneva Convention IV) respectively; Art. 1(2) Protocol I above n 10; Preamble to Protocol I (The Additional Protocols use the term 'principles of humanity' instead of 'laws of humanity'); Preamble to the Convention on Conventional Weapons, above n 26 and Preamble to the Convention on Anti-Personal Mines, above n 25.

[43] Nuclear Weapons, above n 19, para 92.

[44] Coupland (2001, pp. 969, 972).

why it has been accepted as the essential principle from which other humanitarian principles (distinction, unnecessary suffering and proportionality) are derived.[45] While the term "humanity" remains undefined in the law, the restrictions based on this principle "define the absence of humanity in articulating what constitutes inhumane practice."[46]

9.4 Locating the Principles in Hart-Dworkin Exchanges on Rules and Principles

The above description introduces the fundamental principles of the laws of armed conflict. Several rules of the treaties on the conduct of war reflect these principles. It must be noted that the treaties seek to regulate the conduct in war which, otherwise, is generally prohibited by the Charter of the United Nations. Additionally, this body of law is seen as a humanitarian law, whereas it does not prohibit war; rather, it validates infliction of injuries and causing death and destruction of diverse proportion (see Chapter 13 and 14). Thus, there is a likelihood of contradictions and inner-tensions in and around the law. In such a legal architecture, do the principles fit in the jurisprudential analysis of the notion of principle? The discussion below attempts to locate the principles of the laws of armed conflict in jurisprudential framework with the help of Hart-Dworkin debate and raises certain critical questions.

9.4.1 What Was the Hart-Dworkin Debate

Hart and Dworkin were prominent jurists of the second half of the previous century. Dworkin was Hart's student at the University of Oxford. What led to the beginning of the exchanges between them was Hart's influential work, The Concept of Law, first published in 1961. Dworkin wrote a critique of the book in 1967 in his article, "The Model of Rules I."[47] The series of critiques and replies from both the authors continued for almost two decades (1967–1987) and numbered fifteen exchanges.[48] Dworkin intended to present a general attack on positivism, and for this purpose, he used Hart's work.[49] The Dworkinian critique of Hart's theory of legal positivism has many dimensions. The aspect relevant to the present chapter is Dworkin's views on legal principles and rules. Dworkin claimed that Hart's version of law presents law as consisting of rules only, and thus Hart ignores legal principles as a constituent of law.[50] He also maintains that there is a sharp distinction between legal rules and principles.[51] Hart agreed to the former, but not the latter claim.[52]

9.4.2 Jurisprudential Insights to the Principles

Among the basic principles of the laws of armed conflict, the status of the principle of humanity as a principle has been contested frequently. Given the sanctioning of hostilities (e.g. combatants are given the right to participate directly in hostilities),[53] infliction of harm (unless it is superfluous for a combatant or widespread to the environment)[54] and loss to civilians under the law (if it is not exceeding the military advantage),[55] the idea of humanity gets compromised during armed conflicts and gives way to the demands of military necessity. Therefore, adopting a narrow view of the idea of principle, few commentators have

45 Pictet (1979, p. 135).

46 Fast (2016, p. 118).

47 Dworkin (1967–1968, pp. 15–46).

48 Bayles (1991, p. 349).

49 Dworkin (1967–1968, p. 22).

50 Ibid., pp. 22–25 and Hart (2007, p. 259).

51 Dworkin (1967–1968, pp. 23–24).

52 See, Hart (2007, pp. 259–263).

53 Art. 43(2) Protocol I, above n 10.

54 Ibid., Art. 35(2)(3).

55 Ibid., Art. 51(5)(b).

argued that it is not a principle, but a consideration[56] or a "meta-juridical consideration"[57] only. This argument has been substantiated by the view that there is no binding obligation of humanity in the treaty law.[58] The legal impact of the principle of humanity has also been questioned.[59] The denial of the status of a principle to humanity has been justified by comparing it with the other principles of the laws of armed conflict.[60] Besides, there also exist conflicts and overlaps among these principles. To address these fundamental issues pertaining to the nature of the principles and to contribute to the better understanding of the field, the views of Dworkin and Hart on principles and rules may be looked into.

First, let us investigate the broad jurisprudential spectrum of the notion of principle in order to present a deeper understanding of the principles of the law of armed conflict. Generally, law is a combination of two broad categories; legal rules and principles.[61] Legal principles have more than one facet and they perform varied functions. Simply put, a legal principle is the broad reason underlying a legal rule. According to Dworkin, a principle is a standard to be observed because justice or fairness or some other dimension of morality renders it necessary.[62] A principle, according to him, is also a "consideration inclining in one direction or another."[63] Likewise, in the opinion of Hart, principles refer to standards of conduct and include theoretical and practical considerations.[64] He further says that principles refer to some purpose, goal, entitlement or value which are exemplified by rules.[65] As contrast to rules, principles are broad, general or unspecific, and several rules may exhibit a single principle.[66] And sometimes, a rule may represent a compromise between two conflicting and competing principles also.[67] Principles rationalize and justify rules.[68] In respect of the laws of armed conflict, similar position appears from the above introduction of the principles. For instance, the rules prohibiting indiscriminate attacks and attacks causing disproportionate harm to civilians mirror the principles of distinction and proportionality, respectively.

These insights in respect of the idea of principle also offer a response to some of the questions raised in respect of the status of the principle of humanity. Under the common Article 3 obligation to treat humanely the persons taking no active part in hostilities, the concept of humanity appears as a standard.[69] On the other hand, humanity emerges as a consideration from prohibition on adverse distinction founded on sex, race, nationality, religion and the like considerations while protecting and taking care of protected persons.[70] In the similar vein, the rules prohibiting attack on civilians and requiring humane treatment with the protected persons are explained and justified by the principle of humanity. Thus, given the comprehensive approach towards the scope of legal principles, the principle of humanity is reflected from some of the rules of the laws of armed conflict, even if it appears in the form of a standard, consideration or an element. However, locating the principle of humanity in the jurisprudential framework of

[56] Larsen et al (2013, p. 1).

[57] Dinstein (2013, p. 73).

[58] Ibid.

[59] Larsen et al. (2013, pp. 1–8).

[60] Ibid., p. 1 and Dinstein (2013, p. 73).

[61] Some consider it as operating through four distinct categories: principle, policy, standard and rule: J. Dickinson, in Paton (2011, p. 236).

[62] Dworkin (2010, p. 22).

[63] Ibid., p. 26.

[64] Hart (2007, p. 260).

[65] Ibid., p. 260.

[66] Ibid.

[67] Dworkin (2010, p. 77). See. Art. 35 Protocol I, above n 10, on balancing military necessity and humanity.

[68] Hart (2007, p. 260).

[69] See also, Art. 12, 12, 13, 27 Geneva Conventions I-IV, respectively, above n 42; Art. 75 Protocol I, above n 10 and Art. 4 Protocol Additional to the Geneva Conventions of 12 August 1949, and relating to the Protection of Victims of Non-International Armed Conflicts (Protocol II) of 8 June 1977.

[70] Art. 12, 12, 16, 13 Geneva Conventions I-IV, respectively, above n 42; Art. 3 common to Geneva Conventions I-IV; Art. 75 Protocol I, above n 10 and Art. 4 Protocol II, above n 69.

principle does not mean that the status of the principle in the laws of armed conflict is influential and commanding.

Other arguments challenging the status of the principle of humanity relate to its legal impact[71] and doubt the existence of obligations based on the principle.[72] While the latter challenge stands answered above, an inquiry into the legal impact of the principle offers few responses. The laws of armed conflict contain some prescriptions and prohibitions based on this principle. The violations of the legal obligations founded on this principle are referred to as "grave breaches" of the Geneva Conventions of 1949.[73] To illustrate, willful killing, torture or inhuman treatment, or willfully-causing great suffering or serious injury to body or health amount to grave breaches.[74] Moreover, the Additional Protocol I[75] and the Statute of the International Criminal Court[76] recognize the grave breaches as war crimes. Similarly, the International Criminal Tribunal for the Former Yugoslavia also exercised jurisdiction on the grave breaches.[77] Independent of the grave breaches, the Statute of the International Criminal Court declares as war crimes some of the violations of the rules reflecting principle of humanity.[78] Thus, the legal impact of the principle is present to some extent in the laws of armed conflict and international criminal law.

However, this discussion does not answer the larger challenge that humanity is not a fundamental overarching principle of the laws of armed conflict and that there are other principles which take precedence over humanitarian considerations. Importantly, some of the rules and principles operate contrary to the idea of humanity, which are not nullified by the principle of humanity (see Chapter 14).

Second, the exchange of views between Dworkin and Hart are useful to understand and explain the conflicting nature of some of the principles of the laws of armed conflict. Dworkin maintains that an integral part of the concept of principle is the dimension of weight.[79] Hart also did not deny this dimension while replying Dworkin.[80] The element of weight becomes more important when two conflicting and competing principles intersect. For instance, the principles of humanity and proportionality may intersect during an armed conflict and clash because the proportionality principle tolerates what the humanity principle prohibits. In such a situation, Dworkin and Hart suggest that it is the dimension of weight of the principles that acts as a tool to resolve the conflict. It does not mean a principle having weight takes over the one without any weight. Because every principle has some weight, Dworkin says that the resolution of the conflict is done taking into account the relative weight of each of the conflicting principles.[81] In the context of the laws of armed conflict, while both, the principles of proportionality and humanity, carry some weight, the former has relatively more weight because the dominant idea in the laws of armed conflict is winning the war, instead of saving lives and infrastructure. Hart suggests that the principle with greater weight prevails and becomes applicable to decide the problem.[82] The humanity principle thus gives way to the proportionality principle. Similarly, the principle of military necessity prevails over the principle of humanity. Therefore, given the greater military advantage, some amount of incidental loss of civilian life and property is sanctioned by the law.

In this conflict-resolution of principles, it must be noted that the principle having relatively less weight in a given situation and therefore getting compromised does not mean that it will have

[71] Larsen et al. (2013, p. 1).

[72] Dinstein (2013, p. 73).

[73] See, Art. 50, 51, 130, 147 Geneva Conventions I-IV, respectively, above n 42 and Art. 11(4), 85(20), 85(3) Protocol I, above n 10.

[74] See, ibid.

[75] Art. 85(5).

[76] Art. 8(2)(a), Statute of International Criminal Court (1998) (Rome Statute).

[77] Art. 2 Ibid.

[78] E.g. Art. 8(2)(a)(i), (v), (xxi), (xxii).

[79] Dworkin (2010, p. 26).

[80] Hart (2007, p. 261).

[81] Dworkin (2010, p. 26).

[82] Hart (2007, p. 261).

similar less worth in other cases also or that it will not survive. It is obvious from the provisions related to grave breaches and humane treatment. Hart also advocates the view that such a less weighty principle will survive and "it may win in competition with some other principle of lesser weight."[83] An illustration from the laws of armed conflict suitable to this idea is, though, difficult to find.

Third, the insights are also relevant to understand the character of a legal principle. Dworkin in his analysis of the idea of principle says that principle is "a standard that is to be observed, not because it will advance or secure an economic, political, or social situation deemed desirable, but because it is a requirement of justice or fairness or some other dimension of morality."[84] The moral foundations of a principle (e.g. justice and fairness) advocated here by Dworkin become crucial when it comes to the laws of armed conflict, especially because it is marketed as "International Humanitarian Law." The tragedy of the humanitarian law is that it is predominantly founded on the principle of military necessity, and the principle of humanity operates within the boundaries fixed by the principle of military necessity. The law compromises with humanitarian ideas at almost every next step. Therefore, the Dworkinian understanding of the idea of principle may be useful, (1) to question the nature and impact of "basic" principles of the law of armed conflict, (2) to draw the attention towards the crucial role of principles in general in shaping the rules, and (3) to realize the critical absence of such ideas in the "basic" principles of the laws of armed conflict. Translating this understanding of the concept of principle into reality necessitates determination of the principles before the drafting of rules. In the making of an international treaty, however, generally legal principles are deduced from rules, of course, subsequent to the adoption of a treaty.

On the other hand, despite advancing the elements of morality in a principle, Dworkin did not emphasize upon them while explaining the concept of principle as a constituting element of law and also while contrasting principles with rules. He maintained that every principle has a dimension of weight but he did not talk about the character or content of weight. The meaning and scope of weight thus remain open to interpretation and they depend upon the nature of a particular law, rather than the necessary moral requirements. In such a situation, his suggestion to resolve the conflict between two principles on the basis of relative weight of the principles also fails to reinforce the moral foundations of rules. Accordingly, in the context of "international humanitarian law," the principles of military necessity and proportionality override the principle of humanity.

Dworkin's understanding of the nature of principle gets reflected in Paton's views also when he says: "The marks of an efficient legal principle are that it should give cohesion to a particular branch of law by capably explaining the relevant cases; it must be suited to the practical needs and ethical requirements of that particular community and be elastic enough to afford opportunities for development in the rules that are based upon it."[85] Considering the principle of military necessity and its ancillary principles on one side, and the principle of humanity and the title of the discipline, "International Humanitarian Law" on the other, it is evident that the principles do not provide cohesion and consistency to this body of law. There is incessant contradiction and conflict with the humanitarian idea in the rules of "international humanitarian law." Paton's suggestion of a principle being suitable to the practical needs, however, seems vague and misleading too. The nature and extent of "practical needs" are ambiguous. Paton suggests that a legal principle must meet ethical requirements. But, from a purely humanitarian point of view, the dominant principles of "international humanitarian law" do not suit the ethical requirements. For instance, the principle of unnecessary suffering implies that suffering to some extent is acceptable and necessary. Can such deviations from ethical standards find a place in the category of "practical needs"? Can the scope of the expression "practical needs" be determined by the adjacent expression "ethical

[83] Ibid.

[84] Dworkin (2010, p. 22).

[85] Paton (2011, p. 236).

requirements"? These issues remain unclear from Paton's views.

This chapter, thus, gives an overview of the principles of the laws of armed conflict and illustrates how the rules reflect the principles. Subsequently, the ideas of Hart and Dworkin help in locating the principles of the laws of armed conflict in the jurisprudential framework of principles. The discussion helps in developing theoretical understanding of the principles and indentifying certain critical issues.

References

Bayles M (1991) Hart v. Dworkin. Law Philos 10(4):349–381

Brehm M (2014) International humanitarian law and the protection of civilians from the effects of explosive weapons. In: Harvey C et al (eds) Contemporary challenges to the laws of war: essays in honour of professor Peter Rowe. CUP, Cambridge, pp 235–267

Cannizzaro E (2015) Proportionality in the Law of Armed Conflict. In: Clapham A, Gaeta P (eds) The Oxford handbook of international law in armed conflict. OUP, Oxford, pp 332–352

Cohen A, Zlotogorski D (2021) Proportionality in international humanitarian law: consequences, precautions, and procedures. OUP, New York

Coupland R (2001) Humanity: what is it and how does it influence international law? Int Rev Red Cross 83(844):969–989

Crawford E (2015) Identifying the enemy: civilian participation in armed conflict. OUP, Oxford

Dinstein Y (2013) The principle of proportionality. In: Larsen KM et al (eds) Searching for a 'principle of humanity' in international humanitarian law. CUP, Cambridge

Dworkin R (1967–1968) The model of rules I. Univ Chic Law Rev 35(14):15–46

Dworkin R (2010) Taking rights seriously. Universal Law Publishing Co., New Delhi

Fast L (2016) Unpacking the principle of humanity: tensions and implications. Int Rev Red Cross 97(897/898):111–131

Garraway C (2014) Direct participation and the principle of distinction: squaring the circle. In: Harvey C et al (eds) Contemporary challenges to the laws of war: essays in honour of professor Peter Rowe. CUP, Cambridge, pp 169–190

Gisel L (2016) The principle of proportionality in the rules governing the conduct of hostilities under international humanitarian law, report on international expert meeting 22–23 June 2016. ICRC, Geneva

Hart HLA (2007) The concept of law. OUP, New Delhi

Henckaerts JM, Doswald-Beck L (2009) Customary international humanitarian law, vol I. ICRC/CUP, New York

ICRC (2015) International humanitarian law and the challenges of contemporary armed conflicts, 32nd international conference of the Red Cross and Red Crescent, Geneva, October 2015. ICRC, Geneva

ICRC, Fundamentals of IHL. https://casebook.icrc.org/law/fundamentals-ihl#d_iii

Kolb R, Mar KD (2015) Treaties for armed conflict. In: Clapham A, Gaeta P (eds) The Oxford handbook of international law in armed conflict. OUP, Oxford, pp 50–88

Larsen KM et al (2013) Introduction by the editors: is there a 'principle of humanity' in international humanitarian law? In: Larsen KM et al (eds) Searching for a 'principle of humanity' in international humanitarian law. CUP, Cambridge, pp 1–20

NATO (2017) Tallinn Manual 2.0 on the international law applicable to cyber operations: prepared by the international groups of experts at the invitation of the NATO cooperative cyber defence centre of excellence. CUP, Cambridge

Ohlin JD (2016) The inescapable collision. In: Ohlin JD (ed) Theoretical boundaries of armed conflict and human rights. CUP, New York, pp 1–22

Paton GW (2011) A textbook of jurisprudence. OUP, New Delhi

Pictet J (1979) Commentary on the fundamental principles of the red cross. Int Rev Red Cross 210:130–149

Sandoz Y et al (eds) (1987) Commentary on the additional protocols of 8 June 1977 to the Geneva conventions of 12 August 1949. ICRC/Martinus Nijhoff, Geneva

Silvestri A (2019) Direct participation in hostilities: between a rock and a hard place. Perth Int Law J 4:13–19

Sloane RD (2015) Puzzles of proportion and the reasonable military commander: reflections on the law, ethics, and geopolitics of proportionality. Harv Natl Secur J 6:299–343

Solis GD (2010) The law of armed conflict: international humanitarian law in war. CUP, Cambridge

State of Israel (2015) The 2014 Gaza conflict, 7 July–26 August 2014, factual and legal aspects. https://www.gov.il/en/Departments/General/2014-gaza-conflict-factual-and-legal-aspects

10 Feminist Perspective to International Humanitarian Law

Abstract

In this chapter, I try to analyze the laws of armed conflict from a feminist perspective. I try to explain how capitalist patriarchy makes the law stereotypical, gender-biased and hostile towards women. I reemphasize that the treaty-law by and large reflects a male view of armed conflict. It ignores the fact that women experience war in a much more different and atrocious way. Accordingly, I provide a detailed analysis of how the law is based on patriarchal notions and how it makes the conditions of women even worse in some situations during an armed conflict. The chapter argues that from a humanitarian perspective, the notion of humanity in the laws of armed conflict largely means masculinity. Lastly, I ring an alarm in respect of the attempts of dilution and hegemonic appropriation of the feminist movement.

Keywords

Feminism · Women and IHL · Women and armed conflict · Sexual violence during armed conflict · Third World feminism

Questions about gender are rendered so irrelevant during wartime that to raise the subject is to risk public ridicule. Christiansen (1994, p. 206)

10.1 Contextualizing Feminism in International Humanitarian Law

This section tries to explain how feminist perspective of international law in general is relevant to examine laws of armed conflict (international humanitarian law) from a feminist perspective. It also introduces briefly various feminist approaches to international law which are helpful to understand the feminist standpoint of the laws of armed conflict in the next section.

10.1.1 Fragmentation of International Law and Feminism

During last more than fifty years, international law has diversified and expanded through the emergence of specific, self-contained and relatively autonomous bodies of rules. This expansion has occurred in areas, such as human rights, trade, investment, environment, armed conflict and international crimes, to name some of them.[1] Each of these specialized international

[1] Fragmentation of international law: difficulties arising from the diversification and expansion of international law, report of the study group of the International Law Commission, UN Doc A/CN/4/L.702, 18 July 2006, p. 3.

K. Jeenger, *A Humanitarian Critique of International Humanitarian Law*, Sustainable Development Goals Series, https://doi.org/10.1007/978-981-96-8319-2_10

legal regimes is characterized by the proliferation of its own normative and institutional framework.[2] These functional systems dress up in "the most sophisticated form available,"[3] however, they are an integral part of the system[4] of international law. The sophistication, technical vernacular and specialization do not render them immune from the charges usually leveled against general international law, because "they are not randomly but systematically related to general international law."[5] Accordingly, the problems and anxieties attached to general international law are very much obvious in the specialized international legal systems also. For instance, these expertise based normative frameworks are not neutral,[6] determinate,[7] anti-hegemonic,[8] apolitical,[9] objective[10] and free from structural bias.[11] From a feminist perspective, international law and its particularized domains are a spectacle of male domination, gender bias and invisibility of women.

10.1.2 Feminism: A View from Below

The feminist way of looking at international law is a view from below, indicating how social hierarchies shape someone's perception. Generally, international law is projected by (white, elite, heterosexual) men as objective, non-political, neutral and rational.[12] This understanding is an outcome of their (the knowing subjects') dominating position in the society.[13] This is privileged knowledge. Michel Foucault states that those in power and privileged positions determine what is regarded as knowledge.[14] Such knowledge is unavoidably subjective, not neutral.[15] In order to mask these realities, lies are constructed and mainstreamized.

Contrary to the generalized view, the feminist approach maintains that the character of international law is masculine, male-dominated, gendered and structurally biased against women. This is a worldview of those who are at the bottom of the hierarchical social structure. This view is regarded as "more complete view of the oppressive nature of the dominant discourse."[16] The feminist perspective relies on the lived experiences of women. It perceives international law by understanding the impact of marginalization, oppression, subjugation, inequality, discrimination and systemic obstacles on international level. These inhuman experiences are particularly the result of patriarchy, colonization, casteism,[17] global capitalism,[18] or a combination thereof. They shape and structure the society in such a way that subjugation and oppression of women is justified and normalized; women are kept away from intellectual pursuits, and they are reduced to a sex-object and a commodity. However, the gravest impact of patriarchy, casteism, colonization and global capitalism is not the multifaceted victimization and reductionism, but the conditioning of

[2] Broude (2013, p. 285).

[3] Koskenniemi (2011, p. 324).

[4] Fragmentation of international law, above n 2, p. 7.

[5] Fragmentation of international law: difficulties arising from the diversification and expansion of international law, report of the study group of the International Law Commission, finalised by Martti Koskenniemi, UN Doc A/CN.4/L.682 and Add1, p. 14, paras 32–33.

[6] Koskenniemi and Leino (2002, p. 573) and Koskenniemi (2011, p. 68). "…neutrality and determinacy of norms is an ideologically loaded way of disguising the fact that they privilege some views or positions.": Navari, cited in Koskenniemi (2006, pp. 538–539, n. 55).

[7] Koskenniemi (2006, p. 604).

[8] Koskenniemi (2011, p. 320) and ibid., p. 597.

[9] Koskenniemi (2006, p. 597).

[10] Ibid.

[11] Ibid., p. 610 and Koskenniemi (2011, pp. 65, 320, 334, 336).

[12] Bianchi (2016, p. 21).

[13] Davies (2017, p. 17).

[14] Ibid., p. 10.

[15] MacKinnon, in ibid., p. 238.

[16] Ibid., p. 17.

[17] Bhimrao Ambedkar believed that in the context of India, caste discrimination and gender subordination are interlinked: Kapadia (2020, p. 10).

[18] For an account of oppression and exploitation of women in capitalist mode of production, see Gimenez (2005, pp. 11–32) and Gimenez (1975, pp. 61–80).

female-minds in accepting their subordinate position as a "natural phenomenon." It has not only established the moral and cultural authority of the dominant heterosexual male, but has made women internalize their inferior status and prevented resistance also. A feminist critique of international law echoes these realities of approximately half of the population.

10.1.3 Feminist Approaches and International Law

The feminist approaches to international law are multiple and diverse. They try to engage with women's concerns from various directions. Liberal feminism argues in favor of equal rights for women to put an end to unjust and discriminatory treatment.[19] The approach has been subjected to criticism that it again throws women into a world of institutions characterized by male-monopoly and determined by male standards.[20] It does not challenge and seek to overthrow the structural inequality. Rejecting this model, cultural feminism focuses on the essential natural features of women and argues that the institution of law identifies itself with maleness and devalues femininity.[21] Therefore, it needs to be reformed on the basis of essential feminine characteristics.[22] However, this gender essentialism presumes women to be a homogenous category and often considers the problems and experiences of privileged women only.[23] It ignores the intersecting concerns of women at the periphery, such as the black, Muslim, *Dalit*[24] and lesbian.[25] Essentialism also hampers the prospects of restructuring of socio-political settings.[26]

Radical feminists, on the other hand, condemn the equal legal treatment thesis because men and women are situated in a domination-subordination relationship. Catharine MacKinnon maintains that "sexuality is the linchpin of gender inequality."[27] According to her, "A built-in tension exists in this concept of equality, which presupposes sameness, and this concept of sex, which presupposes difference. Sex equality becomes a contradiction in terms, something of an oxymoron ..."[28] On intersecting lines, for instance, Ambedkar and Lohia believe that caste plays an important role in the oppression and sexual exploitation of *Dalit* women.[29]

Contrasting the white feminism, the Third World feminist approach highlights the experiences of Third World women during colonialism, imperialism, global capitalism and post-colonialism.[30] All of them and a few other schools of feminism are relevant to tell the gendered stories of international law because capitalist patriarchy silences women and makes them fade away at different stages and in various ways. It is also because different women have different experiences to share. Therefore, it has been realized that plurality of techniques is "not only valuable, but essential."[31]

The diverse feminist approaches look critically at the history, principles, concepts and categories of international law.[32] This engagement is said to have begun with the International Congress of Women, 1915[33]; however, it

[19] Charlesworth calls it equality on paper and calls for substantive equality. She rejects Tesón's suggestion to be content with formal equality: Charlesworth (1994, p. 8). See also, Tesón (1993, p. 653).

[20] Dalton (1987–1988, pp. 4–5).

[21] Chamallas (2013, pp. 28–29).

[22] Charlesworth and Chinkin (2000, pp. 40–41).

[23] Mohanty (1984, p. 351).

[24] Bhaskar (2020, pp. 66–68). The expression *Dalit* refers to a group of people who are at the lowest level of the social hierarchy in India and who are considered as untouchables.

[25] Kapur (2002, p. 8).

[26] Charlesworth (1994, p. 9).

[27] MacKinnon (1982, p. 533).

[28] MacKinnon (1987, p. 33).

[29] Bhaskar (2020, pp. 66–68).

[30] See, Kapur (2002, pp. 1–37), Mohanty (1984, pp. 333–358) and Chimni (2017, pp. 386–392).

[31] Charlesworth et al. (1991, p. 613).

[32] Chimni (2017, p. 410).

[33] Ibid., p. 358 and Bianchi (2016, p. 183). Women associations used the forums of the League of Nations and International Labour Organisation to draw their attention to women issues: Deborah Stienstra, cited in Charlesworth (2000, p. 64).

gained momentum with the path breaking works of Hilary Charlesworth, Christine Chinkin and Shelley Wright.[34] These and subsequent works made an attempt to unveil and expose the masculine normative and structural framework of international law, and the resultant invisibility and silence of women. These disclosures signal towards something more than the liberal ideas of poor recognition of rights of women or underrepresentation of women in international organizations. Third World scholars maintain that international law is a product of masculine acts of colonization and global capitalism.[35] Others have alleged male domination and gender bias in the making of international law by contending that international law is "made by men for men."[36] It has been highlighted that the making of international law is generally based on consent which itself is a masculine and a patriarchal act. In patriarchal systems, only men are capable of consenting; women can neither freely express their likes or dislikes, nor their choices matter. Feminists believe that the dominant subject of international law is State which is an embodiment of masculinity, patriarchy and capitalism,[37] and hence oppressive to women.[38] It has also been argued that the vernacular of international law is founded on male attributes. Its vocabulary, such as sovereign, States, use of force, consent, conflict, command responsibility, self-determination is manly in nature.[39] "And to be manly is not simply to be manly, but also to be in the more highly valued position in the discourse."[40] It has been alleged that international law has been coded in gendered binaries of male–female, for instance public–private, objective-subjective and international-domestic, wherein the first word is attributed to male characteristics, while the second indicates feminine traits.[41] Accordingly, only the first one qualifies for legitimacy, relevance, importance and precedence.[42] These binary oppositions, thus, carry out structural gender discrimination. Feminists have also contended that the international legal system regards issues of men as common human issues, and women's problems as worthy of limited concern,[43] as if human beings mean only men. Actually, they do. International law is, thus, not just blind, deaf and dumb towards women, but also hostile and biased. Its edifice echoes domination and monopoly of men, and discrimination against and neglect of women.

10.2 Feminist Critique of International Humanitarian Law

The discussion below seeks to offer a feminist critique of the laws of armed conflict touching upon various dimensions of an armed conflict and the relevant law. It exposes the patriarchal language of the law and its implications on the plight of women during an armed conflict. It explains that the law addresses in a very limited manner the concerns of female-victims of an armed conflict.

10.2.1 How Women Experience Armed Conflicts

An important aspect of the laws of armed conflict is protection of civilians. Though, civilian population consists of individuals of different gender, sexual orientation and gender identity, it has been supported by empirical studies that women are worst hit during an armed conflict.[44] They become victims of a completely masculine acts and a show of masculine power called war, which

[34] Charlesworth et al. (1991, pp. 613–645) and Charlesworth and Chinkin (2000).

[35] Chimni (2017, pp. 386–387).

[36] Bianchi (2016, p. 186).

[37] Chimni (2017, pp. 413, 414) and Charlesworth et al. (1991, p. 622).

[38] MacKinnon (1983, p. 644).

[39] Charlesworth and Chinkin (2000, p. 49).

[40] Cohn (1993, p. 229).

[41] Ibid. and Charlesworth and Chinkin (2000, p. 49).

[42] Charlesworth (1999, p. 382) and Charlesworth and Chinkin (2000, p. 50).

[43] Charlesworth et al. (1991, p. 625).

[44] Chinkin (1992, p. 279), Charlesworth (1999, p. 385) and Gardam (1997, p. 60).

is decided without their involvement.[45] While men also suffer from wars,[46] women's experience during and after an armed conflict is multifaceted and stands on a different footing.[47] In the words of Catharine MacKinnon, "Women are violated in many ways in which men are violated. But women are also violated in ways men are not."[48] Armed conflicts affect women more because of patriarchy-driven gender inequality, shackles in the form of less mobility,[49] economic dependence,[50] gender roles of care and household management.[51] Additionally, these experiences get intensified and varied by the intersecting considerations of race, poverty, pregnancy, ethnicity, caste, class, religion and sexuality.[52] As admitted by the International Committee of the Red Cross (ICRC):

> women are likely to have fewer financial resources to cope with injury and property damage, are more likely to be discriminated against because of injury or disability, may face additional barriers to accessing health care when injured and are likely to be less represented in decision-making roles regarding humanitarian aid delivery.[53]

The most common and serious form of harm that women undergo in war is sexual exploitation, sexual abuse and sexual violence.[54] While statistics on sexual atrocities in armed conflicts in the form of rape, forced prostitution, forced pregnancy, sexual slavery is available, many such cases go unreported and undocumented also.[55] Sexual violence reasserts hetero-masculinity individually and also collectively in case of gang-rapes.[56] It is "a product of warped (yet normalized) militarized hegemonic masculinity."[57] It is deliberately committed by heterosexual male soldiers against specific women—enemy women.[58] Historically, sexual abuse of women has been seen as part of the spoils of war,[59] and a privilege of male-troops. Invading and victorious armies even today claim this "war prize." And if they meet with resistance from the women, they subject them to beatings, food deprivation and even execution.[60] Sexual violence not just results in terror, trauma, injuries and pain, but its victims also run the risk of getting pregnant and infected by sexually transmitted diseases. Their re-victimization in the form of socio-cultural consequences *inter alia* extends to "unmarriageability, refusal to accept by family, suicide, shame,"[61] "caring of child born of rape, family treating her as damaged goods and her child as an enemy offspring."[62] In Yugoslav wars, for instance, rape was carried out on mass level to insult and terrify a community. This attitude connects sexual violence with "the idea of women as property."[63] In a "non-technical sense,"[64] on the other hand, sexual violence is also termed as

45 Cohn (1993, pp. 236–237).

46 Charlesworth and Chinkin (2000, p. 251). For impact of wars on men, see ICRC (2022, p. 7) and Durham and O'Byrne (2010, pp. 47–49).

47 Charlesworth and Chinkin (2000, p. 251) and Gardam (1997, pp. 58–62).

48 MacKinnon (1994, p. 184).

49 Gardam and Charlesworth (2000, p. 151).

50 Charlesworth and Chinkin (2000, p. 252).

51 Gardam and Charlesworth (2000, p. 151).

52 ICRC (2022, p. 8) and Charlesworth and Chinkin (2000, p. 252).

53 ICRC (2022, p. 11).

54 Rehn and Sirleaf (2002, pp. 9–18), Women, United Nations (2002, pp. 14–18) and S/RES/1325 (31 October 2000). For a detailed account of various forms of wartime sexual abuses, see Bennoune (2007, p. 366).

55 Gardam (1997, pp. 58–59) and Charlesworth and Chinkin (2000, p. 252).

56 Alison (2007, p. 77).

57 Henry (2016, p. 44).

58 Alison (2007, p. 79).

59 Gardam (1997, p. 59).

60 United Nations (2002, p. 16).

61 For a detailed enumeration, see Bennoune (2007, p. 367).

62 Leatherman (2007, pp. 64, 65–67).

63 Charlesworth and Chinkin (2000, p. 254).

64 Gaggioli (2014, p. 519). Gaggioli further explains that technically, rape cannot amount to a weapon because it is an act in itself, as contrast to a device or an instrument. To consider it a method of combat is also erroneous because it does not add to the absolute prohibition of such an act. See, pp. 518–519.

a weapon and a method of war,[65] because many-a-times rape is systematically committed on mass level in order to terrorize civilians, destroy their morale and challenge the government, for instance rape camps set up in Bosnia with the support of commanders in 1992.

10.2.2 Third World Feminist Perspective

Third World scholars have argued that colonization and imperialism led to the origin and development of international law.[66] During the "long nineteenth century,"[67] ending with the year 1914, a major portion of international law expanded on the rules of war. Increasing colonization and imperialism shaped the form and content of the international law of war. These historical events were apparently manly acts not just because only men used to fight in the battlefield but also because such acts demonstrate an essentially masculine and patriarchal attitude of show of power.[68] The laws of war, thus, were based on gendered foundations.

An essential feature of the growing international law was the exclusionary gendered dyads of colonizer-colonized, and civilized-uncivilized, wherein the first category symbolizes manly characteristics of power and domination, while the second expression reflects the feminine elements of weakness and victimization. The colonies were branded as uncivilized and, thus, considered unworthy of participating in the international law making. In the context of the law relating to war, these opposites were especially employed to exclude the application of restraints in case of war with a colony, on the premise that the uncivilized peoples are unworthy of any fair treatment.[69] In fact, the colonizers were reluctant to incorporate too many restraints in war or compromise with their military power. They wanted to maintain their supremacy and expand their empires unabated. Thus, the complex interface among colonization, patriarchy, global capitalism, imperialism and race significantly wrote the terms of the early laws of war. It must be noted that non-Western women had to undergo horrifying trauma during colonization and armed struggles against foreign domination. White feminism, however, barely takes account of colonial and anti-colonial wars, and the experiences of the Third World women.[70]

10.2.3 Gender Bias in the Protection Afforded by Law

Despite these experiences, the early laws of armed conflict were blind towards these concerns. Before World War II, very little of the laws of war was concerned with civilians.[71] Prohibition of attacks on civilians was missing completely. Excepting few provisions such as prohibiting confiscation of private property,[72] pillage[73] and collective punishments[74] during war, and forceful participation in military operations[75] or oath to the occupying State[76] during belligerent occupation, there were hardly any rules protecting civilian

[65] For rape as a weapon of war, see A/RES/48/143 (1993, para 2) and for rape as a tactic of war, see S/RES/1820 (2008, para 1).

[66] E.g. Anghie and Chimni (2003, pp. 80, 84).

[67] The span of the "long nineteenth century" is not uniform for every commentator. It is 1750–1914, in Koskenniemi and Stråth (2014, p. 11; 1789–1914), in Kennedy (1996, p. 390; 1776–1914), in Hulle and Lesaffer (2019). However, the ending point, 1914, is uniform.

[68] Barbara Ehrenreich rightly mentions that imperialism, militarism and capitalism are simply expressions of male aggressiveness. Cited in Chimni (2017, p. 402).

[69] Vitoria also sought to justify brutal wars in this fashion.

[70] See, Chimni (2017, pp. 386–387).

[71] Best (1979, p. 27).

[72] Art. 46, Regulations concerning the Laws and Customs of War on Land, annexed to the Hague Convention (II) with Respect to the Laws and Customs of War on Land of 29 July 1899 (Hague Regulations 1899/Hague Convention II) and Regulations respecting the Laws and Customs of War on Land, annexed to the Hague Convention (IV) with Respect to the Laws and Customs of War on Land of 18 October 1907 (Hague Regulations 1907/Hague Convention IV).

[73] Art. 47, ibid.

[74] Art. 50, ibid.

[75] Art. 44 Hague Regulations 1899, above n 73.

[76] Art. 45 above n 73.

lives, let alone special provisions for the safety of women and children. Conversely, there were detailed rules addressing various concerns of soldiers who were, of course, men. This includes comprehensive provisions ensuring care, protection and good of prisoners of war,[77] sick and wounded soldiers,[78] troops on the battlefield,[79] spies,[80] and troops and the wounded in neutral States.[81] Thus the pre-World War II laws of war were blind towards women and biased towards men so far as effects of war were concerned. Interestingly, the Hague Regulations require "humane" treatment with prisoners of war[82] and supply to interned troops of basic necessities as required by "humanity."[83] Certainly, in this version of humanity, only men count as human beings.

There are even deeper patriarchal foundations for not prescribing legal protection for civilians as a whole during war. Fighting in war as soldiers and sacrificing life for the country is considered a masculine act.[84] And being a guard of the "fatherland,"[85] they deserve more respect and legal protection. Their lives matter. Conversely, non-participation in war carries images of weakness and femininity and, thus, does not merit legal protection.

10.2.4 Patriarchal Vernacular

The way in which the laws of armed conflict address the issues of women in international as well as non-international armed conflicts, remains inspired by capitalist patriarchal notions. They reflect a predominant male perspective, whereas men and women experience the consequences of armed conflicts differently. To begin with, the laws of armed conflict view women through the lenses of patriarchy in their conventional stereotypical roles. It has been investigated that about half the provisions, which address the concerns of women affected by war, see women in their relational capacities as caring or pregnant mothers[86] and "not as individuals in their own right."[87] Even the provisions seeking to protect women from sexual violence do so from a male perspective. Under the Geneva Convention on Civilians, a provision has been worded in the following vocabulary:

> Women shall be especially protected against any attack on their honor, in particular against rape, enforced prostitution, or any form of indecent assault.[88]

The patriarchal vernacular of the provision has been severely criticized by articulating its basic assumptions.[89] For instance, the provision does not consider sexual abuse as a wrong against her bodily integrity[90] or torture[91] or a crime of violence.[92] Connecting violence to woman's honor fosters the idea of her ownership as property by a male.[93] Connecting sexual offence with honor is to see rape as a social stigma and a fall in women's virtue, rather than an attack against her body and psyche.[94] The provision actually seeks to prevent attack on male members' honor, instead of that of female.[95] The language of the Article finds women's honor in some of her

[77] Sec. I, Ch. II, ibid.

[78] Art. 21, ibid.

[79] Art. 23, ibid.

[80] Sec. I, Ch. II, ibid.

[81] Sec. IV, Hague Regulations 1899, above n 73.

[82] Art. 4, above n 73.

[83] Art. 58 Hague Regulations 1899, above n 73.

[84] Alison (2007, p. 76) and Gardam and Charlesworth (2000, p. 157). It has been named as "masculinity cult": Tetreault, cited in Gardam (1988–1989, p. 265).

[85] Phrase borrowed from Dijk (2022, p. 292).

[86] Gardam (1997, p. 57).

[87] Gardam and Charlesworth (2000, p. 159).

[88] Art. 27 para 2 Geneva Convention relative to the Protection of Civilian Persons in Time of War of 12 August 1949 (Geneva Convention IV).

[89] See generally, Gardam (1997, p. 74), Gardam and Charlesworth (2000, p. 159) and Charlesworth (1999, pp. 386–387).

[90] United Nations. https://www.un.org/womenwatch/daw/public/w2apr98.htm and Sassòli (2019, p. 557).

[91] Gardam (1997, p. 74).

[92] MacKinnon (1987, p. 85).

[93] Charlesworth (1999, p. 386).

[94] Haeri and Puechguirbal (2010, p. 118).

[95] Gardam (1997, p. 68).

sexual attributes, instead of her intellect or personality, which are considered as exclusive male domains.[96] This approach is, thus, a reflection of a "male view of rape."[97] It has been argued that these archconservative provisions were drafted because in World War II, the participation of women in combat roles had destabilized the sex differences.[98]

More importantly, the above-cited provision does not prohibit rape during armed conflicts despite its long history. Multiple theories have been suggested in response to this failure. It has been argued that sexual violence was seen by the male drafters as a natural inevitable outcome of war.[99] Second, the delegates did not deliberate on sexual violence during war so that the Conference does not bring the rapists in their own armies into discussion.[100]

The provisions requiring care, protection and respect of women combatants have been worded in a language that projects them as weak. For instance, the Geneva Convention I provides that the sick and wounded female members of armed forces shall be treated with all considerations[101] or the regard[102] due to their sex. According to the original ICRC commentaries to the provisions, special consideration must be accorded to women because they are weak and their modesty and honor requires respect.[103] However, now the ICRC considers these provisions and their explanations to be discriminatory.[104] In the latest edition of the Commentaries to these articles, the ICRC has distanced itself from this construction by saying that the original interpretation was a reflection of the then social and historical context, and the same is no longer appropriate.[105] Actually, however, the provisions were not just a product of the contemporary settings but also of what the ICRC too believed in.

10.2.5 Gender Blind Law

Although war affects women more severely than men and thereby adds to their vulnerability, the laws of armed conflict, instead of having special provisions for women, often becomes blind to their concerns. Its provisions have been crafted mainly keeping in mind male civilians. For instance, under the precautionary principle, effective advance warning must be given of attacks likely to affect civilians.[106] While men may find it easy to flee, expectant women or women with small babies do encounter problems in sudden shifting and movement. Even after the displacement to refugee camps, women not only become easy target of sexual abuse and male domination, but face the lack of health and hygiene facilities, and nutrition.[107]

Another common sight of contestation in the laws of armed conflict in respect of sexual violence is rules on "grave breaches"[108] of the 1949 Geneva Convention on civilians. It has been repeatedly highlighted that rape and other forms of sexual violence have not been included in grave breaches[109] of the Convention.[110] It must

[96] Gardam and Charlesworth (2000, p. 159).

[97] Gardam (1997, p. 74).

[98] Dijk (2022, p. 294).

[99] Ibid., p. 297.

[100] Ibid., p. 298.

[101] Art. 12, The Geneva Convention for the Amelioration of the Condition of the Wounded and Sick in Armed Forces in the Field of 12 August 1949 (Geneva Convention I) and the Geneva Convention for the Amelioration of the Condition of Wounded, Sick and Shipwrecked Members of Armed Forces at Sea of 12 August 1949 (Geneva Convention II).

[102] Art. 14, Geneva Convention relative to the Treatment of Prisoners of War of 12 August 1949 (Geneva Convention III).

[103] Pictet (1952, 1960a, b).

[104] ICRC (2022, p. 23).

[105] ICRC (2016, 2017, 2020).

[106] Art. 57(2)(c) Protocol Additional to the Geneva Conventions of 12 August 1949, and relating to the Protection of Victims of International Armed Conflicts (Protocol I) of 8 June 1977.

[107] Charlesworth and Chinkin (2016, pp. 174–175) and Charlesworth (1999, p. 385).

[108] See, Art. 146, 147 Geneva Convention relative to the Protection of Civilian Persons in Time of War of 12 August 1949 (Geneva Convention IV).

[109] Ibid., Art. 147.

[110] See generally, Gardam (1997, p. 75), Gardam and Charlesworth (2000, p. 159) and Charlesworth (1999, pp. 386–387).

be noted here that the Convention requires its parties to lay down in the domestic law stringent punishment for those who commit grave breaches of the Convention, and to prosecute them or facilitate extradition for their trial.[111] Consequently, non-inclusion of sexual violence in grave breaches does not compel State-parties to shape their panel laws on such serious issues pertaining to women. In response to this objection of non-inclusion, it has been suggested that in the enumeration of grave breaches, the expressions "torture or inhuman treatment" and "willfully-causing great suffering or serious injury to body or health" are broad enough and may be interpreted to cover sexual assaults.[112] But these explanations are masculine ways of dealing with women's issues: lightly, casually and insincerely. These are attempts to mask the stripped maleness. Nevertheless, the grave breaches provision completely ignores a grave mental and physical trauma specific to women.

10.2.6 Proportionality Principle and Women

As the law is blind towards women's significant matters, it is no surprise when it devalues the lives of women and becomes insensitive towards them. The proportionality principle draws such a picture. It seeks to prevent in few ways,

> an attack which may be expected to cause incidental loss of civilian life, injury to civilians, damage to civilian objects, or a combination thereof, which would be excessive in relation to the concrete and direct military advantage anticipated.[113]

At the first place, the provisions containing proportionality principle approves incidental harm to civilians and damage to civilian property, if the same is not excessive to the direct military advantage anticipated. However, be it the loss of any family member or damage to civilian objects, it makes women more vulnerable so far as economic condition of family, women's own health[114] and household responsibilities are concerned. For instance, destruction of a path regularly used by women to bring water, firewood and food affects women and illustrates gendered impact of military operations.[115]

Further, the proportionality test requires assessment of probable loss to civilians, however, in many cases women stay inside the house to perform domestic activities as dictated by patriarchy. Their invisibility to an attack planner reduces the quantum of likely collateral damage in the calculation beforehand and, consequently, prompts attack. Thus, the probability of women becoming victims of armed attacks increases because of their engagement in gendered domestic roles. Patriarchy often makes them invisible to outsiders, but patriarchal law may make them invisible forever. The concept of incidental civilian harm under the proportionality principle is, therefore, narrow and gendered. The probable hardships to women due to an armed attack are out of its purview. Thus, for instance, it does not take into account the likely problems that women may have to encounter, in particular, loss of health facilities, food and water shortage, displacement and dislocation consequent upon military operations.[116] Such losses are invisible to male commanders. Here, while calculating the probable civilian harm, the foreseeability of a commander has its limits not because of distance or light but because of myopic patriarchal vision.

Another side of proportionality assessment is to anticipate whether an attack is likely to cause more or less civilian damage as compared to the military advantage. It thus involves value-judgment as to the foreseeable loss by predominantly male commanders.[117] It is a subjective assessment of the worth of someone's life, safety and health. The value assigned to the lives and wellbeing of women and female specific objects

[111] Art. 147 Geneva Convention IV, above n 109.

[112] Sassòli (2019, p. 555) and Gardam (1997, p. 76).

[113] Art. 51 (5)(b) Protocol I, above n 107. See also Articles 57(2)(a)(iii), 57(2)(b) Protocol I. See Ch. 13, for more on proportionality principle.

[114] United Nations (2002, pp. 32–46).

[115] ICRC (2022, p. 16).

[116] Gardam and Charlesworth (2000, p. 161).

[117] Gardam (1997, p. 71) and ICRC (2022, p. 15).

(e.g. an exclusive maternity hospital)[118] varies in different cultures and societies. There are societies with practices, like female feticide, witch-hunting, *Devdasi* and *Sati*. In some cultures, boys and other male family members eat first,[119] followed by the female family members. Given the inferior social position of women, a perpetrator, for instance, may consider attack on civilians with male majority disproportionate to resultant military gain, but may find attack on a group of civilians with female majority proportionate to military benefit in similar circumstances. Proportionality assessment may be gender-biased and regard probable harm to women insignificant. Thus, the application of the proportionality principle may have deadly consequences to women.[120]

In the proportionality equation, while the concept of concrete military advantage itself is a masculine one, its application also carries a gendered dimension. The ambit of military advantage extends to saving the lives of own military members who are primarily men.[121] Accordingly, under the proportionality principle, the life, safety, health or property of civilians may be sacrificed in order to protect a belligerent's own soldiers. Such hierarchical value of lives is attributed to the concerns of military necessity.[122] The legal bias and imbalance in the worth and protection of lives of combatants and civilians also illustrates public/private dichotomy.[123] It has been argued that the laws of armed conflict focus more on the protection of combatants as their fighting for the State amounts to a public activity.[124] On the other hand, women's lives matter less as they are mainly engaged in domestic/private roles. The spectrum of military advantage is, thus, gender-biased.

10.2.7 Humanity Principle and Women

Despite validating killings of soldiers and incidental loss to civilians, the laws of armed conflict are glorified as founded on the principle of humanity and popularized as a new discipline in the name of "International Humanitarian Law." Notably, this gendered yet "humanitarian" law contains detailed legal provisions woven in the language of prohibitions[125] in favor of predominantly male combatants in international armed conflicts.[126] However, it provides for relatively general and weaker provisions for the benefit of civilians covering almost all women[127] worded in a vernacular of protection.[128] Vague and flexible terms, such as "as soon as" and "as far as possible" are often employed in the rules protecting civilians, thereby weakening the protection available to them.[129] Principle of military necessity as an overarching idea values the lives of combatants more.

The laws of armed conflict comprise of a legal framework whose conceptual building blocks are masculine; whose claims of neutrality and objectivity are lies; whose protection mechanism is biased in favor of men; whose equal protection promises are fake; whose normative framework presupposes men as default human beings; which seeks to protect men's honor in the name of protecting women against sexual assault; whose vernacular finds women in gendered roles confirming to male standards; whose language is full of default omnipresent male pronoun "he"; which creates smokescreen against women; which betrays women by discriminating against them overlooking their sacrifice, and contribution and

[118] See ICRC (2022, p. 17).

[119] Gardam (1997, p. 61) and Charlesworth (1999, p. 388).

[120] See generally, Fellmeth (2000, pp. 715–716).

[121] Though, Gardam makes the point but does not critique it from feminist perspective. See, Gardam (1993, p. 409; 1997, p. 72) and Stephens and Lewis (2005, p. 72).

[122] Gardam (1997, p. 72).

[123] Ibid.

[124] Gardam (1988–1989, p. 276).

[125] Gardam and Charlesworth (2000, p. 159) and Charlesworth (1999, p. 386).

[126] Charlesworth (1999, p. 389).

[127] Ibid.

[128] Gardam and Charlesworth (2000, p. 159) and ibid.

[129] For example, Art. 16 para 2, 18 paras 4–5, 73 para 2 Geneva Convention IV.

importance of their conventional roles at the backstage of armed conflict[130]; which is deaf towards women's perception and experiences of war; which provides a hierarchical structure of lives with men's lives at the top; wherein men's issues find space as common human issues and women's concerns are conferred selective recognition at the margins. In such a law, human beings primarily mean men and humanity means masculinity. Its excessively marketed and trumpeted title, International Humanitarian Law, is a shameful charade.

10.2.8 Gendered Dimension of Regulating the Conduct in Non-international Armed Conflict

Prior to World War II, the international laws of armed conflict did not address and regulate at all the hostile conduct in civil/internal wars or armed conflicts of non-international character.[131] Even in the 1949 Geneva Conventions, the regulation of conduct in non-international armed conflicts has been confined to one provision, Article 3 common to the four Conventions, with inadequate protection to victims. States including the post-colonial were in favor of domestic legal regulation and control of armed rebellion and civil war.[132] It was strongly argued that it was a private matter and any international regulation thereof would make inroads in sovereignty.[133] After almost three decades, a separate Protocol (Protocol II) dedicated to non-international armed conflicts was adopted in 1977.[134] However, the Protocol provides for objective criteria, and the threshold of applicability of the Protocol has been set so high that it becomes applicable in rare conflict situations.[135] To uncover the gendered foundations of neglect of non-international armed conflicts, feminists trace the oppositional pair of public/private in liberal legal theory.

In the Western liberal thought, private sphere is considered as women's space, while the public world is dominated by men.[136] It demarcates what is public and what is private by further suggesting that the public is suitable for regulation by State, while the private domain occupied by women falls within individual autonomy (of male).[137] Accordingly, it suggests that women's issues and problems of torture and assault at home are to be left unattended. Conversely, violence in public space, of course dominated by men, requires State intervention being a public matter.[138] Feminists therefore argue that public world is a sight of power, maleness and economic and political life, while the domestic arena is seen as consisting of children and home, and thus fit for women.[139] They contend that the continuity of public/private dualism rests on normalization of male–female features: For men, they are aggression, curiosity, ambition and responsibility; while for women, affection, emotions, care and obedience.[140] Correspondingly, they suggest, law is seen from the lens of public or men's world as rational, objective and

[130] Charlesworth and Chinkin (2000, p. 56) and Gardam (1997, p. 72). Shouldn't this role also extend to sexual services provided to soldiers while carrying out a masculine public activity, war? Notably, more than one lac "comfort women" from occupied territories were forced to offer such services to Japanese troops in World War II. On the supply of sexual services during war, see Charlesworth and Chinkin (2000, pp. 56, 253) and Gardam (1997, p. 78).

[131] See Art. 2 Hague Convention II and IV, above n 73.

[132] Final Records of the Diplomatic Conference of Geneva of 1949, vol II Section B. p. 328 (Burma) and Official Records of the Diplomatic Conference on the Reaffirmation and Development of International Humanitarian Law Applicable in Armed Conflicts Geneva (1974–1977), vol VII, p. 64 (Nigeria), p. 81 (India), vol VIII, p. 207 (Germany).

[133] Ibid.

[134] Protocol Additional to the Geneva Conventions of 12 August 1949, and Relating to the Protection of Victims of Non-International Armed Conflicts (Protocol II), 8 June 1977.

[135] See Cullen (2010, pp. 109–112) and Minimum humanitarian standards, Analytical Report of the Secretary-General Submitted Pursuant to Commission on Human Rights Resolution 1997/21, UN Doc. E/CN.4/1998/87, 5 January 1998.

[136] See Tesón (1993, p. 658).

[137] Charlesworth and Chinkin (2000, p. 31).

[138] Fellmeth (2000, p. 668).

[139] Charlesworth et al. (1991, p. 626) and Charlesworth (1999, p. 383).

[140] Charlesworth et al. (1991, p. 626).

powerful, as opposed to private or female's place which is emotional, passive and subjective.[141] International law has been said to be operating in "the most public of all public worlds."[142] Thus, for instance, the United Nations Charter,

> makes the (public) province of international law distinct from the (private) sphere of domestic jurisdiction, … the law of state responsibility sorts out (public) actions for which the state is accountable from those 'private' ones for which it does not have to answer internationally.[143]

Accordingly, the regulation of belligerent conduct in (public) international armed conflicts, and the early non-regulation and the present impracticable regulation of hostile conduct in (private) non-international armed conflicts under international law reproduce the gendered notions of public/private distinction.[144]

10.3 Attempts to Dilute and Appropriate the Feminist Movement

While, the laws of armed conflict are inherently biased and structurally a gendered body of norms, few arguments have been put forward in the recent past in order to counter the feminist critique. Embedded in sophisticated vocabulary, these attempts seek to subvert, dilute and divert the feminist project on the laws of armed conflict. First is denial and burden-shifting. The ICRC believes that the reason behind women suffering from tragic wartime consequences is not any weakness in the law, but its poor implementation.[145] Notably, the implementation of the laws of armed conflict falls within the field of international criminal law where the ICRC appears to be shipping the burden. Similarly, some commentators place the responsibility on State-parties and recommend better respect for the extant rules instead of adopting new rules.[146] It must be noted here that the argument of adequacy of women-centric provisions in the laws of armed conflict is founded on the quantitative examination of the provisions, and not a qualitative one.[147] These are top-down observations. While the due implementation of the prevalent rules is significant, these musings are often used to veil the gendered character and male view of the laws of armed conflict.

The second contention relates to sexual violence on males. It has been suggested that gender perspective of the laws of armed conflict must involve the experiences of men and boys also because they too face sexual abuse of several forms during armed conflict.[148] Though, the law must adequately address male sexual victimization also, however, it must be ensured that the male centric discourse does not eclipse the female perspectives and experiences of war, just because some members of a dominant class (in this case heterosexual males) are targeted whose suffering arguably demands more and immediate attention as compared to the "others." This apprehension is obvious given the patriarchal form of society. Further, it must be understood that the reasons, experiences and consequences of sexual abuse are different for women and men. Where during war, women's sexual exploitation is treated as adversary's shame and defeat, a belligerent would prefer to commit the same more violently and on a larger scale. Similarly, so far as post-abuse trauma is concerned, a husband would be more likely to discard his wife who has been raped. These and many other differences in respect of sexual violence on women and men cannot be ignored.

---

[141] Ibid., p. 627.

[142] Charlesworth and Chinkin (2000, p. 31).

[143] Ibid.

[144] Despite this, however, Marco Sassòli takes a narrow view of public/private dyad and argues that quarrels and violence at home are not a subject matter of law of armed conflict, but that of international human rights law. Sassòli (2019, p. 557).

[145] ICRC (1995, p. 26).

[146] Krill (1985, p. 360). See also, Bennoune (2007, pp. 363–391).

[147] For instance, Krill calculates that out of 560 Articles of the four Geneva Conventions, 1949 and two Additional Protocols, 1977, almost 40 Articles specifically address women's concerns: Krill (1985, p. 360). According to the ICRC, the number is somewhere around 50: ICRC (1995, p. 6).

[148] Carpenter (2006, pp. 83–103) and Durham and O'Byrne (2010, p. 49).

The third deals with patriarchal hegemonic appropriation of feminist movement. To argue this, Gardam cites an article co-authored by Helen Durham and Katie O'Byrne,[149] published in the ICRC's journal, International Review of the Red Cross.[150] She points out that in the context of male sexual abuse, the authors have argued a gender-equal approach under the laws of armed conflict.[151] They have suggested that the comprehensive legal prohibitions of sexual violence are useful in this regard because they do not specifically apply to women and girls, and therefore may be relevant in case of male sexual exploitation. The authors, thus, seek to challenge the perception of the laws of armed conflict, a task which has been done by feminist scholars in the context of the need for better recognition of women's experience of war but of no avail.[152] On the other hand, similar strategies have been readily put to use in the context of male sexual abuse. Gardam notes:

> This example provides a salutary lesson in how the patriarchy can seamlessly appropriate what starts out as a rare positive for women and turn it to the use of men. It is not the fact that men can also benefit from gender equality that is of concern but that, as explained further below, we risk in such a process, albeit often inadvertently, gender becoming a negative for women.[153]

It is worth noting that this appropriation is facilitated and justified not just by citing the incidents of sexual abuse of men and boys, but by portraying the picture of women as combatants, cruel interrogators in Abu Ghraib and perpetrators of crimes (e.g. Pauline Nyiramasuhuko), and that of men as victims.[154] Dominant classes, in the ordinary course of life too, have this tendency of projecting themselves as major victims and, therefore, worthy of immediate and strong attention, and thereby, appropriating the mechanism originally meant for the marginalized classes of people.

Soon, the apprehensions of appropriation of the notion of gender equality became apparent in few of the international initiatives too. Gardam illustrates:

> For example, a conference organised by the ICRC *Responding to rape in armed conflict how can we do better*? that took place on the 25th November 2014, stresses the prevalence of the rape of male refugees and the outcome document of the 2014 UK Global Summit to end Sexual violence in conflict was extremely carefully worded to maintain gender equality. All well and good–who could disagree in theory?[155]

Recently, in an ICRC document on Strategy on Sexual Violence (2018–2022), one of the indicators and activities useful in measuring the achievement of the strategic objective of effectively addressing sexual violence in diverse ways[156] was drafted in this fashion:

> Indicator 1.5. Research and Understanding: Extent to which specific issues of humanitarian concern related to sexual violence are explored/better understood by the ICRC
>
> Means/Example activities: Conduct research on key thematic issues related to sexual violence such as sexual violence against men and boys ...[157]

Although male may also benefit from the legal provisions, and the initiatives of the ICRC and others, Gardam cautions that sexual violence against women during armed conflict is not only quantitatively different but qualitatively too, as already exemplified.[158] Therefore, the matter of concern is dilution of the distinction, the appropriation of feminist ideas and disproportionately diverting the attention from female sexual abuse.

---

[149] Durham and O'Byrne (2010, pp. 31–52).

[150] Gardam, (2014) p. 2.

[151] Ibid.

[152] Ibid. Feminists have contended for long how international law is gender-blind to women and the same fell on deaf ears as unimportant. However, the same argument was conveniently applied in respect of men. The Chair's Summary to Global Summit to End Sexual Violence in Conflict (2014) says that data-collection of victims of sexual violence should not be gender blind to men and boys: OCHA (2014).

[153] Gardam, (2014) p. 2.

[154] Durham and O'Byrne (2010, pp. 37–42).

[155] Gardam, (2014) p. 5.

[156] ICRC (2018, p. 8).

[157] ICRC (2018, p. 9).

[158] Gardam, (2014) p. 5.

References

Alison M (2007) Wartime sexual violence: women's human rights and questions of masculinity. Rev Int Stud 33(1):75–90

Anghie A, Chimni BS (2003) Third world approaches to international law and individual responsibility in internal conflicts. Chinese Journal of International Law 2(1):77–103

Bennoune K (2007) Do we need new international law to protect women in armed conflict. Case Western Reserve Journal of International Law 38(2):363–391

Best G (1979) Restraints on war by land before 1945. In: Howard M (ed) Restraints on war: studies in the limitation of armed conflict. OUP, Oxford, pp 17–37

Bhaskar B (2020) Ambedkar, Lohia, and the segregations of caste and gender. Caster: Glob J Soc Exclusion 1(2):63–72

Bianchi A (2016) International law theories: an inquiry into different ways of thinking. OUP, Oxford

Broude T (2013) Keep calm and carry on: Martti Koskenniemi and the fragmentation of international law. Temple Int'l Comp LJ 27(2):279–292

Carpenter C (2006) Recognizing gender-based violence against civilian men and boys in conflict situations. Secur Dialogue 37(1):83–103

Chamallas M (2013) Introduction to feminist legal theory. Wolters Kluwer, New York

Charlesworth H (1994) Feminists critiques of international law and their critics. Third World Legal Studies 13:1–16

Charlesworth H (1999) Feminist methods in international law. American Journal of International Law 93(2):379–394

Charlesworth H (2000) Martha Nussbaum's feminist internationalism. Ethics 111(1):64–78

Charlesworth H et al (1991) Feminist approaches to international law. American Journal of International Law 85(4):613–645

Charlesworth H, Chinkin C (2000) The boundaries of international law: a feminist analysis. Manchester University Press, Manchester

Charlesworth H, Chinkin C (2016) An alien's review of women and armed conflict. In: Stephens D, Babie P (eds) Imagining law: essays in conversation with Judith Gardam. University of Adelaide Press, Adelaide, pp 171–194

Chimni BS (2017) International law and world order: a critique of contemporary approaches. CUP, Cambridge

Chinkin C (1992) A gendered perspective to the international use of force. Australian Yearbook of International Law 12:279–293

Christiansen AE (1994) Gendering war talk by Miriam Cooke and Angela Woollacott (Book Review). Hypatia 9(2):206–212

Cohn C (1993) Wars, wimps, and women: talking gender and thinking war. In: Cooke M, Woollacott A (eds) Gendering war talk. Princeton University Press, Princeton, pp 227–246

Cullen A (2010) The concept of non-international armed conflict in international humanitarian law. CUP, New York

Dalton C (1987–1988) Where we stand: observation on the situation of feminist legal thought. Berkeley Women's Law J 3:1–13

Davies M (2017) Asking the law question. Thomson Reuters, Sydney

Dijk B (2022) Gendering the Geneva conventions. Hum Rights Q 44(2):286–312

Durham H, O'Byrne K (2010) The dialogue of difference: gender perspectives on international humanitarian law. Int Rev Red Cross 92(877):31–52

Fellmeth AX (2000) Feminism and international law: theory, methodology, and substantive reform. Hum Rights Q 22(3):658–733

Gaggioli G (2014) Sexual violence in armed conflicts: a violation of international humanitarian law and human rights law. Int Rev Red Cross 96(894):503–538

Gardam J (1988–1989) A feminist analysis of certain aspects of international humanitarian law. Aust Year Book Int 12:265–278

Gardam J (1993) Proportionality and force in international law. Am J Int Law 87(3):391–413

Gardam J (1997) Women and the law of armed conflict: why the silence? Int Comp Law Q 46(1):55–80

Gardam J, Charlesworth H (2000) Protection of women in armed conflict. Hum Rights Q 22(1):148–166

Gardam J (2014) More of the same-feminist interactions with IHL. https://regnet.anu.edu.au/sites/default/files/files/CIGJ-%20RecentDevelopFeministThinkingIL&IR-20141203-Gardam-MoreOfTheSame.pdf

Gimenez ME (1975) Marxism and feminism. Front J Women Stud 1(1):61–80

Gimenez ME (2005) Capitalism and the oppression of women: Marx revisited. Sci Soc 69(1):11–32

Haeri M, Puechguirbal N (2010) From helplessness to agency: examining the plurality of women's experiences in armed conflict. Int Rev Red Cross 92(877):103–122

Henry N (2016) Theorizing wartime rape: deconstructing gender, sexuality, and violence. Gend Soc 30(1):44–56

Hulle IV, Lesaffer R (eds) (2019) International law in the long nineteenth century (1776–1914). Brill and Nijhoff, Leiden

ICRC (1995) Women and law. ICRC

ICRC (2016) Commentary on article 12, Geneva convention I. https://ihl-databases.icrc.org/en/ihl-treaties/gci-1949/article-12/commentary/2016

ICRC (2017) Commentary on article 12, Geneva convention II. https://ihl-databases.icrc.org/en/ihl-treaties/gcii-1949/article-12/commentary/2017

ICRC (2018) Strategy on sexual violence, 2018–2022. ICRC, Geneva

ICRC (2020) Commentary on article 14, Geneva convention III. https://ihl-databases.icrc.org/en/ihl-treaties/gciii-1949/article-14/commentary/2020

ICRC (2022) Gendered impacts of armed conflict and implications for the application of international humanitarian law. ICRC, Geneva

Kapadia K (2020) Ambedkar's feminism. Econ Polit Weekly LV(1):10–12

Kapur R (2002) The tragedy of victimisation rhetoric: resurrecting the "native" subject in international/postcolonial feminist legal politics. Harv Hum Rights J 15:1–38

Kennedy DW (1996) International law and the nineteenth century: history of an illusion. Nordic J Int Law 65:385–420

Koskenniemi M (2006) From apology to utopia: the structure of international legal argument. CUP, New York

Koskenniemi M (2011) The politics of international law. Hart Publishing, Oxford

Koskenniemi M, Leino P (2002) Fragmentation of international law? postmodern anxieties. Leiden J Int Law 15:553–579

Koskenniemi M, Stråth B (2014) Creating community, ordering the world and struggling for securing welfare, an introduction. In: Koskenniemi M, Stråth B (eds) Europe 1815–1914: creating community and ordering the world. University of Helsinki, Helsinki, pp 1–15

Krill F (1985) The protection of women in international humanitarian law. Int Rev Red Cross 249:337–363

Leatherman J (2007) Sexual violence and armed conflict: complex dynamics of revictimization. Int J Peace Stud 12(1):53–71

MacKinnon CA (1982) Feminism, Marxism, method, and the state: an agenda for theory. Signs 7(3):515–544

MacKinnon CA (1983) Feminism, Marxism, method, and the state: towards feminist jurisprudence. Signs 8(4):635–658

MacKinnon CA (1987) Feminism unmodified: discourse on life and law. Harvard University Press, Cambridge

MacKinnon CA (1994) Rape, genocide, and women's human rights. In: Stiglmayer A (ed) Mass rape: the war against women in Bosnia-Herzegovina. University of Nebraska Press, Lincoln

Mohanty CT (1984) Under Western eyes: feminist scholarship and colonial discourses. Boundary 2 12(3):333–358

OCHA (2014) Chair's summary to global summit to end sexual violence in conflict, 13 June 2014. https://reliefweb.int/report/world/chairs-summary-global-summit-end-sexual-violence-conflict

Pictet J (1952) Commentary on article 12, Geneva convention I. https://ihl-databases.icrc.org/en/ihl-treaties/gci-1949/article-12/commentary/1952?activeTab=

Pictet J (1960a) Commentary on article 12, Geneva convention II. https://ihl-databases.icrc.org/en/ihl-treaties/gcii-1949/article-12/commentary/1960?activeTab=

Pictet J (1960b) Commentary on article 14, Geneva convention III. https://ihl-databases.icrc.org/en/ihl-treaties/gciii-1949/article-14/commentary/1960?activeTab=

Rehn E, Sirleaf EJ (2002) Women, war and peace: the independent experts' assessment on the impact of armed conflict on women and women's role in peace-building. United Nations Development Fund for Women, New York

Sassòli M (2019) International humanitarian law: rules, controversies, and solutions to problems arising in warfare. Edward Elgar, Cheltenham

Stephens D, Lewis MW (2005) The law of armed conflict—a contemporary critique. Melbourne J Int Law 6(1):55–85

Tesón FR (1993) Feminism and international law: a reply. Virginia J Int Law 33:647–684

United Nations (2002) Peace and security, study submitted by the Secretary-General pursuant to Security Council resolution 1325 (2000). United Nations, New York

United Nations (2000) Sexual violence and armed conflict: United Nations response. Women

Queer Perspective to International Humanitarian Law

11

Abstract

In this chapter, I offer a critique of the laws of armed conflict from a queer perspective. I initially talk about the patriarchal normalization of gender binary and introduce the queer theory. I unearth the fundamental heterosexual-normalcy and binary assumptions, and explain how they are problematic so far as the protection of bodies with different gender identities or sexual orientations during an armed conflict is concerned. Subsequently, I seek to explain how they experience war in a different way, and in spite of this, the law is blind towards these bodies and their concerns. I also try to highlight the blind, deaf and discriminatory nature of the legal provisions from a queer perspective.

Keywords

Queer and IHL · Gender and IHL · Homosexuality and IHL · LGBT and war

11.1 Patriarchal Normalization of Binary

It is essential though common to begin this discussion by introducing sex and gender. It is said that sex is biological and categorizes bodies as male or female. On this biological foundation,[1] patriarchal society constructs gender.[2] It does so by assigning a whole lot of features different for men and women, such as behavior, color-preferences, responsibilities and sexuality. This approach of looking at sex presupposes that sex is natural, pre-political and objective,[3] and gender is socially and culturally created post birth. However, taking into account practices, like categorization of bodies into male or female at birth, crave for pre-natal sex determination, female feticide, mutilation of several bodies for their failure to conform to either category of sex; it has been argued that sex itself is a cultural category and, thus, "gender in disguise."[4]

Thus, the socio-cultural beliefs and practices implant, solidify and normalize the masculine-feminine gender binary. This binary is of course manufactured by social processes, instead of biological ones, as naturalists claim.[5] Bodies are thrown into watertight compartments of typical default gender roles and identities.[6] Beyond these

[1] Dozier, cited in Darwin (2017, p. 319).

[2] Berkowitz et al. (2010, p. 133).

[3] Srinivasan (2021, p. xi).

[4] Ibid., pp. xi–xii.

[5] Rahman (2020, p. 17).

[6] See, Charlesworth (1999, p. 206). On how gender interacts with other discourses and shapes them, see also, Cohn (1993, p. 228).

K. Jeenger, *A Humanitarian Critique of International Humanitarian Law*, Sustainable Development Goals Series, https://doi.org/10.1007/978-981-96-8319-2_11

sexed and gendered boundaries of male-female duality, the patriarchal society recognizes no other human beings. Indeed, "Gender is typically understood as a fixed location, that we can name and claim as an identity."[7] This rigidity and normalization of binary is hegemonic and inhuman. It is not neutral and all-encompassing.[8] A provision in the Statute of International Criminal Court (Rome Statute) illustrates well the international law's binary foundations:

> For the purpose of this Statute, it is understood that the term 'gender' refers to the two sexes, male and female, within the context of society. The term 'gender' does not indicate any meaning different from the above.[9]

Apparently, the provision excludes intersexuals and also bodies with different sexual orientation and gender identity, to say the least. Although, in 2014, the Office of the Prosecutor of International Criminal Court (ICC) released a policy paper and clarified that the Office considers inclusion of these categories.[10]

Sexual orientation towards a person of opposite sex (in short, heterosexuality) is one of the socially attributed essential features and occupies a primary position in the rigid gender binary. The binary labels the persons with different sexual orientations (e.g. gays, lesbians and bisexuals) or different gender identities (e.g. transgenders, intersexuals, and queers) as abnormal, deviant and an aberration, and hence considers them worthy of no dignity, respect and humane treatment. This stigmatization is layered and oppressive to these groups, though not uniformly.

Non-binary groups face more marginalization when they belong to and intersect with a category that is already oppressed, for instance, a bisexual or transgender who belongs to poor, black, tribal, disabled, refugee or *Dalit* community.[11] However, some of these persons belong to the otherwise dominant groups also, and may get identified as a white gay, a transgender born in a rich family, or a forward caste intersexual. These affiliations, though, do not guarantee them a dignified life similar to their binary affiliates; however, their experiences of marginalization differ from the former. These intersections are "sights of difference"[12] and offer a "specific angle of vision"[13] in order to draw attention to multidimensional inequalities and experiences. Thus, during war, civilians encounter violence and inhuman treatment of various sorts; however, the experiences of individuals with different sexual orientation or gender identity are more terrible. Despite that, the narrow vision of the laws of armed conflict (international humanitarian law) provides for restraints keeping in view the male-female binary only.

Therefore, there is suggested a non-binary approach which questions and challenges the normalized, rationalized and dominant understanding of sexuality and gender identity in terms of binary oppositions. This reference is to queer[14] and similar non-binary approaches. The term "queer" was invented in 1991 by Teresa de Lauretis.[15] The queer theory seeks to destabilize and transgress the norm of heterosexuality[16] because it believes in multiple sex identities and sexual orientations.[17] It rejects the idea of a pre-existing concept of gender wherein human beings may be compartmentalized. Instead, it recognizes the production of gender by performance, by doing it in every interaction of daily life,[18] for instance by doing gender-neutral things, or by rejecting gender binary in usual course.[19] In

[7] Faucette (2014, p. 80).

[8] Ibid., p. 86.

[9] Art. 7(3) Statute of International Criminal Court (1998) (Rome Statute).

[10] OTP (2014), paras 15–16. For a detailed comment on the Policy Paper, see Oosterveld (2017–2018, pp. 450–452).

[11] Rallin (2019, p. 373).

[12] Davies (2017, p. 271).

[13] MacKinnon (2013, p. 1020).

[14] The term queer has no definitional essence or content. It does not seek to realize rights because doing so makes identities static. See, Davies (2017, p. 289).

[15] Kepros (1999–2000, p. 281).

[16] Davies (2017, p. 289).

[17] Ibid., p. 288.

[18] Judith Butler, cited in Ghisleni et al. (2016, p. 770) and West and Zimmerman, cited in Smith and Smith (2016, p. 67).

[19] Darwin (2017, p. 318).

short, "we become our gender by the way we live, move, interact."[20] Overall,

> Non-binary activism brings something valuable to the table not because it destroys or eliminates gender, but because it questions the logic behind rigid gender norms, hierarchies, and the state's use of gender as an unnecessary control mechanism. This questioning benefits people of all genders, not only non-binary people.[21]

International law's exclusion of non-binary experiences and identities is also subject to queer scrutiny. In order to carry out this investigation, we need to, in Dianne Otto's terms, ""take a break" from "seeing normally.""[22] Thus, seeing differently, we find how sexual hierarchies structure international law; how international law institutionalizes heteronormativity,[23] and so on. Queer perspective thus seeks to expose, among others, the invisibility and exclusion of non-binary bodies in international law and the normalization of presumed heterosexuality[24] It seeks to shake the heterosexual architecture of international law that is considered as normal. Queer theory brings in fluidity to challenge international law's conceptual foundational rigidity and this foundation's insistence on permanence, boundaries and discipline. A queer critique of international law attempts to "celebrate human sexuality and gender expression in all its diversity and fluidity".[25]

11.2 Queer Critique of International Humanitarian Law

In light of the above backdrop, this section discusses the laws of armed conflict from a queer perspective.

[20] Davies (2017, p. 287).

[21] Faucette (2014, pp. 75–76).

[22] Otto (2007, p. 120).

[23] Buss (2007, p. 123).

[24] Otto (2007, p. 121).

[25] Otto (2018, p. 1).

11.2.1 In the Beginning

During the nineteenth century when the laws of armed conflict began to develop, same-sex sexual acts amounted to a punishable offence in many jurisdictions. It has been observed that this culpability originated in the West by way of moral condemnation of homosexual conduct as sin or vice.[26] Consistent with this moral principle, English enactments criminalized sodomy or buggery from the sixteenth century onwards.[27] The nineteenth century England under the Victorian reign experienced sexual starvation[28] and sexual repression for multiple reasons. It has been maintained that the industrial revolution and machine age also degenerated sexual drive among the commoners.[29] During this epoch, the homosexual Europeans working in the army, administration and trade found a private space free from any moral or legal prohibitions while on colonial adventures.[30] Even heterosexual English men in colonies engaged in fluid "situational homosexuality"[31] due to hot climate[32] and absence of their sexual partners. On the other side, homosexual behavior among the colonized folks, including Indians, was natural and frequent.[33] Therefore, the British Empire imposed anti-homosexuality laws[34] as a measure of social control on all its colonies, containing about a third of world's population.[35] The British intolerance

[26] Kirby (2015, p. 39).

[27] Ibid., pp. 81–82.

[28] Because of, for instance, prohibition of homosexual acts, anti-masturbatory campaigns and repression of woman's sexual response. See Hyam (1990, pp. 56–58).

[29] For a study in Germany, see Crouthamel (2008, pp. 61, 63).

[30] Aldrich (2003, pp. 58, 83).

[31] Ibid., p. 3.

[32] Kirby (2015, p. 95).

[33] Arondekar (2004, pp. 19–20).

[34] E.g. Sec. 377 Indian Penal Code (1860). The Supreme Court of India has declared this provision unconstitutional to the extent it criminalizes homosexual conduct in private space between two consenting adults. See, Navtej Singh Johar v. Union of India, AIR 2018 SC 4321.

[35] Kirby (2015, pp. 86–87).

towards homosexual conduct could also be seen in respect of colonial army. During World War I, England punished more than 230 soldiers[36] on the charges of "gross indecency" (homosexual offences) instead of being grateful to the thousands of gay soldiers[37] who fought for the "fatherland".[38]

The colonial attitude towards homosexuals was not much different in Germany. In the pre-World War I Germany, the top psychiatrists warned about disorders including sexual "deviance" in the industrialized German society.[39] In order to counter these proclivities to homosexuality, the German men were idealized as rational and capable of controlling their "irrational" instincts (homosexuality).[40] During the war, however, the shell-shocked "real men" naturally succumbed to a psychological trauma and breakdown of sexual desires, and developed "perverted" symptoms of masturbation and homosexuality also.[41] These findings were put forward by a famous sexologist, Hirschfeld, through his scientific research.[42] He also recommended decriminalization of homosexual acts; however, he and his organization were targeted soon after the Nazis came to power subsequently.[43]

In this way, the peak times of colonialism were full of homophobic beliefs and practices both in Europe and non-European world. The colonial rulers thus manufactured and concretized a gender identity featuring heterosexual male and normalized the same. It further produced, akin to the duality of civilized-uncivilized, contradictory dyads of normal-abnormal, natural-unnatural, healthy-sick, straight-deviant and rational-irrational, wherein the first term was attributed to the heterosexual males, while the other, to the homosexuals. These dichotomies were different from those related to male-female distinction in that the homosexual bodies representing the second term of these dualities were not just considered unworthy of any dignity and respect, but their natural tendencies were considered unnatural and their engagement in intimate acts was seen as a punishable offence. This attitude cemented the idea of an ambitious and aggressive, and a powerful and heterosexual man. It also got reflected in the content of the pre-World War I treaty law on armed conflict wherein no compromise was made with the aggressive conduct of war and the ambition of winning the battle, disregarding the concerns of civilian victims during war and people of occupied colonies. Given this construction of gender and the hostile attitude of the "civilized" colonial masters towards homosexuals, irrespective of their country of origin, there was no hope for any place for homosexuals in the laws of armed conflict, whatsoever. Thus, in the formative period of the law, the colonial countries built and hardened a "normal" heterosexual gender wherein there was no space for fluidity and sameness. The epoch of colonialism created a hostile environment towards the "others."

In the First World War, thousands of British and German gay soldiers fought for the country and lost their lives or limbs, but the ungrateful yet "civilized" countries continued to treat them as outlaws. Therefore, a striking feature of colonialism-homosexuality connect is related to the European homosexuals who were treated as perverted, heretic and hysteric at home, but who actually had the opportunities to get intimate with the foreign men in the colonies and befriend with them.[44] The hate received from their countrymen and love from foreign men changed their outlook towards European imperialism. It planted the seeds of anti-colonialism among them too. Consequently, a huge majority of them was critical of European rule or had ambivalent approach about it.[45]

The account of homosexuals in the Second World War is even more intense on this subject.

[36] Harvey (2001, p. 313).

[37] Including the two very famous war poets Siegfried Sassoon and Emmanuel Levinas.

[38] Phrase borrowed from Crouthamel (2008, p. 66).

[39] Ibid., p. 63.

[40] Ibid., p. 64.

[41] Ibid., pp. 61, 67, 83.

[42] Ibid., p. 71.

[43] Ibid.

[44] Aldrich (2003, p. 367).

[45] Ibid.

In addition to the criminalization of homosexuality in military law by many countries, the Nazis tortured, jailed or transferred to concentration camps thousands of gays.[46] Relying on the engrained prejudices, gay soldiers were not just presumed to be weak (without any evidence)[47] but a threat to the "masculinity" of heterosexual males. This stereotypical dynamic worked differently in case of dykes who were seen fit for the military.[48] Post-World War II, the "crusaders of humanity" incorporated the idea of human rights for all in the United Nations Charter (1945) and the Universal Declaration of Human Rights (1948), however, it has been observed that while negotiating the four Geneva Conventions (1949), the drafters neither raised the issues of war-time persecution of homosexuals nor, obviously, tried to incorporate provisions prohibiting ill-treatment with them.[49] The reasons of this attitude have been traced in "a perceived threat to the nuclear family and military discipline".[50]

11.2.2 Geneva Conventions Onwards

This section examines the prominent treaty law of armed conflict from a queer standpoint. It tries to explain how the law is based on gender binary. It emphasizes the exclusion of queer bodies from the law.

11.2.2.1 Queer Bodies, Army and Armed Conflict

The post-World War II developments in the laws of armed conflict have been lauded for their "humanitarian" character. In addition to the general provisions protecting those rendered unable to fight (*hors de combat*), non-combatants and civilians, and regulating the means and methods of battle, the treaty law also seeks to address the wartime concerns of specific categories of persons, such as children,[51] women,[52] labour,[53] old people[54] and journalists.[55] But the predominantly heteronormative international community deliberately turned a blind eye to queer soldiers, let alone queer civilians, and their concerns. It came with no surprise given the ban on military recruitment of queer bodies and the law criminalizing homosexuality in army and common masses in majority of countries. The situation on military bans has improved gradually; however, almost half of the countries still prohibit[56] recruitment of queer people in the army, while some countries[57] allow only lesbians, gays and bisexuals in the army.[58] The Additional Protocol I facilitates such a practice under Article 43(1) by subjecting the armed forces to an internal disciplinary system. The expression "internal disciplinary system" has been explained to imply military disciplinary and penal law of a State.[59] Thus, States have the liberty to constitute their armed forces according to their choice. Notably, several domestic army laws criminalize same-sex intimate relations among the members of the troops.[60] Even when the

[46] Dijk (2022, p. 307).

[47] May (1991, p. 257) (reviewed book: Berube [1990]).

[48] Ibid., p. 256.

[49] Dijk (2022, pp. 307–308).

[50] Ibid., p. 309.

[51] Art. 14, 17, 24, 50 Geneva Convention relative to the Protection of Civilian Persons in Time of War of 12 August 1949 (Geneva Convention IV), Art. 77, 78 Protocol Additional to the Geneva Conventions of 12 August 1949, and relating to the Protection of Victims of International Armed Conflicts (Protocol I) of 8 June 1977 and Art. 4(3), 6(4) Protocol Additional to the Geneva Conventions of 12 August 1949, and relating to the Protection of Victims of Non-International Armed Conflicts (Protocol II) of 8 June 1977.

[52] Art. 27, 38, 76 Geneva Convention IV, 76 Protocol I and Art. 5(2)(a) Protocol II, ibid., respectively.

[53] Art. 51, 52, Geneva Convention IV, above n 51.

[54] Art. 17, ibid.

[55] Art. 79 Protocol I, above n 51.

[56] Including India, Pakistan, Myanmar, Turkey, Syria, North Korea and Russia.

[57] For instance, Nepal, Italy, Japan, Columbia.

[58] See Polchar et al. (2014, pp. 57–61).

[59] Sandoz et al. (1987, para 1675).

[60] For instance, India under Sec. 45, The Army Act, 1950.

Indian Supreme Court decriminalized[61] homosexuality, the chief of Indian Army, General Bipin Rawat, promptly reacted that it continues to be an offence in the Indian Army.[62] The Army Act of India punishes homosexual acts by members of the forces under the category of "disgraceful conduct of a cruel, indecent or unnatural kind."[63] These prohibitions and criminalization are usually accompanied by a variety of justifications; such as homosexuality is a mental illness, homosexuals are security risks[64] and same sex intimate relations are detrimental to unit cohesion.[65] Homosexuals are further hypersexualized and presented as uncontrolled sexual predators.[66] Importantly, all these conjectures have been proved false by empirical studies.[67] The real reasons at work include perceived "threat" of involving heterosexuals in homosexual conduct and socio-cultural prejudices.

In modern times, many countries do not discriminate against queer applicants and do not prevent them from joining the army. While there are no separate rules for queer members of army under the laws of armed conflict, the general rules apply to them also. Accordingly, the law provides for care, respect, protection and humane treatment with sick, wounded and shipwrecked members of the armed forces.[68] Of course, the reference to sick soldiers applies to those who fall sick during armed conflict. Furthermore, the treaty law prohibits torture and violence,[69] and acts affecting physical and mental health and integrity of soldiers.[70] The relevant international instruments ban discrimination against the members of the armed forces, but they do not expressly prohibit discrimination and unfair treatment on the basis of sexual orientation and gender identity.[71] After all, how negotiating States could provide for care and respect of and ban discrimination against those whom they were discriminating against and penalizing at home for their being simply what they are.

11.2.2.2 Homosexuality and Prisoners of War

An important category related to troops is prisoners of war. Geneva Convention III seeks to especially deal with the treatment of prisoners of war. It aims at ensuring humane treatment with them at all times.[72] It is also a rule of customary law[73] and international human rights law.[74] Further, a detaining State is also bound to ensure that the prisoners are not subjected to violence, threats, insults and public curiosity.[75] The Convention also entitles all prisoners to respect for their persons and their honor in all circumstances.[76] Respect to their person has been interpreted to denote respect for the physical as well as moral person of a prisoner of war.[77] However, the prohibition on adverse distinction on various grounds is blind towards queer combatants.[78] Additionally, where the Convention permits the detaining State to take away money and valuable articles from prisoners of war, there is no provision as to who

[61] Navtej Singh Johar v. Union of India, AIR 2018 SC 4321.

[62] Dutta (2019).

[63] Sec. 46(a), The Army Act, 1950.

[64] See generally, Gouliquer et al. (2018, pp. 323–335).

[65] HRW (2003).

[66] Winkler (2022).

[67] See HRW (2003, n. 26–32) and Dyer (1990, p. 35).

[68] Art. 12 Geneva Convention for the Amelioration of the Condition of the Wounded and Sick in Armed Forces in the Field of 12 August 1949 (Geneva Convention I), Geneva Convention for the Amelioration of the Condition of Wounded, Sick and Shipwrecked Members of Armed Forces at Sea of 12 August 1949 (Geneva Convention II) and Art. 10 Protocol I, above n 51.

[69] Art. 12 Geneva Convention I, II, ibid.

[70] Art. 11(1), (4) Protocol I, above n 51.

[71] Art. 12 Geneva Convention I, II, above n 51 and Art. 9(1) Protocol I, ibid.

[72] Art. 13. See also, Art. 75(1) Protocol I, ibid.

[73] Eritrea-Ethiopia Claims Commission, Partial Award: Prisoners of War, Ethiopia's Claim 4, 1 July 2003, para 53 and Henckaerts and Doswald-Beck (2009), Rule 87.

[74] Art. 10(1) International Covenant on Civil and Political Rights (1966).

[75] Art.13 para 3 Geneva Convention relative to the Treatment of Prisoners of War of 12 August 1949 (Geneva Convention III).

[76] Art. 14.

[77] Pictet (1960).

[78] See Art. 16 Geneva Convention III, above n 75.

may search a queer military member.[79] While the Convention mindfully mandates separate accommodation for male and female prisoners of war,[80] there is no mention of similar concerns of queer prisoners of war.

But, a queer dimension is necessary not just to shed light on the lack of adequate legal provisions but to understand how (forced) homosexuality may be used as a tool of torture for prisoners of war presumed to be heterosexuals. Torture inflicted upon the Iraqi military personnel and civilians by American prison officers in Abu Ghraib detention camps is a case at hand. A queer perspective to these abuses exposes multiple problematic aspects of the barbaric events and wonders how law can address these issues. In these prisons, among several other ways of abuses, homoeroticism was deliberately employed as an instrument of torture and humiliation against the Muslim detainees whose cultural conservatism does not approve of those acts. The American military personnel, Charles A. Graner and Lynndie England, forced the detainee men particularly to simulate homosexual acts (such as sodomy and fellatio). The active participation of a female officer is evidence of her integration into a masculine institution of power.[81] These compulsions were also driven by heterosexuality as a symbol of power. The selection of homoeroticism as a mode of humiliation displays a heteronormative assumption that the targeted men were by default heterosexual, and that homosexuality is an insulting act. The homoerotic torture was gendered and sexualized in character,[82] and was employed as a cultural instrument to punish. It has been seen as a deliberate war technology used to quash the enemy.[83] Simultaneously, it also presents contradictions in America whose society is providing more space to homosexuals on one hand, while its conservative homophobic army used homosexual performance as a mode of abuse.[84] According to Judith Butler, the homophobic United States army considers itself sexually progressive and open against a conservative Muslim culture, and accordingly is on a civilizing mission: "a homophobic institution against a population that is both constructed and targeted for its own shame about homosexuality."[85] The Bush administration considered some of the detainees as "High Value Detainees" who had been confined to extract some intelligence information. The International Committee of the Red Cross (ICRC) visited some of the detention centers in Iraq and witnessed cases of abuse, however, its report which recorded several torturous incidents of various sorts, did not mention the acts stated above.[86] The report, however, reminded the Coalition Forces that the ill-treatment of diverse proportion amounts to violation of several prohibitions, such as Articles 13 (humane treatment of prisoners), 14 (respect for the person of prisoners), 17 (questioning of prisoners), 87 (penalties) of Geneva Convention on prisoners of war, and Articles 27 (humane treatment), 31 (prohibition of coercion), 32 (prohibition of corporal punishment, torture, etc) of Geneva Convention on civilians.

11.2.2.3 Queer Civilians

Besides prisoners of war, civilian protection during armed conflict has also been a grave concern sought to be addressed by the Geneva law. Aiming at care and protection of civilians during armed conflict, the Geneva Convention IV uses the language of entitlement and obligation, both. Under Article 27, protected persons are entitled, in all circumstances, to respect for their persons, their honor, their family rights, their religious convictions and practices, and their manners and customs. According to the ICRC Commentary, the term "respect for their persons" implies their physical, moral and intellectual integrity; the term "their honor" refers to moral and social quality of individuals; the expression "family rights" include

[79] For rules regarding conduct of search ensuring privacy and dignity of prisoners of war, see United Nations Standard Minimum Rules for the Treatment of Prisoners, (the Nelson Mandela Rules) Rules 50–53.

[80] Art. 25, 97, 108.

[81] Ahmed (2011, p. 16).

[82] Gronnvoll (2007, p. 371).

[83] Winkler (2024).

[84] Rosner (2020).

[85] Ahmed (2011, pp. 17–18).

[86] See for more, ICRC (2004).

right to marry; and the word "manners" here means behavior.[87] Additionally, Article 27(1) puts an obligation on belligerent States to treat protected persons humanely and to protect them from violence. Civilians and military personnel of belligerent States are prohibited from taking any action causing murder, torture, corporal punishment, mutilation, medical or scientific experiments not necessitated by the medical treatment, or any other form of physical suffering.[88] Parties to an armed conflict are also bound to assist the ship-wrecked, wounded and other persons at grave risk, and to protect them against pillage and ill-treatment.[89] Similarly, the belligerents shall also strive to evacuate, by an agreement wounded, sick, infirm, and aged persons, children and maternity cases from besieged areas.[90] Subsequently adopted Additional Protocol I *inter alia* bans infliction of torture[91] and humiliating and degrading treatment[92] on civilians. The law relating to non-international armed conflict[93] too contains similar provisions requiring humane treatment with civilians and prohibiting torture, humiliating treatment and outrages upon personal dignity.[94] They have also attained the status of customary international law.[95]

Queer persons may seemingly benefit from such provisions; however, they do not adequately answer the vulnerable lived experiences of queer people and hostile socio-cultural prejudices against them. The prohibition of rape in the Geneva Convention IV[96] and Additional Protocol I[97] is not gender-neutral. It specifically refers to only woman as a victim. Thus, these instruments are silent about rape committed on queer people. In fact, no provision was specifically drafted with intent to protect queer civilians. The provision prohibiting adverse distinction does not recognize gender identity and sexual orientation as grounds of discrimination.[98] Because of socio-cultural prejudices towards queer bodies, they are more likely to be tortured and subjected to other sorts of inhuman treatment by an invading or occupying army. In the Protocol I, there is no separate provision, akin to that of women, children or old persons, seeking to protect queer bodies. This is despite the barbarism frequently unleashed on homosexuals in occupied territories and during international and non-international armed conflicts.

Historically, Nazi Germany declared homosexuals as "asocials" and persecuted thousands of them.[99] In respect of Iraq, a Human Rights Watch report states that armed groups torture and kill LGBT with impunity.[100] In its anti-gay campaigns, the Islamic State in Iraq and the Levant has thrown off terrace, stoned or shot dead several homosexuals.[101] Once, the fighters of Islamic State executed nine men and a boy in Syria in just one day on the suspicion of sodomy.[102] Thus, persecution of queer people in occupied lands and in non-international armed conflicts is frequent.[103] It has been maintained, that in their torture and killings, the family, community and State authorities[104] are complicit and equally

[87] Pictet (1958).

[88] Art. 32, Geneva Convention IV, above n 51.

[89] Art. 16, para 2.

[90] Art. 17.

[91] Art. 75(2)(a)(ii).

[92] Art. 75(2)(b).

[93] Art. 3 common to Geneva Conventions I-IV, Protocol II, above n 51 and customary international law.

[94] See common Article 3 and Art. (1) Protocol II, ibid.

[95] Humane treatment (Rule 37); murder (Rule 89); torture, cruel and inhuman treatment (Rule 90), Henckaerts and Doswald-Beck (2009).

[96] Art. 27.

[97] Art. 76(1).

[98] Art. 13, 27 Geneva Convention IV and Art. 75(1) Protocol I, above n 51.

[99] Dijk (2022, p. 307).

[100] HRW (2022).

[101] Tharoor (2016). See also Report of the Secretary-General on women and peace and security, 29 September 2016, UN Doc S/2016/822, para 36.

[102] Tharoor (2016).

[103] For situation in Iraq, Columbia, Syrian Arab Republic, see Conflict-related sexual violence, Report of the Secretary-General, 23 March 2015, UN Doc. S/2015/203.

[104] OutRight Action International (2014).

responsible.[105] Often, these acts enjoy social legitimacy. Targeting queer people in this fashion is accomplished of course through weaponization of cultural prejudice[106] which looks at them as "undesirable, immoral, sinful, disordered and criminal."[107] Abusive acts practised on queer people are followed by social stigmatization and family rejection too. War thus attaches new layers of discrimination and violence to these sections.

Yet another form of queer civilian vulnerability must be underlined in relation to the proportionality principle. This principle mainly seeks to prohibit an attack when it appears that the incidental loss of civilian lives or objects due to the attack is likely to be disproportionate or excessive in relation to the military benefit expected.[108] It thus requires an attacker to compare the two variables beforehand and discard the attack if the probable civilian harm is excessive. This subjective comparative calculation depends upon whose lives the perpetrator values more. Due to the inherent social prejudices towards queer people and criminalization of homosexual conduct, an attack-planner may not value their lives equal to that of heterosexuals (male). Consequently, the perpetrator is more likely to launch the attack putting in danger their lives, whereas the attacker might have acted differently, had there been "normal" people around. The queer approach highlights the difference in the worth of lives attributed in these two situations where some lives matter, while the "others" don't.

11.2.3 Colorblind Law-Makers

Mentioning the blind spot on queer concerns in the treaty law of armed conflict, a commentator has tried to argue as to how queer people may benefit from the existing laws of armed conflict.[109] He argues that the references to LGBT persons can be inferred from the principle of humane treatment which applies to all persons not actively participating in hostilities.[110] Similar inferences can be drawn from expressions, such as "the whole of the population," according to him.[111] In relation to the ban on penalties which are inhuman considering an internee's sex, he suggests that the term "internee's sex" by implication covers sexual orientation or gender identity.[112] Regarding prohibition of adverse distinction on the basis of some grounds, he appears to be in favor of the position that sexual orientation or gender identity can also be deduced from the ground of "sex."[113] To some extent, these interpretations may extend the application of the provisions to queer people during an armed conflict. However, such a narration misses out the urgent need to fundamentally challenge the law as a reflection of heteronormativity. This approach perhaps treats the issues of homosexuals as homogenous with that of the "normal" where they are more likely to be rendered unimportant and fade away. This mix-up also disregards the specific attention these people need considering their lived experiences of perceived "abnormality." For instance, general dislike among the masses (such as, to 69% of Ukrainian respondents, homosexuality is unacceptable)[114]; harassment and violence by combatants and civilians[115]; discrimination and exclusion during evacuation and emergency responses[116]; issues of privacy; abuse and assault at health facilities, checkpoints, border crossings, etc.[117]; many times a community considers a homosexual an insult to them[118]; a moral code

[105] Margalit (2018, p. 239).

[106] Report of the independent expert on protection against violence and discrimination based on sexual orientation and gender identity, Victor Madrigal-Borloz, 27 July 2022, UN Doc A/75/235, para 43.

[107] Ibid., para 45.

[108] Art. 51(5)(b), Protocol I, above n 51.

[109] Margalit (2018, pp. 237–265).

[110] Ibid., p. 250.

[111] Ibid.

[112] Ibid., p. 254.

[113] Ibid., p. 251.

[114] Pew Research Center (2022).

[115] Equal Rights Coalition (2022).

[116] Ibid.

[117] United Nations (2022).

[118] OutRight Action International (2014, pp. 3–4).

of a community may declare homosexuals worthy of humiliation,[119] and a religious practice may sanction execution of those engaging in homosexual acts.[120] These matters certainly demand different approach. However, the commentator also illustrates how queer -worries may be specifically addressed with the help of Israeli Prison Service policy.[121]

The Israeli policy mandates that a transgender should be detained in a separate cell meant for transgenders during the initial five days of their detention.[122] It not only ensures their safety but has the effect of inspiring moral solidarity among them. Similarly, the policy also seeks to address queer concerns of privacy and dignity while undergoing search by the prison authorities. The document asks to provide a transgender detainee with an option as to who may search them, a male or a female.[123] It also explores the possibility of search by male and female both, depending on detainee's transitional status.[124] These details of the policy reemphasize the fact that drawing inferences from the law meant for the mainstream "normals" is of limited significance for queer people.

And finally, the commentator's discourse on inferences and deductions also ignores and often covers up the fact that the negotiating parties turned a blind eye towards this category of people. They acted as if such people never existed. In 1978, Gilbert Baker, a United States based gay-rights activist and an artist, created a flag with rainbow colors as a symbol of homosexuals. Rainbow's splendor fascinates and compels everyone to notice it, except for those who see colors also in binary, perhaps, black and white. The binary worshippers cannot notice any other colors. They are color-blind. Their color blindness is visible on the face of the instruments they draft. The invisibility of queer people and their concerns in the treaty law is a sight of color -blindness of the negotiating States.

11.2.4 Intersecting Lines

Queer bodies are not a homogenous category and there are differences within the fluidity which explains that the experiences of all of them are not the same. Distinguishing the lines of privilege and oppression on the basis of class, caste, race and disability cut across the broad type and mark a point of difference. These intersections challenge the ostensible sameness and make us realize that within a marginalized group, there may be people more oppressed than the rest. Thus, intersectionality helps identify multiple factors of oppression of some people within a group.

In the laws of armed conflict, the hierarchy of oppression and privilege among queer bodies becomes apparent on several occasions, for instance, in case of repatriation of foreigners present on the territory of a belligerent,[125] treatment with people in occupied territories,[126] and transfer and evacuation of protected persons from a particular area by occupying State.[127] In the implementation of these provisions, cisgender gays and bisexual men may find themselves in a relatively better position in patriarchal societies. To the contrary, cisgender lesbians and bisexual women may have to encounter dual forms of discrimination, being a woman and a queer, and consequent hardships in availing the legal protection. On the other hand, transgender and intersexual people may face severe forms of exclusion, humiliation and violence. Other factors, such as class, caste and race may further intensify the oppression and unfair treatment for some, but may also favor the others.

However, the significance of intersectionality discourse is not just limited to seeing layers of differences. It has been maintained that this reductionism towards the notion of intersectionality overlooks its "power as a theoretical and practical

[119] Ibid., pp. 4–5.

[120] Ibid., p. 5.

[121] Margalit (2018, pp. 255–256).

[122] Ibid., p. 255.

[123] Ibid., p. 256.

[124] Ibid.

[125] Art. 35–36 Geneva Convention IV, above n 51.

[126] Art. 27, ibid.

[127] Art. 49, ibid.

orientation."[128] The crucial insight that intersectionality offers is about who gets benefitted the most by a movement for the vulnerable groups and who still remains helpless. It has been suggested that it is the least oppressed within a marginalized section of people whom a progressive movement serves the most. Intersectionality, thus, seeks to point out the functional dimension of a liberation movement and the perpetual vulnerability of the weakest among the weaker sections.

References

Ahmed A (2011) When men are harmed: feminism, queer theory, and torture at Abu Ghraib. UCLA J Islam Near East Law I1:1–20

Aldrich R (2003) Colonialism and homosexuality. Routledge, London

Arondekar A (2004) Without a trace: sexuality and the colonial archive. Journal of the History of Sexuality 14(1/2):10–27

Berkowitz D et al (2010) Walk like a man, talk like a woman: teaching the social construction of gender. Teach Sociol 38(2):132–143

Berube A (1990) Coming out under fire: the history of gay men and women in World War II. Free Press, New York

Buss DE (2007) Queering international legal authority. Proc Annu Meet Am Soc Int Law 101:122–125

Charlesworth H (1999) The gender of international law. Proc Annu Meet Am Soc Int Law 93:206–209

Cohn C (1993) Wars, wimps, and women: talking gender and thinking war. In: Cooke M, Woollacott A (eds) Gendering war talk. Princeton University Press, Princeton, pp 227–246

Crouthamel J (2008) Male sexuality and psychological trauma: soldiers and sexual disorder in World War I and Weimar Germany. J Hist of Sex 17(1):60–84

Darwin H (2017) Doing gender beyond the binary: a virtual ethnography. Symb Interact 40(3):317–334

Davies M (2017) Asking the law question. Thomson Reuters, Sydney

Dijk B (2022) Gendering the Geneva conventions. Hum Rights Q 44(2):286–312

Dutta AN (2019) Here's how homosexuals in Indian military can be punished, 11 January 2019. https://theprint.in/theprint-essential/heres-how-homosexuals-in-indian-military-can-be-punished/176500/

Dyer K (ed) (1990) Gays in uniform: the Pentagon's secret reports. Alyson Publications, Boston

Equal Rights Coalition (2022) Aggression against Ukraine and the protection of LGBTI persons and refugees, 6 April, 2022. https://equalrightscoalition.org/publications/erc-statement-on-the-aggression-against-ukraine-and-the-protection-of-lgbti-persons-and-refugees/

Faucette A (2014) Fucking the binary for social change: our radically queer agenda. In: Walton Gerald (ed) The gay agenda: claiming space, identity, and justice. Peter Lang, New York, pp 73–88

Ghisleni L et al (2016) Introduction to "binary binds": deconstructing sex and gender dichotomies in archaeological practice. J Archaeol Method Theory 23(3):765–787

Gouliquer L et al (2018) A Threat to canadian national security: a lesbian soldier's story. Qual Res Psychol 15(2–3):323–35

Gronnvoll M (2007) Gender (in)visibility at Abu Ghraib. Rhetor Public Aff 10(3):371–398

Harvey AD (2001) Homosexuality and the British army during the First World War. J Soc Army Hist Res 79(320):313–319

Henckaerts JM, Doswald-Beck L (2009) Customary international humanitarian law, vol I. ICRC/CUP, New York

HRW (2003) Uniform discrimination: the "don't ask, don't tell" policy of the U.S. military. https://www.hrw.org/reports/2003/usa0103/USA0103FINAL-02.htm#P217_34266

HRW (2022) "Everyone wants me dead": killings, abductions, torture, and sexual violence against LGBT people by armed groups in Iraq, 23 March 2022. https://www.hrw.org/report/2022/03/23/everyone-wants-me-dead/killings-abductions-torture-and-sexual-violence-against

Hyam R (1990) Empire and sexuality: the British experience. Manchester University Press, Manchester

ICRC (2004) Report of the International Committee of the Red Cross (ICRC) on the treatment by the coalition forces of prisoners of war and other protected persons by the Geneva conventions in Iraq during arrest, internment and interrogation. https://www.legal-tools.org/doc/e5324c/pdf

Kepros LR (1999–2000) Queer theory: weed or seed in the garden of legal theory? Law Sex Rev 9:279–310

Kirby MD (2015) Sexual orientation & gender identity: a new province of law for India. Universal Law Publishing, New Delhi

MacKinnon CA (2013) Intersectionality as method: a note. Signs 38(4):1019–1030

Margalit A (2018) Still a blind spot: the protection of LGBT persons during armed conflict and other situations of violence. Int Rev Red Cross 100(907–909):237–265

May ET (1991) Review: history without victims: gays in World War II. Rev Am Hist 19(2):255–259

Oosterveld V (2017-2018) The ICC policy paper on sexual and gender-based crimes: a crucial step for international criminal law. William & Mary J Women Law 24(3):443–457

[128] Srinivasan (2021, p. 17).

OTP (2014) Policy paper on sexual and gender-based crimes. The Office of the Prosecutor, International Criminal Court 1-43

Otto D (2007) "Taking a break" from "normal": thinking queer in the context of international law. Proc Annu Meet Am Soc Int Law 101:119–122

Otto D (2018) Introduction: embracing queer curiosity. In: Otto D (ed) Queering international law: possibilities, alliances, complicities, risks. Routledge, New York, pp 1–12

OutRight Action International (2014) When coming out is a death sentence persecution of LGBT Iraqis. https://www.refworld.org/docid/58c2ba784.html

Pew Research Center (2022) The global divide on homosexuality persists, 25 June 2020. https://www.pewresearch.org/global/wp-content/uploads/sites/2/2020/06/PG_2020.06.25_Global-Views-Homosexuality_FINAL.pdf

Pictet J (1958) Commentary on article 27, Geneva convention IV. https://ihl-databases.icrc.org/en/ihl-treaties/gciv-1949/article-27/commentary/1958?activeTab=1949GCs-APs-and-commentaries

Pictet J (1960) Commentary on article 14, Geneva convention III. https://ihl-databases.icrc.org/en/ihl-treaties/gciii-1949/article-14/commentary/1960?activeTab=

Polchar J et al (2014) LGBT military personnel: a strategic vision for inclusion. The Hague Centre for Strategic Studies, The Hague

Rahman M (2020) What makes LGBT sexualities political? Understanding oppression in sociological, historical, and cultural context. In: Bosia MJ et al (eds) The Oxford handbook of global LGBT and sexual diversity politics. OUP, New York, pp 15–30

Rallin A (2019) Queer and now: A roundtable forum with Dipika Jain, Akhil Kang, Sheena Malhotra, Hoshang Merchant, Shakthi Nataraj, Chayanika Shah, Nishant Shahani, Oishik Sircar and Ruth Vanita. In: Aneja Anu (ed) Women's and gender studies in India. Routledge, New Delhi, pp 357–374

Rosner ED (2020) Abu Ghraib, homonationalism, and the rationalization of modern torture. Inquiries 12:9. http://www.inquiriesjournal.com/articles/1801/abu-ghraib-homonationalism-and-the-rationalization-of-modern-torture.

Sandoz Y et al (eds) (1987) Commentary on the additional protocols of 8 June 1977 to the Geneva conventions of 12 August 1949. ICRC/Martinus Nijhoff, Geneva

Smith JS, Smith KE (2016) What it means to do gender differently: understanding identity, perceptions and accomplishments in a gendered world. Humboldt J Soc Relat 38:62–78

Srinivasan A (2021) The right to sex. Bloomsbury, London

Tharoor I (2016) The Islamic State's shocking war on gays, 13 June 2016. https://www.washingtonpost.com/news/worldviews/wp/2016/06/13/the-islamic-states-shocking-war-on-homosexuals/

United Nations (2022) Ukraine: Protection of LGBTI and gender-diverse refugees remains critical—UN expert, 22 March 2022. https://www.ohchr.org/en/press-releases/2022/03/ukraine-protection-lgbti-and-gender-diverse-refugees-remains-critical-un

Winkler M (2022) A queer eye on the law of armed conflict, 2 August 2022. https://lieber.westpoint.edu/queer-eye-loac/#:~:text=The%20three%20issues%20are%3A%20the,under%20the%20law%20of%20occupation.&text=A%20common%20way%20to%20erase,participating%20in%20the%20armed%20forces

Winkler M (2024) Queering the law of armed conflict. In: Ziegler A (ed) The Oxford handbook of international LGBTI law. Oxford University Press https://doi.org/10.1093/oxfordhb/9780198847793.013.26

12 What Is Blurred in the Principle of Distinction?

Abstract

In the beginning of this chapter, I discuss critically the meaning of civilians and civilian objects, and the principle of distinction. Subsequently, I discuss three important humanitarian challenges to the distinction principle in the contemporary warfare: (1) how to distinguish in asymmetrical warfare; (2) disputed meaning and scope of the phrase "direct participation by civilians in hostilities," and (3) whether child soldiers may be targeted. The analysis refers to the current armed conflicts between Israel and Palestine, and Russia and Ukraine, and contextualizes the problematic side of the principle.

Keywords

Civilians · Civilian objects · Asymmetrical war · Direct participation in hostilities · Child soldiers

12.1 Distinction in International Armed Conflicts

On 5 October 2023, a precision missile launched by the Russian army attacked a cafe in Hroza, a village in the Kharkiv region of eastern Ukraine. The explosion killed 59 people including 36 women and one boy.[1] They had assembled to attend a reburial ceremony of a local member of the Ukrainian military. While the Russian authorities claimed the gathering to be a military target, the Office of the United Nations High Commissioner for Human Rights found no indication of the presence of legitimate military target at or near the funeral reception at the time of the attack.[2] In the report published by the United Nations Mission in Ukraine, it was observed that:

> The fact that the Russian armed forces carried out the attack indicates that they either failed to take sufficient steps to verify that the target was a military objective, or they deliberately targeted civilians or civilian objects, in either event in violation of international humanitarian law.[3]

It appears that the Russian military failed to distinguish between civilians and military targets and carried out an indiscriminate attack.

The incident has been cited in the context of attacking enemy targets during an armed conflict and its regulation by the law. Military attacks raise the probability of hitting civilians and civilian objects as well, alongside enemy soldiers. This goes contrary to one of the core principles of the laws of war which seeks to limit attacks only at

[1] OHCHR (2023, p. 3).

[2] Ibid., pp. 3, 6.

[3] Ibid., p. 4.

K. Jeenger, *A Humanitarian Critique of International Humanitarian Law*, Sustainable Development Goals Series, https://doi.org/10.1007/978-981-96-8319-2_12

those who pose a threat to a belligerent's military capacity. Thus, to protect civilians from the effects of war, laws of armed conflict (international humanitarian law) seek to draw a distinction between civilians and members of armed forces, and prohibit targeting the former. The relevant rule in Protocol I clearly outlaws attacks at civilian population and civilian objects in the following terms:

> In order to ensure respect for and protection of the civilian population and civilian objects, the Parties to the conflict shall at all times distinguish between the civilian population and combatants and between civilian objects and military objectives and accordingly shall direct their operations only against military objectives.[4]

This is the "cardinal"[5] principle of distinction. It offers not only a protection mechanism for civilians but guidance to combatants also. Accordingly, they are informed by the Protocol as to whom they may lawfully target and whom they must spare. The principle, thus, seeks to regulate the conduct of the participants in conflict, so as to protect those not participating.[6] The scope of the Geneva Convention IV on the protection of civilian persons is, however, limited as it does not seek to protect civilians during military operations nor it regulates the means and methods of conducting hostilities.[7]

This prohibition of targeting civilians in the Protocol is inevitable considering the steep rise in civilian deaths during the last century. According to a data released by the United Nations, the civilian loss has increased from five percent at the beginning of the twentieth century to 15% in the First World War, up to 65% during the Second World War and up to almost 90% during the 1990s armed conflicts.[8] Innocent civilians pay the price of being nationals of an adversary. Despite this, very little of the law was concerned with civilians at the end of World War II.[9] While the customary international law was scanty and lacking in detail,[10] The Hague Regulations were also confined only to few aspects of the protection of civilians during war.[11] Post-World War II, the Geneva Convention on Civilians, 1949 provided for humane treatment with civilians and the protection of civilian population against certain consequences of war. But it did not limit the use of weapons against civilians. Supplementing the Convention, the Additional Protocol I prescribe wider guarantees for civilians and also seeks to ban killing civilian population by incorporating the principle of distinction.

The ongoing Israel-Palestine war is also an evidence of wholesale killing of civilians and destruction of civilian objects. The war has so far witnessed killings of more than 30,000 civilians and injuries to more than 75,000 members of civilian population.[12] The attacks by the Israeli Defense Forces have also razed to the ground more than 70,000 dwelling units in Gaza.[13] The totality of various figures stated above explains not only the urgency of the principle of distinction but also its failure, because the Protocol containing detailed rules relating to protection of civilian life and property was adopted in the year 1977 and the incidents of mounting civilian deaths are recent. Though, the Protocol was very lately adopted, civilian casualties kept rising even after its adoption. While the factors contributing to the

[4] Art. 48 Protocol Additional to the Geneva Conventions of 12 August 1949, and relating to the Protection of Victims of International Armed Conflicts (Protocol I) of 8 June 1977.

[5] Legality of the Threat or Use of Nuclear Weapons, Advisory Opinion, (1996) ICJ Rep 226, para 78.

[6] Stern (2019, p. 15).

[7] Wilt (2019, p. 30).

[8] Stern (2019, p. 3).

[9] Best (1979, p. 27).

[10] Miller (1975, p. 71).

[11] E.g. prohibition of confiscation of private property, pillage, collective punishment, compelling the civilians of occupied territories to participate in combat operations. Art. 44, 45, 46, 47, 50, 52, Regulations concerning the Laws and Customs of War on Land, annexed to the Hague Convention (II) with Respect to the Laws and Customs of War on Land of 29 July 1899 (Hague Regulations 1899/Hague Convention II) and Regulations respecting the Laws and Customs of War on Land, annexed to the Hague Convention (IV) with Respect to the Laws and Customs of War on Land of 18 October 1907 (Hague Regulations 1907/ Hague Convention IV).

[12] See the data published by the United Nations Office for the Coordination of Humanitarian Affairs in OCHA (2023).

[13] Ibid.

brazen violation of distinction principle and rising civilian death-toll may be several, the ambiguity and inconsistency in the provisions are equally responsible for the deviations.

12.1.1 Who Are Civilians? Identifying the Gaps

12.1.1.1 Definition Under Geneva Convention IV

The presumption underlying the protection afforded to civilians by the Geneva Convention is that civilians do not conduct belligerent acts, and therefore, the armies must not make the innocent people the victims of war.[14] The Convention uses the expression "protected persons" for civilians, and defines them as those who find themselves in the hands of a Party to the conflict or Occupying Power of which they are not nationals.[15] The definition provides for two conditions: being in the hands of a belligerent and nationality of other State. The condition of "being in the hands" is not merely a question of being in enemy hands directly, like a prisoner.[16] It does not necessitate direct or physical control; rather, indirect or constructive control is also sufficient. Residents of Bosnian village Stupni Do were treated to be constructively in the hands of Croatia by a trial chamber of the International Criminal Tribunal for the Former Yugoslavia (ICTY) because of the control exercised by Croatia over Bosnian Croats close to the village.[17]

The expression of the second requirement, "of which they are not nationals," needs elaboration. The expression may refer to nationals of an adversary, a co-belligerent State or a neutral State. It may include stateless persons also. At the first instance, the expression obviously refers to nationals of adversary. They need protection because they cannot seek diplomatic protection, as the diplomatic ties are severed when armed conflict begins.[18] As regards nationals of a co-belligerent or a neutral State, Article 4 paragraph 2 makes it clear that nationals of such a State are not protected persons if such a State has usual diplomatic representation in the State in whose control the persons are present. Article 4 is silent in respect of stateless persons; however, state practice reflects protection to them, because they do not enjoy diplomatic protection of any State.[19] Moreover, the Additional Protocol I specifically puts stateless persons and refugees in the definition of "protected persons" as defined in the Convention.[20]

However, the nationality test leaves gaps in the protection because it does not cover people falling in the hands of a State of which they are nationals. To illustrate, where some of the nationals of country X flee to a neighboring country Y due to fear of ethnic cleansing, and later on find themselves in the control of the army of X in the occupied territory of Y, they are not protected by the Geneva Convention. Such an approach is quite contrary to human rights regime which seeks to protect people against the actions of their own government.[21] It reflects the spirit of the traditional view of the role of international law.[22] The practice under international criminal law is, however, different. The ICTY has adopted a liberal attitude in respect of the nationality requirement. In the Čelebići Prison Camp case, the accused persons were convicted for killing or mistreating individuals of their nationality but of different ethnicity owing allegiance to some other country.[23] Thus, the tribunal widened the limited scope of "protected persons." However, the protection afforded by the Convention is not limited to those who are covered by the expression "protected persons" only.

[14] Garraway (2007, p. 329).

[15] Art. 4, para 1.

[16] Pictet (1958).

[17] Prosecutor v. Rajić and Andrić, IT-95-12, Trial Chamber, Review of the Indictment pursuant to Rule 61 of the Rules of Procedure and Evidence, 13 September 1996, para 37.

[18] Kolb and Hyde (2008, p. 222).

[19] Ibid.

[20] Art. 73.

[21] Prosecutor v. Delalić et al., IT-96-21-T, Trial Chamber, Judgment, 16 November, 1998, para 266.

[22] Ibid., para 250.

[23] Ibid., paras 263, 265.

While "protected persons" are entitled to specific protection under Part III of the Convention, the Convention provides for general protection under Part II in favor of "whole of the populations of the countries in conflict,"[24] irrespective of their race, nationality, religion, political opinion, language, economic condition, social status, etc. Unlike the former term "protected persons," this expression clearly covers a belligerent State's own nationals. However, neither of them covers nationals of a co-belligerent or a neutral State who have diplomatic representation in the belligerent State in whose control such persons are.

Thus, the Fourth Geneva Convention covers two categories of civilians: protected persons and populations of the countries in conflict, and provides for separate provisions for their protection. Additional Protocol I, however, has further enhanced the scope of civilians as well as the range of protection they are entitled to during an armed conflict.

12.1.1.2 Definition Under Additional Protocol I

Supplementing the Convention, Protocol I also uses two expressions, civilians and civilian population, however, both are neither distinct categories of persons nor entitled to different set of protection. Under the Protocol, civilian population comprises all persons who are civilians.[25] However, the provision further clarifies that the presence within the civilian population of individuals who are not covered by the definition of civilians does not deprive the population of its civilian character. As far as the expression "civilians" are concerned, the Protocol adopts a different way to identify them. The Protocol defines civilians as persons who are, (1) not members of the armed forces under Article 43 of the Protocol, or (2) not entitled to prisoners of war status under Article 4(A)(1), (2), (3) and (6) of the Geneva Convention on Prisoners of War, 1949.[26]

In Article 43, the expression "members of the armed forces" should not be confused with combatants, because medical personnel and chaplains are not combatants, nevertheless, fall within the ambit of members of the armed forces. Generally, those who fight are combatants. However, a person who is not engaged in attack but is authorized to do so is also treated a combatant.[27] Therefore, in terms of international law, a combatant means a person who is authorized by international law to fight in accordance with international law applicable in armed conflicts.[28] Thus, members of the armed forces other than medical personnel and chaplains are combatants under the Protocol I.[29] However, as the Protocol seeks to supplement the four Geneva Convention; few authors[30] prefer the definition of prisoners of war, instead of Article 43 of the Protocol to explain the concept of combatant. Nevertheless, Article 43 indicates that members of armed forces are not civilians.

The other category is persons who are entitled to the status of prisoner of war. It refers to members of the armed forces, members of militias forming part of armed forces, members of other militias having fixed distinctive sign and carrying arms openly, and civilians resisting invading forces spontaneously and carrying arms openly.

Thus, persons other than the above two categories are civilians within the meaning of Article 50. It is a negative expression, but it is believed to have made the notion of civilians "extremely broad."[31]

In customary international law too, civilians are persons who are not members of the armed forces.[32] The negative character of the definition is justified on two premises: (1) the inoffensive character of an individual is more important than one's nationality, and (2) the concepts of civilians and armed forces are contrary to each other.[33]

[24] Art. 13.

[25] Art. 50(2).

[26] Art. 50(1).

[27] Art. 44(5) Protocol I, above n 4.

[28] Ipsen (2013, p. 81).

[29] Art. 43(2).

[30] See Crawford (2015, p. 17) and Crawford and Pert (2015, p. 90).

[31] Summers (2014, p. 15).

[32] Rule 5, Henckaerts and Doswald-Beck (2009).

[33] Sandoz et al. (1987, paras 1909, 1914).

Thus, everybody, except the members of armed forces, physically present in the national territories of belligerents is a civilian.[34] Furthermore, if civilian status of an individual is doubtful, they are treated as civilians under the Protocol.[35] In the opinion of an Appeals Chamber of the ICTY, the definitions of civilians and civilian population as contained in Article 50 may largely be viewed as reflecting customary law.[36]

12.1.2 What Are Civilian Objects? Wartime Motives Decide

Objects other than military objectives, are civilian objects[37] and not targetable. Thus, for instance, civilian houses, schools, hotels and means of transport are civilian objects, while military installations, weapons and military means of transport are not. However, there are some objects which may be of common use and importance to both civilian population and army (also called dual-use objects), such as a tunnel or bridge near a border town. This commonality of purpose is captured by the definition of military objectives in the Protocol. It also unveils the hidden complexity while defining the expression "military objectives." Military objectives, according to the Protocol I are objects "which by their nature, location, purpose or use make an effective contribution to military action and whose total or partial destruction, capture or neutralization, in the circumstances ruling at the time, offers a definite military advantage."[38] These objectives are legitimate targets and, thus, may be attacked during hostilities. Giving a limited scope to the provision, the Commentary of the International Committee of the Red Cross (ICRC) explains that it extends to all objects directly used by the military (e.g. arms and military headquarters), locations beneficial to military action (e.g. bridges), and civilian objects whenever used for armed operations (e.g. school and hotel).[39] The negotiating history of the provision, however, reflects the impact of military necessity and the dominance of powerful States in shaping of the provision.

In the Diplomatic Conference, the draft submitted by the ICRC defined military objectives in almost similar vague fashion as the provision reflects today, but with fewer details:

> objectives which are, by their nature, purpose or use, recognized to be of military interest and whose total or partial destruction, in the circumstances ruling at the time, offers a distinct and substantial military advantage.[40]

Romanian delegate sought to reduce the vagueness in the text by proposing the following definition of military objectives emphasizing upon proximity between an object and military importance:

> All objects which do not directly serve to produce weapons, military equipment or methods of combat, or which are not directly and immediately used by the armed forces shall be deemed to be civilian objects even if some change in their use should later cause them to acquire a predominantly military nature.[41]

The Romanian amendment was certainly beneficial to civilians. Likewise, the Australian proposal of amendment also tried to mitigate the uncertainty introduced by the use of adjectives and adverbs.[42] The amendments collectively recommended by several the Middle East and African countries sought to strictly limit the attacks to military objectives only, and to spare any other object.[43] The proposal definitely intended to reduce civilian damage. However, countries like France appeared to be unwilling to compromise on the question of targeting the adversary. Initially, the French delegation was reluctant to agree with

[34] Ibid., para 1917.

[35] Art. 50(1).

[36] Prosecutor v. Blaškić, IT-95-14-T, Appelas Chamber, Judgment, 29 July 2004, para 110.

[37] Art. 52(1) Protocol I, above n 4.

[38] Art. 52(2), ibid.

[39] Sandoz et al. (1987, paras 2020–2022).

[40] Official Records of the Diplomatic Conference on the Reaffirmation and Development of International Humanitarian Law Applicable in Armed Conflicts Geneva (1974–1977), vol I, Part 3, p. 16.

[41] Ibid., vol III, p. 207.

[42] Ibid., p. 209.

[43] Ibid., p. 211 (Arab Republic of Egypt, Democratic Yemen, Iraq, Jordan, Kuwait, Lebanon, Libyan Arab Republic, Mauritania, Morocco, Qatar, Syrian Arab Republic, United Arab Emirates, Yemen).

the idea of attacking military objectives only.[44] It was stated that:

> there were many situations in armed conflicts in which it was difficult or even impossible to determine precisely the limits of a military objective, particularly in large towns and in forest areas, in either of which enemy armed forces and groups of civilians might be intermingled. His delegation was therefore unable to accept such a restriction, which, by the strictness of its terms, could seriously prejudice the exercise of the legitimate right of self-defence, and it had therefore been obliged to abstain in the vote.[45]

Later on, the French representative proposed by way an amendment to extend the definition of military objective even to those objects which would indirectly contribute to the military capabilities of the adverse party.[46] The text finally adopted is largely based on the amendment offered by the Netherlands in relation to the ICRC draft.[47]

The present definition[48] of military objective contains vague expressions, creates confusion[49] and provides enough leeway to an attack planner, putting civilian objects in jeopardy. While it is true that certain civilian objects may be useful in military operations because of their utility, nature or location; their changing status may render them "immune from targeting on one day, but targetable the following day."[50] Yet, out of the duality of purposes (civil and military), it is the military use that is given importance and the lawfulness of a target is determined accordingly. Moreover, the expressions "circumstances ruling at the time" and "a definite military advantage" are imprecise and open to subjective interpretation and abuse. Russia's continuous strike at Ukraine's vital power infrastructure since March 2024 illustrates this point.

Since 22 March 2024, Russia has launched waves of planned attacks at Ukraine's critical energy facilities, mainly thermal and hydro power plants.[51] The strikes have damaged about 80% of the power plants and resulted into frequent blackouts and power cuts.[52] Energy is a vital resource for civilians, especially for smooth water, health and education services. Russia treats energy infrastructure as a legitimate military target,[53] and calls the strikes lawful being aimed at weakening the enemy's army.[54] While energy services are important for military capacities, comprehensive aerial strikes on nearly all power plants and consequent destabilizing of the energy facilities across the country cannot be justified. It is a sheer abuse of the unclear expressions of the provision.

The flexible interpretation of dual-use objects by powerful countries weakens the very idea of distinguishing. "Indeed, the dual-use exception to Distinction might devour the Principle itself."[55] Given the dependency of modern militaries on civilian contractors, personnel and companies in the domains of production, communication, cyber expertise, transportation and operation of military satellites, it appears that the distinguishing lines are getting blurred. On the other, it has also been apprehended that the strict interpretation suggested by the ICRC Commentary has the potential of "prolonging an otherwise terminable war."[56]

12.1.3 What Helps Distinguish Civilians?

Distinguishable appearance is the hallmark of combatants and fundamental to the principle of distinction.[57] In order to distinguish military

[44] Ibid., vol VI, p. 169.

[45] Ibid.

[46] Ibid., vol III, p. 209.

[47] Ibid., p. 210. For Netherlands' interpretation of draft Article 47, see ibid, vol VI, p. 195,

[48] "...objects which by their nature, location, purpose or use make an effective contribution to military action and whose total or partial destruction, capture or neutralization, in the circumstances ruling at the time, offers a definite military advantage." See Art. 52(2) Protocol I, above n 4.

[49] Swiney (2005, p. 751).

[50] Crawford and Pert (2015, p. 166).

[51] See, UNHRMMU (2024).

[52] United Nations (2024a).

[53] Polityuk (2024).

[54] DD News (2024).

[55] Swiney (2005, p. 751).

[56] Ibid.

[57] Art. 44(3) Protocol I, above n 4.

personnel from civilians, the prominent modes are wearing uniform and having a fixed distinctive sign recognizable from a distance. Combatants are obliged under the Protocol[58] to distinguish themselves from civilians during an armed conflict. Article 44(7) further specifies that this Article does not intend to modify the common practice of States regarding the wearing of the uniform by combatants fixed for the regular, uniformed armed troops. This paragraph has twofold meaning. First, it recalls the State practice that armed forces put on uniform which is also a rule of customary international law.[59] Second, use of the words "regular, uniformed armed units" acknowledges the fact indirectly that irregular armed forces do not generally wear uniforms. Therefore, Article 44(3) simply requires a combatant to appear differently, either by uniform or any distinctive sign visible from a distance.

This requirement is, however, subject to some exceptions. In an armed conflict, armed combatants may not be able to so distinguish themselves because of the nature of combat. In such a situation, the Protocol provides that they shall retain the combatant status, provided that they carry arms openly during each military engagement and while preparing for the launching of an attack.[60] The kind of situations and the nature of hostilities thought of in this paragraph generally include belligerent occupation and war of national liberation wherein the guerrilla fighters cannot so distinguish themselves from civilian population, and also include situations where members of regular armed forces have to wear civilian clothes under a special assignment.[61] Similarly, civilians who spontaneously take up arms against an invading army attain the status as combatants provided they carry their arms openly. Under the Protocol, a combatant who fails to so distinguish is not entitled to the status of a prisoner of war, but to the legal protections available to prisoners of war.[62] Under the 1949 Geneva Convention III, however, the status of combatant and prisoner of war and the corresponding protection were considered for guerrillas and freedom fighters because of their not being able to so distinguish. Their poor status and weak military resources did not let them operate in the manner the European armies do. Thus, during the wars that occurred before the adoption of the Protocol, these Third World fighters were mercilessly treated and killed.[63]

12.2 Distinction in Non-international Armed Conflicts

The answers to the fundamental question of who is a civilian in non-international armed conflicts have been unclear.[64] Unlike international armed conflicts, the treaty law regulating non-international armed conflicts (common Article 3 and Additional Protocol II) does not define the term "civilians." Moreover, in practice it is difficult to distinguish civilians from armed groups because they are seldom organized and they carry out armed operations with a variety of civilian support.[65] While common Article 3 does not use the term civilians, Additional Protocol II does,[66] without giving much guidance as to its meaning and scope. Therefore, its meaning has to be deduced from the text. Common Article 3 incorporates two key points to infer the meaning of civilians. First, common Article 3 is binding on "each party to the conflict," that is, the State through its armed forces as well as the organized armed groups. Thus, those who are not part of the parties of the conflict may be civilians, subject to the second condition. According to the second point of guidance, persons who take no active part in the hostilities are entitled to the protection under common Article 3. Thus, civilians are

58 Ibid.

59 Henckaerts and Doswald-Beck (2009), Commentary to Rule 106, p. 385.

60 Art. 44(3) Protocol I, above n 4.

61 Sandoz et al. (1987), paras 1698, 1703. See also, Ipsen (2013, pp. 90–92).

62 Art. 44(4), Protocol I, above n 4.

63 See, Jeenger (2024).

64 Akande (2010, p. 181).

65 Fleck (2013, p. 591).

66 Art. 13.

those persons who neither form part of a party to the conflict, nor take active part in the hostilities.[67] Similarly, under Protocol II, civilians are those who do not constitute any of the parties to the conflict (armed forces of a State, its dissident armed forces and other armed groups) and do not participate in the hostilities directly.[68]

Here it is imperative to clarify a misconception about the determination of civilian status in non-international armed conflicts. In a non-international armed conflict, the expression "civilian" is often taken to mean every person who is not a member of the armed forces.[69] Such a view creates an impression that members of armed groups are civilians but not immune from direct attack due to their direct participation in hostilities. Common Article 3 helps remove this confusion. It uses the words "each party to the conflict" while asking them to treat humanely "members of armed forces who have laid down their arms and those placed *hors de combat* by sickness, wounds, detention …"[70] It, thus, treats members of armed groups as armed forces for this purpose.[71] Therefore, it is wrong to say that all persons except the State armed forces are civilians. Thus, armed forces, organized armed groups and civilians are mutually exclusive categories.[72]

Another way to define civilians in non-international armed conflict is to follow the negative-definitional approach of Article 50(1) of Additional Protocol I. Thus, the International Criminal Tribunal for Rwanda (ICTR) took the view that a person who is not a member of either party to the armed conflict is a civilian.[73]

12.2.1 Distinguishing Civilians

Common Article 3 is sometimes called a "mini convention"[74]; however, the ICRC[75] is of the view that it does not regulate the conduct of hostilities because there is no provision entailing, for example, the principle of distinction. However, Additional Protocol II puts an obligation to refrain from targeting civilians or civilian objects, to plan attacks distinguishing civilians and civilian objects from the armed forces and military assets, to refrain from using weapons causing excessive harm, and not to locate military objectives at a place surrounded by civilians.[76] In respect of non-international armed conflicts also, the principle has attained the status of customary international law.[77]

12.3 Specific Challenges to the Application of Principle of Distinction

Apparently, the principle of distinction supported by the rules of distinct appearance and protection of civilians reflects its ease of application and human consideration. The rules make us believe the situation in black and white by segregating those who are legitimate targets and those who are not. However, there are situations, such as participation of civilians in hostilities directly and use of human shields, where the grey side of the principle surfaces. These

[67] Melzer (2014, pp. 319–320).

[68] See Art. 1(1), 13(3).

[69] Boothby (2012, p. 69).

[70] Art. 3(1) common to the Geneva Convention for the Amelioration of the Condition of the Wounded and Sick in Armed Forces in the Field of 12 August 1949 (Geneva Convention I) and the Geneva Convention for the Amelioration of the Condition of Wounded, Sick and Shipwrecked Members of Armed Forces at Sea of 12 August 1949 (Geneva Convention II), Art. 33 the Geneva Convention relative to the Treatment of Prisoners of War of 12 August 1949 (Geneva Convention III), Art. 15(a)(b) the Geneva Convention relative to the Protection of Civilian Persons in Time of War of 12 August 1949 (Geneva Convention IV).

[71] ICRC (2020).

[72] Melzer (2009, p. 28).

[73] Prosecutor v. Musema, ICTR-96-13-A, Trial Chamber I Judgment, 27 January 2000, paras 277, 280.

[74] Crawford (2015, p. 37).

[75] ICRC (2016, paras 540–543).

[76] Art. 13(1) and Sandoz et al. (1987, para 4772).

[77] Rule 1, Henckaerts and Doswald-Beck (2009).

conflict situations are largely internal[78] or non-international in nature, but different from revolutionary wars, with increasing involvement of civilians.[79] They are "new wars" which have rapidly replaced the classic warfare with the end of the Cold War.[80] For instance, hostile situations in Somalia, Niger Delta, Bosnia, Sierra Leone and Democratic Republic of Congo. The actors in the new wars are mainly organized and loosely organized armed groups, militias, criminal gangs, paramilitaries and rebel groups who fight for a range of motives (including economic gains and identity politics), or out of ethnic or religious hatred.[81] Their combat resources, mode of operation and purposes differ greatly from the conventional understanding of war between States. The present law of armed conflict does not sync well with them. Further, their direct participation in hostilities blurs the distinction lines and makes it extremely difficult to distinguish them from civilians not playing a direct role in hostilities. And the worst is recruitment and use of child soldiers in such wars which challenge the law relating to targeting. Thus, the three specific challenges relating to asymmetry of warfare, direct participation by civilians in hostilities and targeting of child soldiers are discussed hereunder.

12.3.1 Asymmetry of Warfare

The principle of distinction presupposes war between States and standard combat support in terms of armed forces and advanced military equipments. It is State-centric and it has been crafted for international armed conflicts. States are party to the treaties governing hostile conduct. They formally proclaim their willingness to abide by the law of armed conflict and also possess the wherewithal to comply with the treaty-obligations. However, this commonality is missing in majority of the contemporary wars as they feature armed non-State actors. These actors are dispersed and loosely coordinated.[82] They are certainly weaker in their fighting capabilities and different in their mode of attack, warring interests and ideological foundations. Thus, for instance, the armed groups may employ irregular fighters, conduct surprise operations, prefer adherence to religious texts and deliberately target civilians through hostage taking, the use of human shield, looting, killings, sexual exploitation and damage to property.[83] At times, there may be "imbalance of military power,"[84] and they may also not possess the devices necessary to verify or assess the presence of civilians or existence of a civilian object. The principle of distinction fares miles away from these realities of modern warfare and does not accommodate them. Therefore, it has been seen as based "on an outdated view of the world"[85] and Eurocentric view of wars (i.e. war between States).

12.3.2 Direct Participation of Civilian in Hostilities

As a general rule, civilians are not legitimate targets as they pose no threat to the adversary and, therefore, enjoy immunity from attack under treaty as well as customary law as already explained. Principle of distinction echoes the same idea. However, the immunity from attack is not absolute. Under the laws of armed conflict applicable in international as well non-international armed conflicts, civilians enjoy the protection "unless and for such time as they take a direct part in hostilities."[86] Thus, any direct participation in hostilities disentitles civilians of the protection because it makes civilians and members of armed forces equally hostile to the other belligerent and

78 Lamp (2011, p. 250).

79 Akande (2010, p. 182) and Schmitt (2005, p. 511).

80 Münkler (2005, p. 1).

81 Chinkin and Kaldor (2017, p. 8) and Stern (2019, p. 49).

82 Kennedy (2007, p. 174).

83 See, Swiney (2005, pp. 737, 747) and Lamp (2011, p. 245).

84 Gil (2015, p. 156).

85 Swiney (2005, p. 733).

86 Art. 51(3) Protocol I, above n 4 and Art. 13(3) Protocol Additional to the Geneva Conventions of 12 August 1949, and relating to the Protection of Victims of Non-International Armed Conflicts (Protocol II) of 8 June 1977. Common Article 3 uses the expression 'Persons taking no active part in the hostilities'.

places them on equal footing of legitimate targets. However, it is not a sanction for criminal behavior of civilians but a consequence of military necessity in the conduct of hostilities.[87] Yugoslav wars are appropriate examples of direct participation of civilians in hostilities, wherein organized and unorganized civilian armed groups resorted to armed attacks.

However, the words used in the provisions are vague and pose crucial challenges as to their interpretation. Neither the Protocols offer any definition of direct participation in hostilities, nor there is any otherwise "agreed definition."[88] Therefore, it is unclear as to which acts would amount to direct participation, or at what point of time protection available to a civilian is lost or resumed. There is no detailed list of activities that constitute direct participation in hostilities.[89] The problem surfaces more prominently when a non-State actor is involved in hostilities. The war between Israel and Hamas explains the issue and the lack of clear meaning of "direct participation."

As already noted, thousands of civilians of Palestine have been killed and injured by indiscriminate Israeli attacks, and hundreds of civilians have lost their lives in Israel by Hamas' indiscriminate operations since October 2023. In its 2014 report on Gaza Conflict, Israel has explained that in the absence of any elaboration of the phrase "direct participation of hostilities," the Israeli Defense Forces have issued to the troops a list of activities amounting to "direct participation."[90] The list is based on the Israeli Supreme Court's judgment.[91] The report further clarifies that "civilians affiliated with Hamas are not lawful targets as such." Notably, Israel has not ratified[92] the Protocol; however, it has made it clear that it abides[93] by those provisions of the Protocol which reflect customary international law. According to the ICRC, principle of distinction and loss of civilian protection due to direct participation in hostilities reflects customary international law.[94] This is an ideal position held by the Israeli forces in respect of distinction and direct role of civilians in combat.

However, from the indiscriminate strikes carried out by the Israeli forces and the huge amount of consequent civilian loss, it appears that the forces perhaps loosely presumed the civilian participation (and, arguably, their acquiescence too) in Hamas' armed attacks. This approach may be inferred from the public statements made by the Israeli authorities. The International Court of Justice (ICJ) referred to a statement made by the President of Israel on 12 October 2023:

> We are working, operating militarily according to rules of international law. Unequivocally. It is an entire nation out there that is responsible. It is not true this rhetoric about civilians not aware, not involved. It is absolutely not true. They could have risen up. They could have fought against that evil regime which took over Gaza in a *coup d'état*.[95]

Similarly, the Defense Minister of Israel reportedly said that he had released all restraints and they would eliminate everything. This double standard raises several queries: What did transpire among the Israeli authorities and military? Can the knowledge among civilians about Hamas' operations and their inaction be understood as "direct participation"? Does Israel consider almost every Palestinian to be accomplice in the October 7 attacks by Hamas? Is it an abuse of a vague provision by the Israeli forces? Was Israel already prepared for providing justifications for massive civilian casualties subsequent to attacks? It appears that Israel's approach towards the notion of "direct participation in hostilities" is not only flexible but misconceived also. Arguably, it interprets the provision

87 Melzer (2009, p. 62).

88 Public Committee against Torture in Israel v. Government of Israel, HCJ 769/02, 14 December 2006, paras 34–35 (Public Committee against Torture in Israel).

89 State of Israel (2015, para 317).

90 Ibid.

91 Public Committee against Torture in Israel, above n 88, paras 34–35.

92 See, https://ihl-databases.icrc.org/en/ihl-treaties/api-1977/state-parties?activeTab=default.

93 State of Israel (2015, para 234, n. 397).

94 Rules 1, 3, Henckaerts and Doswald-Beck (2009).

95 Application of the Convention on the Prevention and Punishment of the Crime of Genocide in the Gaza Strip (South Africa v. Israel) ICJ, Order, 26 January 2024, para 52.

as a permission to punish the assumed criminal conduct of Palestinians.

Vagueness in the notion of direct civilian participation has been a persistent issue that calls for a thoughtful attention. Realizing the severity of the matter, the ICRC took the initiative and brought together experts from different parts of the world to deliberate upon and form consensus as to the interpretation of the relevant provisions.[96] However, the experts could hardly arrive at an agreement; therefore, the ICRC published its own views on the subject in a work titled Interpretive Guidance on the Notion of Direct Participation in Hostilities under International Humanitarian Law, in 2009.[97] The ICRC has clarified that the document is an expression of its own views and has no binding legal character. Owing to the similar expressions used in the treaties regulating international and non-international armed conflicts, the interpretation of the notion of "direct participation in hostilities" in both the kinds of conflicts should be same, according to the ICRC.[98] The ICRC study explains the notion of direct participation as under.

12.3.2.1 Time Span of Loss of Protection

Civilians directly participating in hostilities lose the immunity from attack "only for such time" during which they do so. These words used in Article 51(3) suggest that such a civilian does not lose protection from attack permanently; rather, the immunity is regained the moment direct role in hostilities is over. According to the ICRC, the time span of loss of protection covers the time taken in adopting measures preparatory to the execution of a hostile act, execution phase of such an act, and deployment to and return from the location of execution of the act.[99] However, it is not always so easy to draw the line. The beginning and end of direct participation in hostilities can be understood by two factors: (1) the nature of an act, and (2) the nature of engagement. However, both must be considered together to determine the time span for loss of protection to a civilian.

On the basis of nature, an act amounting to direct participation in hostilities may be classified into two categories: (1) a preparatory measure integral to the execution of a specific hostile act, and (2) a specific hostile act. Examples of preparatory measures essential to the execution of a specific hostile act include transportation of weapons and troops, collecting intelligence information or loading ammunition onto a fighter aircraft, but do not cover supplying food to war zones. Thus, for the duration of time a civilian remains engaged in such a preparatory act or in the execution of a hostile act, the person is not immune from direct attack.

Second, the nature of engagement in hostilities may also affect the temporal scope of loss of protection. The nature of involvement in hostilities may be of three types: sporadic, recurrent and open. First, a civilian may sporadically participate in hostilities, for instance, a locomotive pilot running a train carrying tanks to a railway station closest to war zone. The driver remains a legitimate target during the entire journey because his role is preparatory in nature. Second, there may be a civilian who lives peacefully by the day but participates in hostilities by night, famously known as "a farmer by day and a fighter by night."[100] In respect of recurrent participation, the ICRC opines that direct participation in hostilities covers not only every hostile act but also the continued intent to perform hostile acts. However, since it is difficult to gather the intent to engage in future, direct participation in hostilities must be interpreted as restricted to specific hostile acts only, otherwise it would unnecessarily expose the civilians to attack.[101] States like Israel and United States disagree with this position and maintain that such a civilian may be targeted during the interval also.[102] Few commentators also suggest treating a person playing dual role an

---

[96] Garraway (2014, p. 173).

[97] Melzer (2009).

[98] Ibid., p. 44.

[99] Ibid., p. 65.

[100] Ibid., p. 72.

[101] Ibid., pp. 44–45.

[102] Cohen and Zlotogorski (2021, p. 142).

unlawful combatant at all times, and consequently divorced from immunity from attack.[103]

The third category may be broadly called as unlawful combatants. They are members of a regularly or casually constituted armed group of civilians engaged in continuous combat function, without complying with paragraphs 2[104] or 6[105] of Article 4A of the third Geneva Convention. To determine the time span of loss of protection for such civilians, their affiliation to the group is the crucial factor. Thus, a civilian becoming an unlawful combatant loses immunity as soon as such a person joins the group, and regains the same upon unambiguous separation from the group.

However, the ICRC's views on the temporal scope of loss of protection have been found to be too restrictive to make sense on the modern battlefield.[106]

12.3.2.2 Constitutive Elements Suggested by the ICRC

As per the Commentary to the Protocol, direct participation means acts of war which by their nature or purpose are likely to cause actual harm to the personnel and equipment of the enemy armed forces.[107] This view was understood as too narrow because it excludes acts which target civilians.[108] The ICRC Interpretive Guidance provides further clarification in this regard. It says that in order to qualify as direct participation in hostilities, a specific act of a civilian must meet the following cumulative conditions. The explanation to these conditions has been understood as "overly narrow interpretation."[109] In fact, certain States and experts believe the customary definition of direct role in hostilities to be wider and less restrictive.[110]

Threshold of Harm

The first condition displays the very nature of a specific hostile act that it must be of a harming nature. It is a very significant interpretation by the ICRC because the wordings of Article 51(3) do not suggest this. According to the Interpretive Guidance: "The act must be likely to adversely affect the military operations or military capacity of a party to an armed conflict or, alternatively, to inflict death, injury, or destruction on persons or damage to objects protected against direct attack."[111] An important element in this proposition is likelihood of adverse effect consequent upon the act, instead of actual occurrence of such an effect. Therefore, where an act executed by a civilian is likely to damage in all its probabilities the combat capacity of enemy, the act qualifies for direct participation in hostilities. Thus, acts like killing or wounding army personnel, damaging military equipments, capturing an enemy soldier, removing mines laid by enemy, transporting weapons to the conflict area or sharing intelligence of immediate combat use satisfy the threshold of harm. Schmitt, however, believes that even support activities which improve the military

---

[103] Dinstein (2004, p. 177) and Boothby (2010, p. 758).

[104] "(2) Members of other militias and members of other volunteer corps, including those of organised resistance movements, belonging to a Party to the conflict and operating in or outside their own territory, even if this territory is occupied, provided that such militias or volunteer corps, including such organized resistance movements, fulfil the following conditions:

(a) that of being commanded by a person responsible for his subordinates;
(b) that of having a fixed distinctive sign recognizable at a distance;
(c) that of carrying arms openly;
(d) that of conducting their operations in accordance with the laws and customs of war."

[105] "(6) Inhabitants of a non-occupied territory who, on the approach of the enemy, spontaneously take up arms to resist the invading forces, without having had time to form themselves into regular armed units, provided they carry arms openly and respect the laws and customs of war."

[106] Boothby (2010, p. 768).

[107] Sandoz et al. (1987, para 1944).

[108] Public Committee against Torture in Israel, above n 88, para 33.

[109] Schmitt (2010, p. 720).

[110] Cohen and Zlotogorski (2021, p. 139).

[111] Melzer (2009, p. 47).

capacity of a belligerent should also be considered because eventually it adversely affects the adversary.[112]

The ICRC also includes attacks on enemy's civilians or civilian property within the threshold of harm,[113] provided that the other two conditions are also met. However, many harmful acts committed on civilians do not have any belligerent nexus (i.e. favoring one party to the detriment of another). This is particularly in case of new wars wherein targeting civilian population is "frequently a central strategy,"[114] for instance, violent acts committed by Boko Haram on civilians. It has been observed that the ICRC Guidance is silent on this issue as it has been designed to meet the situations of armed conflict as understood in traditional sense.[115]

Direct Causation

This element enunciates the test that whether the highly probable loss to the enemy is a direct result of the act in question, or an indirect or remote outcome. For instance, in both the events where a civilian works in a weapon producing unit or drives a weapon-loaded truck to a war zone, the weapons are ultimately going to cause some loss to the enemy, however, the former is an indirect cause for the loss to the enemy, whereas the latter is a direct one. The ICRC puts forward this test as follows: "There must be a direct causal link between the act and the harm likely to result either from that act, or from a coordinated military operation of which that act constitutes an integral part."[116] For a specific act to qualify as direct, rather than indirect participation in hostilities there must be a sufficiently close causal relation between the act and the resulting harm.[117] Thus, scientific research on weapons, repairing of roads and bridges, or training[118] army personnel do not establish the direct causal link, however, placing mines or communicating critical intelligence information do, according to the ICRC.[119] It shows "one causal step" test, which Schmitt seeks to replace by "integral part" test alone, implying indirect causal effect.[120] According to Melzer, however, "integral part" criterion is appropriate in collective operations.[121]

Belligerent Nexus

Belligerent nexus of the specific conduct refers to its relation with the parties of armed conflict. The feature of a specific act of being favorable to a party to an armed conflict but harmful to the other is belligerent nexus. Thus, combining all the three constitutive elements, it is said that: "The act must be specifically designed to directly cause the required threshold of harm in support of a party to the conflict and to the detriment of another."[122] Therefore, there is no belligerent nexus where a civilian resorts to use of force, for instance, in self-defense, in order to prevent any assault on one's life, dignity or property by an invading army.[123] Such an attack is, though, harmful to the enemy but not intended to benefit one's own country. Similarly, lawful use of force against an escaping prisoner of war or judicial proceedings lawfully initiated against a prisoner of war does not reflect belligerent nexus.[124]

These elements and their interpretation render several acts as amounting to "indirect" participation in hostilities, which are treated by many States as direct. Furthermore, the three elements are derived from an "establishment view of conflict,"[125] whereas in new wars the violent situations are fluid and unclear enough to know exactly the beginning of a non-international

[112] Schmitt (2010, pp. 718–719).

[113] Melzer (2009, p. 49).

[114] Stern (2019, p. 170).

[115] Ibid.

[116] Melzer (2009, p. 51).

[117] Ibid., p. 52.

[118] Training has been treated as "a quintessentially military task": Stern (2019, p. 172).

[119] Melzer (2009, pp. 53–54).

[120] Schmitt (2010, pp. 728–729).

[121] Melzer (2010, pp. 866–867).

[122] Melzer (2009, p. 58).

[123] Ibid., p. 61.

[124] Ibid., p. 62. See also, Art. 42, 82 Geneva Convention III, above n 70 (for escape of a prisoner of war and judicial proceedings against a prisoner of war, respectively).

[125] Stern (2019, p. 172).

armed conflict.[126] In the Democratic Republic of Congo, there are several rebel groups engaged in range of criminal activities of uneven gravity for many years. This fluidity of the situation and range of actors pose a challenge to the ICRC Interpretive Guidance.[127]

12.3.2.3 Human Shields and Direct Participation in Hostilities

During an armed conflict, when civilians protect army personnel or military objectives against a combat operation by their presence nearby or surrounding them, they are said to act as human shields. It, generally, happens in ground operations or urban warfare. It is an abuse of the immunity from attack, irrespective of the fact that they do so voluntarily or they are compelled to act in this manner by the military personnel of their own country or of the enemy. In Gulf war (1990), Iraq allegedly used thousands of involuntary foreign nationals (including enemy nationals) and many of its own nationals to act as human shields.[128] Further, they also placed military equipments near or within the densely populated areas.[129] Using human shields is contrary to the law of armed conflict and punishable under international criminal law.

The Geneva Convention IV as well as Additional Protocol I prohibit the use of the presence of civilians to render certain legitimate targets immune from military strikes.[130] In the opinion of the ICRC, customary international law also echoes the similar prohibition.[131] However, the Statute of International Criminal Court (Rome Statute) prohibits the use of civilians as well as other protected persons, such as prisoners of war as human shields. Thus, "utilizing the presence of a civilian or other protected person to render certain points, areas or military forces immune from military operations"[132] amounts to a war crime under the Statute.

The above obligations are, of course, applicable only to the parties to an armed conflict. However, do the civilians who act as human shields also bear the burden under the law, or put in other way, do they lose the immunity from direct attack otherwise available under the principle of distinction; similarly, will they not be considered for proportionality assessment? For this purpose, classification of human shields into two categories is suggested: voluntary and involuntary.

Voluntary Human Shields

When civilians act as human shields out of their own volition, they are referred to as voluntary human shields, although it becomes difficult for the enemy doing air strikes to identify voluntary and involuntary human shields, as contrast to ground operations. Consequently, a belligerent would prefer not to attack the target or postpone the same. However, since due to such cancelation or postponement, the belligerent did not get the military advantage to the detriment of the enemy, which they might have got, had there been no human shields; will the act of the civilians protecting the legitimate targets amount to direct participation in hostilities within the meaning of Article 51(3) of Additional Protocol I? For this purpose, the ICRC distinguishes between ground military operations and air strikes, and treats human shields in both the situations differently. Where human shields pose an obstacle in carrying out armed operations by a belligerent, it causes the threshold of harm directly.[133] However, in case of air raids, the presence of voluntary human shields does not adversely affect "the capacity of the attacker to identify and destroy the shielded military objective"[134] according to the ICRC. The different treatment in respect of ground operations and air strikes has been criticized as "unrealistic"[135] and

[126] Ibid., p. 169.

[127] Ibid., pp. 168–169.

[128] CIA (2003, pp. 1–10).

[129] Ibid.

[130] Art. 28 Geneva Convention IV, above n 70 and Art. 51(7) Protocol I, above n 4.

[131] Rule 97, Henckaerts and Doswald-Beck (2009).

[132] Art. 8(2)(b)(xxiii) Statute of International Criminal Court (1998) (Rome Statute).

[133] Melzer (2009, p. 56).

[134] Melzer (2009, pp. 56–57).

[135] Garraway (2014, p. 178).

"artificial."[136] It has been suggested that logically voluntary human shields must be treated as directly participating in hostilities.[137] Further it has been observed that: "Still, even assuming that they are direct participants in hostilities, it must be perceived that voluntary human shields cannot be attacked separately from the lawful target since no preparation is required for either their 'deployment' or 'disengagement.'"[138] Irrespective of the nature of their participation (direct or otherwise), a fundamental ambiguity lingers in respect of the degree of free will necessary to become voluntary human shield and the scale of coercion to act as involuntary human shield.[139]

Involuntary Human Shields

Apparently, civilians forced to shield a military target cannot be treated as directly participating in hostilities and robbed of the protection under the law of armed conflict.

12.3.2.4 Presumption of No Direct Participation

Despite the uncertainties and complexities in the interpretation of the concept of direct participation in hostilities, the operational realities may present a situation before a hostile army where it is not quite clear to them whether the conduct of an individual civilian amounts to direct participation in hostilities or not. In such a situation, it shall be presumed that the conduct in question does not amount to direct participation in hostilities, and therefore, the person is entitled to civilian protection.[140] This presumption bears resemblance with the presumption of civilian status under Article 50(1), Additional Protocol I, though the latter is used to determine membership of a civilian to armed forces, while the former helps find out the degree of involvement in hostilities.

12.3.2.5 Tribunals and Direct Participation in Hostilities

When the ICRC was working on the interpretation of direct participation in hostilities, almost during the same time the international tribunals were also struggling with its meaning. However, they had to settle with a case-by-case approach in the absence of a definition of the phrase.[141] The ICTY in Strugar[142] case included the following actions, in addition to the uncontested hostile acts, within the notion of direct participation in hostilities: "transmitting military information for the immediate use of a belligerent, transporting weapons in proximity to combat operations, and serving as guards, intelligence agents, lookouts, or observers on behalf of military forces."[143] On the other hand, the acts treated beyond the term are: "participating in activities in support of the war or military effort of one of the parties to the conflict, selling goods to one of the parties to the conflict, expressing sympathy for the cause of one of the parties to the conflict, failing to act to prevent an incursion by one of the parties to the conflict, accompanying and supplying food to one of the parties to the conflict, transporting arms and munitions, and providing supplies, and providing specialist advice regarding the selection of military personnel, their training, or the correct maintenance of the weapons."[144] Though, the Chamber did not clarify what is meant by "activities in support of the war or military effort," the ICRC, referring to the decision, uses two similar phrases: activities part of general war-effort (such as, design, production and shipment of weapons; construction or repair of roads, ports,

[136] Rubinstein and Roznai, cited in Dinstein (2016, p. 184).

[137] Schmitt (2010, p. 734).

[138] Dinstein (2016, p. 174).

[139] Melzer (2010, p. 871).

[140] Melzer (2009, pp. 74–75).

[141] Prosecutor v. Dusko Tadić, IT-94-1-T, Trial Chamber Judgment, 7 May 1997, para 616. For a detailed account of judicial approach, see Schmitt (2010, pp. 705–708) and Darcy (2014, pp. 123–125).

[142] Prosecutor v. Strugar, IT-01-42-A, Appeals Chamber Judgment, 17 July 2008.

[143] Ibid., para 177.

[144] Ibid. The International Criminal Court also does not include providing food and shelter within direct participation in hostilities. Prosecutor v. Mbarushimana, ICC-01/04-01/10, Pre-Trial Chamber I, Decision on the Confirmation of Charges, 16 December 2011, para 148, cited in Darcy (2014, p. 124).

airports, bridges, railways), and war-sustaining activities (for instance, political propaganda and media activities).[145] The ICRC also considers these activities outside the purview of direct participation in hostilities.

On national level, the Supreme Court of Israel has not only adopted the same approach but also expanded the scope of the notion of direct participation in hostilities by including voluntary human shields within its ambit. As already discussed, it is contrary the views held by the ICRC.[146]

12.3.2.6 Academic Debate Over ICRC Interpretive Guidance

The Interpretive Guidance is an outcome of a unilateral effort of the ICRC, because, as stated earlier, the experts invited by it to prepare a document on direct participation in hostilities could not agree upon number of issues. However, when the ICRC came up with its own conclusions on the subject, it ignited a considerable amount of debate. The commentators, especially from the United States, had several reservations with respect to the legal position suggested by the ICRC, and their publicity was ensured through publication.[147] In response, Nilz Melzer,[148] acting on behalf of the ICRC, wrote a detailed reply to the four major critics. Most importantly, he clarified that the Interpretive Guidance seeks to strike a balance between humanitarian considerations and military necessity,[149] whereas, the criticism was "almost exclusively driven by military necessity,"[150] for example, Schmitt suggests that even in case of doubt, a person should not be considered as civilian, and therefore, may be directly attacked. Similarly, in case of membership of armed organized groups, Watkin proposes that persons providing combat service support, such as unarmed cooks and administrative personnel should also be considered as members of such groups.[151] Israel and United States hold the same view in respect of membership of an armed group.[152]

12.3.3 Targeting Child Soldiers

With the rise of asymmetrical warfare, the recruitment and use of children in hostilities is also increasing. Generally, soldiers below the age of eighteen are classified as child soldiers; however, in legal parlance the age-limit is fifteen because employing children below fifteen as soldiers amounts to a war crime.[153] There are almost 300,000[154] child soldiers involved in various combat roles across the Global South, especially in the sub-Saharan Africa.[155] Forty

[145] Melzer (2009, p. 51).

[146] Public Committee against Torture in Israel, above n 88 para 36.

[147] Four major dissenting views were as follows: (1) A large amount of criticism was written by Prof. Schmitt on the constitutive elements of direct participation in hostilities. See Schmitt (2010). (2) The next dissent was received from Brigadier General Kenneth Watkin, who had disagreements with position taken by the ICRC regarding membership in organised armed groups. See Watkin (2010). (3) The third response is from Air Commodore William Boothby whose dissent focuses on the conclusion arrived at by the ICRC in respect of the beginning and end of direct participation in hostilities. See Boothby (2010). (4) Hays Parks, a retired Colonel challenged Section IX of the document, titled 'Restraints on the Use of Force in Direct Attack', on the ground that the ICRC has crossed its mandate, and the views presented in this Section are not practicable. See, Parks (2010).

[148] See Melzer (2010, p. 831).

[149] Ibid., pp. 831, 914.

[150] Ibid.

[151] Ibid., p. 913.

[152] Cohen and Zlotogorski (2021, p. 142).

[153] Drumbl (2012, p. 90).

[154] OCHA (2017).

[155] Vautravers (2008, p. 96).

percent of them are girls[156] whose proportion is ascending.[157] Children from indigenous[158] and marginalized[159] sections form a major portion of child soldiers. Their tender age, vulnerability, lack of education, unemployment, poverty and victimization by ongoing conflicts are exploited and they are thrown into war zones by abducting or making rewarding[160] promises. They are usually given small arms as they are lightweight, durable and conveniently transferable.[161] Besides performing direct combat roles, they are engaged in drug-abuse, spying, physical labor and sexual slavery.[162]

In legal context, the expression "children" refers to those who have not attained the age of fifteen. Recruiting them as soldiers (voluntarily or forcibly) or making them participate directly in international or non-international armed conflict is prohibited.[163] It also amounts to a war crime.[164] Yet, it is the most prevalent of the "six grave violations against children during armed conflict".[165],[166] In reality, 71% of the child soldiers are aged below fifteen[167] and the average age of child soldiers is fourteen.[168]

The presence of child soldiers on the battlefield or their direct participation in hostilities poses a moral dilemma before an enemy combatant: whether to use lethal force against a child soldier or not. While military necessity may permit it, considerations of humanity might disallow doing so. The laws of armed conflict drafted largely keeping in mind inter-State wars has no answer to this moral predicament. On the question of targeting, the law applicable in international armed conflicts allows attack on combatants subject to at least two conditions: no infliction of excessive[169] harm and no attack on combatants who are sick, wounded and ship-wrecked,[170] or intend to surrender.[171] Given these rules, child soldiers generally enjoy no immunity from attack. This is also in consonance with the principle of distinction as it exists. Child soldiers' voluntary enlistment or conscription becomes immaterial in this regard.

In the context of armed conflicts not of an international character, a civilian not enrolled as a member in an organized armed group may become targetable subject to the fulfillment of the criteria of direct participation in hostilities, as discussed above. On the other hand, a member of an organized armed group is also rendered targetable in case of involvement in continuous combat function, which means "preparation, execution, or command of acts or operations amounting to direct participation in hostilities."[172] Thus, a child fulfilling any of the two conditions is not entitled to any immunity against targeting, except in case of laying down arms or inability to engage

[156] United Nations (2015) "4 out of 10 child soldiers are girls", Office of the Secretary-Generals Envoy on Youth, 12 February 2015, available at: https://www.un.org/youthenvoy/2015/02/4-10-child-soldiers-girls/#:~:text=Up%20to%2040%20per%20cent,for%20Children%20and%20Armed%20Conflict.

[157] United Nations (2024b, p. 22).

[158] Ibid., p. 21.

[159] United Nations (2022, p. 13).

[160] Bosco Ntaganda, chief of a militia group in Congo, told the child soldiers: "... if you are a soldier, the army is a place of happiness and joy for you. You will have women for free, houses for free and everything is free when you are a soldier." See, The Prosecutor v. Bosco Ntaganda, ICC-01/04-02/06, Trial Chamber VI, Trial Hearing, Open Session, 28 August 2018, p. 39. https://www.icc-cpi.int/sites/default/files/Transcripts/CR2018_04129.PDF.

[161] Stohl (2002, p. 281).

[162] United Nations (2024b, p. 21).

[163] Art. 77(2) Protocol I, above n 4, Art. 4(3)(c) Protocol II, above n 86 and Art. 38(2)(3) Convention on the Rights of the Child (1989). However, the Optional Protocol to the Convention does not approve of compulsory recruitment into the armed forces and non-State armed groups of persons who have not attained the age of 18 years: Art. 2, 4(1) Optional Protocol to the Convention on the Rights of the Child on the Involvement of Children in Armed Conflict A/RES/54/263, 25 May 2000.

[164] Art. 8(2)(b)(26) Rome Statute, above n 132.

[165] United Nations (2013).

[166] United Nations (2024b, p. 21).

[167] Vautravers (2008, p. 96).

[168] United Nations (2024b, p. 22).

[169] Art. 35(2) Protocol I, above n 4.

[170] See Art. 12 Geneva Convention I, II, above n 70.

[171] Art. 41(1), (2)(b) Protocol I, above n 4.

[172] Melzer (2009, p. 34).

because of sickness, wounds or detention.[173] The ICRC[174] also approves of this position.

However, this is easier said than accomplished without having been to a war zone. It is perhaps the toughest call to decide whether to strike at a child soldier. The moral intuition that children remain children despite performing direct roles in hostilities influences the applicable norms[175] and shapes an individual's suggestions. Considering the factors responsible for children's participation in hostilities and their tender age, many commentators have put forward range of suggestions advocating a flexible and soft approach towards targeting child soldiers. They include: prefer capturing instead of killing a child soldier, whenever possible, taking into account military necessity and humanitarian considerations[176]; treat them as "super-privileged combatants" or "victimized combatants" deserving special considerations[177]; during split-second ground operations, hit them in self-defense only[178]; use the least injurious means and methods of war against child soldiers[179]; treat them as non-combatants (e.g. medical and religious personnel) and do not target unless they participate directly in hostilities.[180]

However, on targeting child soldiers the following concerns still need to be diligently addressed: First, an enemy combatant is recognized by uniform, carrying of arms and combat roles. There is no legal obligation on a soldier to know the age of an enemy soldier. Even by physical appearance, the age of an enemy soldier may not be known[181] most often because of uniform, helmet, lack of sufficient light and visibility. In the midst of all these practical challenges, how will law help recognize a child soldier and target accordingly? Second, all child soldiers do not take up arms forcefully. In the battlefield, an enemy is hardly able to distinguish child soldiers on the basis of voluntary or forceful participation.[182] In such a situation, how shall the issue of voluntary and involuntary participation be addressed while determining lawfulness of targeting child soldiers? Third, the idea of flexible approach towards targeting child soldiers emanates from human rights discourse; however, the relationship between international law of armed conflict and that of human rights is debated.[183] Thus, the point is which of the two shall prevail. Fourth, rendering child soldiers immune from an attack may amount to perpetuating an illegality because recruitment and use of child soldiers is a war crime. Thus, targeting child soldiers involves number of legal, moral and practical issues awaiting a balanced answer.

The present law of armed conflict, however, provides for no separate legal standards in respect of targeting child soldiers. It does not cater to the huge challenge posed by several ongoing asymmetrical armed conflicts. It is surprising to find that the Additional Protocols of 1977 sought to prescribe a protection mechanism for children during armed conflict, including the ban on recruitment and use of child soldiers; however, they contain no special guidelines in respect of targeting child soldiers. Notably, several provisions on targeting were inserted in the Protocols which relate to the principles of distinction, proportionality and precaution. Did the drafters intend to apply the same norms in respect of child soldiers also? It is important to note that the problem of deploying child soldiers in war existed in 1970s also though at a very rudimentary stage.[184] Additionally, they were largely

[173] Art. 3(1) Common to Geneva Conventions I–IV, above n 70.

[174] Melzer (2009, p. 60).

[175] Provost (2016).

[176] Provost (2016) and Jungfleisch (2020, p. 272).

[177] Sinha (2013, p. 584).

[178] Roughley (2017, p. 79) and Mégret (2013, p. 2).

[179] Provost (2016).

[180] Mégret (2013, p. 3).

[181] Jungfleisch (2020, p. 269).

[182] Radhika Coomaraswamy, UN Special Representative for Children and Armed Conflict, submissions before the International Criminal Court: The Prosecutor v. Thomas Lubanga Dyilo, ICC-01/04-01/16, Trial Chamber I, Decision, 14 March 2012, para 611.

[183] Jungfleisch (2020, p. 273).

[184] For instance, in Columbia 17,865 child soldiers during 1958–2023: United Nations (2024b, p. 21) and Sandoz et al. (1987, para 3183).

the Third World countries struggling with political and economic stability wherein child soldiers began to be thrown into war zones by governments as well as non-State armed groups. Therefore, it appears that these instruments, like many others, carry a West-oriented approach towards the realities of war and do not address the specificities of the Third World. In the context of international legal protection of children in war zones, it has been suitably remarked:

> The social construction of childhood in Africa has inherent difficulties that limit the applicability and relevance of international, often Western, standards relating to the protection of children in conflict zones, even though most African countries are signatories to these international legal instruments.[185]

The author further observes:

> Extensive research fieldwork in Liberia and Sierra reveals that the application of the restrictive and Western-centric definition and construction of a 'child' and 'childhood' raises inherent difficulties in the African context.[186]

Thus, it appears that the treaty law does not address the diversity of the Third World experience. It addresses the problem of child soldiers up to the stage of its prohibition, and it is silent on the question of targeting them.

12.4 Proportionality Principle and Distinction

The factors responsible for the weakness of the principle of distinction are not only the complexity of differentiation but also the overriding effect of the principle of proportionality. Though, targeted attacks on civilian population and property are prohibited, where there is an incidental or unintended loss to civilian life while hitting a legitimate target, the proportionality principle may decide the legality of the collateral damage. Accordingly, no legal liability arises where the expected incidental civilian loss or damage to civilian objects is not disproportionate or excessive to the direct military advantage anticipated by the attack.[187] Thus, the principle of distinction is not a mutually exclusive and absolute principle. It is overridden by the exception created by the proportionality principle.

References

Akande D (2010) Clearing the fog of war? The ICRC's interpretive guidance on direct participation in hostilities. Int Comp Law Q 59(1):180–192

Arondekar A (2005) Without a trace: sexuality and the colonial archive. J Hist Sex 14(1–2):10–27

Best G (1979) Restraints on war by land before 1945. In: Howard M (ed) Restraints on war: studies in the limitation of armed conflict. OUP, Oxford, pp 17–37

Boothby B (2010) "And for such time as": the time dimension to direct participation in hostilities. New York Univ J Int Law Polit 42:741–768

Boothby WH (2012) The law of targeting. OUP, Oxford

Chinkin C, Kaldor M (2017) International law and new wars. CUP, Cambridge

CIA (2003) Putting noncombatants at risk: Saddam's use of "human shields". Central Intelligence Agency. https://irp.fas.org/cia/product/iraq_human_shields/iraq_human_shields.pdf

Cohen A, Zlotogorski D (2021) Proportionality in international humanitarian law: consequences, precautions, and procedures. OUP, New York

Crawford E (2015) Identifying the enemy: civilian participation in armed conflict. OUP, Oxford

Crawford E, Pert A (2015) International humanitarian law. CUP, Cambridge

Darcy S (2014) Judges, law and war: the judicial development of international humanitarian law. CUP, Cambridge

DD News (2024) Russia hits vast dam in war's largest strike on Ukrainian energy infrastructure, Kyiv says, 22 March 2024. https://ddnews.gov.in/en/russia-hits-vast-dam-in-wars-largest-strike-on-ukrainian-energy-infrastructure-kyiv-says/

Dinstein Y (2004) The conduct of hostilities under the law of international armed conflict. CUP, Cambridge

Dinstein Y (2016) The conduct of hostilities under the law of international armed conflict. CUP, Cambridge

Drumbl MA (2012) The effects of the Lubanga case on understanding and preventing child soldiering. Yearbook IHL 15:87–116

Fleck D (2013) The law of non-international armed conflicts. In: Fleck D (ed) The handbook of international humanitarian law. OUP, Oxford, pp 581–610

[185] Francis (2007, p. 210).

[186] Ibid., p. 207.

[187] Art. 51(5)(b) Protocol I, above n 4 and Prosecutor v. Galić, IT-98-29-A, Appeals Chamber, Judgment, 30 November, 2006, para 190.

Francis DJ (2007) 'Paper protection' mechanisms: child soldiers and the international protection of children in Africa's conflict zones. J Mod Afr Stud 45(2):207–231
Garraway C (2014) Direct participation and the principle of distinction: squaring the circle. In: Harvey C et al (eds) Contemporary challenges to the laws of war: essays in honour of professor Peter Rowe. CUP, Cambridge, pp 169–190
Garraway CHB (2007) "Combatants"—substance or semantics. In: Schmitt MN, Pejic J (eds) International law and armed conflict, exploring the faultlines: essays in the honour of Yoram Dinstein. MartinusNijhoff, Leiden, pp 317–334
Gil ED (2015) Trapped: three dilemmas in the law of proportionality and asymmetric warfare. Yearbook IHL 18:153–180
Henckaerts JM, Doswald-Beck L (2009) Customary international humanitarian law, vol I. ICRC/CUP, New York
ICRC (2016) Commentary on article 3, Geneva convention I. https://ihl-databases.icrc.org/en/ihl-treaties/gci-1949/article-3/commentary/2016#146_B
ICRC (2020) Commentary on article 3, Geneva convention III. https://ihl-databases.icrc.org/en/ihl-treaties/gciii-1949/article-3/commentary/2020?activeTab=undefined#_Toc44265113
Ipsen K (2013) Combatants and non-combatants. In: Fleck D (ed) The handbook of international humanitarian law. OUP, Oxford, pp 301–331
Jeenger K (2024) Third world view of the laws of armed conflict: an introduction. RGNLU Student Res Rev 10(2) (forthcoming)
Jungfleisch J (2020) You cannot target child soldiers as if they were adults, can you?—solutions to close the gap between law and morals concerning child soldiers currently under discussion. J Int Law Peace Armed Confl 3(3):261–277
Kennedy D (2007) Modern war and modern law. Univ Balt Law Rev 36(2):173–194
Kolb R, Hyde R (2008) An introduction to the international law of armed conflicts. Hart Publishing, Oxford
Lamp N (2011) Conceptions of war and paradigms compliance: the 'new war' challenge to international humanitarian law. J Confl Secur Law 16(2):225–262
Mégret F (2013) When is it permissible to target child soldiers? Lieber notes. Am Soc Int Law Spring 2–3
Melzer N (2010) Keeping the balance between military necessity and humanity: a response to four critiques of the ICRC'S interpretive guidance on the notion of direct participation in hostilities. New York Univ J Int Law Polit 42:831–916
Melzer N (2014) The principle of distinction between civilians and combatants. In: Clapham A, Gaeta P (eds) The Oxford handbook of international law in armed conflict. OUP, Oxford, pp 296–331
Melzer N (ed) (2009) Interpretive guidance on the notion of direct participation in hostilities under international humanitarian law. ICRC, Geneva
Miller RI (1975) The law of war. Lexington Books, Lexington
Münkler H (2005) The new wars. Polity Press, Cambridge
OCHA (2017) 10 countries where child soldiers are still recruited in armed conflicts, 28 February 2017. https://reliefweb.int/report/central-african-republic/10-countries-where-child-soldiers-are-still-recruited-armed
OCHA (2023) Occupied Palestinian territory. https://www.ochaopt.org/.
OHCHR (2023) Attack on funeral reception in Hroza, 5 October 2023, UN Human Rights Monitoring Mission in Ukraine, p. 3. https://www.ohchr.org/sites/default/files/documents/countries/ukraine/2023/attack-funeral-reception-hroza-report-en.pdf
Parks WH (2010) Part IX of the ICRC "direct participation in hostilities" study: no mandate, no expertise, and legally incorrect. New York Univ J Int Law Polit 42:769–830
Pictet J (1958) Commentary on article 4, Geneva convention IV. https://ihl-databases.icrc.org/en/ihl-treaties/gciv-1949/article-4/commentary/1958?activeTab=
Polityuk P (2024) The Russian attacks that have pounded Ukraine's power facilities, 20 January 2024. https://www.reuters.com/business/energy/russian-attacks-that-have-pounded-ukraines-power-facilities-2024-06-14/
Provost R (2016) Targeting child soldiers. EJIL:Talk!, 12 January 2016. https://www.ejiltalk.org/targeting-child-soldiers/
Roughley C (2017) Mind the gap: child soldiers and the law of targeting. Aust Int Law J 23:65–90
Sandoz Y et al (eds) (1987) Commentary on the additional protocols of 8 June 1977 to the Geneva conventions of 12 August 1949. ICRC/Martinus Nijhoff, Geneva
Schmitt MN (2005) Humanitarian law and direct participation in hostilities by private contractors or civilian employees. Chic J Int Law 5(2):511–546
Schmitt MN (2010) Deconstructing direct participation in hostilities: the constitutive elements. New York Univ J Int Law Polit 42:697–739
Sinha GA (2013) Child soldiers as super-privileged combatants. Int J Hum Rights 17(4):584–603
State of Israel (2015) The 2014 Gaza conflict, 7 July-26 August 2014, factual and legal aspects. https://www.gov.il/en/Departments/General/2014-gaza-conflict-factual-and-legal-aspects
Stern OM (2019) Gender, conflict and international humanitarian law: a critique of the 'principle of distinction.' Routledge, New York
Stohl R (2002) Targeting children: small arms and children in conflict. Brown J World Aff 9(1):281–292
Summers J (2014) Introduction. In: Harvey C et al (eds) Contemporary challenges to the laws of war: essays in honour of professor Peter Rowe. CUP, Cambridge, pp 1–29
Swiney G (2005) Saving lives: the principle of distinction and the realities of modern war. Int Lawyer 39(3):733–758

UNHRMMU (2024) UN Human Rights Monitors voice alarm as Russia renews attacks on power grids in Ukraine, 22 March 2024. https://ukraine.un.org/en/264071-un-human-rights-monitors-voice-alarm-russia-renews-attacks-power-grids-ukraine
United Nations (2013) Office of the special representative of the Secretary-General for children and armed conflict, the six grave violations against children during armed conflict: the legal foundation, working paper No. 1. United Nations, New York
United Nations (2015) 4 out of 10 child soldiers are girls, Office of the Secretary-Generals Envoy on Youth, 12 February 2015. https://www.un.org/youthenvoy/2015/02/4-10-child-soldiers-girls/#:~:text=Up%20to%2040%20per%20cent,for%20Children%20and%20Armed%20Conflict
United Nations (2022) Office of the special representative of the Secretary-General for children and armed conflict, the gender dimensions of grave violations against children in armed conflict. United Nations, New York
United Nations (2024a) Escalating attacks on Ukraine's civilian, energy infrastructure making humanitarian aid delivery even more dangerous, relief chief tells Security Council, 9625th meeting, SC/15695, 14 May 2024. https://press.un.org/en/2024/sc15695.doc.htm
United Nations (2024b) Office of the special representative of the Secretary-General for children and armed conflict, responding to conflict-related sexual violence against boys associated with armed groups during the process of reintegration in Colombia. United Nations, New York
Vautravers AJ (2008) Why child soldiers are such a complex issue. Refug Surv Q 27(4):96–107
Watkin K (2010) Opportunity lost: organized armed groups and the ICRC "direct participation in the hostilities" interpretive guidance. New York Univ J Int Law Polit 42:641–695
Wilt H (2019) Towards a better understanding of the concept of 'indiscriminate attack'—how international criminal law can be of assistance. Yearbook IHL 22:29–42

13 Principle of Proportionality: Disproportionate Vagueness and High Expectations

Abstract

This chapter critically approaches the principle of proportionality and tries to unveil its inhuman side. I begin with the Roman theological underpinnings to the principle of proportionality and then discuss its drafting history in order to explain how several delegates found the draft proportionality provision to be problematic. Thereafter, I discuss in detail the critical dimension of the proportionality principle with special reference to the wars on Ukraine and Gaza. I stress upon the vagueness in the provision and explain how the proportionality assessment is challenging for a commander. I reemphasize that certain effects of war, such as mental harm and reverberating effects do not factor in the assessment. I explain how the vague notion of military advantage may be abused by a powerful belligerent, especially on the ground of self-defense. I also argue that at times the principle may even encourage violence and justify death and destruction.

Keywords

History of proportionality · Incidental civilian harm · Military advantage · Proportionality and human shield · Critique of proportionality

13.1 Introduction

The principle of distinction, though, makes it mandatory to distinguish the civilians from soldiers, and prohibits direct attack on civilians or civilian objects, however, sometimes incidental civilian loss is inevitable. In order to check such incidental civilian loss, Protocol I follows the principle of proportionality and prohibits the following type of attack being indiscriminate:

> an attack which may be expected to cause incidental loss of civilian life, injury to civilians, damage to civilian objects, or a combination thereof, which would be excessive in relation to the concrete and direct military advantage anticipated.[1]

The principle seeks to prohibit a military operation where the probable consequent loss to civilians appears to be excessive and disproportionate to the military advantage anticipated. In the proportionality principle, thus, what is important is the degree of expected military advantage and loss to civilians. The principle finds mention in identical form and content at quite a few places in the treaty law of armed conflict (international humanitarian

[1] Art. 51(5)(b) Protocol Additional to the Geneva Conventions of 12 August 1949, and relating to the Protection of Victims of International Armed Conflicts (Protocol I) of 8 June 1977.

K. Jeenger, *A Humanitarian Critique of International Humanitarian Law*, Sustainable Development Goals Series, https://doi.org/10.1007/978-981-96-8319-2_13

law). Under Article 51 of Additional Protocol I, an attack is declared as indiscriminate and the same is prohibited if it may be expected to cause incidental harm to civilians which would be excessive in relation to the direct and concrete military advantage anticipated.[2] A belligerent is under an obligation to refrain from deciding to launch such an attack.[3] Further, where a belligerent realizes, subsequent to planning an attack, that the attack is likely to cause more harm to civilians and make less military gain, such an attack shall be cancelled or suspended.[4] In a similar way, Protocol II to the Conventional Weapons Convention, 1980 bans the indiscriminate use of the mines and other conventional weapons which is likely to cause comparatively more harm to civilians.[5]

13.2 Philosophical Origins of Proportionality

The idea of proportionality involves a question of morality and ethics which has long been a subject matter of Roman Catholic theology. Under this tradition, the moral correctness of an action is judged by the priority accorded to the good result over the evil result caused by the action. In Summa Theologiae, Thomas Aquinas explains that an act may have two effects: one being the intended and the other, just accidental.[6] Moral backing to an act differs in respect of killing someone with intent to kill and causing death as a side-effect.[7] It is the intended effect that determines the moral side of the act. Thus, deliberately killing a person is not justified but causing death in self-defense stands validated. This is the principle of double effect.[8] Prima facie, it appears to be a consequentialist approach (judging an action by its impact). However, is the principle applicable to every situation including the conduct of military operations? Is the incidental harm to civilians justifiable under the double effect principle?

According to the New Catholic Encyclopedia, the very first condition of applicability of double effect principle is moral rectitude of the act itself.[9] This condition makes the principle deontological (judging an action by fairness of the act itself, instead of its effect) and, therefore, it may not approve of killing civilians incidentally because justness of violence during war is debatable.

An essential part of the double effect principle, however, is the principle of proportionality. Aquinas observes that where the incidental violence in the form of unintended effect is not out of proportion to the intended aim, the action shall be lawful.[10] This is a utilitarian idea (maximizing pleasure and minimizing pain). Though, in the context of armed conflict, it has been argued that the double effect principle and its corollary utilitarian doctrine would not permit bombardment affecting civilians, especially, given the obligations to protect civilians from direct and indirect attacks.[11]

Irrespective of the moral approval, the utilitarian basis of the proportionality principle under the Protocol is manifest. It is based on the cost–benefit calculations. If the military benefit outweighs the cost, the violent action is permissible. According to Jeremy Bentham, maximizing utility is the highest principle of morality useful in moral and political life.[12] By utility he meant the property or tendency of a thing to prevent some evil or to procure some good.[13] In the utilitarian assessment, he did not allow interference of any idea other than pains and pleasures.[14] This

[2] Art. 51(4), (5)(b), ibid.

[3] Art. 57(2)(a)(iii), ibid.

[4] Art. 57(2)(b), ibid.

[5] Art. 3(3)(c), Protocol on Prohibitions or Restrictions on the Use of Mines, Booby-Traps and Other Devices as amended on 3 May 1996 (Protocol II to the 1980 Convention on prohibitions or restrictions on the use of certain conventional weapons which may be deemed to be excessively injurious or to have indiscriminate effects, as amended on 3 May 1996).

[6] Aquinas, vol II, Part II, Question 64, Art. 7.

[7] Finnis (2021).

[8] For more, see Alison (2023).

[9] Ibid.

[10] Aquinas, vol II, Part II, Question 64, Art. 7.

[11] Alison (2023).

[12] Sandel (2009, p. 34).

[13] Bentham (2004, p. 1).

[14] Ibid., p. 2.

consequentialist approach ignores certain basic rights which should command more respect than the cost–benefit calculations.[15] In the context of an armed conflict, the approval of proportionate damage to civilians certainly neglects some of the basic rights of the civilians and the States' obligations towards them. Bentham is responsible for this shift of focus from natural rights.[16] Richard Posner, while commenting on an argument made by a character, Captain Vere, in an unfinished novella Billy Budd, observes that it,

> puts the reader in mind of the most disturbing feature of utilitarianism—that it countenances the deliberate sacrifice of an innocent person for the sake of the general good. Utilitarianism treats the whole society as a single organism whose welfare is to be maximized, which makes it as natural to kill one person for the greater good of society as it would be to remove a cancerous organ.[17]

13.3 Negotiating Proportionality

Historically, the International Committee of the Red Cross (ICRC) was in favour of introducing the proportionality principle in international as well as non-international armed conflicts. Therefore, it inserted alike clauses in the drafts of the Additional Protocol I and II. The draft provisions submitted by the ICRC to the Diplomatic Conference prohibited attacks "which may be expected to entail incidental losses among the civilian population and cause the destruction of civilian objects to an extent disproportionate to the direct and substantial military advantage anticipated."[18] It was certainly a compromise formula between civilian loss and military interests. On the negotiating table, however, the same was not acceptable to several delegates, especially those representing the Third World countries. They recommended by way of an amendment to the draft Protocol I deletion of the phrase "to an extent disproportionate to the direct and substantial military advantage anticipated."[19] Similarly, in respect of the draft provision in Protocol II, some delegations[20] recommended deletion of the entire clause, while some of them suggested deletion[21] of the proportionality phrase. Thus, the disagreement over the proportionality test was apparent at the outset of the Conference. In the Plenary Meeting, the representative from Afghanistan was skeptical about the technical implementation of the provision in the field due to lack of accuracy.[22] On the other hand, despite candid charges of confusion, inaccuracy and difficulty in operation from many weak and post-colonial countries, the delegates from powerful States, like the United Kingdom welcomed the provision as a mechanism to protect the civilian lives and property, and to restraint the military action.[23]

It, thus, appears that although the poor countries wanted precise rules of the game, the colonial States wanted to benefit out of the imprecise wordings. While the newly independent countries realized that the draft rule lacked precision and, therefore, would fail to serve the purpose, the advanced nations found it as a useful tool of legitimizing incidental civilian harm and not as legal restraint on targeting. In the end, 77 countries voted for adopting the draft article, while 16 abstained from

[15] Sandel (2009, p. 34).

[16] Friedmann (2011, p. 314).

[17] Posner (2009, p. 219). The argument made by Vere was: "How can we adjudge to summary and shameful death a fellow creature innocent before God, and whom we feel to be so?".

[18] Draft Art. 46(3)(b), Draft Protocol I and Draft Art. 26(3)(b), Draft Protocol II: Official Records of the Diplomatic Conference on the Reaffirmation and Development of International Humanitarian Law Applicable in Armed Conflicts Geneva (1974–1977), vol I, Part 3, pp. 15, 40.

[19] Ibid., vol III, pp. 200–207. The countries who suggested the deletion were: Czechoslovakia, German Democratic Republic, Hungary, Poland, Romania, Algeria, Arab Republic of Egypt, Democratic Yemen, Iraq, Kuwait, Libyan Arab Republic, Morocco, Sudan, Syrian, Arab Republic, United Arab Emirates, Mali, Mauritania, Philippines.

[20] Romania, Canada, German Democratic Republic and Pakistan. Ibid., vol IV, pp. 75–83.

[21] Arab Republic of Egypt, Democratic Yemen, Iraq, Kuwait, Libyan Arab Republic, Morocco, Sudan, Syrian, Arab Republic, United Arab Emirates, Philippines. Ibid., vol IV, pp. 75–83.

[22] Ibid., vol IV, p. 165.

[23] Ibid., vol IV, p. 164.

voting and one voted against its adoption.[24] The provision was adopted without deleting the words requested by many delegates.

Here, attention must be drawn to the fact that those who sided with the proportionality clause as proposed by the ICRC were aware of the complexities attached to the assessment of civilian loss and military gain. They could also anticipate that at times their attacks may harm civilians disproportionately. A fair number of delegates had already raised concerns of this sort during the negotiating process. Despite these voices, the majority of delegations did not concur on dropping the phrase related to proportionality. Had it been done, the draft provision would have prescribed prohibition of "an attack which may be expected to entail incidental losses among the civilian population and cause the destruction of civilian objects;" plain and simple. However, the majority's insistence on the original ICRC draft once again testified that humanitarian considerations are weaker than military interests during an armed conflict.

In respect of non-international armed conflicts, the draft provision on proportionality was completely rejected during the course of negotiation.[25] In fact, the Plenipotentiaries found the entire ICRC Draft Protocol II as committing States too far and intervening in their internal matters.[26] To simplify the draft, Third World countries took the lead. Pakistan, in collaboration with the Canadian delegation and like-minded ICRC experts, submitted a proposal, close to a new draft of Protocol, containing a series of amendments.[27] On the question of civilian protection, although the Committee draft contained detailed provisions under the draft Articles 24–26 (providing for basic rules, definition and protection of civilian population, respectively), the new proposal reduced everything into one Article containing three clauses and also resulted into the deletion of the proportionality provision.[28] Here, it must be noted that, though, the uncertainty attached to civilian protection was mitigated by the deletion of the proportionality clause, as it had been desired but not secured during the deliberations on Protocol I, at the same time; the comprehensive civilian protection originally suggested by the ICRC under Articles 24–26 of the draft Protocol II was also lost at the hands of those States who once struggled for the safety of their people during the colonial rule. At present, no provision of Protocol II is based on the principle of proportionality.

13.4 Proportionality and Distinction

The provisions based on the proportionality principle in Protocol I as they were adopted by the Diplomatic Conference secured recognition by the international tribunals also. In the Nuclear Weapons Advisory Opinion, it was observed that even a legitimate target may not be attacked if the collateral civilian casualties would be disproportionate to the specific military gain from the attack.[29] The negative expression by Higgins in her dissenting view offers a better explanation to the underlying principle. It also helps understand the link between the principles of distinction and proportionality. Although the distinction principle renders military objectives and armed forces as legitimate targets, it cannot be understood as an absolute permission to hit them. It means an attack on a legitimate target may also be illegal if the collateral damage to civilians is disproportionate to the military gain. In other words, incidental loss of civilian lives is not unlawful if it is not excessive to the concrete and direct military advantage. Thus, proportionality creates a qualification to the distinction principle. Yoram Dinstein prefers to call proportionality as an add-on to distinction.[30] It is also

[24] Ibid., vol VI, p. 163.

[25] Ibid., vol VII, p. 135.

[26] Ibid., vol VII, p. 60.

[27] Forsythe (1978, p. 278).

[28] Official Records (1974–1977), above n 18, vol IV, p. 81.

[29] Legality of the Threat or Use of Nuclear Weapons, Advisory Opinion (1996) ICJ Rep 226, para 587. See also, Prosecutor v. Kupreškic´ et al., IT-95-16-T, Trial Chamber, Judgment, 14 January 2000, para 524.

[30] Dinstein (2013, p. 74).

seen as a corollary to the principle of distinction.[31] The combined effect of both the principles is that it is illegal to target civilians specifically and to cause excessive unintended injury to their lives and objects while targeting military personnel or objectives. The following observation in the context of Israel-Palestine conflict clearly exemplifies this position:

> Even when civilian housing may be used by combatants to take shelter, as alleged in the attacks on the Jabalia refugee camp, launching attacks on entire apartment blocks is prohibited if they will lead to disproportionate damage, death and displacement of a large number of civilians, the UN expert warned.[32]

13.5 Imprecision Syndrome

The provisions mirroring proportionality present a whole lot of difficulties to the State-parties as well as international tribunals, and consequently endanger civilians. While the protection of civilian life and property is the prime concern, the vague language of the provisions creates operational hardships to the military command and the problem of interpretation for the tribunals. In the Diplomatic Conference, the provision was criticized because of imprecise terminology.[33] During the deliberations in the Plenary Meeting of the Conference, the Italian delegation called the text "deficient in clarity because of its generally vague wordings."[34]

According to the ICRC Commentary to the Protocol, the criticism is justified to certain extent.[35] Therefore, it helplessly suggests that belligerents need to act in good faith and with a desire to ensure civilian protection.[36] In its view, the interpretation of proportionality principle is a question of common sense and good faith for army officers.[37] The ICRC's surrender speaks volume of the vulnerable drafting. In respect of the ICRC's suggestion of good faith, it has been aptly remarked:

> There is an unfortunate tendency, encouraged by the ordinary meaning and connotation of proportionality, to conceptualize the question in pseudo-mathematical terms, as though it were susceptible to determination by an algorithm or tit-for-tat calculation.[38]

To begin with, the proportionality rule contained in the Protocol requires a belligerent to do three things in a war zone: One, to foresee whether there may be incidental or unintentional loss to civilians or their property due to an armed attack; two, to anticipate the extent of concrete and direct military advantage that may result consequent upon such an attack, and three, to assess beforehand whether an attack is going to cause excessive harm to civilians as compared to the military gain. Thus, it is all about foresight and assessment *ex ante* (estimation prior to an attack). It is a precaution in itself,[39] though the provision comes with no assistance or guidelines for observing the same. Therefore, the proportionality rule has been found to be inadequately defined,[40] imprecise,[41] notoriously opaque,[42] highly amorphous,[43] difficult in application,[44] notoriously difficult,[45] indeterminate[46] and one of the most complex and misunderstood norms.[47]

---

[31] ICRC (2023, p. 1) and Dinstein (2005, p. 211).

[32] OHCHR (2023). See the full report: Adequate Housing as a "Component of the Right to an Adequate Standard of Living, and the Right to Non-Discrimination in this Context", UN Doc. A/77/190.

[33] Sandoz et al. (1987, para 1977).

[34] Official Records (1974–1977), above n 18, vol VI, p. 231.

[35] Sandoz et al. (1987, para 1978).

[36] Ibid., para 1978.

[37] Ibid., para 2208, Knuckey et al. (2021, p. 376) and Dinstein (2005, p. 216). The principle of *pacta sunt servanda* under Article 36 of the Vienna Convention on the Law of Treaties (1969) also requires the parties to perform a treaty in good faith.

[38] Sloane (2015, p. 322).

[39] Boogaard and Vermeer (2017, p. 184).

[40] Fenrick (2009, p. 272).

[41] Franck (2008, p. 716).

[42] Cohen and Zlotogorski (2021, p. 3) and Knuckey et al. (2021, p. 375).

[43] Gaughan (2015, p. 231).

[44] Fenrick (2009, p. 278) and Kretzmer (2013, p. 236).

[45] Knuckey et al. (2021, p. 375).

[46] Vestner (2024) and Sloane (2015, p. 301).

[47] Vestner (2024) (internal citation omitted).

The ambiguity in language persists in the corresponding rule in the criminal law also. Article 8(2)(b)(iv) of the Rome Statute declare the following as war crime:

> Intentionally launching an attack in the knowledge that such attack will cause incidental loss of life or injury to civilians or damage to civilian objects or widespread, long-term and severe damage to the natural environment which would be clearly excessive in relation to the concrete and direct overall military advantage anticipated

The expressions "clearly excessive" and "overall military advantage" are not only uncertain but also self-contradictory in the sense that it is difficult to *clearly* assess the excessive nature of incidental harm, when compared with *overall* military gain.[48]

Coming back to the provision in the Protocol, it must be understood at the outset that the ambiguity in the language and lack of guiding factors do not matter much in straight-forward proportionality assessments. For example, attack on an entire village to kill a soldier may not be justified, whereas killing one civilian while destroying a convoy of army vehicles may be declared as justified under the provision. However, the war-time situations are not always so clear-cut, like these two extremes. According to Schmitt, complexity arises when the situation lies somewhere between these extreme poles.[49] This is where military officials have to compare the probable losses and gains exercising own subjective judgment amidst the anxieties of a war situation. It is easier said than done, especially, when the language of the rules offers no help.

13.6 Challenges for a Commander

The task to assess the cost and benefit actually presents a variety of issues before an attack planner. To begin with, the anticipation of probable loss and gain depends on several factors. According to the ICRC, the prediction depends on a variety of dynamics, including:

> their location (possibly within or in the vicinity of a military objective), the terrain (landslides, floods etc), accuracy of the weapons used (greater or lesser dispersion, depending on the trajectory, the range, the ammunition used etc), weather conditions (visibility, wind etc), the specific nature of the military objectives concerned (ammunition depots, fuel reservoirs, main roads of military importance at or in the vicinity of inhabited areas etc), technical skill of the combatants (random dropping of bombs when unable to hit the intended target).[50]

Similarly, factors such as light, distance, available equipments and intelligence information may also affect the assessment. While negotiating the terms of the draft provision in the Diplomatic Conference, several delegates raised similar concerns. The Indian delegate categorically expressed that the application of the provision is limited by means and methods available to every country, capabilities, practical possibility and feasibility of each party to conflict.[51] Federal Republic of Germany's delegate specifically underlined the susceptibility of information available to mission planners and stated that commanders have to take a decision "on the basis of their assessment of the information from all sources which is available to them at the relevant time."[52]

In relation to the proportionality principle, a commander is expected to act like a "reasonably well-informed person"[53] using common sense and in good faith.[54] The assessment of the situation must be guided by the available information and not hindsight.[55] However, the warzone realities do not present a situation smooth enough to carry out the calculations accurately. It has been observed that an attacker "simply cannot make an informed assessment"[56] of the incidental harm to civilians. This is mainly because commanders usually operate "under conditions of great stress in

48 Emphasize supplied.

49 Schmitt (1999, p. 170).

50 Sandoz et al. (1987, para 2212).

51 Official Records (1974–1977), above n 18, vol VI, p. 228.

52 Ibid., vol VI, p. 226.

53 Prosecutor v. Galić, IT-98–29, Trial Chamber, Judgment, 5 December, 2003, para 58.

54 Sandoz et al. (1987, para 2208).

55 ICRC (2015, p. 50) and State of Israel (2015, para 317).

56 Cohen (2010, p. 12).

the midst of chaotic circumstances and unfamiliar terrain."[57]

13.7 Ignored Effects of Armed Attacks

Even if, by hypothesis, mission planners are able to assess almost every probable loss, they can measure only the measurable; they can foresee only what is conventionally foreseeable; they value what they subjectively consider to be important; they assess only the direct effects of attack. Eventually, only the obvious types of harms, such as probable physical injuries, deaths and destruction of civilian objects matter the most. Consequently, what is immeasurable is rendered insignificant and, therefore, not considered for the estimation of civilian loss. The provision also offers no guidance in this regards. It uses a "conservative"[58] expression "incidental loss of civilian life, injury to civilians, damage to civilian objects"[59] with no further explanation. The provision, for instance, does not require the perpetrators to consider the hardships caused to a victim or the family subsequent to loss of limb, death of a kin or destruction of civilian objects. Similarly, several crucial aspects of a civilian life have been kept away from the assessment of civilian harm under Article 51(5)(b). For example, psychological impact of attacks, impact on educational and economic activities, death or permanent disablement of a sole breadearner of a family, problems related to displacement and rehabilitation, and loss of water, sewage and electricity systems. Some of these harms have attracted considerable attention and debate all over the world, for instance, serious mental disorders caused by traumatic effects of military operations, and indirect or reverberating effects of armed attacks.

[57] Sloane (2015, p. 302).

[58] Lieblich (2014, p. 197).

[59] Art. 51(5)(b) Protocol I, above n 1.

13.7.1 Mental Harm

The issue of considering mental harm within the purview of incidental injury to civilians has come to the forefront in the last few decades. The point in question is the expression "injury to civilians" under Article 51(5)(b) of the Protocol, which received a conservative interpretation for quite a long time that it refers to physical harm only. To start with, it has been argued that absence of discussion on mental harm in the drafting exercise or lack of reference to such harm in the provision does not mean that the drafters deliberately excluded mental harm.[60] It is believed that with the growing awareness[61] and medical research on traumatic impacts of wartime attacks on civilians' psyche, there are compelling[62] reasons to take into account mental harm in the assessment of incidental civilian injury. This is especially because wartime attacks and violence in populated areas cause severe psychological trauma leading to harmful and long-lasting mental infirmities.[63] There is no need to stay clung to the conservative meaning of the term injury which is confined to bodily harm only.

Recently, it has been argued in a research that exposure to bombardment, shooting, explosions and violence can cause a variety of mental health problems, including post-traumatic stress disorder (PTSD).[64] The disorder is "the most prevalent psychopathological consequence of exposure to traumatic events"[65] which can extend to "significant distress and functional impairment."[66] Children are the most vulnerable and easy victims of such a disorder.[67] Since there is a causal relationship between the disorder and armed attacks, and since the disorder is a reasonably foreseeable

[60] Gillard (2018, p. 32).

[61] Gisel (2016, p. 34).

[62] Knuckey et al. (2021, p. 368). See also, Gillard (2018, p. 32) and Lubell and Cohen (2020, p. 174).

[63] Gisel (2016, p. 34) and Lieblich (2014, p. 203).

[64] Knuckey et al. (2021, pp. 368, 398).

[65] Ibid., p. 381.

[66] Ibid., pp. 368, 382, 384.

[67] Ibid., p. 383.

consequence of exposure to wartime trauma,[68] inclusion of severe mental disorders in the proportionality analysis has been emphatically argued. Similar suggestions have come from some international forums as well.

For instance, the Tallinn Manual 2.0 on cyber military operations considers severe mental suffering within the notion of injury.[69] In an international expert meeting convened by the ICRC, several experts opined that mental health is as important as physical health, and that there is no reason to exclude mental harm from the principle of proportionality.[70]

13.7.2 Reverberating/Indirect Effects

The proportionality provision does not consider indirect effects of military attacks, often referred to as "reverberating, knock-on, indirect or long-term effects".[71] They include displacement of civilians, loss of essential civilian services, illness, loss of jobs and similar less visible but disastrous effects of armed attacks, especially in populated zones. To illustrate, the ongoing Israeli attacks on densely populated areas of Gaza present a glaring example of direct as well as catastrophic indirect and long-term consequences of armed attacks. The attacks have caused huge displacement, lack of basic necessities and complete devastation of civilian infrastructure. Similarly, attacks on Iraq's power grids during the Gulf War disrupted access to water and caused the deaths of between 40,000 to 1,10,000 civilians, according to an estimate.[72] The proportionality rule is silent about such indirect consequences. It has been considered to be a grey area in the laws of armed conflict.[73]

This concern has gained enough support on international level in the recent past and several thoughtful opinions have come up arguing that long-term consequences of armed operations must form part of incidental civilian harm and must factor in the proportionality equation. The Tallinn manual 2.0 considers that proportionality covers both direct as well as indirect effects that are foreseeable.[74] Acknowledging that anticipating all possible effects of armed attacks is both impracticable and impossible, the ICRC agrees to the position that foreseeable reverberating effects must be considered while applying the proportionality principle.[75] Similar opinion was expressed by a majority of international experts in an ICRC meeting.[76] A number of commentators have also argued that taking into account the reasonably foreseeable reverberating effects of attacks in populated areas is essential in proportionality assessment.[77] These submissions are also consistent with the argument of maintaining coherence in Protocol I because in few provisions, the Protocol engages with indirect and long-term harms of military attacks, for instance, prohibition of attacks causing lack of food or water, or leading to starvation of civilians[78]; and prohibition of attacks on works and installations containing dangerous forces, namely dams, dykes and nuclear electrical generating stations.[79]

One of the significant and common wartime indirect consequences is illness caused to civilians due to exposure to toxic material used in weaponry or due to contamination caused by damage to sewerage system or lack of food or water.[80] It has separately drawn attention of the experts globally. The Tallinn Manual 2.0 has recognized serious

[68] Ibid., p. 397. An attempt has been made to make a similar case for traumatic brain injuries (TBI) acknowledging lack of necessary scientific data to make equally sound arguments. See, Schmitt and Highfill (2018).

[69] NATO (2017, p. 417).

[70] Gisel (2016, p. 35).

[71] ICRC (2015, p. 52) and Gillard (2018, p. 35).

[72] Sassòli and Cameron (2006, p. 65).

[73] Robinson and Nohle (2016, p. 109).

[74] NATO (2017, p. 472).

[75] ICRC (2015, p. 52).

[76] Gisel (2016, p. 36).

[77] Robinson and Nohle (2016, p. 109), Lubell and Cohen (2020, p. 174), Cohen and Zlotogorski (2021, pp. 83–88) and Sassòli and Cameron (2006, p. 65).

[78] Art. 54(2) Protocol I, above n 1.

[79] Article 56(1), ibid.

[80] Cohen and Zlotogorski (2021, pp. 83–84) and Gisel (2016, p. 33).

illness as amounting to injury.[81] Along similar lines, majority of experts in an ICRC international expert meeting have expressed their views.[82]

13.8 Concrete and Direct Military Advantage: How to Draw the Line?

On the other side of the proportionality equation is situated the notion of "concrete and direct military advantage." According to the ICRC, the expression refers to foreseeable ground gained and annihilation or weakening of the enemy armed forces.[83] This view mainly deals with "tactical gains"[84] and it has been understood to be a narrow interpretation of the expression.[85] Its meaning and scope are still contested because the expression "concrete and direct" provides "scant guidance."[86] The various meanings and interpretations attributed to the phrase include: interrupting enemy military activities, diverting adversary's combat capabilities and focus, enhancing the security of own army, and weakening the morale of enemy troops.[87] However, it has been found to be complicated to articulate the precise meaning of the term and therefore, it may be misunderstood and misapplied.[88] Looking for military advantage in high-value targets and effects of an attack illustrate the abuse of vagueness.

13.8.1 Assessment in Advance

Above all, the military advantage with all its varying meanings and dilemmas has to be anticipated before launching an attack. This requirement of anticipation includes ensuring not only that the target is lawful, but hitting the same is militarily advantageous too. Therefore, it has been rightly remarked:

> One primary problem with the term "military advantage" is that it is not easy to assess, and does not necessarily have clear instrumental value. Destroying an enemy tank, plane, radar installation, or logistical base clearly gives a military advantage under the current rule of proportionality. However, it might not be apparent to observers that such an attack caused a tangible contribution to the overall military operation.[89]

The correlative description of offence under the Statute of International Criminal Court (Rome Statute) uses the words "concrete and direct overall military advantage."[90] The advantage must be measured in the context of an attack as a whole, instead of an isolated attack or a particular strike.[91] The Elements of Crime relating to the criminalizing provision explain that such advantage may or may not be temporally or geographically related to the object of the attack.[92] This position certainly broadens the interpretation of the ICRC. Thus, even a deception practiced through shelling to divert the attention of the adversary fulfils the criteria of the intended advantage.

13.8.2 Force Protection as a Military Advantage

To begin with, saving the lives of members of own army or force protection is suggested to be worth considering while calculating the military advantage.[93] It presents a moral dilemma which

81 NATO (2017, p. 417).

82 Gisel (2016, p. 36).

83 Sandoz et al. (1987, para 2218).

84 Watkin (2014, p. 280).

85 Cohen and Zlotogorski (2021, p. 60).

86 Sloane (2015, p. 318).

87 Cohen and Zlotogorski (2021, p. 60) (internal citations omitted).

88 Watkin (2014, p. 280).

89 Cohen and Zlotogorski (2021, p. 64).

90 Art. 8(2)(b)(iv).

91 The view was supported by various delegations during the deliberations in the Diplomatic Conference, though in the context of the proportionality clause under Article 57(2)(a)(iii), (Draft Art. 50(1)(b)). See Official Records (1974–1977), above n 18, vol VI, p. 226 (Federal Republic of Germany), p. 231 (Italy), p. 241 (United States of America).

92 Elements of Crimes, International Criminal Court, Element 2, Art. 8(2)(b)(iv), n. 36.

93 Gardam (1993, p. 409) and Stephens and Lewis (2005, p. 72).

asks for attributing value to the lives of soldiers and civilians. The Kasher versus Walzer debate engages with this dilemma.[94] Kasher argues in favour of prioritizing soldiers' lives because soldiers are also human beings and there is no obligation to equally treat enemy's civilians.[95] To the contrary, Walzer sides with protecting civilians because soldiers do not enjoy the protection of the right to life.[96] Thus, the meaning of military advantage is not only uncertain but full of moral questions also. It is noteworthy that the Committee to review the NATO bombing stated that "states are permitted to protect their soldiers by resorting to an aerial campaign, even though it places a greater number of civilian lives at risk."[97] Protection of own military is understood as a military advantage by many States and experts too.[98]

In respect of the ongoing Israeli military operations in Gaza and Rafah, Israel has stated before the International Court of Justice (ICJ) that its military actions are justified because it intends to rescue its civilian hostages illegally held by Hamas.[99] In this situation, can estimated military advantage be sought in releasing civilian hostages too? Recently, on 9 June 2024 a rescue operation of four captives was conducted by the Israeli Yamam Counter-Terrorism Unit along with the Israel Defense Forces in the densely populated Nuseirat refugee camp in Gaza during the day. Reportedly, the raid was planned weeks in advance.[100] During the raid, the Hamas' gunmen opened fire at the extracting team. Due to the heavy exchange of fire from machine guns and grenades, more than a hundred civilians were killed and hundreds of them suffered from severe bodily injuries and infirmities. Commenting on the lawfulness of the attack under the law of armed conflict, few Israeli scholars and international law experts found the following to be military advantage for Israel in this operation: rescue of four civilian hostages abducted by a terrorist group and protection of the rescue force.[101] Therefore, they argued that the loss of civilian life and property was not excessive as compared to the military advantage.

To the contrary, the United Nations High Commissioner for Human Rights[102] and Human Rights Watch raised doubts on the lawfulness of the attack on the ground of non-observance of the principles of proportionality and precaution.[103] It was stated that the probable harm to civilians was clearly foreseeable because the targeted location was an overcrowded civilian area and the operation was carried out in day-time when a large number of people are likely to be around. Given the temporal and geographical specification, it appears that the rescue team failed to observe the principles of proportionality as well as precaution because the mission was planned well in advance.

Such incidents demonstrate, (1) ambiguity in the expression "direct and concrete military advantage" in terms of its meaning and scope, (2) its being prone to manipulation, (3) the dangers attached to unclear and unexplained words of a provision, and (4) possible misinterpretation and abuse of such expressions. Importantly, Israel in not[104] a party to the Additional Protocol, however, it has made its stand[105] clear that it abides by those provisions of the Protocol which reflect customary international law. According

[94] See for detailed debate, Cohen and Zlotogorski (2021, pp. 108–110).

[95] Ibid., p. 109.

[96] Ibid., p. 110.

[97] Cohen (2010, p. 11).

[98] See, Cohen and Zlotogorski (2021, pp. 60), n. 2. The authors cited War Manuals, Statements on Ratification and Program on Humanitarian Policy and Research (HPCR) Manual, 2013. See also, Henderson (2009, p. 205).

[99] Public sitting held on 12 January 2024 at the Peace Palace, President Donoghue presiding, in the case concerning Application of the Convention on the Prevention and Punishment of the Crime of Genocide in the Gaza Strip (South Africa v. Israel), Verbatim Record, p. 16, https://www.icj-cij.org/sites/default/files/case-related/192/192-20240112-ora-01-00-bi.pdf and Application of the Convention on the Prevention and Punishment of the Crime of Genocide in the Gaza Strip (South Africa v. Israel) ICJ, Order, 24 May 2024, para 42.

[100] Sharon (2024).

[101] Ibid.

[102] OHCHR (2024a).

[103] Sharon (2024).

[104] See, https://ihl-databases.icrc.org/en/ihl-treaties/api-1977/state-parties?activeTab=default.

[105] State of Israel (2015, para 234, n. 397).

to the ICRC, the principles of proportionality and precaution constitute the rules of customary international law.[106]

13.8.3 Military Advantage in Weakening the Opponent

Similarly, a belligerent may look for military advantage in weakening the adverse party or in inducing its surrender. In such a situation, however, a more important question is: what is the limit of destruction and violence that would suffice for disempowering adversary or compelling its surrender. The Nuremberg Tribunal condoned the United States' bombing of Japanese cities on the basis of effecting military surrender, though in the context of indiscriminate bombing.[107] Proportionality assessment is more prone to such justifications. In the Gulf War, the Coalition forces killed more than 1.5 lac civilians[108] and destroyed the Iraqi economic and health infrastructure[109] on similar justifications. Therefore, what constitutes military advantage to a warring party is never comprehensible, but in the garb of it belligerents execute unprecedented devastation.

13.8.4 Military Advantage in Self-Defense

Sometimes, military advantage anticipated in respect of the same portion of territory may be different for both the parties, which, in turn, may affect the proportionality assessment. In a hypothetical situation, an aggressor invades and occupies a portion of enemy land. The same area is recaptured by the defending troops. Collateral damage to civilians is caused by both the parties. Can it be argued that taking control of a portion of enemy territory amounts to a greater military advantage as compared to the military advantage gained by recapturing the same ground by defending troops because the land belongs to them? Consequently, can the aggressor justify proportionately greater civilian loss during invasion? Why cannot the territorial State have the same privilege, whereas they have regained their lost ground? Isn't the national defense against invasion more valuable?

Thus, military advantage in such situations may mean different for both the parties to an armed conflict, and may have material bearing on the proportionality evaluation. Such situations reemphasize the fragile nature of civilian protection, and vague expressions and compromised texts, which is not the problem of the proportionality principle alone, but that of nearly the whole body of the laws of armed conflict.

In the context of national self-defence against invasion, strong concerns were raised while negotiating the draft instrument by some of the delegations who challenged draft Articles 46[110] and 50,[111] especially, the proportionality clauses and other restrictions on the means and methods of war contained therein. Supporting civilian protection in substance, they contended that some of the clauses weaken their legal right to self-defense[112] in the event of invasion[113] as they restrain the amount of force that can be used to defend the territory. Delegates from the Third World countries, like Afghanistan and Romania, appeared to be especially concerned on this issue. Expressing the worries of the Third World, the Afghan delegation underlined the significance of the right to self-defense against invasion and also the issue of national defense, especially for the developing countries.[114] In a similar fashion, the Romanian representative argued that international law cannot restrict the legitimate right in the name

[106] Rules 14, 19, Henckaerts and Doswald-Beck (2009).

[107] Jochnick and Normand (1994, p. 92).

[108] Normand and Jochnick (1994, p. 400, n. 46).

[109] Ibid., pp. 402–407.

[110] Official Records (1974–1977), above n 18, vol I, Part III, p. 16.

[111] Ibid., p. 17.

[112] See, Art. 51, Charter of United Nations (1945).

[113] Official Records (1974–1977), above n 18, vol VI, pp. 165, 219 (Afghanistan), pp. 169, 211 (France), pp. 197, 235 (Romania).

[114] Ibid., p. 165.

of proportionality.[115] The delegate went on to plead for a clear distinction between aggressor and its victim, and also for a privileged legal regime in favor of a victim of invasion so far as means of defense and civilian protection is concerned.[116] Thus, some delegates were completely dismissive of the proportionality clauses in the interest of national self-defense. Thus, what contributed to the antagonism is that in the event of invasion, the restriction sought to be put by the proportionality provisions was understood not only as an obstacle to the exercise of the right to self-defense but also of some assistance to an aggressor.

On the other side of the spectrum, a military power, like Israel, may invoke the right to self-defense and seek to justify horrendously excessive killings of civilians (more than 30,000)[117] and complete destruction of civilian infrastructure. Notably, on the allegations of violations of the Genocide Convention,[118] the State of Israel claimed the right of self-defense[119] before the ICJ and sought to clarify that Israel was in a war of defense against Hamas, not against the Palestinian people.[120] In the backdrop, Israel had launched large scale indiscriminate military operations in Palestinian territory after the terror attacks by Hamas and other Palestinian armed groups on 7 October, 2023, resulting in killings of about 1,200 people and illegally taking around 250 captive. This is a brazen abuse of the right to self-defense and, arguably, any amount of civilian loss may be claimed to be proportionate in furtherance of the exercise of the right.

The situation gets more complex and full of uncertainty when it comes to Russia-Ukraine armed conflict. Before the ICJ, the Russian Federation sought to justify its "special military operation" in Ukraine on the basis of its right to self-defense.[121] However, the Russian State organs and its senior officials have issued public statements on national and international platforms that the purposes of the military operation were "protection of people from acts of genocide by Ukraine in Luhansk and Donetsk"[122] and "de-Nazification."[123] Others argue that Russia wants surrender by Ukraine and control over some parts of Ukrainian territory, but does not want Ukraine to become a member of the North Atlantic Treaty Organization.[124] Additionally, it has been observed that Russia seeks "to inflict harm on civilians to compel Kyiv to submit to negotiations favorable to Moscow"[125] and "breakdown Ukraine's resolve."[126] Though, justification of war and military advantage may be different, military advantage anticipated from an attack launched in furtherance of such aims is bound to be subjective and prejudiced. Notably, during the comprehensive and intensified campaign on the Ukrainian territory, the Russian military have not just killed and injured thousands of civilians,[127] but targeted critical civilian infrastructure, including hospitals, grain ports, railways, energy plants[128] and heat supplies.[129] These attacks have been seen as excessively causing

115 Ibid., p. 197.

116 Ibid., p. 235.

117 Reuters (2024).

118 Convention on the Prevention and Punishment of the Crime of Genocide (1948).

119 South Africa v. Israel, Verbatim Record, above n 99, p. 16.

120 Ibid., p. 21.

121 Allegations of Genocide under the Convention on the Prevention and Punishment of the Crime of Genocide (Ukraine v. Russian Federation) (2022) ICJ Rep 211, Provisional Measures, Order of 16 March 2022, p. 220.

122 Ibid., pp. 221–222.

123 Ibid., p. 222.

124 Watling and Reynolds (2024) and Dnevnik (2022).

125 United Nations (2024).

126 Ibid.

127 As at 15 February 2024, 8,898 had been killed and 18,818 injured in such attacks, according to OHCHR. The actual number is likely higher: Report of the Independent International Commission of Inquiry on Ukraine, A/HRC/55/66, 18 March 2024, para 26.

128 UNHRMMU (2024).

129 OHCHR (2024b). See generally, Report of the Independent International Commission of Inquiry on Ukraine, A/HRC/55/66, 18 March 2024.

harm to civilians and civilian infrastructure as compared to possible military advantage.

In such an environment of competing claims, it is indeed difficult to deal with the invocation of self-defense by powerful States, balance national interests of each of the belligerents and draw the line of disproportionate civilian loss.

13.9 Human Shields and Proportionality

Deaths of civilians acting as human shields voluntarily should factor in the assessment of proportionality of the attack at the legitimate target defended by them, as opined by the ICRC also.[130] The loss of civilian life (including civilians acting as human shields) and civilian property consequent upon an attack against a military target should not be excessive in relation to the direct military advantage foreseen. However, few writers dissent to this position. One of them treats voluntary human shields as civilians, but carrying less weight in the proportionality test due to their deliberate participation falling short of direct participation.[131] However, the other completely disagrees with the view of the ICRC and argues that the attacking army cannot be held liable as civilians have deliberately chosen to risk their lives.[132]

In this regard, the uncontested legal position is that, the injury caused to involuntary human shields by an enemy attack against a military objective shall be considered to evaluate the proportionality of the expected military advantage, and the attacker may be held liable for excessively killing forced human shields while hitting a legitimate target. Consequently, an attacker may be held liable for a war crime of causing incidental loss of life or injury to civilians or damage to civilian objects clearly disproportionate to the military advantage anticipated,[133] whereas the adversary, for the war crime of utilizing the presence of a civilian or other protected person to render a military targets immune from attack.[134]

13.10 Comparing the Uncommon

Once the civilian loss and military gain is anticipated before attack, they have to be compared from utilitarian perspective. The provision requiring the comparative assessment puts a perpetrator in a very awkward situation because one has to perform the evaluation between two "unlike quantities or values,"[135] sans any common tool of measurement. Military advantage and civilian harm are like apples and oranges.[136] They have no common denominator.[137] The utilitarian notion requires weighing of available choices on a single scale without judging them.[138] For instance, before launching an attack in order to block a tunnel of military importance, it is anticipated that a few civilians and civilian vehicles may get harmed. In such a situation, how can a commander weigh the death of human beings against the benefit to be secured by damaging a construction? What parameters one may apply to arrive at a conclusion that the civilian loss is not excessive to the military benefit anticipated by blocking the tunnel? Therefore, proportionality assessment is a value judgment, as contrast to factual judgment. While factual judgment is based on facts and common parameters, value judgment relies on subjective reasoning based on one's own belief and "social or cultural background."[139] Thus, in the absence of any common measuring unit, the value assigned to a particular military benefit and civilian loss depends on a commander's own attitude. This subjectivity is bound to be prejudiced and discriminatory and

[130] Melzer (2009, p. 57).

[131] Garraway (2014, p. 179).

[132] Dinstein (2016, p. 183).

[133] Art. 8(2)(b)(iv) Statute of International Criminal Court (1998) (Rome Statute).

[134] Article 8(2((b)(xxiii), ibid.

[135] Fenrick (2009, p. 278).

[136] Yoram Dinstein, cited in Vestner (2024).

[137] Cohen and Zlotogorski (2021, p. 7).

[138] Sandel (2009, p. 41).

[139] Schmitt (1999, p. 151).

may prove to be fatal in a decision-making process during war.

Thus, the absence and impossibility of a common unit of measurement in the proportionality assessment puts the attack planner in a difficult situation, especially, when the situation is not so clear for decision-making and judgment call lies in the middle of proportionality scale. It certainly renders the proportionality assessment arbitrary and subjective.

Consequent upon the questionable and often flawed value judgment, an attacker is required to arrive at a finding as to whether the probable collateral damage is excessive to military advantage or not. In respect of the term "excessive" it has been argued that the scale of excessiveness should be "clearly excessive,"[140] as opposed to ambiguously excessive. However, excessiveness is always not "black and white."[141] The assessment of excessiveness is a "relational value judgment"[142] and not "an exact science."[143] Therefore, like other words used in the proportionality provision, the term "excessive" introduces further indeterminacy.[144] Proportionality principle actually puts "an unrealistic burden on the attacker to make a cost–benefit analysis in the midst of a battle."[145]

13.11 Encouragement to Violence

As noted above, the proportionality principle tolerates[146] civilian casualties and harm to the extent the damage is not excessive to probable military benefit. It bears repetition that the prohibition is not on killing or injuring civilian population, or damaging civilian objects, but on the relatively excessive causing thereof. The principle does not prescribe any maximum limit of civilian loss. Therefore, what an attacker has to take care of is the comparative evaluation only. Once the assessment clears the proportionality test, the law does not prevent an attacker from carrying out violent attacks. There is no liability for the collateral damage.

This privilege and immunity is crucial here. It helps expose yet another and more brutal facet of the principle of proportionality. The principle actually assists an attacker in terms of gravity of armed operations. Instead of discouraging, it motivates, for instance, an invader to plan attacks likely to capture more and more enemy areas and kill more enemy soldiers, consistent with the law. An aggressor prefers to create a perception of lawful attacks. Proportionality principle helps do that. The legitimacy to violence afforded by the principle incentivizes an attacker. It legitimates violence to an extent blur enough to take advantage of. It has the potential of making a perpetrator fearless and more violent, yet law-abiding. An invader may become as lawfully brutal as one may prefer to be, provided that the concomitant civilian damage is relatively less than the often self-conceived notion of military advantage. This is the sole condition. Thus, the principle certainly benefits the countries with more military power and imperialistic tendencies. The Gulf War exemplifies this proposition.

In the Gulf War, the United States-led Coalition forces systematically destroyed Iraq's infrastructure. They went on to target electrical grids, factories, life support systems, and means of transportation and telecommunication.[147] Thousands of civilians were killed, succumbed to war-related health problems and deprived of basic life support systems, due to the Coalition raids and air attacks. The unnecessary destruction paralyzed Iraq, but did not discourage the Coalition. The associated military benefit of the strikes was to incapacitate Iraqi military[148] and to force it to surrender. In relation to such battlefield advantages, collateral

[140] Cohen and Zlotogorski (2021, p. 92).

[141] Henderson (2009, p. 221).

[142] Sloane (2015, p. 317).

[143] Dinstein (2005, p. 215).

[144] Sloane (2015, p. 316).

[145] Cohen (2010, p. 12).

[146] Gaughan (2015, p. 230).

[147] Henderson (2009, pp. 129, 139–140, 142) and Normand and Jochnick (1994, pp. 399–400).

[148] Gardam (1993, p. 409).

civilian damage of any scale might not seem to be excessive. Rather, it becomes lawful under the proportionality principle. Mightier the belligerent, more intense, yet lawful, the civilian harm. The United States military command was reported to have hired more than 200 military lawyers in the warzone to seek legal advice.[149] Coalition military and political authorities created a legal rhetoric by justifying their armed operations on the basis of the laws of war. They made such a strong perception of having respected the law in the war against Iraq that it was agreed to by mainstream media, general public, academia and humanitarian organizations, and, moreover, it earned them the reward of the "most legalistic war ever fought."[150] Thus, the proportionality principle encourages its invocation for justifying and condoning destruction of non-military objects in the most brutal form.

References

Alison M (2023) Doctrine of double effect. The Stanford Encyclopedia of Philosophy. https://plato.stanford.edu/archives/sum2023/entries/double-effect/

Aquinas T, Summa Theologica

Bentham J (2004) Theory of legislation. LexisNexis, New Delhi

Boogaard JC, Vermeer A (2017) Precautions in attack and urban and siege warfare. Yearbook of IHL 20:163–198

Cohen A (2010) Proportionality in modern asymmetrical wars. Jerusalem Center for Public Affairs, Jerusalem

Cohen A, Zlotogorski D (2021) Proportionality in international humanitarian law: consequences, precautions, and procedures. OUP, New York

Dinstein Y (2005) Collateral damage and the principle of proportionality. In: Wippman D, Evangelista M (eds) New wars, new laws? applying laws of war in 21st century conflicts. Transnational Publishers, New York, pp 211–226

Dinstein Y (2013) The principle of proportionality. In: Larsen KM et al (eds) Searching for a 'principle of humanity' in international humanitarian law. CUP, Cambridge

Dinstein Y (2016) The conduct of hostilities under the law of international armed conflict. CUP, Cambridge

Dnevnik JH (2022) Ukraine's six months of resistance, resilience, and resolve, 26 August 2022. https://si.usembassy.gov/ukraines-six-months-of-resistance-resilience-and-resolve/#:~:text=Ukraine%20is%20fighting%20to%20defend,values%20we%20all%20hold%20dear

Fenrick WJ (2009) Applying IHL targeting rules to practical situations: proportionality and military objectives. Windsor Yearbook of Access to Justice 27(2):271–283

Finnis J (2021) Aquinas' moral, political, and legal philosophy. The Stanford Encyclopedia of Philosophy. https://plato.stanford.edu/archives/spr2021/entries/aquinas-moral-political/

Forsythe DP (1978) Legal management of internal war: the 1977 Protocol on non-international armed conflicts. American Journal of International Law 72(2):272–295

Franck TF (2008) On proportionality of countermeasures in international law. American Journal of International Law 102(4):715–767

Friedmann W (2011) Legal theory. Universal Law Publishing Co., New Delhi

Gardam J (1993) Proportionality and force in international law. American Journal of International Law 87(3):391–413

Garraway C (2014) Direct participation and the principle of distinction: squaring the circle. In: Harvey C et al (eds) Contemporary challenges to the laws of war: essays in honour of professor Peter Rowe. CUP, Cambridge, pp 169–190

Gaughan AJ (2015) Collateral damage and the laws of war: d-day as a case study. Am J Leg Hist 55(3):229–285

Gillard E (2018) Proportionality in the conduct of hostilities: the incidental harm side of the assessment. Chatham House, Institute of International Affairs

Gisel L (2016) The principle of proportionality in the rules governing the conduct of hostilities under international humanitarian law, report on international expert meeting 22–23 June 2016. ICRC, Geneva

Henckaerts JM, Doswald-Beck L (2009) Customary international humanitarian law, vol I. ICRC/CUP, New York

Henderson I (2009) The contemporary law of targeting: military objectives, proportionality and precautions in attack under Additional Protocol I. Martinus Nijhoff Publishers, Leiden

ICRC (2015) International humanitarian law and the challenges of contemporary armed conflicts, 32nd international conference of the Red Cross and Red Crescent, Geneva, October 2015. ICRC, Geneva

ICRC (2023) Cyber operations during armed conflict, the principle of proportionality. ICRC, Geneva. https://www.icrc.org/sites/default/files/wysiwyg/war-and-law/04_proportionality-0.pdf

Jochnick C, Normand R (1994) The legitimation of violence: a critical history of the laws of war. Harv Int Law J 35(1):49–96

[149] Normand and Jochnick (1994, p. 395, n. 29).

[150] Ibid., pp. 395, 408.

Knuckey S et al (2021) The proportionality rule and mental harm in war. In: Kreß C, Lawless R (eds) Necessity and proportionality in international peace and security law. OUP, New York, pp 367–408

Kretzmer D (2013) The inherent right to self-defence and proportionality in jus ad bellum. European Journal of International Law 24(1):235–282

Lieblich E (2014) Beyond life and limb: exploring incidental mental harm under international humanitarian law. In: Jinks D et al (eds) Applying international humanitarian law in judicial and quasi-judicial bodies: international and domestic aspects. Asser Press, The Hague, T.M.C, pp 185–218

Lubell N, Cohen A (2020) Strategic proportionality: limitations on the use of force in modern armed conflicts. International Law Studies 96:159–195

Melzer N (ed) (2009) Interpretive guidance on the notion of direct participation in hostilities under international humanitarian law. ICRC, Geneva

NATO (2017) Tallinn Manual 2.0 on the international law applicable to cyber operations: prepared by the international groups of experts at the invitation of the NATO cooperative cyber defence centre of excellence. CUP, Cambridge

Normand R, Jochnick C (1994) The legitimation of violence: critical analysis of the gulf war. Harv Int Law J 35(2):387–416

OHCHR (2023) Gaza: destroying civilian housing and infrastructure is an international crime, warns UN expert, 8 November 2023. https://www.ohchr.org/en/press-releases/2023/11/gaza-destroying-civilian-housing-and-infrastructure-international-crime

OHCHR (2024a) Shock at impact on civilians of Israeli raid in Gaza to free hostages, 11 June 2024. https://www.ohchr.org/en/press-briefing-notes/2024/06/shock-impact-civilians-israeli-raid-gaza-free-hostages

OHCHR (2024b) Ukraine: UN Commission concerned by continuing patterns of violations of human rights and international humanitarian law, 15 March 2024. https://www.ohchr.org/en/press-releases/2024/03/ukraine-un-commission-concerned-continuing-patterns-violations-human-rights

Posner RA (2009) Law and literature. Universal Law Publishing Co., New Delhi

Reuters (2024) Gaza death toll: how many Palestinians has Israel's campaign killed, 14 May 2024. https://www.reuters.com/world/middle-east/gaza-death-toll-how-many-palestinians-has-israels-campaign-killed-2024-05-14/

Robinson I, Nohle E (2016) Proportionality and precautions in attack: the reverberating effects of using explosive weapons in populated areas. International Review of the Red Cross 98(1):107–145

Sandel M (2009) Justice: what's the right thing to do. Penguin Books, London

Sassòli M, Cameron L (2006) The protection of civilian objects: current state of the law and issues *de lege ferenda*. In: Ronzitti N, Venturini G (eds) The law of air warfare: contemporary issues. Eleven International, The Hague, pp 35–74

Schmitt M (1999) The principle of discrimination in 21st century warfare. Yale Human Rights and Development Law Journal 2(1):143–182

Schmitt MN, Highfill CE (2018) Invisible injuries: concussive effects and international humanitarian law. Harvard National Security Journal 9:72–99

Sharon J (2024) Did the Nuseirat hostage rescue operation comply with international law? 12 June 2024. https://www.timesofisrael.com/did-the-nuseirat-hostage-rescue-operation-comply-with-international-law/

Sloane RD (2015) Puzzles of proportion and the reasonable military commander: reflections on the law, ethics, and geopolitics of proportionality. Harvard National Security Journal 6:299–343

State of Israel (2015) The 2014 Gaza conflict, 7 July-26 August 2014, factual and legal aspects. https://www.gov.il/en/Departments/General/2014-gaza-conflict-factual-and-legal-aspects

Stephens D, Lewis MW (2005) The law of armed conflict—a contemporary critique. Melbourne Journal of International Law 6(1):55–85

Taylor A (2023) Israel leans into World War II rhetoric to justify Gaza war, 1 November 2023. https://www.washingtonpost.com/world/2023/11/01/israel-historical-comparison-world-war-two-ii/

UNHRMMU (2024) UN Human Rights Monitors voice alarm as Russia renews attacks on power grids in Ukraine, 22 March 2024. https://ukraine.un.org/en/264071-un-human-rights-monitors-voice-alarm-russia-renews-attacks-power-grids-ukraine

United Nations (2024) Escalating attacks on Ukraine's civilian, energy infrastructure making humanitarian aid delivery even more dangerous, relief chief tells Security Council, 9625th meeting, SC/15695, 14 May 2024. https://press.un.org/en/2024/sc15695.doc.htm

Vestner T (2024) The law of targeting's mechanisation and objectivisation through the use of artificial intelligence (forthcoming). In: Couzigou I, Fromageau E (eds) Technological change and international law: testing the adaptability of international law. Edward Elgar Publishing

Watkin K (2014) Trapped: military advantage: a matter of "value", strategy, and tactics. Yearbook of IHL 17:277–364

Watling J, Reynolds N (2024) Russian military objectives and capacity in Ukraine through 2024, 13 February 2024. https://www.rusi.org/explore-our-research/publications/commentary/russian-military-objectives-and-capacity-ukraine-through-2024

Looking for a Principle of Humanity 14

Abstract

In this chapter, I offer a critique of the much marketed principle of humanity. I try to argue that humanity stays at the periphery of the laws of armed conflict, while military necessity enjoys the prominent position because it dictates the contents of the rules of the game. I question the humanitarian side claimed in respect of the principle of proportionality. I argue that proportionally principle justifies and helps overlook the simultaneous harm to civilians, even when it is huge. Proportionality does not entail an obligation about minimizing civilian loss. Considering the overall architecture of the law, I argue that it compromises with humanitarian considerations and validates violence and suffering in several ways. Lastly, I argue that the name of the discipline (International Humanitarian Law) is flawed, deceptive and political.

Keywords

Military necessity and humanity · Proportionality and humanity · Validation/legitimization of violence

14.1 Military Necessity and Principle of Humanity

There exists a principle, if at all, at the periphery of the laws of armed conflict—the principle of humanity. Periphery is a site of neglect. Things managing to survive at the fringes are insignificant and subordinate to those constituting the core. They do not guide and influence the system. On the contrary, what is at the core is the locus of power. It enjoys prestige, sway and respect, and, thus, determines the way a system works. In the context of laws of armed conflict (international humanitarian law), humanity sobs at the peripheral spaces, while military necessity rules arrogantly at the center. This position, however, does not reflect from the mainstream understanding and recognition of the concepts of humanity and military necessity in the international legal literature.

The International Committee of the Red Cross (ICRC) and many commentators recognize both humanity and military necessity as fundamental principles of the law.[1] The ICRC has also used the term "core principles" and excluded humanity

[1] ICRC, https://casebook.icrc.org/law/fundamentals-ihl#d_iii (The ICRC also calls them general principles and names the principle of military necessity as the principle of "necessity." However, the reference is to the principle of military necessity as it is apparent from the bibliography attached to the principle.), Crawford and Pert (2015, p. 42), Kolb and Hyde (2008, p. 43) and Solis (2010, p. 250).

K. Jeenger, *A Humanitarian Critique of International Humanitarian Law*,
Sustainable Development Goals Series, https://doi.org/10.1007/978-981-96-8319-2_14

and military necessity from the category.[2] This classification has nothing to do with the center-periphery analysis. Actually, what is crucial in this investigation is the dominant idea underlying the rules of armed conflict. The principles of distinction,[3] unnecessary suffering[4] and proportionality[5] respectively permit targeting soldiers, infliction of injuries felt to be inevitable and loss of civilian life and property. It is the military necessity which determines and shapes these rules. It has been maintained that every single norm in the laws of armed conflict implies a balance between humanitarianism and military necessity.[6] The principle of humanity is subordinate to military necessity.[7] It has been argued that "The laws of war permit virtually any form of military conduct as long as such conduct is directed towards achieving clear military objectives."[8]

Thus, to say that the three principles mentioned above are based on the considerations of humanity is to manipulate. This proposition conceals the principal factor, military necessity, which predominantly controls the form and content of the rules. Furthermore, this emphasis on the humane or positive side of the rules is deceptive as it veils the violent and inhuman side of the provisions. Arguments stressing on drawing attention towards positive side of something often benefit the dominant, deceive the inferior and discourage opposition. In fact, the three principles seeking to prevent certain injuries, certain loss of lives or certain damage to environment while tolerating the remainder cannot seek refuge under the principle of humanity. Moreover, considerations of humanity as a restraint on the conduct in hostilities occupy a very weak place in the so called humanitarian rules because there is no yardstick to measure, for instance, how much civilian loss is excessive to the military advantage,[9] how much suffering is necessary[10] or how much damage to environment is widespread, long-term and severe.[11]

Military necessity dominates the whole body of the laws of armed conflict. It so dictates the rules that combat capabilities and military advantages are never compromised, and achievement of military ends is not hampered even at the cost of civilian damage. For instance, it permits incidental loss to civilian life and objects while hitting military objectives.[12] Such civilian damage may be of any scale provided that it is not excessive to the military advantage estimated. Besides that, in the event of invasion, the principle allows destruction or removal of objects essentials for the survival of civilians, such as edible items, crops, drinking water installations, in that part of one's own territory which has not yet been invaded or occupied, in order to make the survival of the invading or occupying army difficult.[13] Some important provisions meant to prevent or

[2] Melzer (2016, pp. 17–19).

[3] Art. 48, 51 Protocol Additional to the Geneva Conventions of 12 August 1949, and relating to the Protection of Victims of International Armed Conflicts (Protocol I) of 8 June 1977.

[4] Art. 35(2), ibid.

[5] Art. 51(5)(b), 57(2)(a)(iii), 57(2)(b), ibid.

[6] Larsen et al (2013a, b, p. 9).

[7] Chinkin and Kaldor (2017, p. 256).

[8] Normand and Jochnick (1994, p. 389).

[9] This is by virtue of principle of proportionality which seeks to prohibit an attack which may be expected to cause incidental loss of civilian life, injury to civilians, damage to civilian objects, or a combination thereof, which would be excessive in relation to the concrete and direct military advantage anticipated. See Art. 51(5)(b), 57(2)(a)(iii), 57(2)(b) Protocol I, above n iii.

[10] Article 35(2) of the Protocol I says that it is prohibited to employ weapons, projectiles and material and methods of warfare of a nature to cause superfluous injury or unnecessary suffering.

[11] The Protocol seeks to ban the use of methods or means of warfare which are intended, or may be expected, to cause widespread, long-term and severe damage to the natural environment. See, Art. 35(3), 55 Protocol I, above n iii.

[12] See previous chapter, for details.

[13] Art. 54(5) Protocol I, above n iii and Sandoz et al. (1987, para 2122). For other provisions shaped by military considerations, see Art. 8, 32, 33, 42, 50 Geneva Convention for the Amelioration of the Condition of the Wounded and Sick in Armed Forces in the Field of 12 August 1949 (Geneva Convention I); Art. 8, 28, 51 Geneva Convention for the Amelioration of the Condition of Wounded, Sick and Shipwrecked Members of Armed Forces at Sea of 12 August 1949 (Geneva Convention II); Art. 8, 23, 126 eneva Convention relative to the Treatment of Prisoners of War of 12 August 1949 (Geneva Convention III); Art. 16, 83, 108, 143, 147 Geneva Convention relative to the Protection of Civilian Persons in Time of War of 12

minimize civilian damage have been diluted by the use of flexible terms, such as "so far as possible," "feasible." These expressions are bound to be interpreted prioritizing military necessity. This possibility had been realized while negotiating the Protocol. In the Diplomatic Conference (1974–77), the Canadian[14] and German[15] delegates stated that: ""feasible," refers to that which is practicable or practically possible, taking into account all circumstances existing at the relevant time, including those circumstances relevant to the success of military operations." Thus, military interest is an important factor while deciding what is practicable or feasible. Additional Protocol I, for instance, requires a belligerent to take feasible steps and precautions to protect civilian population from damage.[16] Here, the demands of military considerations determine the degree of effort to be put in to verify an object.

Military necessity subverts the rules of criminal liability also. An act of violence may not amount to an international crime if the same is indispensable owing to imperative military requirements. The Grave Breaches regime under the Geneva Conventions remains limited by military necessity. Accordingly, acts, like willful killing, torture or inhuman treatment against protected persons amount to a grave breach only if not justified by military necessity.[17] Similarly, the Statute of International Criminal Court (Rome Statute) does not criminalize the incidental loss to civilians or environment unless it is excessive to the military benefit in an international armed conflict.[18] On similar footing, it does not penalize the destruction of enemy property in international as well as non-international armed conflict if military considerations require the same.[19]

Thus, military necessity dictates uncompromisingly the key provisions regulating military operations and criminal liability. It is only the residue of the rules that echo some elements of humanity. The rules prohibiting direct attack on civilians and civilian objects, and those requiring humane treatment with a variety of persons do not adversely affect the war-effort and military strength of parties at war. Such rules occupy a space in the laws of armed conflict only to the extent the necessities of war can accommodate them. This is, if at all, humanitarianism by convenience, to say the least. It has been aptly stated that the principle of military necessity does not require a State to use force and cause violence; rather it simply allows it to do so.[20] It creates an environment where parties at war can justify their destructive and violent armed operations on the basis of military considerations. Radhabinod Pal, in his dissenting opinion at the Tokyo Tribunal very aptly remarked that it is impossible to set bounds to the demands of military necessity.[21]

Thus, military necessity provides a legal wrap to violence in armed conflicts. Principle of military necessity reflects the maxim that necessity is the limit of legality.[22] In such a setting, the

---

August 1949 (Geneva Convention IV); Art. 62(1), 71(3) Protocol I, above n iii; Preamble Hague Convention (II) with Respect to the Laws and Customs of War on Land of 29 July 1899 (Hague Convention II); Art. 22(g), 49 Regulations Concerning the Laws and Customs of War on Land, annexed to Hague Convention (II) with Respect to the Laws and Customs of War on Land of 29 July 1899 (Hague Regulations 1899); Preamble Hague Convention (IV) with Respect to the Laws and Customs of War on Land of 18 October 1907 (Hague Convention IV) and Art. 15, 23(g) Regulations Respecting the Laws and Customs of War on Land, annexed to Hague Convention (IV) with Respect to the Laws and Customs of War on Land of 18 October 1907 (Hague Regulations 1907).

[14] Official Records of the Diplomatic Conference on the Reaffirmation and Development of International Humanitarian Law Applicable in Armed Conflicts Geneva (1974–1977), vol VI, p. 224.

[15] Ibid., p. 226.

[16] Art. 57(2) Protocol I, above n iii.

[17] Art. 50 Geneva Convention I, Art. 51 Geneva Convention II and Art. 147 Geneva Convention IV, above n iii.

[18] Art. 8(2)(b)(iv) Statute of International Criminal Court (1998) (Rome Statute).

[19] Art. 8(2)(a)(iv), 8(2)(b)(xiii), 8(2)(e)(xii), ibid.

[20] Horowitz (2016, p. 183).

[21] The United States of America et al. v. Araki Sadao et al., International Military Tribunal for the Far East, (Decision of 12 November 1948), Dissentient Judgment of Justice Radhabinod Pal.

[22] Sandoz et al. (1987, para 1395).

humanity principle stays at the margins, neglected and repeatedly violated.

14.2 Proportionality Principle and Humanity

The provisions[23] demanding proportionality assessment contain no guidelines as to how much civilian harm is excessive and what amounts to military advantage. To find out whether the harm to civilians is disproportionate or not, it has to be measured only against the military gain that may be estimated. It follows that the greater the military advantage a belligerent is likely to secure, the more loss to civilians may be condoned. However, there is no "metric in mind for comparing"[24] and the assessment is "rarely that straightforward."[25] To understand the situation with a hypothetical situation, while destroying a bridge of military utility, killing of two civilians walking over the bridge may not be excessive under the proportionality principle. In the same vein, suppose the target is a convoy of enemy military trucks carrying battle tanks, troops and armor, which are passing through a border village. While attacking the trucks, almost fifty civilians are likely to be killed and equal number of civilians may get harmed. The damage may also extend to civilian property. Proportionally principle might consider the loss to the civilians proportionate in relation to the huge military advantage and, therefore, approve of the attack. Thus, proportionally principle helps overlook the simultaneous damage to civilians, even when it is too much, and absolves a belligerent of it. The only condition is that the harm to civilians, howsoever intense and widespread, must not be deliberate and greater than the probable military advantage. Proportionality principle is not an obligation about minimizing civilian loss as far as possible. Rather, all it mandates is ensuring relatively less civilian loss. Does it reflect the principle of humanity?

In the relativity test, the proportionality principle mandates comparing civilian life and objects with military advantage (in the form of killing or disabling enemy soldiers, destroying weaponry, military equipments and constructions of military importance, and grabbing enemy land). This utilitarian comparison is blind towards the things being weighed in terms of their moral worth. It provides no guideline as to what may be weighed. It looks at the quantitative value of the things being compared, instead of their qualitative side. Consequently, often a military commander has to decide whether few enemy-civilian lives may be sacrificed to destroy a bridge or other constructions of critical military importance. Of course, "there is no background exchange rate for civilian life."[26] In such a situation, what value a commander would attribute to a construction and human lives? Is it possible and justified to compare a human life with a concrete structure or heap of arms? Which common unit of measurement can make this comparison possible?

The proportionality principle necessitates measuring the available choices on a single scale. In respect of this Benthamite utilitarian approach, Michael Sandel aptly asks: "Is it possible to translate all moral goods into a single currency of value without losing something in the translation?"[27] He significantly notes that every value cannot be calculated by a common currency of value.[28] Proportionality principle approves of giving less importance to the moral worth of human life. It declares civilian life inferior to military advantage, despite its being qualitatively higher.[29] It permits valuing the military benefit more than a loss of civilian life by applying an inappropriate parameter of excessiveness. Actually, no such comparison can be drawn between two entirely different categories. They have no common denominator.[30]

---

[23] Art. 51(5)(b), 57(2)(a)(iii), 57(2)(b) Protocol I, above n iii.

[24] Kennedy (2006a, p. 141).

[25] Stephens and Lewis (2005, p. 68).

[26] Kennedy (2007, p. 192).

[27] Sandel (2009, p. 41).

[28] Ibid.

[29] John Stuart Mill opposes the assessment of all pleasures and pains on a single scale, and declares that some pleasures are more worthy and desirable. Sandel (2009, p. 54).

[30] Cohen and Zlotogorski (2021, p. 7).

The comparison under the proportionality principle also makes value judgment inevitable. The discretion in this relativity test is exercised by ascribing values to the gains and losses. Since both the points to be compared are disparate, there cannot be any objective and value free criteria of comparison. A mission planner has to ascribe values based on personal preferences which depend on an individual's own socio-cultural surroundings. In some societies the lust for economic and political gains may be so tempting that life, safety and dignity of human beings, especially, that of the Third World people, may carry less weight. It is very much clear from the way the Third World people were enslaved, tortured and killed based on the distinction between civilized and uncivilized, modern and savage, and white and black (or colored) during colonization.[31] It is testified also by the fact that the restraints in war were not made applicable to anti-colonial armed encounters.[32] In some social settings, Schmitt explains, hunger, poverty, human-mortality and civil wars are so frequent and common, that it ordinarily makes their masses desensitized to human deaths and suffering.[33] Similarly desensitized people, it is argued, may also be found in advanced capitalist countries that provide military support to armed groups operating in the Third World countries; send troops to countries like Iraq and Afghanistan; engage in proxy wars; destabilize or keep destabilized weak but natural resource-rich countries; supply weapons to countries, such as Israel, enabling it to launch indiscriminate attacks at Palestine, and have a barbarous history of colonizing and enslaving the Third World peoples. Equally true, that some not-so-advanced communities may attribute relatively higher value to human lives and their well-being.

Thus, the value ascribed to the probable civilian harm because of an armed operation cannot be universal. It may vary with a commander's affiliation to a particular socio-cultural environment. This relativism affects the judgment in proportionality test and increases the likelihood of more human suffering. Ultimately, the principle allows securing military benefit at the cost of innocent human lives. Sadly, the international "humanitarian" law has made such comparisons and judgments based on military necessity possible.

14.3 Looking for Principle of Humanity

As discussed in Chap. 4, the incorporation of restraints on war in the form of binding international instruments started in the second half of the nineteenth century. These instruments were adopted by the self-proclaimed civilized nations who were actually engaged in afflicting suffering on the colonized masses and crushing their struggles for freedom by unrestricted means and methods. They took over Henry Dunant's humanitarian plan and wrote the limitations on their conduct in war as suited to their imperialist motives. Armed anti-colonial struggles were kept away from the ambit of the rules on belligerent conduct. The limitations were of course a show of military necessity, instead of humanity.

Humanitarian considerations in war are so weak that they are compromised for one or the other reason. During the first Hague Peace Conference, a question arose as to how the law of war should regulate the conduct of an occupying army in the event of resistance from within the occupied territory.[34] Since the imperialist powers were reluctant to restraint their use of force during armed resistance in colonies, a Russian jurist and diplomat Fyodor Martens formulated the following paragraph which formed part of the preamble to the Hague Convention II on Convention with respect to the Laws and Customs of War on Land, of 1899 and later on attained popularity as Martens Clause:

> Until a more complete code of the laws of war is issued, the High Contracting Parties think it right to declare that in cases not included in the Regulations adopted by them, populations and belligerents remain under the protection and empire of the principles of international law, as they result from the usages established between civilized nations, from

[31] See Chap. 5.

[32] Ibid.

[33] Stephens and Lewis (2005, p. 76).

[34] Bryant (2016, p. 124).

the laws of humanity and the requirements of the public conscience.

This vagueness served no purpose favorable to the people of the occupied colonies. Instead, under the ineffective and deceptive preambular paragraph, the imperialist project and violence in colonies continued without any legal restriction. Still, the notion of humanity is so catchy that States are more inclined towards using it, at least in principle. For instance, the preamble to the Hague Conventions of 1899 and 1907 expressed that the contracting parties are desirous to serve the interests of humanity[35] (though, not by banning war, but by adopting selective restraints on war). In the Diplomatic Conference of Geneva, 1949, the Mexican delegate referring to a draft provision of the Civilian Convention stated that it implied principles of humanity.[36] Similarly, the representative from Czechoslovakia called the draft Geneva Conventions as basic principles of humanity.[37] What has made the rhetorical principle of humanity so popular in the context of laws of armed conflict is the treaty-provisions echoing humanitarian considerations, like provisions exempting from attack persons who do not participate in hostilities[38]; provisions limiting the choice of means and methods of carrying out armed operations and thereby mitigating the loss caused by war[39]; provisions requiring humane treatment with wounded and ill soldiers,[40] and prisoners of war[41]; and provisions regarding the role to be played by the ICRC in ameliorating the conditions of victims of war.[42] Similarly, the principle is also seen in the prohibition of directly targeting civilians or their property and inflicting excessive harm or causing disproportionate collateral damage. In other words, the principle of humanity does not question killing soldiers, inflicting harm considered to be necessary and causing proportionate civilian harm. Instead, it has the effect of legitimizing and normalizing this suffering. Kennedy argues that the fluid vocabulary and vague calculations implicit in the principles were "designed for making distinctions and simply eroding them."[43]

There are several direct references to different shades of humanity in the Geneva Conventions of 1949 and their Additional Protocols. For instance: "humanitarian protection of civilians and civilian objects,"[44] "human person remains under the protection of the principles of humanity,"[45] requirements of health and humanity,[46] and various references to humanitarian activities of the ICRC.[47] However, considering the principles of military necessity, proportionality, distinction and unnecessary suffering, it is clear how weakly represented the humanity principle is in the laws of armed conflict. What this legal position tries to suggest is that a belligerent may have to suffer from death and destruction for an act committed by the adversary because the same has been legitimated by the law. Thus, the laws of armed conflict have set new ethical standards of necessary suffering and proportionate harm. It has displaced one's own sense of judging morally the rightfulness of causing harm to somebody or targeting hospitals and schools. Instead, the task of judging has been assigned to the law. It is also a typical mix of positivism and natural law.[48] The ideas of morality

[35] Hague Convention II 1899 and Hague Convention IV 1907, above n 13.

[36] Final Records of the Diplomatic Conference of Geneva of 1949, vol II Section B, p. 408.

[37] Ibid., p. 305.

[38] Art. 51(1)-(3) Protocol I, above n 3.

[39] Art. 35, 51(4)(5), 55(1), ibid.

[40] Art. 3(1), common to Geneva Conventions I-IV, above n 13.

[41] Art. 13, Geneva Convention III, above n 13.

[42] Art. 3(2), 9, Geneva Conventions I-III; Art. 3(2), 10, 59, 61, Geneva Convention IV, ibid.; Art. 5(3), 22(2)(b), Protocol I, above n 3 and Art. 18(1) (national relief societies) Protocol Additional to the Geneva Conventions of 12 August 1949, and relating to the Protection of Victims of Non-International Armed Conflicts (Protocol II) of 8 June 1977.

[43] Kennedy (2006b, p. 119).

[44] Art. 72 Protocol I, above n 3.

[45] Preamble Protocol II, above n 42.

[46] Art 108 Geneva Convention III, above n 13.

[47] E.g. Art. 9 Geneva Convention I, II, above n 13 and Protocol I, above n 3.

[48] Mégret (2016, p. 772).

and justice probably fail to answer this curious legal position.

The expression "principle of humanity" has been found to be vague, uncertain and less like a legal obligation and more of a moral obligation.[49] It has been challenged on the ground whether the violation of humanity as a principle would invite some form of reaction as the violation of other humanitarian principles does.[50] It has been found to be "loose and partly misleading."[51] Alternatively, the term "consideration of humanity" has been suggested.[52] The International Court of Justice (ICJ), on the other hand, uses the term "principle of elementary considerations of humanity" in Corfu Channel case,[53] whereas in Nuclear Weapons advisory opinion,[54] it used the expressions "principle of humanity" and "considerations of humanity" interchangeably. Thus, it still remains unsettled as to which expression is appropriate and workable. Yoram Dinstein's reflections in this regards explain well the standing of the "principle of humanity" in the laws of armed conflict:

> Humanity is not an obligation (or a set of obligations) incorporated per se in positive IHL. There is no overarching, binding, norm of humanity that tells us what we must do (or not do) in wartime. What we actually encounter are humanitarian considerations, which pave the road to the creation of legal norms and thus explain the evolution of IHL. While impacting on the law, these considerations do not by themselves amount to law: they are meta-juridical in nature.
>
> Considerations of humanity are inspiring and instrumental, yet they are no more than considerations. And they do not monopolize the field. If benevolent humanitarianism were the only factor to be weighed in hostilities, war would have entailed no bloodshed, no human suffering and no destruction of property; in short, war would not be war. IHL must be predicated on a subtle balance – and compromise – between conflicting considerations of humanity, on the one hand, and the demands of military necessity, on the other. Differently phrased, IHL generally takes a middle road between military necessity and considerations of humanity, reconciling them in one form or another.[55]

Thus, is appears that whatever is marketed as a "principle of humanity" does not actually have a binding legal obligation of its own. It is actually about few humanitarian considerations that are taken into account, subject to the overarching military necessity, in the process of norm–formulation and their interpretation. The idea of an independent "principle of humanity" is a farce. None can be identified as such.

14.4 Legitimating Violence

During past few decades, the proposition that the laws of armed conflict legitimate violence has been strongly put forward by few commentators. This proposition seeks to counter the dominant rhetoric of the law trumpeted day and night by the ICRC, States, international organizations and tribunals. It tries to unearth some of the terrible aspects of the laws of armed conflict and argues that the law has the effect of legitimating violence.

During an armed conflict, belligerents try to validate their armed attacks by contending compliance with the law. They even propagate their respect for the law through media. In this way, actions "are validated by simply being legal."[56] It helps manage the public perception also around the military operations and the law. General public is made to believe the significance of the law that it actually protects innocent civilians and helps the victims of war. They sympathize with the State army about the enemy's civilian loss but feel proud of them for launching legitimate attacks. David Kennedy, however, argues that: "We need to remember what it means to say that compliance with international law "legitimates." It means, of course, that killing, maiming,

[49] Larsen (2013, p. 143).

[50] Crawford and Pert (2015, p. 47) (internal citation omitted).

[51] Dinstein (2013, p. 73).

[52] Ibid.

[53] UK v. Albania (1949) ICJ Rep 22.

[54] Legality of the Threat or Use of Nuclear Weapons, Advisory Opinion (1996) ICJ Rep 226, paras 92, 95.

[55] Dinstein (2013, p. 73).

[56] Jochnick and Normand (1994, p. 57).

humiliating, and wounding people is legally privileged, authorized, permitted, and justified."[57] More precisely, the law legitimizes and normalizes[58] killing and harming people in the name of proportionality principle and renders some amount of suffering necessary. The law thus acts as a "strategic partner" in determining legitimacy of attacks.[59] Chinkin and Kaldor argue that from the victim's perspective it makes no difference whether they were killed or harmed lawfully or unlawfully.[60] The morally questionable legal logics are no answer to the innocents' suffering. The law not only overlooks this aspect, but also makes people ignore it under the impression of lawful operations.

The proponents of the legitimacy thesis connect the laws of armed conflict with the legitimacy of war also. For instance, Kennedy argues that the law has become the dominant vocabulary for articulating the legitimacy of war.[61] They further trace the origin of the thesis in the fact that the law of armed conflict "is based on the assumption that wars will happen and its primary objective is to mitigate their worst aspects and in so doing tacitly endorses their legitimacy."[62] Thus, by assuming the inevitability of war, the law of armed conflict "enables, constitutes and perpetuates war".[63] The law has also been seen as a part of reification and even fetishization of warfare.[64]

Because of these problematic foundations, the laws of armed conflict accommodate the demands of military necessity and deliberately "disregard humanitarian considerations."[65] The law has been woven in a vocabulary of legitimating targeting, and proportionate deaths and destruction.[66] It permits violence which is necessary and proportionate. It does not prohibit, for instance, killing of soldiers, and in certain circumstances killing or injuring civilians and destruction of civilian objects. Thus, the narrowly formulated rules legitimate "what is permitted"[67] or "what is not prohibited".[68] Sadly, violence legitimated does not count much. It is soon forgotten, rarely questioned. Thus, the law of armed conflict has become a "global political discourse of legitimacy".[69] In the Gulf War, deaths were sought to be legitimated by adhering to the legal standards.[70] Consequently, the United States military authorities claimed the reward of the most legalistic war ever fought.[71] Indeed, "legitimacy is currency of power."[72]

The legitimacy of military operations is assessed in the context of international criminal law also. The international criminal law declares numerous violations of the laws of armed conflict as war crimes and seeks to prosecute individuals accused of their commission. The Rome Statute determines legality of an attack or a hostile conduct. Thus, the Statute also reinforces attention on the much-sought-after legality of belligerent conduct. It compels parties to war to evaluate their actions on the parameters set by law, instead of moral or humanitarian standards. Thus, only law is the legitimizing tool.[73]

Coming back to Kennedy's thesis, some of his arguments reflect a unique pattern of justification. Consider the following for instance, "To be legitimate is to be powerful, to be powerful is to be legitimate"[74]; "Action legitimates norms,

57 Kennedy (2007, p. 185) and Kennedy (2004, p. 140).

58 Chinkin and Kaldor (2017, p. 259) and Lamp (2011, pp. 225–226).

59 Kennedy (2006b, p. 41).

60 Chinkin and Kaldor (2017, p. 259).

61 Kennedy (2004, p. 328).

62 Chinkin and Kaldor (2017, p. 255). Judith Gardam also argues that IHL assumes that war is inevitable: Gardam (1997, p. 72).

63 Mégret (2016, p. 773).

64 Ibid., p. 774.

65 Normand and Jochnick (1994, p. 409) and Jochnick and Normand (1994, p. 50).

66 Kennedy (2007, p. 178).

67 Kennedy (2006a, p. 138) and Jochnick and Normand (1994, p. 50).

68 Chinkin and Kaldor (2017, p. 256).

69 Kennedy (2006b, p. 120).

70 Kennedy (2006a, p. 144) and Alexander (2015, p. 130).

71 Normand and Jochnick (1994, p. 395).

72 Kennedy (2006b, p. 45).

73 Kennedy (2006b, p. 141).

74 Kennedy (2004, p. 337).

norms legitimate action,"[75] and "using law is also to invoke violence … To use violence is to invoke the law."[76] In philosophy, this way of arguing is known as circular reasoning because the second argument refers back to the first one. It is believed that the aim of reasoning is to rationally convince others of a position.[77] Logical validity is "a sign of maximum argument strength."[78] Circular arguments are poor in achieving that. Therefore, circularity in reasoning is often seen as a defect in logic and an "ultimate intellectual flaw."[79] It affects the logical validity of an argument and weakens it. However, it will be premature to discard Kennedy's arguments on the charge of circularity. Circular reasoning is not always fallacious or vicious.[80] It has been argued that circularity may not necessarily be a defect in logic.[81] Moreover, mere labeling of something as circular is not sufficient; it has to be supported by arguments[82] and reasonable justification.[83] Kennedy's arguments on law-violence linkage are based on the normative framework of the laws of armed conflict, and therefore, cannot be dismissed merely on the ground of circularity.

The laws of armed conflict also legitimize hierarchy among human lives and introduce graded inequality among human beings. Judith Butler recognizes[84] this hierarchy, and the same has been illustrated by Chinkin and kaldor.[85] Assuming an armed conflict between State X and State Y, they argue that as per the laws of armed conflict, X would value the human lives in the following hierarchical order: On the top priority of protection is X's civilian population, next is members of X's armed forces, third are civilians of Y, and the most vulnerable are members of Y's army. Y's soldiers are legitimate targets under the law. Y's civilians may be killed or harmed under the proportionality principle. Military advantage is also claimed in protecting own army at the cost of incidental enemy-civilian loss. This hierarchy of lives is validated by the laws of armed conflict. It defies the basic principle of equality before the law and establishes that law may discriminate against human beings and discriminately assign values to human lives. It is of course determined by the principle of military necessity. This is despite the fact that the Geneva Conventions themselves obligate States to refrain from observing any adverse distinction on specified grounds.[86] The principle thus subverts the principle of humanity in many indirect ways also.

Thus, the impact of the legitimizing function of the law is both overt and covert. Its subtle effect can be seen on legal categories also. It has been argued that "as law became an ever more important yardstick for legitimacy, legal categories became far too spongy."[87] This is explicit from the ambiguous notions of direct participation in hostilities, proportionate loss, superfluous injury, and so on.

14.5 International Humanitarian Law: What's in a Name?

In the context of the laws of armed conflict, it is noteworthy that the principle of humanity and the name of the discipline, International Humanitarian Law, try to mutually reinforce each other. At present what is known as International Humanitarian Law, was first called as law of war in the nineteenth century.[88] The relevant Hague Conventions and the annexed Regulations were also named using this phrase.[89] Law of war is perhaps the first to emerge as an important

[75] Ibid., p. 336.
[76] Kennedy (2007, p. 178).
[77] Hahn (2011, p. 173).
[78] Ibid.
[79] Ibid., p. 180.
[80] Walton (1985, p. 263).
[81] Burgess (2008, p. 216).
[82] Hahn (2011, p. 180).
[83] Walton (1985, p. 180).
[84] Butler (2009).
[85] See, Chinkin and Kaldor (2017, p. 255).

[86] E.g. Art. 3, 12 Geneva Convention I and II, above n 13 and Art. 16, 75 Protocol I, above n 3.
[87] Kennedy (2007, p. 175).
[88] Oppenheim (1952, p. 226) and Hall (1917, pp. 63–65).
[89] Hague Regulations 1899 and 1907, above n 13.

component of international law.[90] Though, its spectrum is certainly broader than international humanitarian law because it extends to other war-related issues, such as neutrality, enemy property, enemy character and termination of war. The expression "international humanitarian law" came into practice after the World War II. Page Wilson maintains that the term "humanitarian law" was employed for the first time by Jean Pictet in the commentaries to the Geneva Conventions of 1949.[91] Another early use of the term is found in an ICRC's conference. In the XIXth International Conference of the Red Cross (1957) at New Delhi, the ICRC named its commission as International Humanitarian Law Commission.[92] Subsequently, it was strongly pursued by the ICRC in 1960s. Resolution XXVII adopted during the XXth International Conference of the ICRC (1965), referred to the 1949 Geneva Conventions as Humanitarian Conventions in its title: "Protests regarding Alleged Violations of the Humanitarian Conventions."[93] Resolution XXVIII used the phrase international humanitarian law in its text.[94]

Similarly, in the preparatory works for the two Additional Protocols of 1977, the ICRC was simultaneously using the expressions law of armed conflict and international humanitarian law. During its XXIst International Conference (1969), it had a Commission working in the field of humanitarian law.[95] The President of the ICRC introduced a report titled Reaffirmation and Development of the Laws and Customs Applicable in Armed Conflicts, which was submitted by the ICRC to the participants of the Conference.[96] However, the official theme of the Conference of Government Experts, 1971[97] and the Diplomatic Conference (1974–1977),[98] which were held in the context of the Additional Protocols, was "Reaffirmation and Development of International Humanitarian Law Applicable in Armed Conflicts." In its submission to the Government Experts Conference (1971), the ICRC declared that the abbreviation IHL stands for the expression International Humanitarian Law Applicable in Armed Conflicts.[99]

The ICRC started pushing the false notion of international humanitarian law so hard that soon the international community witnessed a fresh body of international rules and principles emerging, namely, International Humanitarian Law.[100] The words "Applicable in Armed Conflicts" were also lost in the transition from law of war/armed conflict to international humanitarian law. The ICRC sought to explain the move by arguing that abandoning the use of the expressions Law of War/Armed Conflict reflects the "legally exceptional nature of war."[101] These are certainly political maneuvers. Actually, both, the introduction of the new name and the removal of the reference to armed conflicts tend to create a false impression and mask the realities of the law and war. In reality, the so called humanitarian foundations of the law are questionable and its political undercurrents are visible. In the name of a "humanitarian" law, it masks the legitimization of violence and normalizes suffering. It neglects the concerns of subalterns and privileges the dominant. The façade of international "humanitarian" law helps do that.

[90] Holland (1898, p. 40).

[91] Wilson (2017, p. 567).

[92] Alexander (2015, p. 117).

[93] ICRC (1965, p. 588).

[94] Ibid., p. 589.

[95] ICRC (1969, p. 599).

[96] Ibid., p. 600.

[97] Conference of Government Experts on the Reaffirmation and Development of International Humanitarian Law Applicable in Armed Conflicts (1972), Report on the Work of the Conference, vol I (ICRC, Geneva).

[98] Official Records of the Diplomatic Conference on the Reaffirmation and Development of International Humanitarian Law Applicable in Armed Conflicts Geneva (1974–1977).

[99] Wilson (2017, p. 569).

[100] See, Art. 2 Convention on prohibitions or restrictions on the use of certain conventional weapons which may be deemed to be excessively injurious or to have indiscriminate effects (1980), Art. 36(3)(b)(ii) Rome Statute, above n 18 and UNSC/RES/764 (1992).

[101] Wilson (2017, p. 568).

References

Alexander A (2015) A short history of international humanitarian law. Eur J Int Law 26(1):109–138

Bryant M (2016) A world history of war crimes: from antiquity to the present. Bloomsbury Academic, London

Burgess JA (2008) When is circularity in definitions benign? Philos Q 5(231):214–233

Butler J (2009) Frames of war: when is life grievable? Verso Books, London

Chinkin C, Kaldor M (2017) International law and new wars. CUP, Cambridge

Cohen A, Zlotogorski D (2021) Proportionality in international humanitarian law: consequences, precautions, and procedures. OUP, New York

Crawford E, Pert A (2015) International humanitarian law. CUP, Cambridge

Dinstein Y (2013) The principle of proportionality. In: Larsen KM et al (eds) Searching for a 'principle of humanity' in international humanitarian law. CUP, Cambridge

Gardam J (1997) Women and the law of armed conflict: why the silence? Int Comp Law Q 46(1):55–80

Hahn U (2011) The problem of circularity in evidence, argument, and explanation. Perspect Psychol Sci 6(2):172–182

Hall WE (1917) A treatise on international law. OUP, London

Holland TE (1898) Studies in international law. Clarendon Press, London

Horowitz J (2016) Ending the global war: the power of human rights in a time of unrestrained armed conflict. In: Ohlin JD (ed) Theoretical boundaries of armed conflict and human rights. CUP, New York, pp 157–191

ICRC (1965) Resolutions adopted by the XXth international conference of the Red Cross. International Review of the Red Cross 65:570–598

ICRC (1969) The XXIst international conference of the Red Cross, Istanbul, 1969. International Review of the Red Cross 104:599–607

ICRC, Fundamental principles of International humanitarian law. https://casebook.icrc.org/law/fundamentals-ihl#d_iii

Jochnick C, Normand R (1994) The legitimation of violence: a critical history of the laws of war. Harv Int Law J 35(1):49–96

Kennedy D (2004) The dark sides of virtue: reassessing international humanitarianism. Princeton University Press, Princeton

Kennedy D (2006a) Reassessing international humanitarianism: the dark sides. In: Orford A (ed) International law and its others. CUP, New York, pp 131–155

Kennedy D (2006b) Of war and law. Princeton University Press, Princeton

Kennedy D (2007) Modern war and modern law. University of Baltimore Law Review 36(2):173–194

Kolb R, Hyde R (2008) An introduction to the international law of armed conflicts. Hart Publishing, Oxford

Lamp N (2011) Conceptions of war and paradigms compliance: the 'new war' challenge to international humanitarian law. Journal of Conflict & Security Law 16(2):225–262

Larsen KM (2013a) A 'principle of humanity' or a 'principle of human-rightism'? In: Larsen KM et al (eds) Searching for a 'principle of humanity' in international humanitarian law. CUP, Cambridge, pp 124–148

Larsen KM et al (2013b) Introduction by the editors: is there a 'principle of humanity' in international humanitarian law? In: Larsen KM et al (eds) Searching for a 'principle of humanity' in international humanitarian law. CUP, Cambridge, pp 1–20

Mégret F (2016) Theorizing the laws of war. In: Orford A, Hoffmann F (eds) The Oxford handbook of the theory of international law. OUP, New York, pp 762–278

Melzer N (2016) International humanitarian law: a comprehensive introduction. ICRC, Geneva

Normand R, Jochnick C (1994) The legitimation of violence: critical analysis of the gulf war. Harv Int Law J 35(2):387–416

Oppenheim L (1952) International law, vol II: disputes, war and neutrality. Longmans, Green & Co, London

Sandel M (2009) Justice: what's the right thing to do. Penguin Books, London

Solis GD (2010) The law of armed conflict: international humanitarian law in war. CUP, Cambridge

Stephens D, Lewis MW (2005) The law of armed conflict—a contemporary critique. Melbourne Journal of International Law 6(1):55–85

Walton DN (1985) Are circular arguments necessarily vicious? Am Philos Q 22(4):263–274

Wilson P (2017) The myth of international humanitarian law. Int Aff 93(3):563–579

15 Conclusion

It is ritualistic to say that the body of laws of armed conflict is a pragmatic arrangement, a compromise. Despite the general prohibition on resort to war, it intends to regulate the conduct of war realizing that wars are inevitable and the effects of war must be mitigated. The critique of the laws of armed conflict goes beyond this admission.

The materialist perspective to the laws of armed conflict has explained that historically the law was conditioned by economic and political realities of that time. Fracisco de Vitoria sought to justify brutalities on the "barbarians" during war because of economic interests and cultural differences. Vitoria laid the foundation of the European cultural superiority and consequent monopoly in making universal claims and prescribing prejudiced norms. Thus, economic and political concerns took over humanitarianism very early. Before the Battle of Solferino, the emerging colonization and growing capitalism led to several wars in Europe. The Industrial Revolution not only revolutionized the production process, but gave a fillip to militarism too. However, the development of the laws of war was slow in this epoch.

Subsequent to the Battle of Solferino, few international treaties were adopted to regulate the belligerent conduct, ostensibly in the interest of humanity. It was ensured that the treaties do not compromise with the warring capacity of the States. Considering the colonial competition and trade rivalry, no regulation weakening the combat capabilities of the States was adopted. They refrained from assuming extensive restraints on their behavior during war (e.g. in the Brussels Conference, 1874). Instead, they relied on selective humanitarianism. They preferred to prohibit weapons which were obsolete and outmoded but not the latest and barbaric, and capable of killing indiscriminately. Moreover, the scope of the treaties was narrow. They were based on the distinction between civilized (colonizers) and uncivilized (colonies). They were not made applicable in case of war with the colonies. The logic of the exclusion was three-fold—cultural, economic and political. Colonies were considered culturally inferior to the Europeans and therefore unworthy of any humanitarian treatment. Accepting restraints in war with them might weaken their control over colonies. It was not acceptable to the colonial masters because the colonies contributed to the wealth and empire of colonizers as markets, sources of precious raw-material and places of establishing manufacturing units.

Additionally, the treaties were subjected to general participation clause which further limited the applicability of the treaties. The Hague Regulations were also similarly infected. No Convention on civilian protection could be enacted before World War II. Military necessity prevailed over any other consideration. World War I unleashed unprecedented violence despite the Hague Regulations, and caused civilian deaths in great proportion. The war exposed the façade of humanitarianism.

K. Jeenger, *A Humanitarian Critique of International Humanitarian Law*,
Sustainable Development Goals Series, https://doi.org/10.1007/978-981-96-8319-2_15

The Geneva Conventions adopted after World War II appeared to be extensive in that they provided for the protection of victims in armed conflicts not of an international character also and they included a Convention on civilian protection too. However, the imperialist nations did not compromise with their political motives in the adoption of the instruments. They dominated the negotiating space in the Diplomatic Conference and shaped the drafts favourable to them. Their interests took central stage and the Third World kept waiting at the periphery. Their ambitions reflected in the negotiated texts. They deliberately kept the wars of national liberation out of the ambit of international armed conflict which were dealt with by four separate Conventions. It was a crucial time because several colonies were revolting against the colonizers. However, the lack of any legal obligation helped the flag-bearers of humanity in brutally suppressing the revolts. Additionally, the Conventions display humanitarian discrimination because the conduct of non-international armed conflicts was subject to only one article. The powerful European nations succeeded in limiting the "humanitarian" protection available in non-international armed conflicts. Even the Additional Protocol II, which contains wider restraints in respect of non-international armed conflicts, actually provides for an unworkable higher threshold of applicability.

The international instruments adopted post-World War II greatly contributed in earning the title International Humanitarian Law. However, the texts hardly contribute in justifying the name. None of the four Geneva Conventions regulated the means and methods of war, leading to perpetual threat, especially to the civilian life and objects. The so called humanitarian provisions were made dependent upon the convenience of the warring parties. They were qualified by flexible expressions, such as "as far as possible" and "as far as military considerations allow." These expressions certainly diluted the "humanitarian" obligations assumed by the parties to the Conventions and facilitated discretion, arbitrariness and subjectivity. They especially proved to be helpful to the advanced countries and prejudicial to the Third World nations. Since the number of weak nations in the making of the Geneva Conventions was less due to colonial rule, the powerful nations used the opportunity to mold the provisions to suit their military and political interests. The only option available to the subsequently decolonized Third World countries was to accede to the treaties without any bargaining power.

The nature of the "humanitarian" protection, if at all, provided by the post-World War II instruments is Eurocentric, racial, patriarchal and gendered; in short, exclusionary, instead of inclusive. The freedom fighters of the Third World nations, who would prefer to adopt guerilla tactics of war because of weak military resources, were not entitled to the status of prisoner-of-war under the 1949 Geneva Convention. While women were absolutely excluded from any protection in the pre-World War II instruments, the subsequent agreements were founded on patriarchal language, biased towards heterosexual men and oblivious of specific female-concerns. The bias and exclusion surface more prominently in the "humanitarian" law in case of queer bodies. It is silent, blind and deaf in respect of their specific needs and the hardships faced by them during war. It illustrates that the connotation of humanity in the laws of armed conflict is very limited. It privileges some, and disenfranchises and excludes the "others."

At many places, the law also seems to be reflecting inhumanity and legitimating violence. The instruments are said to be based on the principles of military necessity, proportionality, distinction and humanity. Out of the four principles, military necessity is actually the overarching idea. It determines the content of rules and rest of the principles. It has the tendency of allowing any form of attack aiming at achieving military objectives. It permits violence in certain situations and weakens whatever protection the law offers. In the principle of proportionality, for instance, there is plenty of scope for misinterpretation and subjective assessment. It permits and hence legitimates killings of civilians and destruction of their objects provided that the same is not relatively excessive than the military advantage estimated. While the phrase military advantage is ambiguous and prone to expansive interpretation, its comparison with human lives is not a humane exercise. Moreover,

the only restriction the principle imposes is not to cause comparatively higher civilian loss. It does not aim at minimizing the civilian harm. Thus, the principle validates any amount of loss of civilian life and objects provided it is comparatively less.

The principle of distinction appears to be based on the assumption of inter-State wars. The term "direct participation in hostilities" is an example of careless and problematic drafting. Its interpretation, especially in non-international armed conflicts, exposes the loopholes. Considering the ascending number of asymmetric wars these days, the ambiguity of the phrase is felt the most. The principle of unnecessary suffering also comes with no guideline as to the scale of injury and pain in order to become applicable as a prohibition. In general, the principles of the laws of armed conflict are broad and vaguely worded, and consequently they facilitate manipulation. And it appears that only on the basis of the ostensible, vague and abstract shades of humanitarian considerations, the law has been popularized as International Humanitarian Law.

Much of the misconception and fallacy in and around the discipline may be attributed to the invention and popularity of the title International Humanitarian Law. It has created a false impression that the law has been structured on humanitarian foundations, and that the notion of humanity in this law encompasses every human being. It has also been argued that the law seeks to humanize the war. Such claims are actually misleading and veil the real character of the law. The title of the discipline embodies political undertones. It successfully masks its inhuman side and validation of violence. The language it employs is ostensibly humanitarian, but, it normalizes suffering and killings under the garb of law. The law is a covert instrument of achieving political ends. As usual, it sides with the powerful and helps target the weak.

From the Third World view, the laws of armed conflict originated during the colonial era. Their genesis lies in colonization, trade rivalry, colonial competition, invention of advanced weapons and militarization during the nineteenth century. Historically, the international laws of armed conflict have been exclusionary, discriminatory and disastrous to the peoples of the Third World. They suffered enormously because of the deliberate marginalization of colonies from the creation and application of the laws of armed conflict. They ruthlessly ignored the lived experiences of the Third World. The extension of the law to the wars of national liberation was deliberately delayed by the imperialist States. Even today, the law fails to address the concerns of the Third World. Its provisions are largely based on a Global North's view of war. It is mainly founded on the assumption that every State is as advanced as the former colonizers and every armed conflict is fought by disciplined and well-organized armies. Its vague language benefits the powerful countries and jeopardizes the Third World. Its frequent invocation of the interests of "humanity" reflects mainly the interests of the North.

Index

K. Jeenger, *A Humanitarian Critique of International Humanitarian Law*, Sustainable Development Goals Series, https://doi.org/10.1007/978-981-96-8319-2

MIX
Papier aus verantwortungsvollen Quellen
Paper from responsible sources
FSC® C105338

If you have any concerns about our products,
you can contact us on
ProductSafety@springernature.com

In case Publisher is established outside the EU,
the EU authorized representative is:
Springer Nature Customer Service Center GmbH
Europaplatz 3, 69115 Heidelberg, Germany

Printed by Libri Plureos GmbH
in Hamburg, Germany